Techniques for Coding Imagery and Multimedia:

Emerging Research and Opportunities

Shalin Hai-Jew
Kansas State University, USA

A volume in the Advances in
Knowledge Acquisition, Transfer, and
Management (AKATM) Book Series

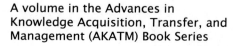

Published in the United States of America by
  IGI Global
  Information Science Reference (an imprint of IGI Global)
  701 E. Chocolate Avenue
  Hershey PA, USA 17033
  Tel: 717-533-8845
  Fax: 717-533-8661
  E-mail: cust@igi-global.com
  Web site: http://www.igi-global.com

Library of Congress Cataloging-in-Publication Data

Names: Hai-Jew, Shalin, author.
Title: Techniques for coding imagery and multimedia : emerging research and
   opportunities / by Shalin Hai-Jew.
Description: Hershey, PA : Information Science Reference, [2018] | Includes
   bibliographical references.
Identifiers: LCCN 2017008840| ISBN 9781522526797 (hardcover) | ISBN
   9781522526803 (ebook)
Subjects: LCSH: Metadata. | Information retrieval. | Content analysis
   (Communication)--Data processing. | Database searching. | Interactive
   multimedia. | Digital media. | Online social networks.
Classification: LCC Z666.73.D54 H35 2018 | DDC 025.3/16--dc23 LC record available at https://
lccn.loc.gov/2017008840

This book is published in the IGI Global book series Advances in Knowledge Acquisition, Transfer, and Management (AKATM) (ISSN: 2326-7607; eISSN: 2326-7615)

British Cataloguing in Publication Data
A Cataloguing in Publication record for this book is available from the British Library.

All work contributed to this book is new, previously-unpublished material.
The views expressed in this book are those of the authors, but not necessarily of the publisher.

For electronic access to this publication, please contact: eresources@igi-global.com.

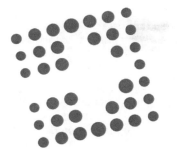

Advances in Knowledge Acquisition, Transfer, and Management (AKATM) Book Series

ISSN:2326-7607
EISSN:2326-7615

Editor-in-Chief: Murray E. Jennex, San Diego State University, USA

MISSION

Organizations and businesses continue to utilize knowledge management practices in order to streamline processes and procedures. The emergence of web technologies has provided new methods of information usage and knowledge sharing.

The **Advances in Knowledge Acquisition, Transfer, and Management (AKATM) Book Series** brings together research on emerging technologies and their effect on information systems as well as the knowledge society. **AKATM** will provide researchers, students, practitioners, and industry leaders with research highlights surrounding the knowledge management discipline, including technology support issues and knowledge representation.

COVERAGE

- Cognitive Theories
- Cultural Impacts
- Information and Communication Systems
- Knowledge acquisition and transfer processes
- Knowledge management strategy
- Knowledge sharing
- Organizational learning
- Organizational Memory
- Small and Medium Enterprises
- Virtual communities

IGI Global is currently accepting manuscripts for publication within this series. To submit a proposal for a volume in this series, please contact our Acquisition Editors at Acquisitions@igi-global.com or visit: http://www.igi-global.com/publish/.

Titles in this Series

IGI Global
DISSEMINATOR OF KNOWLEDGE

701 East Chocolate Avenue, Hershey, PA 17033, USA
Tel: 717-533-8845 x100 • Fax: 717-533-8661
E-Mail: cust@igi-global.com • www.igi-global.com

This is for R. Max.

Table of Contents

Section 1
Coding Imagery for Sensemaking

Section 2
Exploring Social Phenomena

Section 3
Image and Multimedia Coding in Academia

Preface

The book stacks are dark, and the library itself is quiet, locked, and empty. Inside, there is the ticking of electronic shelving sensors and the hum of vending machines with square doughnuts and colorful packages of candy and chips. Here is yet another weekend spent voraciously in pursuit of data, the processed articles, the massive downloads of images and multimedia, the gray literature. The thinking goes like this: it is impossible to know what, in retrospect, will be relevant, so all of it gets swept up and compiled in folders. In the initial stages, the mass of data holds all sorts of promise. Then, as the pieces are considered, the possibilities start to dwindle, and ideas come into form, and then, it is much easier to be brutally selective. While nothing is discarded, only some items from the collected data and information are deemed useful. For all the possible overlays of meaning, only a few now are possible. Everything else is left in the unused digital bins. For all the odds and ends of data, ultimately, there is only a stark binary: yes, there is some patterned coherence, or no, nothing, 1 or 0.

What determines the value of raw data? What is that in-between state between the collection of data and the judgment call of whether there is something relevant there? And if so, what is of particular interest? In between is coding.

CODING UNSTRUCTURED DATA

"Coding" takes on a variety of meanings in various research contexts, but the core one is to extract meaning from raw data. This is so whether the coding is pre-defined and top-down (*a priori* coding, based on theory, frameworks, and predefined approaches) or emergent and bottom-up, with most coding falling somewhere in-between. This issue of how to code imagery and multimedia has come to the fore because of the wide public availability of social data on the Web and Internet.

Such plentiful data is available because of socio-technical factors. For social media data, the commercial companies collecting that data and making it available do so because it is a business model that can be highly lucrative, based on value from advertising streams and data analytics (and the sale of data). People share personal information because they can connect with others and gain friendships and meet other needs online. Researchers can access publicly available social data to contribute to their respective fields and enhance their professional curriculum vitae. Everyone gets a cut.

The mass abundance of publicly shared social text, imagery, videos, and multimedia on the Web has enabled computer scientists to capture large sets of unstructured data for machine learning and other analytical approaches. Their research is widely available in the academic literature. Parallel to this effort has been smaller on-ground work to learn from shared social data by digital humanities practitioners and those from the arts and social sciences. These efforts are often at smaller scale (not "big data" or complete sets of N), often with selected cases, and often with both commercially available technologies and free and open-source technologies.

When data scientist Seth Stephens-Davidowitz (2017) writes of the potential of big data, particularly the search feature in Google, he waxes eloquent:

In fact, at the risk of sounding grandiose, I have come to believe that the new data increasingly available in our digital age will radically expand our understanding of humankind. The microscope showed us there is more to a drop of pond water than we think we see. The telescope showed us there is more to the night sky than we think we see. And new, digital data now shows us there is more to human society than we think we see. It may be our era's microscope or telescope—making possible important, even revolutionary insights. (p. 10)

How to harness the generous outpouring of shared contents is very much an "open problem" in a number of fields, with bottom-up innovations combining expert analysis, human close reading, various technologies, evolving methods, and debated professional ethics.

JEALOUS PROTECTION OF DATA

This is not to say that data is not jealously protected and guarded. A recent experience emphasizes this point. I had been working with a professor at my university on and off for the past decade-plus. In one project, I was training her and a doctoral candidate on how to use a high-end qualitative data analysis tool. She and her student were interested in coding a collection of text-based transcripts from online courses that went back a number of years. After several initial meetings and a flurry of emails, I heard a little bit about the project apparently starting, and then, as is typical, it all went to silence. We all went our own ways and focused on our respective work lives. Then, the faculty member and I had occasion to speak again about a different topic, and she mentioned that the project with that student had ended. As sometimes happens in academia, several principals had had a disagreement, and this professor had ultimately been removed from the doctoral students' committee, and she in return reclaimed her dataset that was to be used in the co-research—the assumption being that the student would help with some of the coding and would earn her doctorate ultimately, and the professor would have a shared byline. Broadly, one would bring the effortful work of coding, and the other would share expertise and the data. The academic kerfuffle, the graduate student's committee shuffle, the lightly mean rumors…were all mundane.

What was initially remarkable to me about this was the scramble over the data and the unceremonious retraction by the faculty member, with far reaching implications for the student but also herself (since the dataset was fairly massive and she did not have much experience with coding). The data itself was collected from learners over multiple years. Its collection was approved by the institutional review board (IRB), and the discussion board records were not yet de-identified (it was possible to see which student posted what). The faculty member and student had a theoretical framework that they were working off of, and they had already started a theory-informed top-down *a priori* codebook for the analysis. In other words, they had already started going operational. With the pulling of the data, the risk going forward was that the faculty member would continue with her pattern of slow to no progress on the actual work, and the student herself would have to start from scratch. One lesson: nothing is done until it is done.

More importantly, a lesson about data: Even in this day and age of "big data," it is no small thing to have access to data. Professional reputations can be made or broken from access to data. Even though there are many datasets released by democratic governments, published authors, and citizen scientists, data are jealously guarded and owned. Practically, they are expensive to collect and maintain, and these efforts occur in complex environments with legal constraints, professional and ethical guidelines, policy guidelines, and other considerations. To extract meaning from data requires high-level expertise and expensive technological tools. Data may be approached any number of ways (theoretically, methodologically, and technologically) and in various combinations of approaches, and numerous interpretations may be extracted from a single dataset or mix of datasets. As may be seen in the academic literature, interpretations from data may even be diametrically opposed. When people share data, it is because they have something to gain from the share; if not, the naïve altruism of that share ends up being costly to the sharer and beneficial to competitors. In some markets, such data giveaways (or losses, such as from illegal hacks) mean loss of market share, and what's at stake is very much zero sum.

Another point is that methods designed for analyzing imagery and multimedia do not only necessarily apply to social data but apply in other research and analytics contexts…including on proprietary and private unstructured data datasets.

SOME TECHNIQUES FOR CODING

Techniques for Coding Imagery and Multimedia: Emerging Research and Opportunities describes some of the applied methods to code imagery and multimedia for research value. "Coding" here is used in a broad way to mean the interpretation and labeling of contents…to know what is in hand and what it means…for particular research contexts. This text consists of three sections:

Section 1: Coding Imagery for Sensemaking
Section 2: Exploring Social Phenomena
Section 3: Image and Multimedia Coding in Academia

In total, there are seven chapters in this work.

Section 1, "Coding Imagery for Sensemaking," contains two chapters. Both are focused on analytical sensemaking based on engaging with social imagery.

The first chapter, "Exploring Identity-Based Humor in a #Selfies #Humor Image Set From Instagram," describes an effort to harness both manual and computational means to understand captured images in a unique image set. Informed by theories on humor, this work involved close analysis of the collectively shared #selfie #humor social image set to understand what people perceive as humorous, the memes shared around this topic, the thematic elements of humor, and other features. Also, this work includes documentation of the research and analytical methods.

In the first chapter, the image coding was informed in part by theory and in part by features of the image data. In Chapter 2, "Snacking Around the World: Evolving an Inductive Image Categorization and Research Query Approach for Image Sets from Social Media," a more purely emergent coding approach was followed. In this non-theoretical approach, two image sets from the #snack hashtag (on Instagram) were used for a systematic and open inductive approach to identify image categories. This bottom-up approach to image categorization enables researchers to achieve three main objectives: (1) describe and assess the image set contents and categorize them in multiple ways independent of a theoretical framework (and its potential biasing effects); (2) conceptualize what may be knowable from the image set by the defining of research questions that may be addressed in the empirical data; (3) categorize the available imagery broadly and in multiple ways as a precursor step to further exploration (e.g. research design, image coding, and development of a research codebook). This work informs the exploration and analysis of mobile-created contents for open learning.

Section 2, "Exploring Social Phenomena," contains three chapters. All three are focused around exploration of social issues through the uses of unstructured data using rich coding techniques.

"Engaging Technology-Based Manifestos Three Ways: (1) Manual Coding, (2) CAQDAS-Supported Manual Coding, and (3) Machine Reading and Autocoding" (Chapter 3) focuses on textual analysis...three ways. This shows that the method of data analytics surfaces different insights about a shared topic, and this makes the case that using multiple and different means of data collection and analysis may be beneficial to deeper knowledge of a phenomenon.

Chapter 4 also involves a topic-based research approach. In this case, "mass surveillance" is studied as a trending "thing" in this current age wherever one stands on the topic. This chapter, "Exploring 'Mass Surveillance' Through Computational Linguistic Analysis of Five Text Corpora: Academic, Mainstream Journalism, Microblogging Hashtag Conversation, Wikipedia Articles, and Leaked Government Data" focuses on the observable differences between writing genres in their approach to this particular topic. This work shows certain genre tendencies, even with smaller text sets.

The fifth chapter is "See Ya! Exploring American Renunciation of Citizenship Through Targeted and Sparse Social Media Datasets and a Custom Spatial-Based Linguistic Analysis Dictionary." One of the hallmarks of a great tool is its ability to accommodate custom features. In this work, a custom spatial-based dictionary was created to run in LIWC2015 in order to study U.S. expat messaging and U.S. renunciation of citizenship as related phenomena. The geospatial aspect focused on both spatial and place senses and used natural language captured through social media platforms: a microblogging site, a social networking site, an image-sharing site, a crowd-sourced encyclopedia, and a news-sharing and discussion board site. This work combines human close reading and machine reading to create the dictionary and included light analysis of the custom spatial-based dictionary.

The third and final section, "Image and Multimedia Coding in Academia," focuses on the practical coding and analytics of imagery and digital learning objects.

This next chapter involves a more classic and structured focus on how instructors may evaluate image and multimedia submittals from learners, given the broad availability of "file upload" options for assignments and the broad proliferation of mobile devices among university and high school students. Chapter 6 is titled "Coding Online Learner Image and Multimedia Submissions for Assignment Fulfillment: An Early Assessment Rubric."

Finally, the last chapter is "Coding Digital Learning Objects for Adoption for Online Teaching and Learning" (Chapter 7). This is about how potential adopters of digital learning objects (DLOs) assess various works and how these features affect their decisions of whether or not to use them. Also, this studies what features instructional designers build to when they create digital learning objects in a local context. Finally, there is analysis of the gap between what DLO adopters want and what DLO creators create, and ways to narrow the gap. Some major challenges are identified, though, in the LO economy given structured incentives. This work includes a first draft of the "DLO Adoption Survey" instrument.

A LIMITED TREATMENT OF MULTIMEDIA CODING

This book is a limited treatment of this large and fast-changing topic. The available technologies are myriad, and these works only tapped some of the more accessible ones. None of the works require scripting or coding, for example. (Scripting and coding are logical next steps for custom analysis tools.) The manual coding involved both qualitative and quantitative methods. In one case, an *a priori* model was used (Chapter 1), but otherwise, bottom-up emergent approaches were taken. This book is not prescriptive in terms of technologies or methodologies, but the idea is to apply different technologies and techniques at different points for different outcomes. It is important to be aware of what is going on at each phase and what the affordances and constraints are for each step and to document these transparently for fellow researchers. It is important to apply professional ethics and principled effort to the work.

This area, though, will continue to be of interest well into the near-future. (Some computational means—computer vision and AI, in combination—make the differences between textual vs. image and multimedia data less present and less onerous.) For all the glitz of computational analyses, there is huge space for human visual and experiential analysis. Where machines generalize, humans can specialize and bring particular expertise and combinations of expertise to bear.

There is power in learning from single examples and low-Ns, with analytical means originated and honed by researchers on the ground in their respective fields. Of course, then, too, there are challenges with the "law of low numbers" simultaneously.

In each of the chapters, a nexus was found between the human researcher and computational affordances to solve real-world challenges. I hope this work contributes something to the work of others.

REFERENCES

Stephens-Davisdowitz, S. (2017). *Everybody lies: Big data, new data, and what the internet can tell us about who we really are*. New York: Harper Collins.

Acknowledgment

Thanks are in order. Courtney Tychinski, Assistant Managing Editor of Book Development at IGI-Global, shepherded this work through the book development process. This was a multi-year effort, and the book has improved because of our shared efforts and contributions. Thanks also to Kaitlyn Kulp and Mike Brehm for the expert typography and assistance during proofing. I am grateful to Research Insights of IGI-Global for supporting the publication of this work. Their adaptability and supportiveness are much appreciated.

Also, Kansas State University is a wonderful place to work. The work projects provide interesting challenges, and my colleagues are a fun group. My work colleagues—fellow researchers, writers, and editors—go well beyond the boundaries of a university campus. Their smarts, high energy, and good will have been critical to my work for many decades, and I am thankful to them.

Section 1
Coding Imagery for Sensemaking

Chapter 1

Exploring Identity–Based Humor in a #Selfies #Humor Image Set From Instagram

ABSTRACT

On a social level, identity humor may be pro-social, anti-social, or more often, both. The research in this chapter examined three basic research questions based on the study of social imagery: (1) What does identity-based humor look like in terms of a #selfie #humor- tagged image set from the Instagram photo-sharing mobile app? (2) What earlier findings and theories about humor apply to the more modern forms of mediated social humor? Is it possible to effectively apply the Humor Styles Model to the images from the #selfie #humor Instagram image set to better understand #selfie #humor? If so, what may be discoverable using this approach? and (3) What are some constructive and systematized ways to analyze social image sets in a naïve and emergent way using manual and computer-supported techniques?

INTRODUCTION

This current time is labeled "the age of selfies." The "selfie" phenomenon in social media interactions basically involves on-the-fly digital self-portraiture as individuals (solo selfies), duos (duo selfies), or groups (group selfies, groupies, we-fies), and in still images as well as videos. The individual, at its most basic form, conveys information about himself or herself, his or her

DOI: 10.4018/978-1-5225-2679-7.ch001

personality, a context, a moment-in-time, and sometimes a message, in the image. Others on the same social media platforms will comment on such shared images, and they may share their own.

Selfies are often considered harmless social phenomena of people sharing aspects of themselves and their lived experiences with others. In the benign view, the main risks of selfies are tastelessness in the overshare and TMI (too much information). Social media platforms serve as amplifiers of messages, so selfies have taken on a syndromic quality, with various ways the self manifests. As a form of user-generated contents, selfies have been studied in various disciplines: sociology, anthropology, human-computer interactions, communications studies, media studies, psychology, emergency management, law enforcement, gender studies, public health, data science, image processing, and education.

Researchers have found aspects for concern, such as teen sexting that may harm the adult selves given the persistence of online information and imagery (Solecki & Fay-Hillier, 2015, p. 934). Another researcher highlights how the sexualization of youth culture has been a long-term challenge and is exacerbated by sexting on social media, which may start chains of events that they cannot control (Gabriel, 2014, p. 105).

There are also risks of data leakage, or the unintended release of private information that may be mis-used. Caught up in the selfie moment, some people have compromised their own financial well-being through unintentional data leakage, such as through #myfirstpaycheck imagery (Lee, 2015). Another type of selfie, what one researcher calls "self-pornification," involves DIY porn, with sites that cater to sharing these types of contents (Tziallas, 2015). Then, there are the potential physical harms of selfies: People's focus on capturing the perfect recorded images and videos of themselves to share have led to injuries and deaths. This "death by selfie" is attributed to people's distraction, with "photo-takers falling off cliffs, crashing cars, being hit by trains and shooting themselves while posing with guns," to the extent that policymakers have had to step in to restrict the taking of selfies in both Mumbai and Pamplona (Salie, Mar. 6, 2016). The self-imperilment of the selfie taker is sometimes part of the design to express something autobiographical; this risk may be from circumstance or design (Saltz, 2014, p. 7).

Based on the research of a #selfie #humor image set from Instagram, the uses of humor in selfies are yet another area of risk. #humor, both in the real and in cyberspace, comes in a variety of forms. There are different formulations for what people find funny. One formula reads: tragedy + time = comedy. The intertwining of tragedy (Melpomene) and comedy (Thalia) is reflected in the comedy and tragedy masks represented in theatre. Collectively, theatre is a space that societies and collectives go to to have discussions about collective social and historical issues. The most common structural component of most humor is incongruity—elements that do not seem to fit in a context based on expectations (Rappoport, 2005, p. 27). People have a hard-wired mental faculty for observing the ludicrous and the incongruous and responding with surprise and laughter. There have been areas of the brain identified to respond to jokes, such as word-play and punning (Kelland, 2011). (While some people will laugh and say, "That's just so wrong!" when they encounter a rude joke or surprising context, people will not respond with laughter at something that is absurd and actually perceived as ethically wrong. In that case, people become angry.)

The research involves two main areas of inquiry. The first is how #selfie #humor manifests in a social image set in Instagram; the latter involves effective ways to code social imagery in a manual and computer-assisted way. Three main research questions (with related sub-questions) were addressed in this work:

1. What does identity-based humor look like in terms of a #selfie #humor-tagged image set from the Instagram photo-sharing mobile app?
2. What earlier findings and theories about humor apply to the more modern forms of mediated social humor? Is it possible to effectively apply the Humor Styles Model to the images from the #selfie #humor Instagram image set to better understand #selfie #humor? If so, what may be discoverable using this approach?
3. What are some constructive and systematized ways to analyze social image sets in an emergent way using manual and computer-supported techniques?

REVIEW OF THE LITERATURE

"Selfie" was the Word of the Year in 2013 in the Oxford English Dictionary. In early March 2016, a Google search of "selfie" brings up 220 million results (in 0.39 seconds, no less). On the Google Android platform alone, in 2014, over 93 million selfies were taken daily, according to Google (Kennemer, June 25, 2014). In a study of millions of photos on Instagram, a research team found that the amount of selfies increased 900-fold from 2012 to 2014, and these types of images were 1.1 to 3.2 times more likely to be liked and commented on than other types of visual content on Instagram contexts (Souza, de las Casas, Flores, Youn, Cha, Quercia, & Almeida, 2015, p. 221). They found Instagram users engaging with others in a homophilous way (based on age and gender). Of most interest, they found that the most common selfies were of young females except in Nigeria and Egypt "that show male dominance" (p. 222). Souza, et al. (2015) found some connections between a country's culture and the types of selfies posted:

There is a complex relationship between taking selfies and a country's culture. The chance of using selfie-related hashtags was higher for cultures with stronger local community membership as well as weaker perception of privacy. (Souza et al., 2015, p. 222)

What a "selfie" is is not clearly defined (Dinhopl & Gretzel, 2016, p. 130). Saltz (2014) suggests that digital self-portraits without the hands in a picture are not actually selfies but also suggests that the phenomenon of selfies is "in its Neolithic phase" (Saltz, 2014, p. 9); in other words, "selfies" are still being defined by practice. Another suggests that the selfie is its own "cultural category" and an outgrowth of digital social networks (Frosh, 2015, p. 1607). The implication is that selfies have a long way to go and will likely evolve as a phenomenon. Taking selfies is a practice that has gone global, and its popularity has not been missed by commercial interests. As a case in point, selfie-takers have become part of the tourist landscape and are catered to by commercial entities in the tourist industry (Dinhopl & Gretzel, 2016).

While selfies may be interesting as a cyber phenomenon, it is most often studied because it has reflections on the real world. A number of studies have found that online behaviors mimic people's offline personalities (Eftekhar, Fullwood, & Morris, 2014, p. 162). There is a cyber-physical confluence or overlap. Also, personal photographic images are shared based on various social uses, including three higher order ones: "constructing personal and group *memory*; creating and maintaining *social relationships*; and *self-expression and self-presentation*" (Van House, Davis, Takhteyev, Ames, & Finn, 2004, p. 1). A research team conducted two studies on selfie-sharing on multiple online social networks (OSNs). The 1,296 men and women who responded reported "sharing anywhere between 0 to 650 selfies per month on various OSN sites, and were found to post, on average, 2.9 selfies of themselves, 1.4 selfies with a romantic partner, and 2.2 group selfies to Facebook each month. Women posted more selfies of each type than did men. Regardless of sex, our results indicate that social exhibitionism and extraversion generally predicted the frequency of online selfie-posting in men and women, however we found no strong evidence for a relationship between self-esteem and selfie-posting behavior among women, and only weak evidence among men" (Sorokowska, Oleszkiewicz, Frackowiak, Pisanski, Chmiel, & Sorokowski, 2016, p. 119).

While selfies may have an impact on individuals' inner states, the actual selfie objects can take on some pretty banal forms. Given the awkwardness of many early selfies, there have been trainings on how to properly frame and capture a selfie image (Jain, Vijay, Maguluri, Sorathia, & Shukla, 2014). The informational value of selfies may be low in many cases, too. J. Saltz writes:

Let's stipulate that most selfies are silly, typical, boring. Guys flexing muscles, girls making pouty lips ("duckface"), people mugging in bars or throwing gang signs or posing with monuments or someone famous. Still, the new genre has its earmarks. Excluding those taken in mirrors—a distinct subset of this universe—selfies are nearly always taken from within an arm's length of the subject. For this reason the cropping and composition of selfies are very different from those of all preceding self-portraiture. (Saltz, 2014, p. 2)

Self-portraits, of course, are not a new phenomenon. They have had a long history in mediums like painting and then photography. As a closer precursor to the modern digital selfie, the first photographic selfie was taken in 1839 in the early days of photography by Robert Cornelius, an American innovator ("Selfies," Jan. 30, 2016, n.p.). The first use of the term "selfie" was in 2002 in an Australian blog. It was not until the broader publics were able to access smartphones with front-facing cameras and to share their images on image-sharing social media platforms that selfies really became popular. "Selfie" is seen as both social practice and object, or "sociomaterial practice" (Svelander & Wiberg, July – Aug. 2015, p. 38). These concepts are unpacked:

First and foremost, a selfie is a photographic object that initiates the transmission of human feeling in the form of a relationship (between photographer and photographed, between image and filtering software, between viewer and viewed, between individuals circulating images, between users and social software architectures, etc.). A selfie is also a practice—a gesture that can send (and is often intended to send) different messages to different individuals, communities, and audiences. This gesture may be dampened, amplified, or modified by social media censorship, social censure, misreading of the sender's original intent, or adding additional gestures to the mix, such as likes, comments, and remixes. (Senft & Baym, 2015, p. 1589)

5

The persistence of selfie practice is not simply an outcome of technological determinism. Some researchers suggest that selfies meet human needs for (social) identity performance (Zhao, Grasmuck, & Martin, 2008, as cited in Eftekhar, Fullwood, & Morris, 2014, p. 163). Social performance through social media is seen as self-agency and self-expression. The exchange of messaging enables people to bond, such as through time-limited (non-persistent, disappearing) snapchats (Piwek & Joinson, 2016). People have a psychological need for social recognition.

Socially Mediated Agentic Engagements With the World

Some point to the power of selfies in allowing people to display themselves in an authentic way and find acceptance. One example is in among "women with a difficult past or existing relations with their bodies and body-image (eating disorders, body-dysmorphism, stress from ageing)" who can express themselves in a self-affirming way and outside the social strictures of youth and thinness (Tiidenberg & Cruz, 2015, p. 12). The authors (2015) write:

For our participants, selfies shape the ways of knowing, understanding and experiencing their bodies. Taking and sharing selfies, combined, make possible to experience a body in ways that merge elements of both how we experience our bodies in photographs taken by others and how we observe our bodies in mirrors. This double axis helps with experiencing and internalizing both corporeal and conceptual transformations. (Tiidenberg & Cruz, 2015, p. 18)

People do not directly create their own senses of the world, but they interact with their environments socially in order to understand it" (Charon, 2004, p. 31). People have social power in affecting both their own lives and others,' and this power is magnified in social media. P. Frosh writes of the selfie as a gestural image, in which the producer of the image and its referent are the same:

The selfie is a preeminent conductor of embodied social energy because it is a kinesthetic image: it is a product of kinetic bodily movement; it gives aesthetic, visible form to that movement in images; and it is inscribed in the circulation of kinetic and responsive social energy among users of movement-based digital technologies. As a kinesthetic image, then, the selfie makes visible a broader kinesthetic domain of digital culture that is relatively overlooked as an object of analysis. (Frosh, 2015, p. 1623)

Selfies are part of what Frosh (2015) calls "phatic communion," a speech act that requires social responses as a matter of course. In conceptualizing selfies as social practice, they enable community maintenance—such as in the sharing of life experiences with one's ego neighborhood (those with direct ties). While selfies are "one-way communication," those who share expect their Instagram followers to "communicate back to them through likes and comments" (Svelander & Wiberg, July – Aug. 2015, p. 37), resulting in two-way and multi-way communications. This is not about passive image consumption. [One education-based research project used the metaphor of the selfie in the learning of science. Here, elementary-age students take selfies of themselves engaged in scientific experiments, and they also interview their friends. Selfie-taking here is an act of technology learning and co-teaching and co-learning in communities of practice (Bonsignore, et al., 2014, p. 135).]

Wannabes Attracted to Celebrity Culture

Some find the "selfie" practice as a metaphor for a generational narcissistic self-regard to the exclusion of broader social interests. Two psychologists have observed a generational "narcissism epidemic" of youth who pursue adulation and affirmation of their own importance, leading to antisocial behavior and incivility (Twenge & Campbell, 2009). These authors find a contemporary analog of Narcissus (of Greek mythology), who so loved his own image reflected in a pool that he is unable to leave it, and eventually dies of this self-obsession; Echo, whose love for Narcissus goes unrequited, ends up alone and bereaved, with her only traces in sound energy.

Selfie-taking is a sign of personhood run amuck, a syndrome of self-directed practices that draws from celebrity culture and self-promotional practices used media for amplification. The majority of individuals who post selfies are engaging in "aspirational production"; they are creating personal brands that show them as high-status individuals or "microcelebrities" (or "subcultural celebrities" or "niche celebrities") based on particular niches. A.E. Marwick writes, "While nobody may actually be paying attention, aspirational producers want the audience to think that they are being snapped by the paparazzi even if their pictures are actually taken by a best friend or boyfriend" (Marwick, 2015, p. 156). Teen users of social media, though, judge self-photographs based on the subject's nonverbal, and they evaluated as follows:

Snapshots of people were considered authentic whereas posing for the camera or imitating role models from celebrity culture was evaluated as inauthentic.

7

The category of "meta-photographs" (Mitchell, 1995), including selfies, was intrinsically inauthentic for this group of people. Overall, factor 1 rejected the styles of current juvenile visual self-representations as being inauthentic. From these findings, it can be concluded that participants in factor 1 consider selfies a gratuitous, useless form of representation. The second group, factor 2, estimated authenticity based on the photo situation. If the situation seems to be set up in order to take pictures, the resulting self-photographs were considered as inauthentic. In contrast, for the third group, factor 3, not the content but the stylistic features—and thus the "how"—determined authenticity whereas the "what" (e.g., motifs, situations) was of less relevance. Thus, stylistic features are particularly important to teenagers familiar with currently popular picture editing practices, photo filters, and photo apps. The last group of participants, factor 4, again focused on the conditions of taking photos. These respondents appreciated photographs showing people in natural, everyday situations depicted in a nonprofessional "amateur way" instead of artistic and visually scripted or composed pictures. (Lobinger & Brantner, 2015, p. 1856)

"Instafame" is the faux version of actual fame. (In terms of user accounts on social media, most if not all follow a power curve, with a few attracting the majority of followers and the rest part of the "long tail," with few followers and maybe many imaginary ones.) The ones who achieve high follower numbers on Instagram, a photo-sharing app, are those who fairly closely emulate mainstream celebrities:

While Instagram makes it possible for "regular people" to attract the mass audiences historically limited to broadcast media, the Instafamous tend to be conventionally good-looking, work in "cool" industries such as modeling or tattoo artistry, and emulate the tropes and symbols of traditional celebrity culture, such as glamorous self-portraits, designer goods, or luxury cars. I argue that Instagram represents a convergence of cultural forces: a mania for digital documentation, the proliferation of celebrity and microcelebrity culture, and conspicuous consumption. Instafame demonstrates that while microcelebrity is widely practiced, those successful at gaining attention often reproduce conventional status hierarchies of luxury, celebrity, and popularity that depend on the ability to emulate the visual iconography of mainstream celebrity culture. This emulation calls into question the idea that social media are an egalitarian, or even just a more accessible, way for individuals to access the currency of the attention economy. (Marwick, 2015, p. 139)

In an attention economy, those who can compete socially emulate those real-world celebrities (musicians, actors, models, and athletes) who are actually able to monetize their social sharing (turn their fame into money).

Most public figures of note are represented by public relations agencies that work to groom their public image and to turn their unsung positive activities into news (and to hide or downplay negative activities). (A majority of news covered in newspapers today are as the result of publicity releases, for example.) Real-world celebrities "socially reproduce" themselves in some of their followers. Selfies (as practiced) further enable the reproduction of social norms and hierarchies in terms of gender representations that show females in positions of "weakness, subordination, and seduction," "objectification," and "loss of control" and with sparse clothing while males are shown with "muscle presentation" (Döring, Reif, & Poeschl, 2016, p. 955). In this content analysis, the research team explained gender expression on two levels: how the persons in the selfies "a) bring certain gender expressions with them (e.g. through their styling and attire) and…b) create gender expressions while taking the selfies (e.g. through choice of posture, facial expression or gaze in the photo)" (Döring, Reif, & Poeschl, 2016, p. 955). These findings elaborate on those of a prior one that showed selfies emulating the self-objectification of the female body in broader mass media and celebrity culture (Walrave, Ponnet, Van Ouytsel, Van Gool, Heirman, & Verbeek, 2015).

Besides copying celebrities, there are other ways to attract social media attention and become popular. An inference-based study of a selfie set of 46,000 images resulted in insights about what makes selfies popular, in terms of objects and sentiment-based contents.

We observed that among ImageNet object categories: mail-lot, lab coat, jersey, fur coat, brassiere, wig, abaya, hair spray, suit, sunglasses, and lipstick (in decreasing order) are the most relevant objects to the popularity of selfies. Among different ANPs (adjective-noun pairs) in SentiBank: sexy dress, lovely dress, fancy dress, traditional tattoo, smiling baby, shiny hair, sexy girls, cute baby, strong legs, stupid hat and happy baby (in decreasing order) are the most relevant concepts to the popularity score. (Kalayeh, Seifu, LaLanne, & Shah, 2015, p. 925)

They also observed that "more positive sentiment, on average, results in a higher popularity" (Kalayeh, Seifu, LaLanne, & Shah, 2015, p. 926). Having a good laugh is one common way people may raise their mood.

Humor, as professionally practiced in the West, can at first seem like all comedian id and no superego. Comedians can share whatever comes to mind—profane, sacrilegious, and irreverent—as they're riffing on stage. The interaction with the audience can be sharp and aggressive, and occasionally, even the most practiced practitioner of the dark arts of comedy will hit a nerve, mis-time whether a sensitive issue may be addressed, and be held to account in public with accusations of poor taste—or worse—discrimination based on racism or sexism. Researchers have suggested that identity-based humor may have historically had prosocial benefits, such as enabling minority populations to practice coping against racism from those in the majority and survive persecution (Rappoport, 2005, p. 67); however, appropriation of such humor by outside groups can be highly offensive and may perpetuate "internalized oppression" and "system justification" for existing social power structures. Humor has had links to social change in part because they help people to see in new ways (Rappoport, 2005, pp. 66, 72) and to engage in social discourse; the practice of humor may support hope over cynicism (p. 70). Ideally, social norms would restrain the worst impulses in people—as individuals and as groups—to control against selfishness, harmful behaviors, deceptions, defamations, and rumor mongering; ideally, social norms would be in place to protect people's human rights and enable societies to progress.

THE SELFIE PHENOMENON AS OBSERVED ON SOCIAL MEDIA PLATFORMS

So what are some ways to understand selfies in terms of social media. A few data extractions were culled to highlight some of the richer evocations of selfies. These approaches involve various types of link analysis, network graphing, and related data visualizations. Figures 1 – 4 are all network diagrams, which are node-link structures. Here, the respective nodes represent entities, and the lines represent links, and the arrow heads (if present) represent directionality.

First, a one-degree article network was extracted from the Selfie page (located at https://en.wikipedia.org/wiki/Selfie) on Wikipedia. An article network shows the outlinks from the target "selfie" page. These outlinks are actual human-made links to other related articles on Wikipedia. In Figure 1, the "selfie" is linked to public figures, social media platforms, media outlets, technologies, and at the left, "comedic." There are 131 nodes and 130 links.

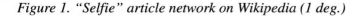

Figure 1. "Selfie" article network on Wikipedia (1 deg.)

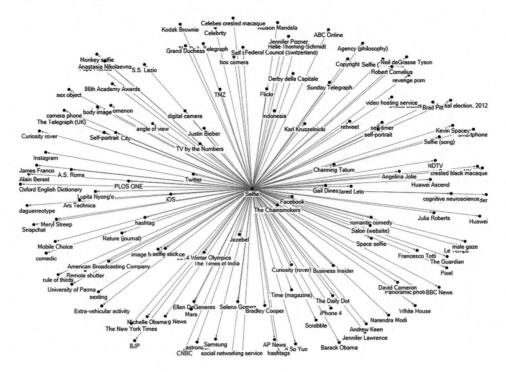

(Figures 1 – 4 and Tables 1 – 4 were achieved using Network Overview, Discovery, and Exploration for Excel or NodeXL.)

Table 1 shows the graphic metrics related to Figure 1.

To capture some of the social media accounts using #selfie to tag their messages on the microblogging site Twitter, a #selfie hashtag network was extracted. A #hashtag network captures some of the social media user accounts engaged in recent conversations labeled with the target hashtag (in this case, #selfie). This graph has 297 vertices with 229 unique links. In this network, there are 220 groups (based on the Clauset-Newman-Moore clustering algorithm). In other words, those engaging in this discussion are not deeply inter-connected but are linked in a number of smaller connections, such as dyads and triadic groups. This may be seen in Figure 2.

Table 2 shows the underlying graph metrics for Figure 2.

A keyword network graph shows the social media user accounts linked to messaging around a particular shared keyword, even if the messaging is not interrelated (such as when social media account users are messaging

Table 1. Graph metrics table for the "Selfie" article network on Wikipedia (1 deg.)

Graph Metric	Value
Graph Type	Directed
Vertices	131
Unique Edges	130
Edges With Duplicates	0
Total Edges	130
Self-Loops	0
Reciprocated Vertex Pair Ratio	0
Reciprocated Edge Ratio	0
Connected Components	1
Single-Vertex Connected Components	0
Maximum Vertices in a Connected Component	131
Maximum Edges in a Connected Component	130
Maximum Geodesic Distance (Diameter)	2
Average Geodesic Distance	1.969582
Graph Density	0.007633588
Modularity	Not Applicable
NodeXL Version	1.0.1.336

independently on an issue). The graph relatedness of a #hashtag network vs. a keyword network is often denser in the first case and less dense (less connected) in the latter. [Interestingly though, in this case of the #selfie hashtag network graph vs. the keyword network graph, the graph density of the latter is denser or more connected. This is generally anomalous at least based on graph explorations of the past few years by the author.] In terms of a "keyword search" for "selfie" on Twitter, a network of 119 vertices was extracted; within this network, there are 72 groups (based on the Clauset-Newman-Moore clustering algorithm), which shows again low connectivity within the social graph and small clusters of small groups sharing around "selfies".

Table 3 shows the extracted graphic metrics for Figure 3.

Finally, "selfie" was used as a seeding term to extract a related tags network from Flickr (an image and video-sharing site). Tags are "related" by co-occurrence in their application in describing shared visuals on this content-sharing site. Whenever the #selfie tag was used to describe a particular shared image, other tags were also used. The co-occurrence means that the

Figure 2. #selfie hashtag network on Twitter

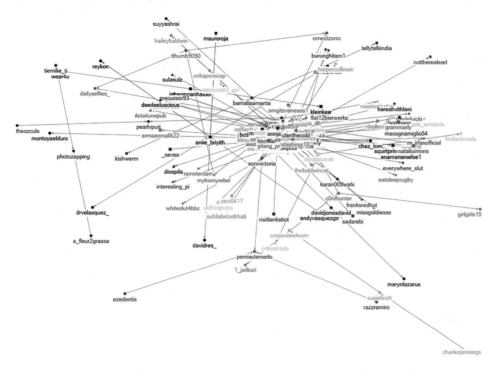

tags tend to appear together to describe the same image. In this case, there are references to people types (woman, self), emotions (love, happy, fun), body parts (eye, face, hair, hands), clothing (jeans), colors (red, orange, pink, bw, light, dark), technologies (canon, photoshop), and so on. The graph at Figure 4 includes some related thumbnail images. This related tags network has 56 vertices (nodes) and 55 unique links.

Table 4 shows the underlying graph metrics data for Figure 4.

The platform from which the selfies in this study are extracted is Instagram. Instagram was launched in 2010 as a free mobile app around the idea of an "instant telegram" built around image sharing (Systrom, Jan. 12, 2011). Facebook purchased Instagram in September 2012 ("Privacy Policy," 2016). It currently has over 300 million active users as of December 2014 (Fiegerman, 2014). This platform has attracted a young demographic, with over 90% of its users under 35; on this platform, teens tend to be more active socially (Jang, Han, Shih, & Lee, 2015, pp. 4039 - 4040). Many of its highly followed accounts "are packed with selfies" (Marwick, 2015, pp. 141 – 142). [A comparison set of "humor" "selfie" imagery was captured from Flickr

Table 2. Graph Metrics Table for the #selfie Hashtag Network on Twitter

Graph Type	Directed
Vertices	297
Unique Edges	229
Edges With Duplicates	82
Total Edges	311
Self-Loops	228
Reciprocated Vertex Pair Ratio	0
Reciprocated Edge Ratio	0
Connected Components	220
Single-Vertex Connected Components	170
Maximum Vertices in a Connected Component	9
Maximum Edges in a Connected Component	12
Maximum Geodesic Distance (Diameter)	2
Average Geodesic Distance	0.670194
Graph Density	0.000910001
Modularity	Not Applicable
NodeXL Version	1.0.1.336

using the Flickr Downloadr web app on Google Chrome, and the 61 images were qualitatively different than those on Instagram. In this latter set, there were a number of self-mocking selfies—with people playing dress-up or finding sublime ridiculousness in daily life. There was only one selfie set up as a meme, with an illustration and textual commentary. In a sense, on Flickr, the selfie "humor" phenomenon did not seem as much of a "thing". Its focus as an image and video content-sharing site seems somewhat less about selfie-ness and more about other in-world phenomena. This may be an issue of demographics of users as well.]

Messaging is complex, and it is possible to come away from #selfie #humor with a range of overlapping and incongruent understandings and misunderstandings. It is the inherent provocative nature of humor that makes its expression in wholly public spaces so socially risky and potentially offensive. The boundaries and lines-not-to-be-crossed differ among people. What is non-jokable for some is totally fair game for others. Online is not a "safe space" for such explorations, in a sense, because there are not direct ways to mitigate for offenses (such as comedy clubs or movie theatres). In live comedy settings, the comedians are testing their audiences for readiness

Figure 3. "selfie" keyword search network on Twitter (in a spiral graph)

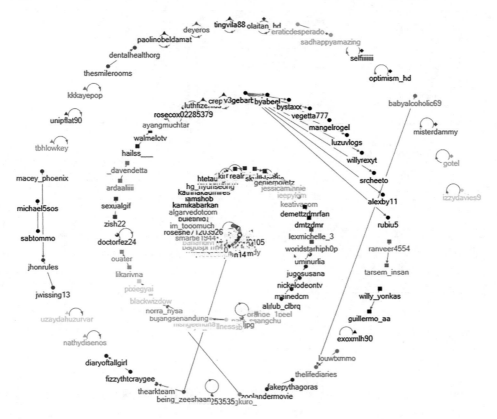

for certain riffs and jokes, and they will make adjustments as needed. The dynamic for online selfies is somewhat different because of a distinct lack of shared context (except cyber). The joke tellers are not identifiable comedic personalities (mostly). Some jokes may appeal to a particular demographic but not others; as a case in point, physical humor (like falling down) and fart jokes may appeal to young adult males but maybe less so for other groups.

Six Theories of Humor

Currently, there are six general theories of humor that are sufficiently broad as to be universal (Rappoport, 2005, pp. 15–30): (1) superiority, (2) incongruity, (3) surprise, (4) ambivalence, (5) cognitive, and (6) release and relief. Humans are socially conscious beings, and they appreciate feeling superior at the expense of others; they appreciate the creation of vertical distance with others when

Table 3. Graph metrics for the "selfie" keyword search network on Twitter

Graph Metric	Value
Graph Type	Directed
Vertices	119
Unique Edges	88
Edges With Duplicates	2
Total Edges	90
Self-Loops	43
Reciprocated Vertex Pair Ratio	0
Reciprocated Edge Ratio	0
Connected Components	72
Single-Vertex Connected Components	42
Maximum Vertices in a Connected Component	10
Maximum Edges in a Connected Component	9
Maximum Geodesic Distance (Diameter)	4
Average Geodesic Distance	0.958199
Graph Density	0.003347102
Modularity	Not Applicable
NodeXL Version	1.0.1.336

others are insulted or ridiculed, punked, or fooled. In this thinking, people's inherent *schadenfreude* emerges—with people experiencing pleasure at others' pain or misfortune. Another cause for humor is "incongruity" or the surprise at observing something that shouldn't go together. In this category are such things as animals engaged in human activities or unexpected scenarios. In the third case, surprise (sudden positive things) may lead to the perception of humor; as an example, random obscenities and pratfalls may strike people as funny. Ambivalence—simultaneously feeling positive and negative feelings about an issue—may produce humor. One example in this category is gallows humor. A "cognitive" component may also be important to humor because appreciating some types of humor will require an intellectual and rational understanding vs. just an emotional response. In this sense, humor has a strong cultural component, which requires some cultural understandings in order to "get" and appreciate a joke. [Humor involves "cognitive, emotional, behavioral, psychophysiological, and social aspects" (Martin, 2000, as cited in Martin, 2001, p. 505)]. Finally, the "release and relief" aspect suggests that some issues arouse tension (an aversive state), and to relieve that tension, the

Figure 4. "selfie" related tags network on Flickr (with thumbnail images included)

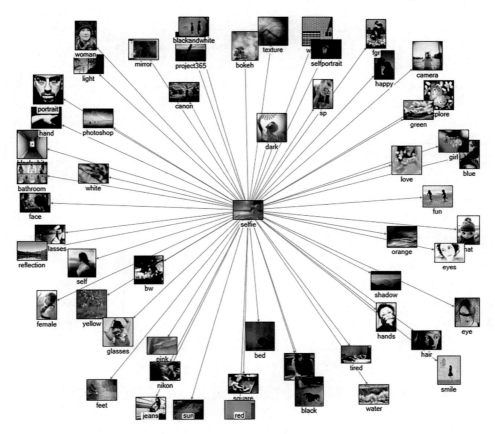

socially acceptable way to relieve that is sometimes to laugh. Humor helps moderate stress, relieve the perception of pain (Rappoport, 2005, p. 26), and may have long-term positive health effects (Martin, 2001, p. 506). Jokes may be made about socially loaded topics—politics, religion, sex, finances—in order to engage difficult issues. Each of the theories is plausible, but their effects overlap, and these effects may be hard to separate.

What creates an individual's sense of humor involves both biological brain features as well as cultural influences (based on lived experiences), so this involves both nature and nurture (to use the colloquial reference). Babies as young as four months old will laugh instinctively; humor is an inborn human capability (Rappoport, 2005, p. 15, 129). Laughter itself may be voiced or unvoiced; in a social context, it is often voiced. Laughter itself tends to be highly social, and is 30 times more likely in social than solitary situations "in

Table 4. Graph metrics table for the "selfie" related tags network on Flickr (1 deg.)

Graph Metric	Value
Graph Type	Directed
Vertices	56
Unique Edges	55
Edges With Duplicates	0
Total Edges	55
Self-Loops	0
Reciprocated Vertex Pair Ratio	0
Reciprocated Edge Ratio	0
Connected Components	1
Single-Vertex Connected Components	0
Maximum Vertices in a Connected Component	56
Maximum Edges in a Connected Component	55
Maximum Geodesic Distance (Diameter)	2
Average Geodesic Distance	1.929209
Graph Density	0.017857143
Modularity	Not Applicable
NodeXL Version	1.0.1.336

the absence of stimulating media (television, radio or books)" (Provine, 1996, p. 41). Laughter is 46% more likely by those speaking than those listening; in other words, speakers tend to laugh at their own jokes. Laughter itself often follows comments not necessarily intended to be funny but is used to punctuate particular points in speech (Provine, 2004).

Shared senses of humor bode well for long-term and happy relationships (Rappoport, 2005, p. 26). Indeed, a psychometric tool measuring humor styles, the Humor Styles Questionnaire (HSQ), has been used to study how humor styles align with personality measures. The HSQ suggests that there are four predominant humor styles: affiliative, self-enhancing, aggressive, and self-defeating. Affiliational humor (sharing humorous anecdotes, sharing witticisms) helps connect the individual with others in a constructive way; self enhancing humor (using humor to deal with stress) benefits the individual's psychological well-being; aggressive humor (using ridicule, using sarcasm) is off-putting to others, and self-defeating humor (using self-disparagement or self put-downs) tends to harm psychological well-being. The first two humor styles tend to be adaptive, and the latter two are maladaptive. Certain types of humor behaviors are linked to each of the four categories. In a study involving 450 pairs of adult twins, one research team found connections between the four humor styles and the so-called Big 5 Personality Traits: extraversion, agreeableness, openness, conscientiousness, and neuroticism. They found that affiliative and self-enhancing humor correlated positively with extraversion and openness to experience (Vernon, Martin, Schermer, & Mackie, 2008, p. 1124). They add:

In contrast, aggressive and self-defeating humor correlated positively with neuroticism (consistent with previous findings of associations with negative moods such as depression, anxiety, and anger) and correlated negatively with conscientiousness (suggesting lower levels of thoughtfulness and impulse control, which might contribute to inappropriate uses of humor in social situations). Furthermore, only self-enhancing humor correlated negatively with neuroticism and positively with agreeableness, providing additional evidence that this perspective-taking humor style is particularly associated with emotional and social well-being. Finally, aggressive humor was most strongly negatively correlated with agreeableness, indicating that it is particularly associated with low levels of empathy and concern for others, and potentially contributing to poorer interpersonal relationships. In sum, these findings provide further support for the view that individuals' humor styles are colored by their broader personality traits. (Vernon, Martin, Schermer, & Mackie, 2008, p. 1124)

These findings have strong implications for using humor to reverse-engineer the personality traits of the person engaging in that humor. Another study used the Humor Styles Questionnaire to see if there were alignments between humor styles and the so-called Dark Triad personality traits (which include narcissism, Machiavellianism, and psychopathy). These traits are known as an "antisocial trinity". Narcissism involves feelings of superiority, Machiavellianism with manipulativeness of others, and psychopathy with a disregard for others, impulsivity, and selfishness. This research team found the following:

Results revealed that participants who scored higher on sub-clinical psychopathy and Machiavellianism exhibited a greater tendency to employ negative humor styles (aggressive, self-defeating), whereas individuals who obtained higher scores on narcissism were more prone to employing a positive affiliative humor style. (Veselka, Schermer, Martin, & Vernon, 2010, p. 772)

This research team also found that narcissism did not show correlations with negative humor styles (aggressive humor, self-defeating humor), and psychopathy and Machiavellianism showed no correlations with the positive humor styles (affiliational humor, self-enhancing humor) (Veselka, Schermer, Martin, & Vernon, 2010, p. 774).

Even without probing the types of humor expressed, there are other channels in selfies that enable some fairly accurate "zero-acquaintance" judgments of the individual through a kind of remote profiling. On research team lists some of the cues:

An accumulating body of research indicates that personality can be judged by unfamiliar others with reasonable accuracy. Such zero-acquaintance judgments (Kenny & West, 2008) are made possible by the presence of personality-related cues, such as facial expressions (Kenny, Horner, Kashy, & Chu, 1992), physical appearance (Borkenau & Liebler, 1992; Naumann et al., 2009), choices of footwear (Gillath et al., 2012), living environment (Gosling et al., 2002), musical preferences (Rentfrow & Gosling, 2006), and linguistic patterns (Holleran & Mehl, 2008; Mehl, Gosling, & Pennebaker, 2006; Qiu, Lin, Ramsay, et al., 2012). (Qiu, Lu, Yang, Qu, & Zhu, 2015, p. 443)

Some of the cues may be more effective than others for an accurate interpretation of the personality behind the social selfie.

People learn social stereotypes as a shorthand about the world, so they can engage it more easily without having to think-through each social context. Stereotypes simplify the world, and heuristics may be applied to the stereotypes for fast (and maybe not better) decision-making—which require less cognitive energy investment. Socially, there are many problems with stereotypes. By definition, these are over-generalizations, with some aspects of truth and falsity. Stereotypes (whether positive or negative) categorize people into groups without acknowledging their unique aspects. The use of stereotypes may discourage individuals from exploring further or considering possible exceptions and outliers.

Stereotypes may communicate negative messages to the targets of those stereotypes by discouraging them from pursuing particular ambitions or expressing other parts of themselves. In acting on their understandings of others, those who use stereotypes may misunderstand who they are dealing with and shortchange others. Humor, when combined with stereotypes, is even more distorting than a straight stereotype. Humor is not observational truth but has a component of exaggeration and absurdity (what George Carlin describes as "one thing way out of proportion" or Sid Caesar suggests is truth with "a little curlicue at the end").

Social Groupings

Beyond geography and history, there are biological explanations of the persistence of social groupings. Social groups, with shared evolved cultures, have formed as a response to pathogens. In-group members share knowledge and learned behaviors to avoid pathogens, which explains in part the sense of risk of strangers who are not aware of the careful behaviors to avoid infections (Shah, 2016).

Ethnicity is one way that individuals may group into social units; an ethnic group may be one based around race, religion, nation, region, language, or other types of national or cultural grouping. Ethnic humor, like other types of humor, many be polysemic, with both shallow surface insights and deeper ones. To extract the deeper messaging, it is important to bring critical thinking and sophistication to the humor, but most people do not have formal humor training, and they may not have the time to mull what the humor means. They may not be able to tease out explicit and implicit contents. The subtext itself may be elusive. Research on how people respond to humor shows that people often misread jokes—their meanings and their targets. There is a lack of clarity between perceived intensions and actual ones. When people react to jokes, they are bringing to bear their own backgrounds, life experiences, pre-existing knowledge, and social expectations. How people respond to humor may also depend on what they are doing at the moment they are engaging with the humor. If they are engaging actively with their full cognition, that may result in a different understanding than if they were processing the information passively.

In humor studies, certain cultures have defined justifiable targets for humor. In the U.S., these have included the following: sexual minority groups, political groups, immigrants, regional groups, groups based on lifestyle, religious groups, overweight people, those from poorer or lower social classes, feminists, and "groups perceived to be threatening." Those who would argue against ethnic humor point out that it may be used to teach stereotypes of others and may reinforce prejudice and existing social imbalances in power. It may create a norm of prejudice (Ford & Ferguson, 2004). Others suggest that there may be prosocial aspects to ethnic humor by opening up dialogues among groups and populations. Ethnic humor may be used to ridicule stereotypes. It may empower ethnic groups by enabling them to better cope with prejudice; small doses of micro-aggressions may serve as inoculation against future experiences with prejudice. Ethnic humor may relieve intergroup tensions by providing a cathartic outlet of laughter. Shared humor may promote intergroup affiliation.

EXPLORING #SELFIE #HUMOR IN AN INSTAGRAM IMAGE SET

The initial intuition for this work is that an image set (seeded from "#selfie #humor Instagram") may provide some insights about identity-based humor. After all, there are manifestations of cyber in the real and of real in the cyber. The research broke out into three main prongs:

1. What does identity-based humor look like in terms of a #selfie #humor-tagged image set from the Instagram photo-sharing mobile app?
2. What earlier findings and theories about humor apply to the more modern forms of mediated social humor? Is it possible to effectively apply the Humor Styles Model to the images from the #selfie #humor Instagram image set to better understand #selfie #humor? If so, what may be discoverable using this approach?
3. What are some constructive and systematized ways to analyze social image sets in an emergent way using manual and computer-supported techniques?

The first two questions relate to online selfie humor, and the third question deals with insights on how to code and analyze social imagery for research.

The research was set up as follows. First there was conceptualization of using a #selfie #humor image set from Instagram for research. To see if this work had been done before and to see where new territory may be explored, a review of the literature followed, with focuses on Instagram, social image analysis, and humor. Then, there was an extraction of the image set (mostly as small-sized thumbnail images) using first Google Images and then Microsoft Bing Images. The image set was identified using #selfie and #humor and Instagram, and then the images were captured from the web browser. Two web browser add-ons were used to extract the images: Google Chrono Download Manager (on Google Chrome web browser) and DownThemAll (on Firefox).

While the add-ons enabled extraction of uniform resource locators (URLs) and other file types from the Instagram site, these additional data types were not extracted. In total, there were 675 images from the Google Image collection and 266 from the Microsoft Bing Images one, for a total of 941. In total, 694 images (or 74%) from the 941 were original and non-duplicative. From the initial extractions already, the set of images was a partial sample (without an N of all). The extracted set is apparently recent, but not likely random nor "representative" because of its non-randomness. (For an actual "baseline," it would be necessary to capture a random sample of imagery that is sufficiently large to represent the whole set. For imagery from social media, the sample image set sizes would have to potentially be "big data"-sized sets.)

The images were collected over two days in order to try for time-based variation. The extracted imagery—downloaded in numbered format (without the retention of the original image file names or related metadata)—was then ingested into NVivo 11 Plus, into two folders (one for the set from Google Images and one from Bing Images).

In terms of analysis, there were two general approaches: (1) descriptive (qualitative and quantitative), and (2) interpretive and analytical. The descriptive approach entailed first an extraction of emergent themes using a basic grounded theory approach. Here, spelled-out #hashtagged campaigns and memes were lightly explored for understanding. Images without clear provenance were placed into TinEye (a reverse image search capability with a web-facing interface available at https://www.tineye.com/) for possible identification. Images in different languages were translated in Google Translate to aid in meaning interpretation. Public figures were identified, and their online profiles were lightly perused. In a few cases, particular messages and images were pursued, which led to some questionable websites (that might have been used for phishing or the distribution of malware, such as keyloggers). Underlying both descriptive and interpretive / analytical approaches is the common practice of perceptual analysis, or analysis by unaided ear and eye first, and then some computer-aided approaches based on initial leads generated by human perception.

The idea though was to capture meaning from the images in as simple a way as possible and not to get in too far into qualitative interpretation. Some images had untranslatable text in foreign languages. Some images were too pixelated to make out. Some images had cultural references that were not readily decipherable. Some images were blurry in an unintended way, while others seemed to have been blurred for artistic effect (such as one urban shot of snow on the ground and water condensation on a window with tight depth of field, which blurred the people in the frame in the snow). One image was deeply under-exposed and would require some recovery work in Adobe Photoshop® to possibly make out. If something was utterly befuddling and indecipherable, the image was left out of the image set count and the interpretation count. A further descriptive approach involved describing the image set involved a quantitative approach. Here, the images were categorized based on several features: the number of people in each image (none, single, duo, or group), the gender of the depicted individuals, the various objects used to represent people in selfies (animals, objects, text, and others), and some cross-references of these various descriptors. Once the basic set was described, the findings from the #selfie #humor image set were analyzed in the context of humor research to see what initial exploratory comparisons and contrasts could be made. This follow-on research was more interpretive and analytical. The research may be conceptualized in five general recursively sequenced steps (as depicted in Figure 5):

1. Review of the Literature
2. Extraction of (Targeted) Imagery from a Social Media Platform(s)
3. Ingestion of Imagery into NVivo 11 Plus
4. Analysis and Interpretation
5. Consideration for Future Research (and Methodologies)

Figure 5. Analyzing social imagery: An overview of the research design and approach

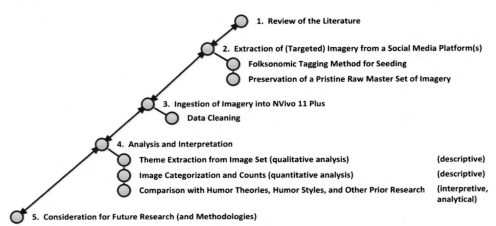

The point of the process-based recursion is to show that this is not a sequentially lock-step process but an adaptable one that may be changed up based on needs.

For this research, an image set of #selfie #humor was extracted from Instagram using two different extraction times. The resulting image set is depicted in Figure 6 as the middle section of this Venn diagram (#selfie AND #humor AND Instagram).

Some General Features of the #Selfie #Humor Image Set

As an image set, the visual depictions were not necessarily sophisticated nor complex. Many images seemed to have been taken on-the-fly or create by happenstance, with little in the way of setup, except for maybe a dozen or so of the images. Some of the images also appeared to be found ones, including screen grabs of television sitcoms and movie trailers. In a few cases, drawings seem to have been usurped for the expression of a concept, with abstracted representations of people. Of these, one was of a person dressed up as Batman and holding up a sign to hitch a ride to Gotham City. Another was of a guy taking a selfie in a bathroom over the wall in order to show a couple having sex standing up in the next cubicle. A few involved pranks, such as a young man urinating on a drunk guy passed out (drunk of intoxicated) on the grass. (This prank—and some others—seemed to involve targets who may not have been in on the joke. In some, there is a sense of a doer and a done-to, in the

Figure 6. #selfie #humor image set from Instagram

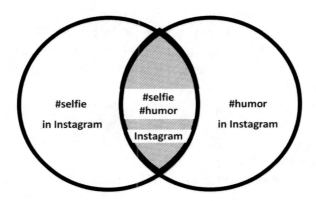

classic sense of a troll context.) The prior photo may also fit in the category of "antic photos" (Saltz, 2014, p. 8), which focus on the grotesque.

There was a few that likely involved some image editing. From a glance, it looked like a majority of the images were captured with smart phones, camera phones, web cams, digital cameras, cameras on tripods, cameras on selfie sticks, screen capture software, and probably some other devices. Certainly, various commercial entities have selfie kiosks and wall stations; some tourist destinations have designated selfie spots—places to stand to take selfies with memorable backgrounds. Some images were "found" ones on the Internet and repurposed for #humor.

The technological savvy to create the images varied. On the higher end would involve the application of tinting, vignetting (darkening outside edges of an image in order to focus viewer eyes on the center of the image), gradient mask application, and superimposing images in layers. The messaging in this image set seemed more to be about wit and insight, the one-up and the "gotcha," and social commentary than about digital image artistry. On the lower end would be uploading an image with a quip or a tag. Some of the images in this collection seem to have started off with a funny image, and then the person puts a humorous spin on it. For example, a pregnant woman is shown along with the caption, "when you accidentally swallow a watermelon seed." In another cropped image, a young girl is facing the camera but looking right, with a stuffed giraffe framed behind her: "There's something behind me isn't there?"

Some of the #selfie #humor images involve word play (wit or punning with words). For example, one involved the polysemic nature of the word "high." The image read: "If a midget smokes weed, does he get high or medium?" Another one, somewhat more risqué, involved a play on the word "watch": "My lesbian neighbors asked me what I want for my birthday. They gave me a Rolex. I think they misunderstood when I said, 'I wanna watch.'" One drawing showed a cell taking a "cell-fie"; this latter one was a play on pronunciation. One road sign for a church read: "It's spring. We're so excited we wet our plants."

Visual gags were also very common. Some visual gags show fictional characters acting out-of-character. There is a Disney Cinderella smoking a splif and looking high, and Kermit (frog) smoking while holding his middle digit to the camera. In another, an image of a stern Meryl Streep (in character) saying, in Portuguese, "I do not like, and I do not disguise" or maybe "I do not disguise my dislike." Several of the #humor #selfies involved both known characters and common folks making funny faces: Mr. Bean with his wide-eyed funny face, and others engaging the camera to express humor.

Another type of visual gag involved side-by-side comparatives, such as one with a cartoon figure on one side and a baby with a somewhat similar intense look on the other. The caption: "I am honestly on the floor crying @ this picture" (This was presented as a social share of a found object.) The side-by-side visual structure invites comparisons. Another visual tag uses the diptych structure as a before and after. There are other visual gags, showing images as sequences, with a starting image…an ending image…and implied actions in between. In terms of numbers of images for such sequences, the highest seemed to be about six.

The visual gags in selfies can be fairly complex. In one, a litter of puppies with curly brown hair was overlaid on the surface of an outdoor grill. The text reads: "If you saw fried chicken instead of cute dogs you have fat mind." The joke here is on the viewer depending on how they decoded that image. At a first and fast glance on a mobile device, the image could have looked like fried chicken pieces on a grill (although fried chicken is deep-fried and not grilled). In another visual gag, a man is lying in bed, but he seems to be riding a bicycle in a spliced photomontage image: "Doing my morning cardio like…" He could be bicycling but thinking of sleep, or he could be sleeping and thinking about bicycling. In another, an ostrich is shown with the text: "Ermahgerd! Strarberries!" or translated "Oh, my God! Strawberries!" (or "OMG…") The joke is partially in imagining what an ostrich might sound like but also in what is astonishing or interesting to an ostrich.

Selfies (Literally) Taken Out of Original Context

These images, while originally portrayed in an original context—a user account, a series of images, a reply to another user—were scraped from Instagram in a de-contextualized way. These #selfie #humor images were without name and without the relational interaction context. If these were used to call out others or reply to challenges, that was not generally ascertainable with the stand-alone selfie image. If the context were investigated and preserved, there would be additional color and meaning. As such, these images seem to be pieces of social discourse that on their face can be difficult. After all, people have to work on relationships to build the history, sense of safety, trust, and intimacy, in order to share difficult truths. Otherwise, false intimacy notes may ring untrue and come across as manipulations. This tension may be observed on social media when a stranger's comment is unwelcome and offensive; common responses to such social intrusions are, "Who (the ***) are you to…?" Even if comments are made in a generic way, comments are often interpreted as personal (related directly to the hearer as a form of "direct address"). The thinking goes like this: "Why is this person discussing this (generic) issue with *me? There* must be something in this discussion that applies to me." This lack of context may affect the core meaning of the selfie. It may be true that "You had to be there" to fully understand and appreciate the humor.

Image Vetting

Images that were obvious advertisements were not used. (There is a bifurcation between commercial/professional and amateur uses of #selfie and #humor images on Instagram, in terms of messaging contents and the quality of the imagery. [As noted in other research, selfie images created by non-professional photographers do not follow any of the three tenets of professional imagery: the rule of thirds, the golden ratio rule, or the eye centering principle. This research team posits that none of these three features "is strongly rooted in spontaneous perceptual preferences," so these must be learned skills (Bruno, Gabriele, Tasso, & Bertamini, 2014, pp. 45 - 46) and are not fundamental principles of visual perception (p. 56). So-called "naïve aesthetics" were a common feature of the image set.] Public service announcements were also not generally used. Two of the selfies looked like potential screenshots from pornographic videos, and those were not directly included. While some of the selfies were racist, sexist, and / or offensive in other ways, they were still included because to omit them would remove a large portion of the image set. The author did use care not to allow the chapter to be a conduit for hate messaging. If an image appeared more than once, it was not counted twice. If an image was used with different messaging and text overlays, those were counted separately. If an image fit multiple categories, it was counted in both categories; however, in terms of actual summaries, the work would generally be summarized once in depth and referenced thereafter. In Figure 7, "High-Level Topic-Based Image Categories in the #selfie #humor Image Set (a spider chart)", none of the 180 or so images showing just human faces but without any obvious humor were included. There were images of women wearing unusual hats, dresses, and makeup. There was an actual scan of a passport (with probably sensitive information). There were images of people at a graduation. There were several images of men standing next to their cars. A 17-image subset of the 180 faces only showed smiling people, which may have referred to "good humor." There was a separate count of figures used to represent people or some aspect of the self (21). For example, there were movie posters and movie characters (multiple images of minions, Spongebob Squarepants, Homer Simpson), digital avatars from digital games, photos of food dishes (mussels, a plate of artichokes with Brussels sprouts), a cat playing with a roll of toilet paper, a part of a car, running shoes, and posed glasses of wine with a bottle of wine. There were also various textual messages, which represent people by what they think. What was realized in the research was that these objects can be stand-ins for the self. There were varying levels of difficulty in drawing out a message. If messages were found, these were included in a theme summary that follows. Also, there were six (6) baby images in this set, which were not included. One other initial category that did not make it into the high-level image categories was one on "word play" since this was one type of way humor was built. The coded humor was mentioned elsewhere in other categories. Also, there were some text-only #selfie #humor images in the image set. Some of these were mere soliloquys or musing by the author; others were dialogues between characters.

The high-level topic-based visualization is drawn from the more broadly interpreted set of images (583) culled from the 941 initial social images captured. At first, 53 images were culled as actual #selfie #humor, meaning individual self-related humor, but that was only 6% of the original image set. [This may be because people "folk" tag images incorrectly and hurriedly; they may apply batch labels. Folk tagging is known for its noisiness and inaccuracy. There may also be challenges with data selection from the Instagram app, search capabilities from Google Images and Microsoft Bing Images, and then also limitations from the uses of the respective web browser applications (DownThemAll on the Firefox web browser and Chronos Download Manager on the Chrome web browser) that enable mass image downloads.]

Initially, this 53-item set was treated as its own theme category, but further analyses of the contents showed that the contents did not fully fit that description, and the messaging of those selfies fit better in other thematic categories. A broader definition of #selfie and #humor would include a much broader percentage of the set: 583 (62% of the original full set); in this latter case, the "self" could be any human individual, human group, animal(s), figure(s), and / or text…and any attempt at humor would count. This approach aligned more with the available images, and this approach is supported theoretically by the extended self, which William James (the founder of psychology) first addressed in 1890, in conceptualizing the "me" as also a person's belongings, extended family, ancestors, friends, reputation, work, land, and moneys (James, 1890, p. 291). On social media and the digital realm, the "extended self" may be conceptualized as being "composed of a person's mind, body, physical possessions, family, friends, and affiliation groups" (Belk, 2016, p. 50), and these are many of the elements shared via selfies and social media Tweetstreams. Belk explains, "The extended self formulation envisions that certain possessions and certain other people are seen to be a part of us. They extend our identity beyond our mind and body alone" (2016, p. 50). Also, the selfies were conceptualized in the following ways:

- Selfie as individual "I" (solo selfie)
- Selfie as collective "we" (dual and group selfies)
- Selfie as individual "other" (solo selfie)
- Selfie as collective "other" (dual and group selfies)

Key to this sense of self or other was the sense of empathy and sympathy as contrasted to non-empathy and antagonism. The self is seen in much more understanding light than others, in many cases. Also, these conceptualizations separate out selfies as solo individual ones vs. dual and group ones.

Finally, generally speaking, the various #humor selfies involved creating pleasure and entertainment for both the self and usually also others. As such, these selfies enable stress relief. The eight theme categorizations were built up around apparent clusters of meaning. The themes are based around three main types:

1. The purposes of the selfies (1. Truth-telling about the self, 4. Inspirational, and 8. Spectacle);
2. The messaging [2. Un-selfie (counter-messaging), 5. Human sociality and social media (meta), 6. Human tensions (and issues)], and
3. The types [3. Animals (as self and others), 7. Funny faces].

As such, these are not all "of a type" in the way clean categorizations should be designed—such as all categorizations based on purposes OR messaging OR type, not usually AND, but suffice it to say that the image set was complex and multi-meaninged. The categories also were not mutually exclusive; in other words, a particular selfie could possibly be both an "animal" selfie and an "inspirational" one, or a "funny face" selfie could also be part of the "spectacle" and "truth-telling about the self" categories. Creating absolute coherence (through the mutual exclusivity of categories) would have meant that other information would be lost, and the actual image set would not be as well described. This is not to say that there are not other ways to conceptualize the contents of this image set. Also, the requirements of parsimony made it less desirable to have more granular categories.

The underlying data for Figure 7 may be seen in Table 5. In this particular #selfie #humor image set from Instagram, many images offered commentary on human sociality and social media (78). The second most popular category by count was the inspirational one (57), in which people encouraged each other. Human tensions and issues (54) were another common topic. The un-selfie (40) was the fourth most common topic; this category involved messaging *against* selfies. The fifth most popular category was of animal-focused selfies (31). Then, there were some spectacle selfies (12), which showed unusual sights for attention-capture. There were an equal number of individual truth-telling (8) selfies and funny face ones (mugging for the camera) (8).

It may help to see some descriptions of the contents of each of these eight categories. While counts have been included with the main themes

Figure 7. High-level image categories in the #selfie #humor image set (a spider chart)

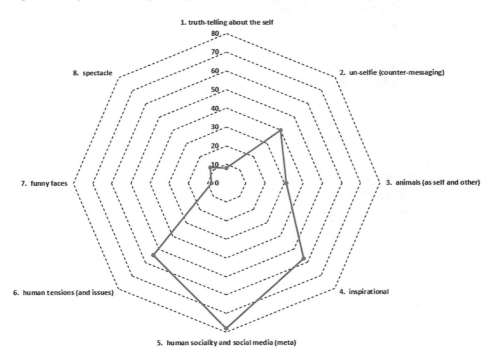

Table 5. *High-level image categories in the #selfie #humor image set*

1. truth-telling about the self	2. un-selfie (counter-messaging)	3. animals (as self and other)	4. inspirational	5. human sociality and social media (meta)	6. human tensions (and issues)	7. funny faces	8. spectacle
8	40	31	57	78	54	8	12

and subthemes, not every image was summarized in the section below. Also, as early versions of Figure 7 were created, it became clear that they could be folded into larger theme categories. To that end, smaller groupings were subsumed into larger categories. Also, in the categorizing, overlaps were avoided as much as possible.

DRAFT OUTLINE OF EXTRACTED CATEGORICAL THEMES

- **Category 1:** Truth-telling about the self
  - Owning one's own reality
  - Owning one's own laziness
  - Avoiding gullibility
- **Category 2:** Un-selfie (counter-messaging)
  - Calling out humble-brags
  - Mistaking the virtual for the real
  - Using others to see the self
- **Category 3:** Animals (as self and other)
  - A literal animal selfie
  - Animal selfie humor
  - Straight animal images
- **Category 4:** Inspirational
  - Going forth and conquering
  - Human predicaments
  - Not Monday!
  - Text manifestos about life
  - Time
  - Expressions of gratitude

- **Category 5:** Human sociality and social media (meta)
  - ○ Over-focusing on looks
  - ○ Relating around money and purchases
  - ○ Social exclusion and inclusion
  - ○ Lots of talk and word play
  - ○ Social media socializing
    - ▪ But first, let me take a selfie!
    - ▪ Sharing food…images
    - ▪ Dismissing others.
  - ○ Truth behind the screen
- **Category 6:** Human tensions (and issues)
  - ○ Racial tensions
  - ○ Gender group tensions
  - ○ Critiques of and comments about celebrities
  - ○ No drunkenness please
  - ○ Contemporary social and political issues
- **Category 7:** Funny faces
- **Category 8:** Spectacle

Foremost, this analytical approach to social imagery was naïve and emergent, with categorization of the imagery in a way decontextualized from the original context to first just "see what's there". Then, in later iterations, the images were further informed by theory (Humor Styles Model) and studied in more depth. There is a value to a naïve and emergent approach, which is refined further through a model, which is used to filter the findings.

Disclaimer: In the following section, specific summary details about the respective extracted selfies are shared. Some of the language and described depictions are graphic and possibly offensive. For the sake of accuracy, the full descriptions were included without censorship. However, the author is also aware that such language is not often used in academic writing. The intention here is not to cause offense. The strictures of content analysis are such that inferences must be made as objectively and systematically as possible. That means offensive contents should be included along with anything else of note.

CATEGORY 1: TRUTH-TELLING ABOUT THE SELF

Definition: Images that highlight self-truths that may be embarrassing.

Selfies are seen as tools of self- and group-empowerment because they enable people to express themselves with apparent free agency, autonomy, personality, and style. People can select what they find appealing about themselves to depict and share to a narrowcast audience or even a much broader global one. Truth-sharing and self-deprecating humor can help individuals progress in their own awareness and development. The human condition itself has some inherent comedy, often described as "funny because it's true". The self-mockery, to a degree, may be enjoyable both to the self and to others while serving as a coping mechanism (providing a non-threatening or less-threatening way of talking about difficult issues).

Owning One's Own Reality

Another visual highlights a discrepancy between one's own reality and others' perceptions of it, related to money. This one shows three phrases: "Salary what I get" (shown with a handful of change), "What my friends think" (shown with a wallet of bills), and "What my relatives think" (shown with a giant pile of money). Another is captioned "My iPhone 6" and shows an iPhone 4 box on which "+2 = 6" is written. This, too, shows the view of the have-not (or at least the have-lesser). There are moments of social awkwardness described: one shows Kermit at a meeting and realizing that the "brother" sitting next to him was wearing a certain type of pants.

Owning One's Own Laziness

Some are self-deprecating truths. One selfie reads: "I'm super lazy today. It's like normal lazy, but I'm wearing a cape." Another tries to capture a truism about money. Another one that highlights the lack of satisfaction with work reads: "Why do people ask 'how was work/' Like work is work…I would rather be naked on a yacht right now while eating some pizza but here I am." Another reads: "I hate when Netflix stops & asks if I'm still watching…like yeah, you think I got up and started doing something with my life?! Put on my show!" There is an accompanying image of a young girl apparently out of a sitcom screengrab.

Avoiding Gullibility

There is a lesson about not always believing what others tell you. There is an image of a young woman with a large amount of frizzy hair. This is captioned: "Leave your hair natural they said; it's not that humid they said." This #humor #selfie is set up a visual gag.

The next category shows some of the shortcomings of selfies.

CATEGORY 2: THE "UN-SELFIE" (COUNTER-MESSAGING)

Definition: Images that deride those who take selfies and share them on social media platforms and which criticize social posing on social media.

One of the themes involves the un-selfies, the messaging against the inherent vanity and falseness of selfies. In the tradition of humor, these visualizations are transgressive, and they break up the dominant narrative of the selfie as something self-empowering. One text-only selfie reads: "If showing up in a robe & tiara with a bottle of wine is wrong, then maybe I don't fully comprehend how casual Friday actually works." (Text-only selfies are often somewhat styled with certain font types, layouts, background colors, and border edges. Some include light clip art. Many of these lack the visceral impact of an image or visualization though.) The sharer here is shown as somewhat clueless about the world outside his or her individual interests.

Calling Out Humble-Brags and Social Posing

If the rear end of a celebrity was shared in order to "break the Internet" (and x-rays taken to show that there was no artificial enhancement of that said body part), it can still be taken to the extreme. One selfie shows a triptych, with the labels 2014, 2016, and 2024. In each of the images, there is the same woman standing in front of a gym mirror looking at herself and capturing an image, and in each, her back end is getting larger and larger. By 2014, the woman in the selfie looks like a centaur with a horsey back end and a second set of feet in tights and leg warmers. At some point, the personal brags become ridiculous. Another one comments on the uses of gym mirrors. Overlaid over a photo of actor Lawrence Fishburne (Morpheus in *The Matrix* trilogy) are the words: "What if I told you gym mirrors are for posture checking, not instagram (sic) photos." In another, a woman's face is shown but with an edited-in flap of skin, suggesting an extreme face peel—maybe alluding to superficiality. In another image, two toddlers are sitting next to each other in a shopping cart, with one digitally altered to look like an alien. The toddler next to her is looking at her with consternation. The text reads: "When you finally meet your crush but she left her Filters at home." The message highlights the fragility of social media illusions because the truth is revealed at some point if people ever meet face-to-face. Another selfie involves a drawing of a female with her hair in a bun and dark shades on her face and a smart phone held up in one hand to capture her image, with the label, "Snapchat stupid filter face."

Social posing goes well beyond looks. Several selfies highlighted how people pose in exercise contexts only to look fit but are actually downing large bowls of food or leaving the gym as soon as the image is taken. It's one thing to look the part but another to actually do the hard work to get and stay fit. In yet another #selfie #humor image, a Caucasian male in a suit jacket and black turtleneck points at the viewer: "From the sounds of it, you're an expert at not knowing what the fuck you're talking about. Tell me more." This is about calling out people for their lack of expertise but still listening and wanting to know more, which captures part of the quandary of social media communications. Another selfie image shows the faux seriousness of the speaker: "I dream of a better world where chickens can cross the road without having their motives questioned." Another selfie takes exception with the effort to be profound or deep. It reads: "Stop coming up with fake 'deep' picture captions. Just be honest with yourself and caption your pic 'Look at my cleavage and give me attention.'" This is about calling out people for their latent and hidden intentions; ostensibly they are showing one thing but really reaching for another. Another suggests that selfie-image capturing behavior is repetitive and does not offer new information: "FYI: That picture you just took of yourself and uploaded to Facebook looks just like the one you took yesterday, and the day before, and the day before that"; accompanying this text is a drawing of a made-up young woman with cleavage showing: Exhibit A. In another, there is a group of four ghouls in a black-and-white image, with the message: "You can't sit with us." The message evokes the petty social competition of the playground, with social ostracism as a tool of sociality.

Here, people are being called out for their pretensions, vanities, and hypocrisies. A text-only selfie reads: "I'm on Tinder to make friends." "Sure, and I'm on PornHub to see if this plumber manages to fix this sink." Another reads, "You sir...are a bitch..." The accompanying visualization shows an arrogant male. "Singer, celebrity, photographer, genius all that and much more right in your BATHROOM!" reads one selfie. The message is that people should not take themselves so seriously. Another message reads: "She a model on Instagram but she's just a hoe from my town." Another similar one reads: "Oh, you model? Who is your agency? Instagram?" This latter one highlights the difference between self-claims and amateurism as compared to professional standing. In a split-screen image, a woman is shown in the top half of the image, with the words, "Only god can judge me." Directly below is a picture of a calendar Jesus, with the pronouncement: "You're a whore." This prior selfie is a parody not only of people who would be vain and self-righteous but also for those who would speak for God. Neither side of this comes out looking dignified. A common thread on the Internet involves public shaming, in part to establish social mores, and in part to one-up another who has opened himself or herself to being publicly called out for social wrongdoing (or the breaking of social norms). This phenomenon, known as "selfie-shaming," is applied to selfies as well. These take on various forms:

Aesthetically, it takes the form of easy dismissal of "hipsters" and their self-referential modes of engagement that seem to be embodied in the inward-turned camera that looks at the subject rather than the "real world." However, selfie shaming also takes up more sinister forms, when it is not the mocking of the selfie, but the collective mocking of an individual's selfies. (Shah, 2015, p. 87)

Some Internet shaming rituals result in #memes and campaigns counter-shaming the initial shamer; for example, those who call out others for being overweight are countered by those who extol a wide range of body types as beautiful. Another critiques the social preening; it reads: "It's too bad your selfie stick isn't long enough to capture how ridiculous you look using a selfie stick." A similar one reads, "Friends are a convenient, cost-effective alternative to selfie sticks," suggesting that those who preen so much socially are not very adept at making actual friends.

The "un-selfie" category takes issue with people's inherent egotism or vanity. In one scene, there is first a drawing of a couple taking a selfie of themselves. A guy comes up and asks, "Would you like me to take that for you?" The couple says, "Thanks!" The guy then photobombs the couple by including himself in their image, which he helps to take. This turns on its head the historical consideration for others by helping them take their image. Another highlights how people may over-focus on appearance. It shows a made-up woman with the text: "I thought I had a stroke, but it was my false eyelashes were (sic) making one eye smaller than the other."

Some of the messages are somewhat disparaging of those sharing their images as selfies. One shows a duck holding a camera to take a picture of itself, with the following text: "I remember when selfies were just called 'No one else wants to take my picture.'" Another reads, "If Instagram had a filter called "Paper Bag", your daily selfies might just be a little more appealing." The purpose of these seem to be to take those sharing selfies of themselves down a few notches. Another selfie in this category shows a drawing of an individual with a stretched-out nose and mouth; in other words, the self in the selfie is not "all that." Another message reads: "It appears you suffer from a desperate need for constant attention. The cure? Stop posting bad daily selfies on Instagram & get back to living in the real world." The prior message was delivered with clip art decorations and not a lot of effort at being aesthetically pleasing. In another, a patrician older woman is portrayed, with the message: "My dear, nobody cares about your Year in Facebook." In another message, the text provides advice: "Instead of snapping Facebook selfies all day long, how about cleaning your awfully messy room in the background of the picture?" The idea is that there are more worthwhile activities elsewhere.

Mistaking the Virtual for the Real

A sub-theme involves people mistaking the virtual for the real and therefore shortchanging themselves. One selfie shows a person exercising in a gym but with the quote: "I forgot to post on Facebook (that) I was going to the gym. Now this whole workout was a waste of time." The idea here is that if it didn't happen on social media, then it didn't happen at all. "Just a reminder that mammogramming (sic) your boobs is more important than Instagramming them" goes one apparent public service announcement. The underlying messaging is that there are more important things than digital image appearances, which are fairly easily faked, and actual health (which requires attention).

If the selfie is about this self, the messages of un-selfies militate against the exploitation of the self for self-vanity or others' entertainment or giving over the self to commercial interests. The message is that people taking selfies are subsuming their real lives for vacuous cyber ones. In a drawing, a woman talks to her husband: "Your food is over there. This is for Facebook!" She is setting up food more for the camera and not actual consumption. Another image in the #selfie #humor image set from Instagram reads: "When I get a text from you, I stop whatever I'm doing then reply with 'Hei (sic) buddy…' Welcome to the Friendzone." The text is overlaid over the photograph of a young, blonde female. That messaging suggests something counter-productive about going to virtual spaces to trying to get beyond the Friendzone, which is not a place that males are supposed to want to attain in mainstream pop culture.

Using Others to See the Self

If people need to see an "other" in order to understand themselves, that may be achieved with stand-ins like mass media characters, dolls, and animals. In a digital image of Sheriff Woody from *Toy Story,* he is taking a snap of a sushi platter, with the text comment: "This is everyone on istagram (sic)." (This image seems to be a part of a #selfie series with Woody, who is seen in another image spraying glass cleaner on a mobile computer device screen.) In other words, here's looking at you, Instagrammers. Not only are people investing their own efforts into setting up selfies, but there are pets and other animals used to feed the selfie movement. In one, there is an image of a dressed-up cat with cynical eyes, with the message, "Are you happy now?" The cat looks put-out at being put on display for human entertainment, with meta-meta messaging. A man holding his head and looking concerned laments: "Right now, parents across America are thinking, 'Man, the teachers WERE right about my child all along." In this scenario, parents may have come across what their youngsters have posted, and they are frustrated at what they see.

Next, animals may be conceptualized as having their own theme category of selfie.

CATEGORY 3: ANIMALS (AS SELF AND OTHER)

Definition: Images that show animals playing central roles in the image as selves or egos (stand-ins for humans) or entities (stand-ins for groups of humans).

Thirty-one images in which animals were front and center and which involved humor were identified in the #selfie #humor image set. In an animals image set, there are images that are humorous and others that are just photos of pets. In the first group, colorful puppies are shown on an outdoor grill with a joke that if the viewer saw fried chicken that they had a "fat mind." There is a #humor #selfie of an ostrich commenting about strawberries with a funny "ostrich" accent. There are "funny face" equivalents for animals as well: a cat who has just had a bath and its lower half is waterlogged and skinny compared to its head; a cat in a shower cap; a cat wearing a large monocle; a "hungover" cat regretting his or her drinking, a cat looking intently at a beer label with the caption, "Mmmmm...beer," and others. Pets are used for all sorts of dress-up. In one, a well-groomed dog wears sunglasses and a giant rubber fruit-decorated turban on its head. In another, a dog is wearing prescription glasses (but without glass in the frame). Another #humor #selfie reads, "Girls be taking butt pics like..." and shows a dog stretching with its behind in the foreground and a split screen with a dog showing its face in the foreground and its stretched and raised behind in the background.

A Literal "Animal Selfie"

The first documented animal selfie involved a macaque in Indonesia who picked up a remote trigger to a camera on a tripod and snapped some images of itself. The British photographer David J. Slater argued that he owned copyright to the image, but several entities (including the Wikimedia Commons) suggested that this was in the public domain since non-human animals cannot hold copyright (Phillip, 2014). Several of the monkey selfies may be seen on Wikipedia at https://en.wikipedia.org/wiki/Monkey_selfie.

Animal Selfie Humor

A cat is apparently holding up a camera to take a selfie while there is a structure / building fire in the background. [A similar one shows a little girl looking at the camera in a sinister way while a house burns in the background. The caption: "Next time you will let me use your wi-fi." Part of the humor here involves the disparity between the image of the child and the apparent arson in the background.] A cat looks in wonderment at the camera, and the words read: "Christmas tree O Christmas tree Your ornaments are history," in a full rhyme. Overlaid with an image of a seal: "Talking with co-workers about who could be a serial killer at work...They all agree, it's me." There is a pug with its paw up as if it is pushing a camera shutter release to take its own photo.

There is a duo picture of two dogs together as if they were smiling and taking a shared selfie. There are two dogs standing together. One dog looks like it is whispering into the ear of the other, who wears a shocked expression: "When she whispers "I want it raw.""

In one animal-only scenario, a cat is sitting on a toilet with another cat looking at it from the doorway. The one on the toilet has a bubble thought: "Susan will not stop stalking me. I seriously need some me time." In another, there is an orangutan and dog sitting together, with odd couple dynamics: "When ur friend is really weird but you guys get along really well." The different species here may represent any number of people characteristics that may divide people.

There was one elicitation for Instagram participants to share more photos on National Cat Day. The message read: "Happy National Cat Day to your Instagram account." The accompanying image shows a cat sitting on a person's lap, with the person taking a photo of the cat. This is a form of straight-up imaging, as a call to action for sharing.

One selfie seems to play on the dignity of an animal and the cluelessness of humans. In this one, a dog is looking at a flower held in front of its nose by a guy, and the dog's expression is one of repulsion. The text: "Dude, I just peed on that." Here, the joke is on the human, who doesn't realize that the flower is not only undesirable but also contaminated with dog pee.

Sometimes, there is a philosophical message attached: "The great tragedy of life is not that cats perish but that they cease to love" (with a photo of a cat who has appeared in several #selfie #humor Instagram images). One subtext in some recurring animal selfies is the relationship between the pet and the human. For many, pets are a member of the family.

Straight-Up Animal Images

As with the human images in the #selfie #humor set in Instagram, there were a number of animal images that were simply visuals, without the humor component. There were the following: a tagged cow in a field with a fence in the background, a stretching cat, multiple sloth video screen clips, a cat with an unusual fur pattern on its face, a cat playing with a roll of toilet paper, a cat lying on its back, and others. Several straight images show people and an accompanying animal facing the camera: a smiling woman with a mammal on her shoulder, a smiling woman with a kangaroo behind her which looks like it is stretching its head around to look at the camera from an awkward angle, a human with a camel, a man and a llama, a man posing with his dog stretched out on the back of a sofa, and others. There is a lazing cat with long fur who sits next to a bowl of fruit as part of a still life image. (There is a kind of inherent humor in showing people and animals interacting. The differences between human and animal faces are also points-of-comparison.)

The next category involves messages of inspiration and support in facing the challenges of life.

CATEGORY 4: INSPIRATIONAL

Definition: Images that communicate messages of support, encouragement, understanding, empathy, and affiliation.

A common thematic category of #selfie #humor imagery was the inspirational one, in which people acknowledge life's challenges, commiserate with each other's problems, and send out encouragement and empowering thoughts. In such selfies, oftentimes the text and the image work together to lift spirits.

Going Forth and Conquering

Some messages involved conquering the world. One straightforward one showed a man putting a pizza into an oven, with the message: "Your GPA will open many doors for you." Another showed a giant boot stepping out into the world, with the text: "When you are too short to reach the top shelf... turn an UM of Awkwardness into Awesomeness and Parkour!" ("Parkour" refers to the activity of moving quickly through an urban space, usually by running and climbing, with as little wasted effort as possible. On YouTube, it might be mistaken for a form of gymnastics on urban structures. There are elements of physical competition and performance.) Another conveys a message of support to "follow your arrow," written in cursive and illustrated with two drawn arrows in different directions. One is an expression of religious faith, with Kermit the frog depicted and a textual message: "sometimes I get sad when I have problems then I remember that God loves me and I forget." Another shows three individuals silhouetted in a rainstorm, with the message: "Life isn't about waiting for the storm to pass, it's about learning to dance in the rain." (This one is apparently part of an ad campaign for a fitness routine.) There is a screen grab of the Tin Man from the Wizard of Oz, and this is captioned: "I just need a few dabs of oil and I'll be fine."

Some inspiring #selfie #humor callouts are to apparently actual people; one was a snapshot of an encouraging note for a server at a restaurant who was "awesome." One pure text message summarizes the gist of these: "Believe in your #selfie." One selfie encourages emotional resilience; it reads simply: "inspiration—the ability to start over."

Human Predicaments

There are humorous ways to highlight human predicaments (as a form of empathy and commiseration). In one, there is a photo of a very fit-looking man holding a soggy roll of toilet paper: "When you forget your towel so you use toilet paper to dry yo self". Another one featured an image of the actor Samuel L. Jackson, with the comment: "I'd rather have Samuel L. Jackson narrate my life. No offense Morgan Freeman…my life just requires multiple uses of the word motherfucker." This #selfie provides commentary about a person's lived life but also brings in a sense of rich movie culture.

One image is labeled with "mess-up", but the mistake is not clear. The image looks like three singers who may have somehow gotten out-of-sync. A message of making a mistake lets others off-the-hook because people are not claiming perfection.

Not only is it okay to not be perfect, but around February 14, it is okay to not go with commercial suggestions for how to celebrate Valentine's Day. One selfie reads, "How I plan on spending Valentine's Day" and shows a person sitting alone with a hot cup of coffee in an empty booth at a café.

Another selfie, in German, showed a crumpled traffic light lying on its side; this read: "In red, please switch off the engine" (according to the Google Translate translation). This one seems to comment on the resulting traffic problems once the traffic light turns red. This selfie commiserates with others who can relate to traffic jams.

A woman styled as a 1950s icon from a more idyllic time is depicted, along with the text: "Killed cancer and still had time to bake a cake!" This can be interpreted in multiple ways—as a send-up against the cheery message of being able to do-it-all or as a straight message of inspiration.

Another sub-theme involves financial lack and the difficulties of making ends meet. One shows a man sitting back, with the words, "Naw, I'm not goin' out. I'm on a new diet called, 'I have 50 pesos till payday.'" The key term is *"pesos,"* which suggests a particular context and background. In a drawing, an individual is holding a few bills: "Looking at all the car parts

I want like…I have $3" Another creator of a selfie made a play on public figures' names to wryly comment on the state-of-the-world: "20 years ago we had Johnny Cash, Bob Hope, and Steve Jobs. Now we have No Cash, No Hope and No Jobs. Please Don't let Kevin BACON die." This selfie plays off broad name recognition. In another, there is the photo of an actor and the caption: "The look you give the Chipotle worker when they give you a baby scoop of chicken." Here, an actor's facial expression conveys the feeling of being shorted of something good at a popular national-brand restaurant.

Another example goes like this: "When you ask your mom can she buy you a selfie stick n she say 'Boy we got selfie sticks at home.'" The image is of a young man who is bare-chested and is using a plastic hanger to hold up a smart phone to take a picture of himself. The joke is funny, and the image is memorable. There is a sense of superiority at play in terms of humor because people can laugh at someone who considers a plastic hanger as a selfie stick. There is also some additional layers of humor—how many who may be hard-pressed for funds still have smart phones and who need to keep up social media site presences. There may well be other interpretations of this particular image and text.

In terms of incongruity, there is a drawing of a cat petting a goldfish. This is not a classic selfie, but it may show something about advantage-taking and conflicting interests. One of the themes in the #selfie #humor set is to not get used, which suggests something about the importance of testing assumptions and using caution. In other words, don't be the goldfish.

Not Monday!

Another subtheme to this inspirational category is about facing Monday after a weekend. One selfie reads: "Shortest horror story: Monday." Overlaid on an image of a minion: "I'm not ready for Monday. Can I have another Sunday?" A kitten holds its paw to its head: "Ah shit. Tomorrow's Monday!!" There is a photo of a little girl trying to put on a pair of large rubber gloves on her foot: "Me every Monday morning." In another, a new blended word is coined: "Smonday: The moment when Sunday stops feeling like a Sunday and the anxiety of Monday sets in." In some cases, the messaging is a kind of slacker narrative, but in others, it's about real anxieties about the world. One cartoon shows a big-eyed individual who wants to stay in bed and not face the world. The text reads: "I don't want to get up. If I get up, I have to see PEOPLE…and DO THINGS! Noooo." In the illustration, it seems safer to hide under the covers. Another text-only selfie reads: "I'm super lazy today. It's like normal lazy, but I'm wearing a cape." A minion's image is used with the following text: "I go to sleep so late and wake up so early that I almost cross myself in the hallway!" In another, there is a photo of a sleeping cat stuck between the cushions of a sofa, with the following text: "Now ai (sic) know how Wednesday feels Stuck in the middle and waitin' for teh (sic) weekend." The spelling is sloppy, but that may have been purposefully done to simulate a cat (in part). In this grouping, there is also a diss against Mama June, Honey Boo Boo's mother. Her face is shown along with the following text: "Hey what do you like to do? I love to sleep, sleep and eat, and sleep a little more!" This critique may be personal to the individual or her public persona; it may be taken as a general class observation.

Text Manifestos About Life

Within this category of life-focused text manifestos, there are short text "manifestos" about life. These tend to be text-based and include a list of observations. One provided a list of ideas on how to get started writing. Another (unsigned) offered insights on how to read the messages behind people's communications:

"There's always a little truth behind every 'JUST KIDDING'
A little knowledge behind every 'I DON'T KNOW'
A little emotion behind every 'I DON'T CARE'
And a little pain behind every 'IT'S OK'"

The "5 cardinal rules for life" provide advice:

1. "Make peace with your past so it won't disturb your present.
2. What other people think of you is none of your business.
3. Time heals almost everything. Give it time.
4. No one is in charge of your happiness. Except you.
5. Don't compare your life to others and don't judge them, you have no idea what their journey is all about."

Indeed, people's extracted understandings of life and the world are a kind of #selfie, in the sense that people live in a way that makes sense to themselves.

One social sharer (identified as Bill Hicks) writes: "This is where we are at now, as a whole. No one is left out of the loop. We are experiencing a reality based on a thin veneer of lies and illusions. A world where greed is our God and wisdom is sin, where division is key and unity is fantasy, where the ego-driven cleverness of the mind is praised, rather than the intelligence of the heart."

The messaging is not only in text-based visualizations and text overlays. Sometimes, the messaging is on t-shirts and cups. A young female sits at the foot of a bed; her tank top reads "whiskey & coffee & beard & tattoos," and she is holding something in her hands (but the pixelated image is not clear). In another selfie, it shows a cup with the message: "Keep calm and go fuck yourself." The cup with a brochure in it looks like a typical marketing fodder in professional conferences, but for the aggressiveness of the counter-message.

Another sub-theme addressed body image. One described a weight gain through snacking with a playful wordplay: "I didn't mean to gain weight. It happened by snaccident." Another was affirming: "You are beautiful no matter what shape you are," illustrated with three different types of potted plants (a kind of selfie by representation).

Time

Several selfies engage the issue of time. In one image, a tire is seen on a lawn. The text reads: "Good bye, cruel world." In the next frame, it is hanging from a tree; for all intents and purposes, the image alone is an innocent one… of a tire swing. In the lead-up to a new year, one selfie sharer posted the following text: "A small reminder! Don't be too excited about this New Year stuff…Only the Calendar has changed. The spouse, job and targets remains (sic) the same." Yet another drawing shows some head stones in a cemetery, with the following caption: "In the News: Inventor of the bar code has died." On a headstone is a bar code, which is a play on the text that people put on gravestones to signify people's achievements. A bar code, by contrast, makes the person seem to have been just another part of a large-scale system and only unique in how he or she was digitally stamped, if you will.

Expressions of Gratitude

Several #selfie #humor examples show expressions of gratitude. One is a drawing of a young African male without clothes sitting on top of a blue dolphin, with the message: "Thank you for saving my life." Other contextual details were not readily available. In the set, there was a sense of gratitude to an Uber driver for helping an individual from a high-intoxication situation. There were shared images of a friendly note shared with a server at a restaurant.

Another category of #selfie #humor imagery involved observations about human socializing via social media.

CATEGORY 5: HUMAN SOCIALITY AND SOCIAL MEDIA (META)

Definition: Images that show how humans socialize with each other through social media and other means in the current age.

A number of the images shared comments about human sociality and social media, as part of the messaging. Some messages are mere observations, and others tend to share more of sentiments, emotions, and judgment.

Over-Focusing on Looks

The critique of looks is a common theme in #selfie #humor. The #nomakeup series, which is supposed to show people looking great *au naturel,* is turned on its head with a female zombie image (balding head, straggly hair, desiccated face, dead eyes, and threatening teeth) and the hashtag label. In another, there is an image of two women, with the text overlay: "I thought I had a stroke, but it was my false eyelashes were (sic) making one eye smaller than the other." Another played on a famous old saying: "Diamonds are girl's best friend. False. Squats are girl's best friend." This suggests that the females need to lose weight and get into shape more than they needed diamonds—with all the implications of male attention and marriage. There is a photo of a plastic doll reaching out to various plastic helmets of play hair, with the caption: "Girls be like…how should I do my hair today?"

Relating Around Money and Purchases

Another image highlights something of relationship dynamics. There is a photo of a young girl who seems deeply embarrassed. The caption reads: "When the price is right and your mother starts to ask for a discount." The girl looks like a model in an ad, and the message is a commercial one, something like giving permission to spend a little more so as not to embarrass children who have material wants. Another selfie (mentioned elsewhere) referred to a cheap date, with a guy taking his girlfriend to a street vendor for food.

Social Exclusion and Inclusion

While the concept of social media is that anyone can find his or her community given the "long tail" and niche features of connectivity, social media can be used to exclude others. In one selfie, there is an image of a group of people partying together on one side and a singleton on the other side, with the text: "When your friends hang out without you and post tons of pictures on snapchat." In the multi-audience realities of social media, there are those included and excluded in the same messaging.

Lots of Talk and Word Play

There is a lot of talk on social media. One text-only selfie reads: "People talk so much shit that the ass is envious of the mouth." In social media, talking itself is raised to a high art form. In terms of coining new words, there were several in this collection beyond the portmanteau term "snaccident" for "snack" and "accident." "Hangry" is a combination of "hungry" and "angry" to describe a person's mood from not having sufficient blood sugar. Another is "hair-itated" to describe irritation when a person's hair doesn't go right, as in a form of a "bad hair day." (Of course, when applied to only one gender, it becomes sexist.) In Net culture, #hashtags, too, are also common inventions.

Social Media Socializing

A group of images shed light on social media practices. Several use direct address. One reads: "Right now you have: 3 fingers behind your phone, your pinky tucked under for support and your (sic) scrolling with your thumb! Like if I'm right!!!" In other words, the "call to action" is for respondents to "like" the Instagram image if they agree with the image's creator. The immersion of people into social media is a common sub-theme. In one drawing, a child points at a blue bird and tells his mother, "It's Twitter!" Another #selfie #humor image contains the text: "so lives in diary and then lives lived on Instagram". Another spells out "T.G.I.F." (which stands traditionally for "Thank God it's Friday!") using the logos of Twitter, Google Plus, Instagram, and Facebook—to suggest that people socialize and relax through social media platforms. Another visualization that alludes to the important role of social media offers an image of "vintage social networking" and links various tools to analog equivalents: LinkedIn to a paper rolodex, foursquare to a physical globe, Imgur and Instagram to photos in frames, Word Press to paper, Twitter to sticky notes, Facebook to an address book, Tumblr to pastebooking, Skype to a rotary dial phone, reddit to cartoons, YouTube to looking out the window, and Pinterest to a bulletin board with snippets of text and images. The image was created by John Atkinson of Wrong Hands. Another image shows the respective social media logos on painted Easter eggs. Even people's internal mental points-of-reference related to social media: "I'm not sure whether my current thought is a tweet or a Facebook update." One visual depiction shows a young person huddled under the covers in a kind of digital cave; he is wearing headphones and interacting with a lit screen. Another visual in the image set is of the Instagram logo with a face inside it and scratching to get out; this may have been part of a larger campaign related to Instagram, but for the purposes of this work, the images are seen in isolation.

An observational sort of humor may be seen in another, in which two little cell phones are running up to an older rotary dial phone and calling out "*Abuela*!" (Grandma!) Whereas modern phones are smart and nimble, the older generation corded ones were a lot less agile and not mobile. One shared selfie image reads: "Some of us are so old, we can remember going through a whole day without taking pictures of anything!!" The younger generations have something to teach the older ones, but the learning is not necessarily pro-social. An image from The Cosby Show shows the youngest Constable child talking to her father: "Ppl (people) need to make Instagram names that fit them like @nojobnofuture, @dirty_hoe4life, …" and the list that follows is a list of disses of people like @jailbait14 and @deadbeatdad6. The words are arguably race- and class-based stereotypes.

But First, Let Me Take a Selfie!

The deep integration of social media with people's lives may be seen in a number of images. In one, a minister intones to a couple: "I now pronounce you husband and wife! You may update your Facebook status." In another, a surgeon says: "When I asked a patient what her code status was she said "Do Not Remember." Sounds like DNR to me!" This alludes to how social media culture has infused physician-patient relationships.

Another shows a young man sitting in a movie theatre and drinking from a large soda; he is wearing an attentive expression on his face. The related text reads: "When people argue on social networks." One message is that people are constantly observing on social media.

Indeed, those who are not so enamored of social media do not respond well to those who are caught up in the charms of the mediums. In another, a cartoon, there is a visualization of a female taking a selfie in front of a cartoon male who then takes out a gun and blasts her head off. There are no words exchanged, only violence. Problem solved. (That short-sightedness of that cartoon solution is partly reminiscent of the rushes to judgment seen online, with decisions made based on fast impressions and few facts—if any.)

There are two people in colonial era clothing who are about to spar: "*En garde!* But first, let me take a selfie." The two are holding selfie sticks with smart phones on the ends. There is a comic of three dogs in a field. Two of the dogs have sticks in their mouths, and a third is holding a selfie-stick; this third dog is standing on its hind paws and taking a selfie, and in so doing holding up the game. Two dinosaurs with short arms commiserate, "Oh, forget it--all our selfies are just close-ups of our nostrils." In this context, they stand in for people. A zombie is taking a selfie. In the background is a man standing there obliviously (that man plays the role of the "straight man" in comedy but looking as if everything is just part of a regular day and not noticing that he is being stalked by a zombie with flesh falling off its body). The zombie goes, "Gonna eat that guy behind me but first…let me take a selfie."

In another scenario, the text reads as follows:

Mom: *Get off Instagram.*
Me: *I can't. No, no, I'm not doing that! I'm sorry.*

This context is reminiscent of videos on YouTube that parents have posted that show emotional meltdowns of their children who are denied access to their social media accounts or smart phones.

People may be too full of their own self-importance. One #selfie #humor image reads: "singer, celebrity, photographer, genius all that and much more right in your BATHROOM!" Another message reads: "People talk so much shit that the ass is envious of the mouth."

One visualization depicts humanity as evolving to the present in order to be able to multitask via social media. Early visualizations show a monkey, and as it walks into time, the hunch is less pronounced, and then the human can walk straight up, and the current state of humanity is sitting in a chair with access to all sorts of digital devices.

Several images convey the idea that social media may have more negative effects than positive. [As a side note, researchers suggest that Instagram "is the most detrimental social networking app for young people's mental health," in a study by the Royal Society for Public Health, because of the unrealistic depictions of others, leading to feelings of body image inadequacy and disturbed sleeping patterns (Fox, May 19, 2017). Instagram was the main source of the images in this exploration of #selfie #humor.] In one, a female is sitting in front of a computer. The caption reads: "Checked email, Facebook Twitter, and Pinterest. Ready to start my day. Oh, look, it's lunch time." Another also addresses how people spend their time:

A toilet = 5 min
A toilet and a smart phone = 15 min
A toilet and a smart phone and wireless = 55 min
A toilet, a smart phone, wireless, and electricity = ∞ (infinity symbol)

Social media is a time sink. In other, two drawn rabbits are walking together. One says: "I worry that Facebook is killing meaningful communication." The other responds: "Like." A polished young female admonishes others: "That's the secret, girls. I don't take naked selfies." She has made it by not disrespecting herself…and there are ways to use social media that do not result in compromising images. Another composite image shows a young woman in various stages of well-being, with the message, "good things take time." One of the images shows a hand with a wedding ring on the ring finger; another shows a thrown bouquet. The images are inside a classic-looking frame. One selfie shows a female primping in the car, but the expression on her face seems to belie the action—with her eyes rolled up as if she is finding this unnecessary. In another dialogue, social media platforms are shown to be flattering:

Mirror: You look cute today
Camera: Lol no
Instagram Filters: I got you

Social media are seen as distractions that discourage people from focusing on what is actually more important. One photo shows a fake poster that emulates a fire warning: "In case of fire: Please leave the building before posting it on social media." Another similar selfie reads: "Just a reminder that mammogramming your boobs is more important than Instagramming them." In other words, health before showing off. One image shows a person with his arm coming from inside a crocodile—to take a selfie. Another shows a young couple dressed up for an event. The male is seated in a selfie kiosk, and his female friend is standing next to him, looking a little impatient. The text reads: "Hey babe, before we go to the dance I have to make a quick stop…"

Some images convey a sense of hostility at those who engage on social media (if not also as social media platforms themselves). Accompanying a winking smiley face: "Sometimes I wish Facebook had a PUNCH in the face button instead of a POKE button!" In another, Charlie Brown's visage is used with the text: "I think Facebook needs an 'eye roll' button." Such messages also have push-back or counter-messages. One wrote: "the only people mad about selfies are ugly people." In other words, those who would spoil the fun on social media have little to show off. Overlaid on a drawing of a person: "The only things I bring to social gatherings are excuses to leave early." This is the ultimate in being anti-social on hyper-social media.

Another selfie suggests that sex burns the equivalent number of calories as a 5 km. run, continuing, "I know, you're wondering who the hell can do 5 km in 40 seconds…"

Sharing Food…Images

Another subset of images shares an insight about food images: "the only thing that does not improve in the world when you apply a filter instagram is the food you get on the plate." Another wordplay shows the following text: "Becoming a vegetarian is a huge missed steak" (mistake). Another one made a play on the word "snack": "I didn't mean to gain weight. It happened by snaccident." Another selfie highlights the practice of eating to stuff emotions of loneliness. It reads: "I have a boyfriend. Oh wait no, no that's a fridge. I have a fridge." In a drawing, a little cup runs up to a larger cup and asks, "What is in that cup?" maybe approximating, "What are you thinking?" or "What's on your mind?"

Dismissing Others

Some of the selfies expressed contempt of others. One image of a straight-laced young man in a plaid vest was coupled with the text, "Goes on double date, other guy gets a threesome." The message is that women do not want to date a clueless guy. Another decries over-reactions: this one reads "When she blows up the house because you need a haircut" and shows a woman walking away from an exploding house.

One of the images touches on an issue of trolling and people hating on others. Brene Brown advises, "Don't try to win over the haters. You are not a jackass whisperer." The humor in this work is captured in the idea of "whisperers" who have an inside line on dogs, for example, but if people do not have an empathic link to jackasses, there is no loss there.

To be social requires lie-telling in order not to hurt others' feelings and sense of dignity. "We should have a way of telling people their breath stinks without hurting their feelings like, 'I'm bored, let's go brush your teeth!'" The quip is illustrated with two well-groomed Caucasian men in close proximity interacting as if they were at a party.

Another image consists of two people standing side-by-side, one in a Darth Vader mask and one in a Yoda one—with the message maybe involving something about reconciliation. To mention an upcoming celebration of Christmas: "Jesus be like steppin out tonight" #bdayflow."

There is a photo of two queen characters, with the note: "people who love a selfie with friends." In another image, a bespectacled and white-haired doctor in a white jacket is showing Mr. Potato Head an x-ray. The doctor says, "I think we may have found the cause of your sudden memory loss." The black-and-white x-ray shows a spike going from Mr. Potato Head's skull and into his brain.

Some of the creators of selfies step out of their own spaces of cultural comfort to make observations (even if the observations are minute ones). One photo shows a sense of formality of the table setting, with the observation: "Napkin folding game is strong here." The comment is wry and in the moment, but it is also sufficiently "outside" as to be insightful. The photo shows a from-the-side view of U.S. military men in uniform pointing their respective submachine guns at something off camera to the right. The text reads: "Look!! Justin Bieber." The joke here suggests something about clashes between military and Hollywood culture. While military men may compete with their fighting skills, Bieber is winning over women with his boyish good looks and singing voice.

In a cartoon image, worms start to dance when they realize that it's starting to rain. The text goes, "Hey everyone it's raining, Then we shall dance." A bit later, the worms are all sodden squiggly masses underground. The humor here is that the readers know better than the worms what a heavy rain means. There may be something of a "be careful what you wish for" message.

Truth Behind the Screen

Another #selfie #humor image is set up to reveal the truth behind the screen. In this scenario, a newscaster is delivering the news on television from a studio. Behind him is a large framed image of the city. He is over-dressed on top but is underdressed below the table. This does not convey the sense of a high-end news operation, but the broadcast seems to be about illusions and appearances. This may have been an actual selfie or an extracted image from a film or something else.

In another image, a man in his 20s is going through toys in a plastic container, and leaning against his back is a young boy playing games on a mobile device. The photo caption reads: "This photograph sums up the current Generation Gap."

There is a large cardboard image of the actor Daniel Craig (Bond, James Bond) in *Skyfall,* and he is on his side with his gun pulled. A girl stands in front holding up her hands as if she is being threatened by 007. The caption reads: "The girl's sense of humor is far beyond her age…" Indeed, there is some sophistication here in terms of her putting herself into a 007 scene but also playing to the viewers and the person wielding the camera. This image gives the sense of a found image.

Another selfie uses a navy battleship to stand in for the entity of the U.S. Navy. The image shows a rainbow over the ship. The message reads: "There's the Navy testing their new laser." There is a sense of surprise given that a warship is often connected to fighting, not keeping the peace; however, a standing military can help keep the balance of powers in balance and may be a deterrent against breakouts of violence.

The next category captures some human tensions depicted in the #selfie #humor image set.

CATEGORY 6: HUMAN TENSIONS (AND ISSUES)

Definition: Images that show human tensions and shared issues.

In this category, common human tensions are explored. Some are of apparently perennial ones like racial and gender group tensions. Others critique celebrities, who are seen to embody or represent particular social issues. There is a sub-set of images against drunkenness. Also, there are comments on various social and political issues.

It takes real finesse to handle sensitive social issues through humor. Those comedians who joke about social issues need astute social awareness to make the humor work (Rappoport, 2005, p. 119), with the proper insights, framing, and delivery. Audiences tend to dislike jokes about religion (Rappoport, 2005, p. 105). While issues raised may raise tensions, the resulting laughter from the humor is supposed to relieve the tension. Humor is a coping mechanism that enable people to face issues that discomfit them.

When controversial issues spark on social media, the original prompt may be a message or an image or other forms of "fighting words". The original prompt may be intentional or not; the original poster may be an *agent provocateur* or just a person sharing an observation. Others will take positions on the issue by posting their stances and observations. The issue, at any point-in-time, takes one of three directions: it continues to escalate, attract attention, raise emotions, and heat up, or it plateaus, or it starts to simmer down and resolve. Issues are sometimes unpredictably bursty while other types of social conflagrations are somewhat predictable. While issues may spark and die down and are forgotten, the messaging on social media platforms exist in a digital forever or permanence, enabling people to review and re-review chains of digital interactions. (Computers are also used to surveil and observe social media interactions, often for law enforcement purposes, in blistering speeds and near real-time analysis.) Some messaging encourages calls-to-action, such as boycotting certain businesses or voting a certain way on a certain measure or showing up at a certain hearing and various other types of mass action. Some calls may stroke inter-group or intra-group frictions and rivalries. Some forms of issue-based humor are educational and consciousness-raising, and these often propose corrective functions.

Racial Tensions

Racial tensions are a part of this image set, whether as a central issue or on a backgrounded one. The most blatant racial tensions in this image set came from apparent sexual competition. One selfie, with the text "when white girls who only mess with n--s get old," shows a caricature of a person with tin on her teeth and a darkened complexion. Another image, labeled "White dads (sic) worst nightmare," shows a young Caucasian woman sharing an image on her phone with a group of young black men standing around her. A Caucasian female and a black male are depicted in an image, with the racist and sexist text: "Proof that females will do anything if they think you're famous."

Another selfie made the observation that African American characters often do not last long in a major film but are treated as throwaway characters. The text went: "Missed Call" calls back. No answer. Damn nigga did you die within 3 seconds?"

Gender Group Tensions

While a number of selfie images tend to be somewhat suggestive, some placed edgy sexual dynamics centrally. In one image, a young man stands in an office supplies aisle of a grocery store and is looking at his penis. The label reads: "When your crabs are on fleek," which suggests that his case of pubic lice is uncontrolled and itching. "Fleek," though, is defined as "smooth," "awesome," and "fabulous," and pronunciation-wise, it evokes "fly" and "chic." It is a form of newly coined terminology based on those who interact online.

One #selfie #humor image reads: "There is so many trannys now a days (sic) I'm going to start dating pregnant girls to be safe." Another shows a young male looking at his web cam and reading "when it's 2 a.m. and she's liking all yo pics"; the messaging seems to be positive on the one hand because his pics are being appreciated, but he is still after all just sitting alone in front of his computer in a tee and looking bored.

In another selfie, identity is tied in to sexuality. There is curiosity. "My lesbian neighbors asked me what I want for my birthday. They gave me a Rolex. I think they misunderstood when I said, 'I wanna watch.'" Several #selfie #humor images showed something of a personal dilemma. One image showed a structure of interlinked scissors, with the accompanying text: "when a lesbian friend speaks about his love life." Notice the use of "his" instead of "her." The scissors evoke something about awkwardness and risk and pain. In another, a man with dyed blond hair was shown behind the text (translated from Spanish): "No, lass, I cannot with you."

In another, the famous screengrab of Shelly Duvall (as Wendy Torrance) in *The Shining* is reprised albeit with an outsized packaged condom coming through the door and the words: "Here's Johnny." There is a crass image of a heterosexual couple having sex in a bathroom stall; they are "accidentally" captured when a male one stall over is taking a high-up selfie over the wall into the next stall. This image reads as a setup, but there is always the interplay between the accidental selfie and those that require a fair amount of setup. A more relatively tame one shows three different types of bra straps, with the label: "Easy, medium, (and) hard" (as in to get off, apparently).

In this image set, there was social skewering of both males and females. The capturing of male-female strife came out in various forms. A screen grab from a film shows a Caucasian man who seems bored with a Caucasian woman who is in front of him. (It should be noted that all images have a degree of ambiguity. There are sometimes borderline cases in which a work may fit several categories. For the analyst, it may help to keep a record of such cases that are non-obvious and fuzzy.) The text reads: "A crazy girl with bad pussy is equivalent to a fat girl with little titties. Why are u here?" This suggests that males and females only interact around issues of sexual interest. When that intense interest is gone, the civility quickly disappears. One selfie reads: "When your ex says 'You'll never find no one like me," duhh bitch! That's the whole point!" Another is fairly similar in terms of the dynamic even though this is early in the relationship (apparently). In this one, a man and a woman are seated across from each other:

He: You are the funniest and most beautiful woman I have ever met!
She: You just want to fuck me!
He: Wow, and smart, too!

This messaging is a sharp counter-narrative against the sappy Valentine's messages of romance. The image seems to be from a video still. In this sex-driven social economy, women are valued for "good pussy" and "big titties," in the lingo of the image. In another, a young female is shown to make herself sexually available when she thinks her partner is famous.

In a tamer version, the girlfriend asks her "Bae" to go to a restaurant "where they make the food in front of you," evoking maybe a teppanyaki chef.

GF: *Bae (baby) can you take me to the restaurant where they make the food in front of you*

Me: *(a street vendor photo below)*

The boyfriend answers with a photo of a street vendor selling street food made streetside. He is a low-rent date and ironically proud of it.

Another image shows a woman lying on her back on the floor and playing with her dog. From the angle of the cameraperson, it looks like the woman and the dog are committing bestiality. The word overlay reads: "Bitches be like I don't need a man." In the #selfie #humor dataset from Instagram (extracted both with Google Images and Microsoft Bing Images), there was only one clear part of a trending hashtagged meme, #WasteHisTime2016. The thinking behind this one is that women waste men's time by not responding to his advances or hiding their own true intentions or planning to leave him. One image related to this involve a dry toilet bowl with all sorts of makeup objects thrown into it.

Females are depicted as moody and emotionally mercurial. One selfie reads: "Girls on they period be like, 'Okay, fine, fine. I'm cool. I'm fine.'" This selfie is illustrated with the image of a witch on fire and the cooling off into an icy blue demeanor. Some life lessons focus on relationship challenges: "if u wanna stay with your girl u gotta accept the fact that some days she's gonna have an attitude cause her eyeliner didn't come out right." What is seen as superficial to one partner in a relationship may be important—for all sorts of reasons—for the other.

Females are jealous: "Girlfriends be looking through your photos like… 'Who's that whore?'" A scantily clad female laments, "Why can't I find any decent guys? Ugh!" A stick figure below shrugs. Another selfie reads: "If your legs open up faster than Google's homepage you are not girlfriend material." This selfie suggests something about human dignity and self-respect. A 1950s styled female says, "My favorite position is called 'The Zombie'. I just lie back and get eaten." This may be in contrast to the modern woman who is seen as more concerned about actively pursuing her own interests in this area. The jealousy and competition are not only in the realm of females. The caption reads: "When your man say he going to the market but you gotta make sure he's not cheating." For this, there is an image of a woman hiding in the vegetables with a man looking directly at her while looking for her. She is camouflaged as a figure hidden in the display of fruits and vegetables (based on digital image editing).

They are seen as vain. A woman wearing torn jeans is portrayed next to the text, "Girls be like I just got my brows done."

A selfie in Bulgarian showed two images of a dog: in a nightclub, it has teeth-baring fierceness, but at the dentist, it is a humble pup. As such, this gave a sense of how people themselves are different in different contexts. A context may create a sense of bravado in one context, and another context may create a sense of fear. This concept is explored in another selfie, which reads, "After the club bitches be like…" and the image shows a man who is pooping by garbage dumpsters outside. In other words, a man who was hot inside the club is now just a homeless guy without a place to use the bathroom except outside by the dumpsters. The magic of the dance club has disappeared.

Another image was captioned with "9 months after this snow storm"… and shows a lot of babies lying on a white sheet and their parents all hovered around.

In a visualization titled "Evolution von Frau & Mann," women are seen to evolve to the point where they stand and ride motorcycles; men themselves are not really advancing, just lying on their backs through generations. (This visual may have been part of an ad campaign.) This does suggest though that the sexes are not keeping pace with the other.

Yet another depicts a pretty deplorable state of male-female relations, often in explicit terms: "When you deepthroat his entire dick & balls while swalloin (sic) his nut as he convulses, now he won't stop textin u (sic)." Here the female is depicted as servicing the male's sexual needs but then whining about having too much male attention as part of her social media shtick. Hers is a dominated or losing strategy, in game theory terms. The writing here also shows that "go-to" of a crass street conversational style to speak hard truths, in some social contexts. The two individuals in the image are both apparently African American. In a risqué cartoon, a male with his genitals pulled out says to a woman, "Try the one in the center; it's cream filled…" Both are Caucasians. There is yet another drawing, of anatomically correct male and female teddybears (in terms of male- and female- electrical plugs), with the male bear propositioning the female one. A text message reads: "I do not want evil, but hopefully you escape a fart when you do 69," in reference to a sexual position. Male sexual bravado is another recurring theme. One #selfie showed a dialogue: "In bed, I am like a dragon." "The heat?" "No, the Komodo dragon." Ba da bum! An image of some young male toddlers dancing were labeled with "muevelo (move your body) baby so today paid a fortnight". In yet another edgy selfie, an angry looking guy faces the camera, and the words read: "Because the bitch was sleeping under a tree."

Another calls out men for exaggerating their penis size: "When u bragging bout your dick size and she say 'Lemme see it.'" The accompanying photo shows a sweating man. A similar message is shown but with two toddlers: one toddler shows shock at the appearance of another, because she looks different in the real than in the filtered imagery of Instagram. There is a drawing of an

African American man as a sex machine in an exaggerated drawing, rolling together a racial and gender stereotype.

In a play on the periodic table of elements, the public figure Bill Nye the Science Guy was depicted with the table of elements spelling out a derogatory term for women. (Images like this can cause double harm given the sense of challenge in recruiting women for STEM fields—science, technology, engineering, and math—and the hostile message here of a lack of welcome. Indeed, there were quite a few misogynistic messages in the image set. A race car is shown burning rubber on the race track, and a woman in a helmet says, "Oh, lawd Jesus, it's a fire!" as if she cannot take in the realities of the situation.

There is a drawing of a woman's back end. She is pulling away her undergarment to show an image of a vacation spot. A young man is depicted delivering a pickup line online: "I already have my dream if you give still online." (The translation was a little awkward.)

One of the more complex #selfie #humor images seems to be a send-up of Murad Osmann's entrancing series—of himself following his girlfriend who holds his hand and leads him into various adventures. This sendup consists of four sequential images, of a woman leading this photographer forward. I the second and third pictures, a giant male foot is kicking her into the surf face-down. The text reads: "Cuddle season is over, time to be single." This shows something of a throwaway culture and the transience of romantic relationships. Relationships are not easy. One image showing a young man's face is captioned: "Not realizing that a wrong answer can sour relationships for a while."

Only a few of the images conveyed a message maybe showing something constructive going on between men and women. It was a simple drawing of a clean-cut young woman with an innocent devilish self reflected in a mirror. The words read: "Every woman has a crazy side that only the right man can bring out." One selfie (in Indonesian) read: "love at first typing." In another, a man looks towards a camera as he is walking down a street; he boasts: "My girlfriend is always trying to sneak pics of me!!!" In this context, even a little innocence or niceness actually reads warmly and in a welcoming way.

Critiques of and Comments About Celebrities

There are critiques of public figures who are not living up to their public images. There is a photo of "Dog the Bounty Hunter" walking along the beach.

He has a belly in the photo, which is captioned, "Dog, the Brownie Hunter." Kanye West is called out, with the following text: "When you're watching a movie for the first time and someone keeps asking you questions about it" Another quips: "If your man don't like cars you have a Bruce Jenner," in reference to the running star who changed himself to Caitlyn Jenner through sexual reassignment surgery. Some comments about celebrity are admiring. One wrote: "Morgan Freeman walked away from that plane crash like," and this is overlaid on an image of Freeman with a halo around his head. Another shows Drake lifting weights: "Drake be like…I need a spotter. It's too hard to do these things alone." Kermit, a perennial favorite, is shown along with the quote: "Sometimes I don't feel like going to work…but then I remember I was born cute not rich…" Dr. Phil (McGraw) is brought in to show how inaccurate auto-captioning can be: "when haters think u a Hassidic hillbilly with a snoot full of bees," which apparently refers to an episode in which Dr. Phil was captioned as saying: "I ain't some Hassidic hillbilly with a snoot full of honeybees." One used an image of the world famous tattooed boxer Mike Tyson, with one word: "Thelfie" as a play off his gap-toothed smile.

A number of Hollywood celebrities and animated characters appeared in the selfies, their images obviously usurped for the aim of broad public expression—with some appearing multiple times with different messages. They include the following: Disney's Cinderella, Morpheus in Matrix, Kermit, Sheriff Woody of Toy Story, Mr. Bean, Chrissy Teigen, Samuel L. Jackson, Spongebob Squarepants, Woody Harrelson, Will Ferrell, Klay Thompson (basketball player?), Amy Winehouse, Jordan Peele, Bill Nye, Ricky Criest (wrestler), Kourtney Kardashian, Zayn Malik of One Direction, Bruce Jenner, Daniel Craig, Drake, Duane "Dog" Chapman ("Dog the Bounty Hunter"), Mike Tyson, Mama June, Magic Johnson, and others. For example, one selfie-sharer wrote: "Megastar Ricky Criest be like: Niggas only hate Monday because that is the day they have to return their rentals." This was framed as an insight about African Americans. Another one identified an actor who has passed away in a car crash, and asked, "Guess who hasn't seen *Fast & Furious 7*?" in reference to a movie that that actor had starred in. In a play on *Jurassic Park*, a "Giraffic park" series involves a number of screen grabs with giraffes edited into the role of the carnivorous dinosaurs. There is humor in the word play with the film title, and then the image of slow-moving and docile-appearing giraffes in the place of ravenous dinosaurs leaves an impression.

No Drunkenness, Please

Some images conveyed derision at people who cannot hold their own alcohol. One image shows a hand holding up a pink smart phone to a bathroom mirror but with the individual lying on the floor and out of view, unable to stand to take a selfie. The text reads: "When you're too drunk to be in your own selfie." One elicitation type of #selfie #humor begins: "You know your boyfriend is drunk when..." One image shows a "hungover" cat ruing having gotten drunk. Another is a text selfie: "I'm not clumsy. It's just the floor hates me, the tables and chairs are bullies, & the wall gets in the way." Another social sharer writes, "Talking to the Uber driver after getting fucked up at a party." This evokes the chance meetings between strangers, sometimes in a time of need. Another followed a common joke structure: "I just read an article on the dangers of heavy drinking…scared the hell out of me. So that's it. After today, no more reading." One image shows a man passed out (apparently drunk) on a lawn and another taking a leak on his head. [Interestingly, the first recorded use of the word "selfie" involved alcoholic intoxication. This message was by Nathan Hope on Sept. 13, 2002 on an Australian Internet forum in Karl Kruszelnicki's "Dr Karl Self-Serve Science Forum." In this post, the writer described his own drunken behavior, in the following posting: "Um, drunk at a mates 21st, I tripped ofer (sic) and landed lip first (with front teeth coming a very close second) on a set of steps. I had a hole about 1cm long right through my bottom lip. And sorry about the focus, it was a selfie." ("Selfies," Jan. 30, 2016, n.p.)]

Contemporary Social and Political Issues

Some selfies engaged timely social and political issues. One highlighted the sense of excessive forced used by law enforcement per the #BlackLivesMatter movement narrative. The text read, "May the excessive force be with you" with an image of the diminutive Yoda holding up a light saber and a uniformed police officer in a hard hat and leather gloves using pepper spray on Yoda (from Star Wars). In another, a man who looks like he is in papal robes peeping through a keyhole into someone else's business being kicked on the behind by another man in regular garb. This may reference the issue of misconduct among the ranks of Catholic clergy. Also, there is an image of a stack of healthcare brochures for various ailments: "low back pain, high blood pressure, breast cancer." There is one in the foreground for "Donald

Trump" who is shown with a sneer. There was a Europe-based selfie with a photo of the former Greek Prime Minister Alexis Tsipras, famous for advocating for Greek rebellion against the European Union terms for Greek acceptance of yet another bailout in 2015. The Spanish language selfie reads (in translation): "If you get off at capitol, salts vine frames." This warning may be from the Spanish experience—that if runaway spending is not controlled, the future will not be bountiful (salt ruins plants). Another selfie touched on child marriages still practiced in some traditions: "If she fasts all 30 days of Ramadan, she's too young for you bro."

CATEGORY 7: FUNNY FACES

Definition: Images that show people mugging for the camera by making "funny" faces.

Some of the individuals in the selfies are making a funny face (mugging) to the camera. One shows a man with his mustache shaved as the bat signal to call Batman. An older woman mugs with a squished face. A man has an ice cream bar in his mouth and some white chalky powder on his face, and he is looking at the camera with large eyes. Another shows a man with a large piece of fried chicken in his mouth. Another man simulates sneezing into the camera (or is just about to sneeze into the camera). Another form of a funny face involves side-by-sides, with a human being compared to a cartoon character or animal with a "similar" facial expression. Another shows a man looking cross-eyed at a drill that is coming towards his forehead. Another shows a side-by-side image of a female wearing an Under Armour sweatshirt and making funny faces at the camera while standing in front of a bulletin board.

CATEGORY 8: SPECTACLE

Definition: Images that were designed to capture human attention in a competitive attention economy; "made you look."

If people do live in an attention economy, then the "made you look" phenomenon is a valuable one. In terms of imagery, the attention-capturing aspects may come from real-world acts of daring, such as through illegal "buildering" of skyscrapers. Others may come from creative photomontage work. Yet others include image setups that create a sense of surprise through incongruity.

A dozen images involved digital image editing to create eye-catching effects: a roller coaster view superimposed on an aerial view of a city scape, a man taunting an alligator with food in front of a seated audience, a man with a gun in his hand, two teddy bears with "male" and "female" plugs in their crotches and the male teddy bear propositioning the female one, toys hanging off the ends of ropes, people who have their faces situated above a dog's furry muzzle (as if they were half-human, half-dog), a person standing on an elevated exterior pedestrian walkway and taking a selfie with an unnaturally long and curved arm serving as a selfie stick, a pilot taking a photo of himself outside the window of a jumbo jet (with an ocean with islands in the background), and others. Online, many who participate in social media (such as Reddit) are invited to "photoshop battles" to create noteworthy images that can capture the larger imagination. For these, there may be initial seeding images to start, and people can go from there. Some of these are done in good fun, but some may also turn malicious.

Another attention-getting image shows a man in camouflage pants and shirt walking a headless child mannequin. One Spanish language selfie reads: "falling off a painful way so stupid but you do not know whether to laugh or mourn" (in translation), and this quote gives the sense of an antic gone wrong and causing pain but also something possibly view-worthy.

Another count was done of male, female and unclear-gender characters that were depicted visually—in various types of representations. "Implied" people—off-camera as it were—were not counted. cross-referenced to categories of singleton images [showing one person in the image(s), even if there was a split screen or multiple screens, such as in diptychs, triptychs, quadtychs, and so on], duo images (showing two people foregrounded), and group images (three or more people in the image). The signaling for gender would result in a count for that particular category, no matter if the image was a human or a fictional cartoon character or a body part—as long as the physiological and / or cultural signaling for gender was clear. Some imagery involved visual synecdoche, or the use of a part of the human body to represent the whole person; in other cases, visual metonymy was used to represent a person, such as the use of a pair of sneakers to represent an athletic individual or group or a condom package to represent a sexually active male.

If there was any lack of clarity, the selfie was categorized in the "Unclear Gender" category. (For example, a dog dressed up in a bonnet would be treated as "Unclear Gender" because dress-up of pets for a selfie does not necessarily indicate gender.) The idea was to capture what is obvious in the visual context. In terms of counts of the respective characters, particularly in the group image category (three or more), a serious effort was made for an accurate count; however, in some cases, given low image resolution, those individuals in the image were not included. In other words, either an accurate count was made from the image, or the image itself was left out of the count altogether. Babies and children were counted as their own characters, but their gender was not generally clarified unless it was in the accompanying text. Every effort was made to be as accurate as possible but in a surface interpretation without interpreting too much into the imagery. In terms of the gender counts in singleton images, the male-female count was close (189 – 180). In terms of gender counts in duo images, there were more males (83) depicted than females (61); in other words, there were more images of two males together as "buddies" or "brothers" than females duos in the #selfie #humor image set. Finally, in terms of gender counts in group images, there were slightly more males (82) than females (68). The simple

Figure 8. Gender counts and number presentation in selfies in the mixed set

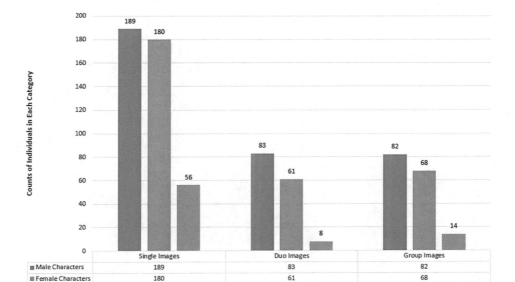

table ("Exploring a Selfie Image Set with Basic Features Extraction") used for Figure 8 is available in Appendix A.

While race and ethnicity are common demographics captured for social sciences research, this was not systematically captured here because visuals can be highly misleading and ambiguous as a factor of race. Very broadly speaking, in this limited image set, those of Caucasian and African American background predominated, and there were much fewer Asians and Hispanics.

Of the full initial image set, only 526 (56%) of the images had humans in the visualization. There were text-only selfies, figurative selfies (think watches, shoes, computers, cups, stuffed animals, food, wine, artwork, and other subjects alone), and animal-only selfies. The basic table ("Selfie Types and Counts") used for Figure 9 is available in Appendix B.

Using the same data in the prior figure (Figure 10), a spider chart was drawn to give a summary sense. Most images in the #selfie #humor image set were comprised of photographs showing individual people foremost, followed by groups and then by duos. While drawings and illustrations and mixed images and text were also used, these categories were much less common than photos alone. Besides people, there were also the employment of animals and figures and text-only to convey identity or "self."

Figure 9. Selfie types and counts

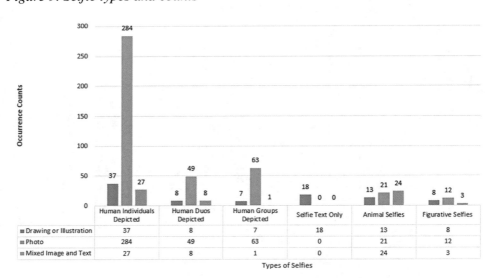

Figure 10. Selfie types and counts (as a spider chart)

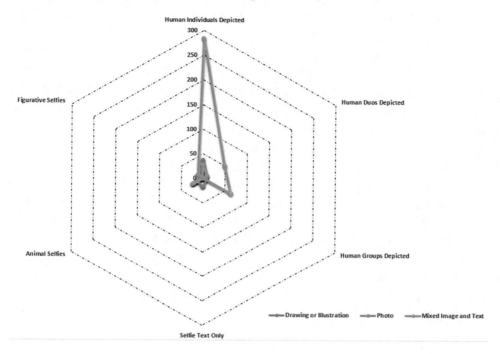

Figure 11. Humans by general age categories in the #selfie #humor image set from Instagram

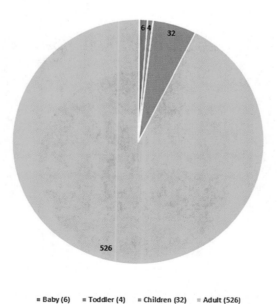

In Figure 11, it's clear that a majority of the #selfie #humor images show adults, with only a few babies and toddlers shown, and some children. The children depicted were often public figures in their own right as actors in television sitcoms and some apparently the children of the photographer. One image of a child was apparently a screenshot from a sports game with the child's image taken from a Jumbotron. Whoever posted that #selfie wrote: "when your home team is losing and you need a haircut," evoking the spiteful thoughts that some may have of others in passing. In other words, babies, toddlers and children were 7% of the extracted imagery in this image set, and the rest were adults. The relative lack of babies, toddlers, and youth in the image set may be because of legal privacy protections in the uses of children's imagery as well as the intellectual property protections. Of course, it is possible that it is just easier to snap a photo of one's actual self in order to communicate a concept instead of finding or creating an image of a child. Also, in terms of the adult imagination, it may be easier to relate to another adult than to a child. In the selfie imagery, children are actually adults: for example, a young girl wearing heavy makeup and a pout, says, "Don't make me go ghetto on your ass."

Figure 12. Types of common imagery in the #selfie #humor image set

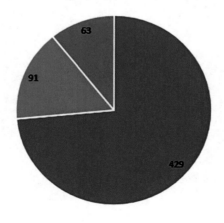

■ Photographs (429)   ■ Drawings or illustrations (91)   ■ Mixed image and text set (63)

IMAGE CATEGORIZATION INTO FOUR MAIN INSTRUMENTED HUMOR STYLES

One of the most salient humor styles instruments that has been applied to people is the Humor Styles Questionnaire, which categorizes the humor styles into four dimensions: affiliative, self-enhancing, aggressive, and self-defeating.

These are: relatively benign uses of humor to enhance the self (Self-enhancing) and to enhance one's relationships with others (Affiliative), use of humor to enhance the self at the expense of others (Aggressive), and use of humor to enhance relationships at the expense of self (Self-defeating). Validation data indicate that the four scales differentially relate in predicted ways to peer ratings of humor styles and to measures of mood (cheerfulness, depression, anxiety, hostility), self-esteem, optimism, well-being, intimacy, and social support. (Martin et al., 2003, p. 48)

These categories highlight the instrumented uses of humor—or practical ways that humor is used, whether consciously or unconsciously. While individuals may have more than one humor style, they tend to have one that predominates. Since the release of the instrument, research has found support for some aspects of the model:

Emotional management ability was positively correlated with self-enhancing humor and trait cheerfulness, and negatively correlated with trait bad mood. Ability to accurately perceive emotions was negatively related to aggressive and self-defeating humor. Positive humor styles and trait cheerfulness were positively correlated with various domains of social competence, whereas negative humor styles and trait bad mood were negatively correlated with social competence. Finally, the emotional management facet of EI (emotional intelligence) was positively correlated with several social competence domains. (Yip & Martin, 2006, p. 1202)

The interrelationships between the humor styles may be seen in an expanded 2 x 2 table. In the respective cells are some categories of apparent humor styles by those sharing those particular selfies. In the top left, truth-telling about the self can be freeing and positive. The un-selfie messaging enables people to not participate and still maintain self-esteem and a sense of value. At the top right cell, many of the #selfie #humor images fell into the affiliational category. In other words, these selfies helped people connect. Animal images are highly popular (think cat videos on YouTube). Inspirational selfies encourage others to do better and to not be discouraged. Human sociality and social media (meta-perspective) enables people to form a sense of critical thinking and awareness about the various mediums. Funny faces evoke smiles. Spectacles leave viewers with something to talk about and often a sense of awe and appreciation for others' skills. At the bottom left, the "human tensions (and issues)" category captures much of the hostility between people, particularly (at least in this image set) between males and females. In terms of the far right bottom cell, the theme category there was also "6. human tensions and issues," which suggests that hostile and aggressive types of humor not only cause harm to the psychological well-being of the selfie creator but also his or her ability to engage with others in a constructive way (affecting social well-being).

Table 6 is summarized after an in-depth analysis of the image set, but it is based on inferential analysis only. After all, it is hard to ascertain the original intentions of those sharing a #selfie labeled as #humor; the analysis is based only on the #selfie #humor imagery, and some 38% of the extracted images were not even found to be #selfie #humor even with a broadened "extended self" type of analysis. The images themselves are ambiguous and multi-meaninged, and the interpretive lenses of the researcher clearly have an effect on the qualitative and quantitative coding. There is not a practicable way of double-checking the codes. Even if there are multiple individuals coding, consensus understandings are not necessarily correct. If the original posters of the #selfie #humor images may be contacted, they may have an interpretation of their purposes, but even that may not be fully accurate given

Table 6. An expanded 2 x 2 table representation of the four dimensions of humor style with linked #selfie #humor image themes

	Enhance Self	Enhance (Social) Relations
Benign	**Self-enhancing (adaptive)**	**Affiliational (adaptive)**
	1. truth-telling about the self 2. un-selfie (counter-messaging)	3. animals (as self and other) 4. inspirational 5. human sociality and social media (meta) 7. funny faces 8. spectacle
Injurious	**Aggressive (mal-adaptive)**	**Self-defeating (mal-adaptive)**
	6. human tensions (and issues)	6. human tensions (and issues)

subjectivity and challenges with memory and lack of clarity about intentions at times. (Self-reportage problems are very common in human research.) In this research, the original individuals who shared the selfies were not captured (neither their names nor their online handles).

An affiliative style involves the use of humor to connect with other people; a self-enhancing humor style involves using it to cope with the stresses and challenges of life; an aggressive style involves using humor to feel better about the self by putting others down, and a self-defeating humor style involves ingratiation of the self towards others at the cost of one's dignity (and ultimately resulting in the loss of self-respect). The first two are seen as related to the person's positive psychosocial well-being (healthy psychological state and healthy social relationships with others), and the latter two are seen as related to that person's negative well-being. While the instrument is applied for the study of personality types, the general model is helpful particularly in shedding light on some of the humor dynamics within each of the theme categories. What this may suggest is that the sharing of #selfie #humor can be highly positive, if people are careful about how they harness humor for their own well-being and the well-being of others.

While there are social pressures to avoid engaging others with prejudice, based on both internal motivations (like personal beliefs and the importance of non-prejudice as part of an individual's self-concept) and external ones (social pressures to conform to social norms), many people's biases have become more implicit rather than explicit (Plant & Devine, 1998).

Real Risks to Some Types of Humor

According to prejudice norm theory, if biases are institutionalized into humor and other social practices, it may increase tolerance for discriminatory acts against targeted groups. The constant presence of biased depictions may desensitize people and encourage acceptance of discrimination. Ethnic, racial, and gender humor—if disparaging—may result in oppression of various social groups. This is one of the major risks of disparagement humor (Ford & Ferguson, 2004). Other researchers have found empirical evidence for people's preferences for disparaging humor towards those they dislike. In social contexts where demeaning humor is applied to low-status outgroups, the social harms are magnified. Cavalier Humor Beliefs (CHB) can mask social biases and affirm falsehoods about social power:

The group-dominance model of humor appreciation introduces the hypothesis that beyond initial outgroup attitudes, social dominance motives predict favorable reactions toward jokes targeting low-status outgroups through a subtle hierarchy-enhancing legitimizing myth: cavalier humor beliefs (CHB). CHB characterizes a lighthearted, less serious, uncritical, and nonchalant approach toward humor that dismisses potential harm to others. As expected, CHB incorporates both positive (affiliative) and negative (aggressive) humor functions that together mask biases, correlating positively with prejudices and prejudice-correlates (including social dominance. (Hodson, Rush, & MacInnis, 2010, p. 660)

Being the target of a joke—as an individual or as a social group—can open the way for continuing bigotry and mistreatment instead of social equality. There is a fine line between laughing at differences between people and subscribing to stereotypes of people that can cause social harm.

DISCUSSION

To recap, three main research questions (with related sub-questions) were explored in this chapter, and some high-level insights were extracted.

1. What Does Identity-Based Humor Look Like in Terms of a #Selfie #Humor: Tagged Image Set From the Instagram Photo-Sharing Mobile App?

Identity-based humor includes the following eight general categories: (1) truth-telling about the self, (2) un-selfie (counter-messaging), (3) animals (as self and other), (4) inspiration, (5) human sociality and social media (meta-perspective), (6) human tensions (and issues), (7) funny faces, and (8) spectacle. The most common type of selfie involved individual images of individuals in photograph format, followed by group selfies, and then duo selfies. There were other types of selfies, including animal selfies, figurative selfies, and text-only selfies (in descending order). Selfies were comprised of photographs (429), drawings or illustrations (91), and mixed image and text sets (63).

2. What Earlier Findings and Theories About Humor Apply to the More Modern Forms of Mediated Social Humor? Is it Possible to Effectively Apply the Humor Styles Model to the Images From the #Selfie #Humor Instagram Image Set to Better Understand #Selfie #Humor? If so, What May Be Discoverable Using This Approach?

Some of the early work in identity-based humor were found to apply to the #selfie #humor image set. Of particular application were insights about racial and ethnic humor as well as gender-based humor. The risks of dehumanizing jokes (as hate speech) were made clear through several salient theories: the creation of prejudicial norms (according to prejudiced norm theory in 2004) and Cavalier Humor Beliefs (2010). Disparagement humor, no matter the original intentions of the #selfie creators, may add to the sidelining of particular socially disenfranchised people groups. Finally, the psychometric humor styles questionnaire's underlying model has application to the segmentation of the #selfies categorized into the eight themes. In this categorization, many of the types of humor found were beneficial to the psychosocial health of the sharer except for those engaging in hostile humor within the "(6) human tensions (and issues)" category.

3. What Are Some Constructive and Systematized Ways to Analyze Social Image Sets in an Emergent Way Using Manual and Computer-Supported Techniques?

The sequence described in Figure 5, "Analyzing Social Imagery: An Overview of the Research Design and Approach, summarized this work in five recursive steps:

1. Review of the Literature
2. Extraction of (Targeted) Imagery from a Social Media Platform(s)
3. Ingestion of Imagery into NVivo 11 Plus
4. Analysis and Interpretation
5. Consideration for Future Research (and Methodologies)

Review of the Literature

While the formal academic literature is an important place to explore thoroughly (to saturation), it is also important to explore the informal social media space, which is dynamic and constantly changing.

Extraction of (Targeted) Imagery From a Social Media Platform(s)

- The extracted image set, while large-size for more traditional research, is quite miniscule in the age of big data. What was extracted was nowhere near an N=all, and there is no verifiable way to tell how much of the tagged set was captured from Instagram.
- The extracted social imagery, based on #selfie #humor tags, resulted with only about 62% (583/941) that could be interpreted as related to #selfie AND #humor. In this coding approach, the "extended self" was considered, enabling the uses of imagery of animals, figures and objects, and text messaging to be part of the "self." Folk tagging is noisy and often inaccurate.
- How images are captured affects not only how much data is captured but also whether the set is accurate to the seeding terms. There are benefits to extracting imagery using multiple browsers, multiple data extraction tools, over multiple time periods—to collect as broad a set as possible. [Those who will use non-manual or automated approaches may strive for even larger datasets using machine scraping and machine analysis.]
- In this particular use case, Google Images was more effective at extracting a large number of #selfie #humor images from Instagram and with more original non-duplicative images.
- The #selfie images captured contained quite a few co-opted images of public figures, movie characters, toy characters, and screen grabs, as might be expected in a mash-up culture.
- The image set contained fairly small images, not quite thumbnail size, but small none-the-less. When zooming in to them, they often pixelated into meaninglessness, especially when there were finer details like small texts or highly complex imagery. If at all possible, it is important to use tools to track an image and to maybe find the original larger-size image (if available on the Web or Internet).

- It is important to keep a pristine master set of the raw images before any sort of data cleaning or de-duplication, in order to protect the contents against destructive or non-recoverable changes.
- Also, it was clear that quite a few of the selfies were digitally edited. In a publication context and in a photojournalistic one, these would be considered digital forgeries. In publication, images cannot be factually changed but only very judiciously cropped and output for publication or website hosting or some particular use. In photojournalism, image colors may be "jumped" for publication, but nothing factually may be changed. S. Lian and Y. Zhang (2010) provide a number of ways that images may be analyzed for potential forgery through multimedia forensics (including "correlation, double compression, light, and media statistical" approaches), but their methods suggest some minimum image resolution. It is not clear if these selfies have sufficient digital details for higher end analysis.

Ingestion of Imagery Into NVivo 11 Plus

NVivo 11 Plus is a data analytics tool that enables the curation of digital image data. It also enables manual coding, along with various data queries and autocoding features. The images that are ingested into NVivo are already pre-named by the web browser add-on used to copy the data on a particular Web page. (Whatever the original names of the images were on the web pages are lost.)

- Data cleaning may involve common efforts, such as de-duplication of the image set (not counting repeat images). There may be other data cleaning methods as well, based on the specific research that is being done.
- While coding, it is helpful to use the image names and numbers to track back to a particular image in order to revisit it for further analysis.
- In this case. MS Professional Suite tools such as Word and Excel were also used, as well as Microsoft Visio. Using a wide range of software tools to describe and record data enables a more flexible method of analysis, even though NVivo 11 Plus does enable a wide range of approaches.
- Once the image set was coded and analyzed in depth, the author conducted some initial autocoding for sentiment and theme, but neither actually turned up much in the way of insights because of the sparsity

Figure 13. Coding in NVivo 11 Plus and in MS Word

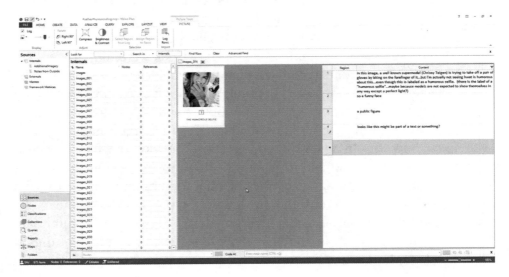

of the text and the fact that much of the coding was also done in outside tools with files not ingested into the NVivo 11 Plus project. This is not to say that these additional analytics and related data visualizations would not be helpful if more text were recorded image-by-image in this project.

Analysis and Interpretation

There were a number of early insights about the manual coding of social image sets using two commonly accessible software programs.

- **Meticulous Attention:** Experientially, for the human coder, coding imagery requires meticulous attention. Particular sets of imagery have their own unique grammars and graphical lexicon, and those have to be observed. This is especially so for emergent coding, which is a bottom-up method. In other words, a coder does not begin with an *a priori* coding model (based on theory or framework or model), but instead engages directly with the data first (in a grounded theory approach). To stay fresh, it is important for coders to break off the coding work once they are not able to maintain an intense level of accurate focus. Also, it is important to iterate through an image set multiple times to reinforce the initial coding but also to look for fresh insights missed in prior iterations.

- **Qualitative Coding Approaches While Embracing Polysemous Messaging in Imagery:** Social imagery is many-meaninged. When coding in a qualitative way for themes, it is helpful to capture as many possible applications of the image as possible…and then to iterate over the image set again several times, so that meaning is not missed. (In more complex projects, it would be highly helpful to have team coding, for example, and to push for as low a Cohen's Kappa as possible— so that there is dissimilarity in the coding for the broadest possible interpretations of the image set as possible.)

- **Categorizing by Theme:** Also, in terms of categorizing social images, this will often take multiple tries. Initially, the granularity of the coding may be too coarse (broad-scale) or too granular (specific). If categories are too coarse, they are not particularly meaningful, and there may be too much spillover and non-exclusivity in the classifications. If categories are too granular, then the problem of overfitting occurs, and the categorizing applies mostly to the actual data set and does not apply to other contexts.

- **Comfort With Some Messiness:** The extraction of themes and categorizing the images by themes was useful, but did not result in a clean classification structure where all the categories were aligned around particular aspects, such as (a) the purposes of the selfies, (b) the messaging, and (c) the types.

- **Research Topic Background:** It is important to have some background with the imagery in order to bring insights to it. That may be seen in the application of some of the theories of humor and also those of prejudice.

- **Quantitative Counts:** Quantitative types of assessments are helpful, too, because they offer ways of understanding magnitude and intensity (such as through frequency counts). These approaches also offer some sort of *objective* reproducibility. During the work, it is important to create labeling tables for quant counts. Also, it is important to use coding features (such as in NVivo 11 Plus) to take notes about the respective imagery (through several iterations). In part, this is a form of reliability check—do the notes still apply at a later date when the researcher is looking at the imagery with fresh eyes?

- **Avoiding Guess-Ti-Mating at Numbers:** When counting, it is critical not to guess-ti-mate. During initial qualitative coding, this researcher strove to keep a rough count of image types initially. Then, she went back and did actual specific counts. The guestimates, in her case, tended towards under-counting.

- **Using an Initial Image Set to Create Tools:** It is advisable to begin with a small image set and to iterate over it multiple times in order to help create some initial coding categories and tools for coding. These categories and tools may be evolved over time. The initial set helps train the researcher's eyes to what he or she is actually looking at and dealing with—for more effective work.

- **Anticipating Image Ambiguity:** Imagery can be quite ambiguous. While people may think gender identification is clear, it is not actually so in every case. There was very much a need for an "unclear gender" category—simply because a visual image may not contain sufficient information to show gender. This is in part because of physical appearances for some. For others, there were only partial body parts showing, such as a pair of legs in shoes, which were sufficiently non-descript and non-branded to indicate gender.

- **Setting Standards for What is Left Out:** Social media data, while it is empirically captured and "in the wild" and "in vivo," do contain direct ads and people free-riding the #selfie message to sell goods and services. There should be ways to identify out images that do not fit with the research questions and to define clear rationales for their exclusion.

Consideration for Future Research (and Methodologies)

The above approach, because of the costly requirements for human attention, is costly. Other researchers have used combinations of computational means and crowd-sourced coding to study cyber bullying (vs. cyber aggression) instances on Instagram (Hosseinmardi, Mattson, Rafiq, Han, Lv, & Mishra, 2015). Their method seems more scalable but also somewhat coarser vs. granular in terms of detail. There is no current publicly known recognition algorithm that can accurately identify humor, given the visual complexities and nuances, and the reality that humor often refers to realities outside the actual image frame. Step 5 is explored in more depth in the following section.

FUTURE RESEARCH DIRECTIONS

This chapter explored some of the ways people visually conceptualize #selfie(s) and #humor in a combined image set from the Instagram image-sharing mobile application. In this naïve exploration, there were extracted insights not only about the specific question of humor and identity through social imagery but also about how to analyze social imagery in a systematic and emergent way, especially given how the Web and Internet have become increasingly visual mediums. What are some next steps to this research?

One simple extension is to begin with the original three research questions and see what other researchers find…with their own image sets from different image-sharing social media platforms or apps. #memes are also constantly changing and time-dependent.

If this same method were applied to an N=all dataset, what could be discovered? Or if this approach were applied to an N=all with time segments broken out from the founding of Instagram to the present, what could be discovered? Could this image coding approach be integrated into an algorithm and to what insights and findings?

Another research approach could explore the pro-social to anti-social aspects of certain types of #selfie #humor, in terms of messaging and then attitude and behavior effects respectively.

Also, other researchers have observed "joke selfies" (Senft & Baym, 2015, p. 1589) which would benefit from research but which were not directly addressed as a category here.

Effective questions can lead people on quests, and the findings may vary depending on the different social media platforms, different image extraction techniques, different coding techniques, different people groups (culturally, geographically, linguistically, and others). The concepts of "selfie" and "humor" are very broad, and semantically, and by practice, these keyword terms do not necessarily limit practices to particular geographies. Selfies are "a phenomenal ubiquitous convention of online culture" (Souza, de las Casas, Flores, Youn, Cha, Quercia, & Almeida, 2015, p. 221); this is a global phenomenon with different manifestations in different sub-populations.

As #dronie- and "selfie bot"-captured imagery come online (as high tech-enabled selfies), there may be interesting insights about #selfie #humor there. [The "selfie bot" is a self-following video drone that is anticipated to be a new technology particularly favored by "sports enthusiasts" (Schneider, 2015).] People have posted self-videos as seen from the backs of their pet dogs, with the dogs acting as a living "selfie bot" of sorts. There are public relations events that are set up as photo opportunities, which are selfies by instrumentation, with the instrumentation being mass and niche media organizations. A fairly new feature in social media—the ephemeral disappearing post based on timed self-destruct features—is also understood to have effects on how people share selfies (Charteris, Gregory, & Masters, 2014, n.p.).

CONCLUSION

To conclude, this chapter addressed three research questions (and related sub-questions) based on exploration of a social image dataset. They were the following questions: (1) What does identity-based humor look like in terms of a #selfie #humor- tagged image set from the Instagram photo-sharing mobile app? (2) What earlier findings and theories about humor apply to the more modern forms of mediated social humor? Is it possible to effectively apply the Humor Styles Model to the images from the #selfie #humor Instagram image set to better understand #selfie #humor? If so, what may be discoverable using this approach? (3) What are some constructive and systematized ways to analyze social image sets in an emergent way using manual and computer-supported techniques?

This work resulted in qualitative and quantitative descriptions of a 941-item image set, with descriptions of various aspects of the image set. #selfie #humor may be seen as an outgrowth of real-space identity humor with the attendant challenges of avoiding false stereotyping and stigmatization of others. In terms of analyses of social image sets, this exploratory work also offered some basic insights. It may be that in retrospect that this multi-layered emergent social image coding approach may be seen as naïve and even superficial; however, this approach may have value as a precursor step to more in-depth and latent insights from more targeted social (media) image analysis. Using an emergent image coding approach enables some loose baseline descriptions of a social image set as an initial somewhat theory-free zone from which to layer theory-based research and coding. A few analytical tools have been shared in the Appendices.

ACKNOWLEDGMENT

This work evolved from a graduate-level summer course I took several years ago on the social and psychological aspects of certain types of humor. Thanks to Dr. Don Saucier at Kansas State University for an engaging and provocative course. A digital poster session based on this chapter was included in the 3rd Annual Big 12 Teaching and Learning Conference at Kansas State University in Manhattan, Kansas, on June 2016. A related slideshow is available on SlideShare at https://www.slideshare.net/ShalinHaiJew/coding-social-imagery-learning-from-a-selfie-humor-image-set-from-instagram.

REFERENCES

Belk, R. (2016). Extended self and the digital world. *Current Opinion in Psychology*, *10*, 50–54. doi:10.1016/j.copsyc.2015.11.003

Bonsignore, E., Pauw, D., Ahn, J., Gubbels, M., Clegg, T., Lewittes, B., . . . Rhodes, E. (2014). *Selfies for science: Collaborative configurations around ScienceKit*. Poster presented in CSCW 2014, Baltimore, MD.

Bruno, N., Gabriele, V., Tasso, T., & Bertamini, M. (2014). Selfies reveal systematic deviations from known principles of photographic composition. *Art & Perception*, *2*(1-2), 45–58. doi:10.1163/22134913-00002027

Charon, J. M. (2004). *Symbolic Interactionism: An Introduction, An Interpretation, An Integration*. Boston: Pearson.

Charteris, J., Gregory, S., & Masters, Y. (2014). Snapchat "selfies": The case of disappearing data. Rhetoric and Reality. Paper presented at ASCILITE 2014, Dunedin, New Zealand.

Dinhopl, A., & Gretzel, U. (2016). Selfie-taking as touristic looking. *Annals of Tourism Research*, *57*, 126–139. doi:10.1016/j.annals.2015.12.015

Döring, N., Reif, A., & Poeschl, S. (2016). How gender-stereotypical are selfies? A content analysis and comparison with magazine adverts. *Computers in Human Behavior*, *55*, 955–962. doi:10.1016/j.chb.2015.10.001

Eftekhar, A., Fullwood, C., & Morris, N. (2014). Capturing personality from Facebook photos and photo-related activities: How much exposure do you need?. *Computers in Human Behavior*, *37*, 162–170. doi:10.1016/j.chb.2014.04.048

Fiegerman, S. (2014, Dec. 10). Instagram tops 300 million active users, likely bigger than Twitter. *Mashable*. Retrieved March 12, 2016, from http://mashable.com/2014/12/10/instagram-300-million-users/#1glRTbvU7Pq0

Ford, T. E., & Ferguson, M. A. (2004). Social consequences of disparagement humor: A prejudiced norm theory. *Personality and Social Psychology Review*, *8*(1), 79–94. doi:10.1207/S15327957PSPR0801_4 PMID:15121541

Fox, K. (2017, May 19). Instagram worst social media app for young people's mental health. *Cable News Network (CNN)*. Retrieved June 4, 2017, from http://www.cnn.com/2017/05/19/health/instagram-worst-social-network-app-young-people-mental-health/index.html

Frosh, P. (2015). The gestural image: The selfie, photography theory, and kinesthetic sociability. *International Journal of Communication*, *9*, 1607–1628.

Gabriel, F. (2014). Sexting, selfies and self-harm: Young people, social media and the performance of self-development. *Media International Australia*, *151*(1), 104–112. doi:10.1177/1329878X1415100114

Hodson, G., Rush, J., & MacInnis, C. C. (2010). A joke is just a joke (except when it isnt): Cavalier humor beliefs facilitate the expression of group dominance motives. *Journal of Personality and Social Psychology*, *99*(4), 660–683. doi:10.1037/a0019627 PMID:20919777

Hosseinmardi, H., Mattson, S. A., Rafiq, R. I., Han, R., Lv, Q., & Mishra, S. (2015). Analyzing labeled cyberbullying incidents on the Instagram social network. *LNCS, 9471, 49 – 66*. doi:10.1007/978-3-319-27433-1_4

Jain, A., Vijay, P., Maguluri, S., Sorathia, K., & Shukla, P. (2014). Exploring tangible interactions for capturing self photographs. *Proceedings of IHCI '14*, 116 – 121. doi:10.1145/2676702.2676721

James, W. (1890). *The Principles of Psychology* (Vol. 1). London: Macmillan. doi:10.1037/11059-000

Jang, J.-Y., Han, K., Shih, P. C., & Lee, D. (2015). Generation Like: Comparative Characteristics in Instagram. Proceedings of CHI 2015: Crossings, 4039 – 4042.

Kalayeh, M.M., Seifu, M., LaLanne, W., & Shah, M. (2015). *How to take a good selfie?*. Academic Press.

Kelland, K. (2011, June 28). Brain scan reveals how brain processes jokes. *Reuters*. Retrieved March 13, 2016, from http://www.reuters.com/article/us-brain-jokes-transmission-embargo-idUSTRE75R7GL20110628

Kennemer, Q. (2014, June 25). Android has 1 billion active users in the past 30 days (and other interesting numbers from IO). *Phandroid*. Retrieved Mar. 12, 2016, from http://phandroid.com/2014/06/25/android-has-1-billion-active-users-in-the-past-30-days-and-other-interesting-numbers-from-io/

Lee, N. (2015). Cyber Attacks, Prevention, and Countermeasures. In N. Lee (Ed.), Counterterrorism and Cybersecurity: Total Information Awareness (2nd ed., pp. 249-276). Springer. doi:10.1007/978-3-319-17244-6_10

Lian, S., & Zhang, Y. (2010). Multimedia forensics for detecting forgeries. In P. Stavroulakis & M. Stamp (Eds.), *Handbook of Information and Communication Security. Springer*. doi:10.1007/978-3-642-04117-4_37

Lobinger, K., & Brantner, C. (2015). In the eye of the beholder: Subjective views on the authenticity of selfies. *International Journal of Communication*, *9*, 1848–1860.

Martin, R. A. (2000). Humor. In A. E. Kazdin (Ed.), Encyclopedia of psychology (Vol. 4, pp. 202 – 204). Washington, DC: American Psychological Association.

Martin, R. A. (2001). Humor, laughter, and physical health: Methodological issues and research findings. *Psychological Bulletin*, *127*(4), 504–519. doi:10.1037/0033-2909.127.4.504 PMID:11439709

Martin, R. A., Puhlik-Doris, P., Larsen, G., Gray, J., & Weir, K. (2003). Individual differences in uses of humor and their relation to psychological well-being: Development of the Humor Styles Questionnaire. *Journal of Research in Personality*, *37*(1), 48–75. doi:10.1016/S0092-6566(02)00534-2

Marwick, A. E. (2015). Instafame: Luxury selfies in the attention economy. *Public Culture*, *27*(1), 137–160. doi:10.1215/08992363-2798379

Phillip, A. (2014). If a monkey takes a selfie in the forest, who owns the copyright? No one, says Wikimedia. The Intersect. *Washington Post.* Retrieved February 17, 2016, from https://www.washingtonpost.com/news/the-intersect/wp/2014/08/06/if-a-monkey-takes-a-selfie-in-the-forest-who-owns-the-copyright-no-one-says-wikimedia/

Piwek, L., & Joinson, A. (2016). What do they *snapchat* about? Patterns of use in time-limited instant messaging service. *Computers in Human Behavior, 54,* 358–367. doi:10.1016/j.chb.2015.08.026

Plant, E. A., & Devine, P. G. (1998). Internal and external motivation to respond without prejudice. *Journal of Personality and Social Psychology, 75*(3), 811–832. doi:10.1037/0022-3514.75.3.811

Privacy Policy. (2016). Instagram Help Center / Privacy & Safety Center. *Instagram.* Retrieved March 12, 2016, from https://help.instagram.com/155833707900388

Provine, R. R. (1996). Laughter. *American Scientist, 84*(1), 38–45.

Provine, R. R. (2004). Laughter, tickling, and the evolution of speech and self. *Current Directions in Psychological Science, 13*(6), 215–218. doi:10.1111/j.0963-7214.2004.00311.x

Rappoport, L. (2005). *Punchlines: The Case for Racial, Ethnic, & Gender Humor.* Westport, CT: Praeger.

Salie, F. (2016, Mar. 6). Death by selfie. Sunday Morning. *CBS News.*

Saltz, J. (2014). Art at arm's length: A history of the selfie. *Vulture.* Retrieved Feb. 12, 2016, from http://www.vulture.com/2014/01/history-of-the-selfie.html#

Schneider, D. (2015). Flying selfie bots. Spectrum: Top Tech 2015, 48 – 51.

Selfies. (2016, Jan. 30). In *Wikipedia.* Retrieved Feb. 14, 2016, from https://en.wikipedia.org/wiki/Selfie

Senft, T. M., & Baym, N. K. (2015). What does the selfie say? Investing a global phenomenon. *International Journal of Communication, 9,* 1588–1606. Retrieved from http://ijoc.org/index.php/ijoc/article/viewFile/4067/1387

Shah, N. (2015, April 25). The selfie and the slut: Bodies, technology and public shame. Review of Women's Studies. *Economic and Political Weekly, L*(17), 86–93.

Shah, S. (2016). *Pandemic: Tracking Contagions, from Cholera to Ebola and Beyond*. New York: Farrar, Straus & Giroux.

Solecki, S., & Fay-Hillier, T. (2015). The toll of too much technology on teens mental health. *Journal of Pediatric Nursing*, *30*(6), 933–936. doi:10.1016/j.pedn.2015.08.001 PMID:26364771

Sorokowska, A., Oleszkiewicz, A., Frackowiak, T., Pisanski, K., Chmiel, A., & Sorokowski, P. (2016). Selfies and personality: Who posts self-portrait photographs? *Personality and Individual Differences*, *90*, 119–123. doi:10.1016/j.paid.2015.10.037

Souza, F., de Las Casas, D., Flores, V., Youn, S., Cha, M., Quercia, D., & Almeida, V. (2015). Dawn of the selfie era: The whos, wheres, and hows of selfies on Instagram. *Proceedings of COSN '15*, 221 – 231.

Svelander, A. & Wiberg, M. (2015, July-August). The practice of selfies. *Interactions,* 34 – 38.

Systrom, K. (2011, Jan. 12). What is the genesis of Instagram? Blog entry. *Quora*. Retrieved March 12, 2016, from https://www.quora.com/What-is-the-genesis-of-Instagram

Tiidenberg, K., & Cruz, E. G. (2015). Selfies, image and the re-making of the body. *Body & Society*, 1–26.

Tsiallas, E. (2015). Gamified eroticism: Gay male social networking applications and self-pornography. *Sexuality & Culture*, *19*(4), 759–775. doi:10.1007/s12119-015-9288-z

Twenge, J. M., & Campbell, W. K. (2009). *The Narcissism Epidemic: Living in the Age of Entitlement*. New York: Atria. Simon & Schuster, Inc.

Van House, N.A., Davis, M., Takhteyev, Y., Ames, M., & Finn, M. (2004). *The social uses of personal photography: Methods for projecting future imaging applications* (working paper). University of California, Berkeley.

Vernon, P. A., Martin, R. A., Schermer, J. A., & Mackie, A. (2008). A behavioral genetic investigation of humor styles and their correlations with the Big-5 personality dimensions. *Personality and Individual Differences*, *44*(5), 1116–1125. doi:10.1016/j.paid.2007.11.003

Veselka, L., Schermer, J. A., Martin, R. A., & Vernon, P. A. (2010). Relations between humor styles and the Dark Triad traits of personality. *Personality and Individual Differences*, *48*(6), 772–774. doi:10.1016/j.paid.2010.01.017

Walrave, M., Ponnet, K., Van Ouytsel, J., Van Gool, E., Heirman, W., & Verbeek, A. (2015). Whether or not to engage in sexting: Explaining adolescent sexting behavior by applying the prototype willingness model. *Telematics and Informatics*, *32*(4), 796–808. doi:10.1016/j.tele.2015.03.008

Yip, J. A., & Martin, R. A. (2006). Sense of humor, emotional intelligence, and social competence. *Journal of Research in Personality*, *40*(6), 1202–1208. doi:10.1016/j.jrp.2005.08.005

ADDITIONAL READING

Rappoport, L. (2005). *Punchlines: The Case for Racial, Ethnic, & Gender Humor*. Westport, CT: Praeger.

Selfiecity. (2014). Retrieved May 24, 2017, from http://selfiecity.net/

KEY TERMS AND DEFINITIONS

Dronie: A digital self-portrait taken from a drone.

Ethnicity: A category of belonging based on shared cultural practices, history, language, and sometimes values.

Ethnic Humor: Something meant to be funny that references ethnicity or ethnic groups (culture-based group membership).

Gender: A social or cultural identification as male or female (vs. biological maleness or femaleness).

Group Selfie: A group self-portrait showing more than one individual.

Humor: Something considered amusing or laughter-inducing because of an inherent ludicrousness, incongruity, or unexpectedness.

Instrumentation: The use of a mechanism or tool to achieve particular ends.

Laughter: Giggling, an expression of humor.

Meme: On the Internet, a popular unit of culture expressed as a phrase, a hashtag, an image with a textual overlay, or a snippet of video (typically).

Perceptual Analysis: A practice in multimedia research that involves the use of human perception channels (sight, smell, taste, touch, hearing, and proprioception, classically).

Race: A category of belonging based often on physical characteristics, with humankind divided into particular divisions.

Selfie: A digital self-portrait, often created by amateur photographers.

Sense of Humor: A tendency to find particular things funny, formed based on biology, culture, personality, cognition, and other factors.

Social Media Platform: The type of social sharing application, such as wiki, blog, microblog, social networking, photo-sharing, video-sharing, short messaging service (SMS), and others.

Solo Selfie: A self-portrait depicting only the individual photographer by himself or herself.

User-Generated Content: The digital information created by people and shared via social media in various forms (text, audio, imagery, video, and other forms).

Visual Metonymy: The use of a visual symbol to represent a referent.

Visual Synecdoche: The use of a visual part of a thing to represent the whole.

APPENDIX A

Exploring a Selfie Image Set With Basic Features Extraction

Table 7 enables researchers to ask some simple questions:

- Of the extracted image set, are there more single, duo, or group #selfie and #humor images? What is the numerical breakdown in terms of humans in the #selfie #humor image set? Why?
- What is the balance of male-female-unclear gender representation in single (solo) images (showing one person), duo images (showing two people, forefronted), and group images (showing three individuals or more). What could this mean?

Table 7. Exploring a selfie image set with basic features extraction

	Single (Solo) Images	Duo Images	Group Images
Male Characters			
Female Characters			
Unclear Gender			

APPENDIX B

Selfie Types and Counts

Table 8 enables researchers to ask some simple questions:

- What mode of illustration is most common overall in the image set: drawing or illustration, photo, or mixed image (visual) and text?
- Given the various types of selfies—human individuals, human duos, human groups, selfie text, animal selfies, and figurative selfies—what type of image (drawing or illustration, photo, mixed image and text) is used in the representations of those particular categories? (What is the most common way for depicting human individuals? Human duos? Human groups?...) Why?
- What types of styling are applied to the respective data table cells? Is it possible to generalize the general look-and-feel of a selfie text that is a photo? An animal selfie that is a mixed image and text image? A human group that is shown in a photo?

Table 8. Selfie types and counts

	Human Individuals	Human Duos	Human Groups	Selfie Text	Animal Selfies	Figurative Selfies	(Totals of General Image Types)
Drawing or Illustration							
Photo							
Mixed Image (visual) and Text							

APPENDIX C

Coding #Selfie #Humor Images as Affiliative, Self-Enhancing, Aggressive, Self-Defeating, or Other Humor Styles

Table 9 enables researchers to ask some simple questions:

- What are the most and least common types of humor styles used in the #selfie #humor image set?
- What are some common themes within the affiliative #selfie humor style? The self-enhancing #selfie humor style? The aggressive #selfie humor style? The self-defeating #selfie humor style? The "other" #selfie humor style?
    - ○ In what ways are the images affiliative, self-enhancing, aggressive, and self-defeating respectively?
    - ○ Are there common visual cues that are indicators of the respective types of humor styles?
    - ○ Are there common textual terms that are indicators of the respective types of humor styles?

Table 9. Coding #selfie #humor images as affiliative, self-enhancing, aggressive, self-Defeating, or other humor styles

	Affiliative #selfie Humor Style	Self-enhancing #selfie Humor Style	Aggressive #selfie Humor Style	Self-defeating #selfie Humor Style	[Other #selfie Humor Style]
(Formal) Definition of the Code Category					
Project-Based Definition of the Code Category					
Counts					
Examples and Descriptions					

Further research may be done to analyze whether there are gendered (and other demographic-based) representations that predominate in particular categories.

This research suggested in the Appendix C table was not done in this particular chapter.

What patterns may be seen?

- What do individual selfie images most tend to be in terms of humor styles? Least likely in terms of humor styles? Why?
- What do duo selfie images most tend to be in terms of humor styles? Least likely in terms of humor styles? Why?
- What do group selfie images tend to be in terms of humor styles? Least likely in terms of humor styles? Why? (Do group #selfie images tend to be mostly affiliative?)
- In terms of the selfies labeled "affiliative," how would that image set best be described? Likewise for "self-enhancing," "aggressive," and "self-defeating"?
- What about the "other" category of humor styles? Should the model include additional humor styles?
- Both "affiliative" and "aggressive" humor styles are obviously social, and "self-enhancing" and "self-defeating" tend to be more individual self-focused. Are there patterns that may be seen among the social humor styles vs. the more individual-focused humor styles?
- "Affiliative" and "self-enhancing" humor styles are seen as positive for people's psychosocial health, and "aggressive" and "self-defeating" humor styles are seen as negative for their psycho-social health? Are there patterns that may be seen in the positive and negative image sets?

Chapter 2

Snacking Around the World:
Evolving an Inductive Image Categorization and Research Query Approach for Image Sets From Social Media

ABSTRACT

Social media platforms enable access to large image sets for research, but there are few if any non-theoretical approaches to image analysis, categorization, and coding. Based on two image sets labeled by the #snack hashtag (on Instagram), a systematic and open inductive approach to identifying conceptual image categories was developed, and unique research questions designed. By systematically categorizing imagery in a bottom-up way, researchers may (1) describe and assess the image set contents and categorize them in multiple ways independent of a theoretical framework (and its potential biasing effects); (2) conceptualize what may be knowable from the image set by the defining of research questions that may be addressed in the empirical data; (3) categorize the available imagery broadly and in multiple ways as a precursor step to further exploration (e.g., research design, image coding, and development of a research codebook). This work informs the exploration and analysis of mobile-created contents for open learning.

DOI: 10.4018/978-1-5225-2679-7.ch002

INTRODUCTION

In a common conceptualization of the different phases of the World Wide Web, Web 1.0 was about the Read Web, Web 2.0 as the Read/Write Web or Social Web (with users writing to the Web by sharing contents socially), and Web 3.0 is the machine-readable Web, which enables computers to exchange data in an automated way via web services. At every stage, new technological affordances have enabled people to interact with each other and with each other's data in new ways. In parallel with these changes, more and more people have been going online. According to Internet Live Stats, there are 3.3 billion Internet users in the world as of late 2015. An estimated 74% of all Internet users also use social networking sites ("Social Networking Fact Sheet," January 2014). By 2016, it is estimated that there will be some two billion social network users globally (Bennett, 2013). With so many people communicating online, social media platforms are rollicking spaces for various types of research.

With the wide availability of publicly-released imagery from content-sharing social media platforms (and other types), researchers have access to an abundance of information-carrying still images for their potential work. However, in the research literature, there is little in the way of non-theoretical approaches for organizing and coding such visuals for research applications. Having a systematic way to summarize image set data may be useful not only for data organization purposes but to potentially enhance research design, image coding, and the creation of a research codebook. Sets are simple groupings of objects, and new objects may be evaluated as to whether they belong in a set or not (a Boolean "true" or "false"). The basic rules of set-making are simple: the rationale for the set building should be clearly defined, and the sets themselves should be sufficiently comprehensive to include all potential members into one mutually exclusive category or another. To explore how this might work, one image set was extracted from Instagram, and the images were lightly analyzed to ultimately test three hypotheses.

Hypothesis 1: From a sufficient topic-based image set from social media, there will be emergent natural categorical breaklines that may be inductively observable by researchers (without *a priori* reference to theoretical frameworks).

Hypothesis 2: From a sufficient topic-based image set from social media, there will be some research questions that may be inductively and inferentially extracted by researchers.

Hypothesis 3: For research analysts using imagery from social media platforms, exploring some of the available imagery through categorization may enhance the work of research design, image coding, and developing a research codebook.

The first hypothesis is a precondition for inductive and emergent analysis of imagery. An underlying assumption is that digital images are socially created communications from people to people, and in that interpersonal dynamic, receivers of the image data may be culturally trained to identify meaning-based image clusters. A "breakline" is conceptualized as apparently natural points of separation or differentiation between image objects. The second hypothesis offers a kind of reverse engineering from data to potential askable questions. The third hypothesis is a broadscale one that encapsulates the first two and underpins the entire chapter. It is included here because it will need to be revisited once this initial exploration is complete.

To test these hypotheses, a real-world dataset of nearly 700 images and another of over 900 images were extracted from the Instagram image-sharing social media app in December 2015. The topic selected—based on convenience

Figure 1. #snacks: A popular topic on Instagram

and inherent (apparent) simplicity—was #snack. The use of a hashtagged topic would mean that there would not be one "owner" of a social media account that would be the one sharing all the images; a diversity of voices would be enabled. The use of the #hashtag by whomever posted the image would indicate the users' sense of the particular topic (although multiple hashtagged labels may be applied to one image). This topic is something that people can relate to, as the practice of snacking likely cuts across geographies and cultures. [Some researchers have suggested that Instagram "is known to have high rates of photos that contain geotags" (Souza, de Las Casas, Flores, Youn, Cha, Quercia, & Almeida, 2015, p. 223), but that assertion was not directly attributed in the source.] Snacking is also a practice that is readily represented through imagery. The DownThemAll browser add-on was used to extract the image data (which is extracted from the most recent images in reverse chronological order); this tool requires that the target website be fully expanded in order to extracted the images as thumbnails, which means that only a small percentage of the collected images would be collected. (For a number of social media platforms, researchers who want to use an N=all must access imagery through commercial companies, and the N=all imagery and videos are hosted in the cloud and analyzed through "big data" methods and technologies.) While there have been recent advancements in autocoding of imagery (in terms of "machine vision" and various artificial intelligence and machine learning applications), all the work described here is manual but machine-enabled. This means that the approach is not as scalable as fully automated processes, but these approaches may be transferred to qualitative data analysis software with multiple coders (and the application of Cohen's Kappa to test for statistical similarity in coding), which may increase coding speed.

REVIEW OF THE LITERATURE

In October 2010, Instagram was founded by Kevin Systrom and Mike Krieger. It was conceptualized as an iOS app for posting photos from iPhones to user accounts. In 2012, it was acquired by Facebook for $1 billion, and it had 100 million active users at the time of sale. Instagram was seen as a software tool to enable access to the mobile marketplace. Using this camera phone mobile app, users of smartphones with camera capabilities may snap an image, apply some filters or effects, and then share broadly in a convenient and spontaneous way, using this app. In a generic sense, Instagram is a content-sharing social media platform and application. A more nuanced descriptor may be as a "photo-sharing social networking service" (PSNS). As a platform, it enables the sharing of short videos as well. In 2015, Instagram had 300 million users worldwide with 80 million pictures shared daily (Lee, Bakar, Dahri, & Sin, 2015, p. 133). Instagram's press page claims 400 million active users as of September 2015 ("Celebrating a Community of 400 Million," 2015). According to the Pew Internet Survey, some 28% of Internet users use Instagram. Instagram's users tend to be young: 55% within the 18 – 29 age group, 28% within 30 – 49 years old, 11% in the 50 – 64 age group, and 4% over 65 ("Instagram Demographics," Aug. 17, 2015). Instagram is known to be popular among "tweens" and "teens" (Derby, 2013, p. 161).

Compared to other online social networks (OSNs), Instagram tends to be used more for personal uses than professional ones (Lim, Lu, Chen, & Kan, 2015, p. 118), with its users "extremely active during weekends" (p. 117). In terms of cross-sharing information and contents, users of Instagram tend to overlap with Tumblr because of easy sharing mechanisms (Lim, Lu, Chen, & Kan, 2015, p. 115). The authors write:

Taking a closer look, we notice that Google+ exhibits higher levels of activity during working hours (09:00-18:00) on weekdays; but exhibits lower and more evenly distributed activity during and after working hours on weekends. Interestingly, Instagram shows an opposite trend, peaking in activity after working hours (>18:00) on weekdays, and showing a decline after working hours on weekends. This hints, albeit subtly, at the contrasting nature of these two social networks – Instagram is a platform more frequently used during nonworking hours, while Google+ is used more during working hours. (Lim, Lu, Chen, & Kan, 2015, p. 116)

Early work in visual studies suggested that people use photography for themselves (to serve memory, narrative, and identity) as well as socially, such as to sustain relationships, self-represent to others, and to express one's aesthetics, creativity, and point-of-view to others (Van House, 2007, p. 2718). More recently, researchers have identified four main motives for sharing photos through such sites: "informativeness, community support, status-seeking, and self- representation," with self-representation and status seeking as predominant motivations (Lee, Bakar, Dahri, & Sin, 2015, p. 132). How people self-present on social media has been analyzed to understand the personalities behind the social media accounts. For example, people who are narcissistic tend to be attention-seeking and exhibitionistic. Males who post selfies (photographic self-portraits) tend to rank high on narcissism metrics:

In two studies with a pooled sample of 1296 men and women, we tested the prediction that individuals who score high on four narcissism sub-scales (Self-sufficiency, Vanity, Leadership, and Admiration Demand) will be more likely to post selfies to social media sites than will individuals who exhibit low narcissism. We examined three categories of selfies: own selfies; selfies with a romantic partner; and group selfies, controlling for non-selfie photographs. Women posted more selfies of all types than did men. However, women's selfie-posting behavior was generally unrelated to their narcissism scores. In contrast, men's overall narcissism scores positively predicted posting own selfies, selfies with a partner, and group selfies. Moreover, men's Vanity, Leadership, and Admiration Demand scores each independently predicted the posting of one or more types of selfies. Our findings provide the first evidence that the link between narcissism and selfie-posting behavior is comparatively weak among women than men, and provide novel insight into the social motivations and functions of online social networking. (Sorokowski et al., 2015, p. 123)

As social beings, people often show a deep interest in other people. They are especially drawn to images of others' faces, which are rich in social details. Photos with faces were found to be "38% more likely to receive likes and 32% more likely to receive comments, even after controlling for social network reach and activity" based on study of a million-image set of Instagram images (Bakhshi, Shamma, & Gilbert, 2014, p. 965). Between 2012 and 2014, the number of selfies posted online has increased "900 times," with the most common sharers of selfies as young females ("except for certain countries such as Nigeria and Egypt that show male dominance") (Souza, de Las Casas, Flores, Youn, Cha, Quercia, & Almeida, 2015, p. 222). People's self-portraits draw outsized attention and communicate something about the individual but also his or her cultural context:

Selfies are an effective medium to grab attention; they generate on average 1.1–3.2 times more likes and comments than other types of content on Instagram. Compared to other content, interactions involving selfies exhibit variations in homophily scores (in terms of age and gender) that suggest they are becoming more widespread. Their style also varies by cultural boundaries in that the average age and majority gender seen in selfies differ from one country to another. (Souza et al., 2015, p. 221)

Even planetary scale data starts local and is grounded in the world and lived experiences. Beyond personal reasons for image sharing, many share online in order to promote word-of-mouth (WOM) enthusiasms about commercial brands, products and services; maintain relationships with customers; publicize commercial events, and ultimately present a positive public image. Images themselves may "trend" or attract intense broad popular attention for a period of time. Image trends result from two main factors:

Firstly, major social events such as protests, civil unrests, and festivals create image trends with many people sharing images related to the event. The second category is when a popular person posts a controversial or a unique image, tags of the image became a trend with many re-sharing the same image in quick succession due to the high interest. (Ahangama, 2014, p. 158)

Those who use social media often do not only use one platform exclusively. There are often cross-postings in order to drive traffic, particularly to image and video resources. For example, when an image is posted on Instagram, a summary and a URL (uniform resource locator) of this post can be shared on the Twitter microblogging automatically. On social media, the currency of value is often "attention," and the potential audiences for social media contents is, while potentially large, also inherently limited. In the vernacular, there are only 24 hours in a day. Images themselves may be memorable in an intrinsic way based on their features and human visual hard-wiring. Visual "interestingness" has been described as "the power of attracting or holding ones (sic) attention" (Amengual, Bosch, & de la Rosa, 2015, p. 65).

A grounded empirical study of the types of photos posted on Instagram, a research team identified eight photo categories: friends, food ("food, recipes, cakes, drinks, etc."), gadgets, captioned photos (with texts and memes), pets, activities, selfies (self-portraits), and fashion ("shoes, costumes, makeup, personal belongings, etc.") (Hu, Manikonda, & Kambhampati, 2014, p. 3). Many use hashtags on Instagram as "image annotation metadata," which describe image contents (Giannoulakis & Tsapatsoulis, 2015). Hashtagging is also used to collect related imagery based on common themes. While images may be shared for personal fulfillment reasons and for local objectives, socially shared images, singly and in collections, may also be used in a de-contextualized way. In other words, while image contents are shared in an ego-based and subjective context, the actual shared materials are also usable in an objective way.

The varying tagging policies (and their enforcement) on social media platforms affects how tagging may be understood. For example, Flickr released machine tagging which applies various tags based on machine vision. While these tags may be removed manually, they are applied by default. Instagram does not show tagging on the top level but does show some people's commenting, likes, and view counts. Research into tagging habits have shown that social networks may share "folk" tagging habits and terminology (Mika, 2005; Anagnostopoulos, Kumar, & Mahdian, 2008). (The labeling of social media contents with amateur-originated tags is known as folksonomic labeling. In this context, no formal taxonomy or formal ontology is used to label the contents. Rather, people use free-form and common language and whatever is top-of-mind to describe their uploaded imagery and videos. Free-text labels, while noisy, may be informative of user intentions and points-of-view, among other insights.)

Warming to the Topic

Finally, on social media, people have posted a variety of images of food. This has been called "foodtography" (a portmanteau term from "food" and "photography") as well as "foodagramming" (a blended word from "food" and "Instagramming") and resulted in the practice of sharing "food porn" (Salie, Dec. 1, 2013). Research suggests that there are intimate ties between images of food and people's lived behaviors (even such extremes of over-eating and non-eating). One researcher studied "pro-anorexia" and "food porn" on the Web and noted that while such depictions are virtual, they have potent impacts on people's physical selves. She writes:

It traces how eating in, and through, cyberspace shapes the biological materialities of bodies whilst also collapsing neat distinctions between offline and online worlds. Virtual vectors of spectating, salivating and digesting are disembodied and yet corporeal. Eating is seen to take place beyond and among bodies and to be dissipated both spatially and temporally. As such, cyberspace is outside and other to lived corporeality, and yet also folded into and productive of the intimate geographies and embodied subjectivities of everyday lives. As eating takes myriad forms across the de-materialised viscerality of the Internet, it also emerges as central to the production and 'matter(ing)' of cyberspace itself; this is (an) eating space in which what is eaten, by whom and with what bodies, perpetually shifts. Thus, seeking to contribute to geographical scholarship on affect and food, this paper engages with eating as both the subject of enquiry and also as a productive pathway into an interrogation of cyberspace and its place within the affective productions of the everyday. It suggests that this is a key site in which to explore the intimate socialities, materialities and biopolitics of food. (Lavis, 2015)

Another work involved the specific study of Instagram food posts and applied a computational method to extract nutritional information and calorific content. The researchers explored how the online community reacted to healthy vs. non-healthy food postings and found "Instagram as a platform where sharing of moderately healthy food content is common, and such content also receives the most support from the community" (Sharma & De Choudhury, 2015, p. 115). In contrast, a different research team studying Instagram images taken in restaurants in the U.S. actually found social approval for unhealthy foods high in sugar and fat (Mejova, Haddadi, Noulas, & Weber, 2015). Yet another clever project captured near real-time Instagrammed postings of restaurant-based food images and sentiment analysis of their comments in order to create maps of restaurants favored by local residents vs. those favored by travelers (Kuo, et al., 2014, p. 202); ultimately, this team is developing a social food recommender system based on shared imagery and messaging about food on Instagram. During their research, the team found that food was a very common subject of the images uploaded in Instagram. Further, they found that the tagging applied to the images tended towards inaccuracy. They wrote:

A large proportion of the images in social media contains food (e.g., more than 100 million images contains hashtag "food" in Instagram). To mine information from these images, it is insufficient to simply use tags to decide what is in the image since tags are really noisy (in our preliminary study, only about 30% of images tagged food on Instagram are correct). Therefore, we adopt state-of-the-art recognition method, convolution neural network (CNN), to recognize food in images. By analyzing different social media sources, we found that Instagram contains more images that can represent users' daily life, but images in Instagram also contain more noises (our experiment shows that about 26% of images tagged food are selfies instead of food images, while the same number is 7.5% in Flickr). (Kuo, et al., 2014, p. 203)

Still another engaging work involved the types of food images that 14-year-olds posted on Instagram with the finding that a majority of the images showed foods "high in calories but low in nutrients," and many images emulated "food advertisements" albeit with the suggestion of personalized peer recommendation (Holmberg, Chaplin, Hillman, & Berg, 2016, p. 121).

#Snack in Social Media

To be clear, this work does not engage the more serious issues of #snack(ing) or food. Rather, this is more of an incidental topic used to explore the open coding or inductive labeling of social imagery based on a common subject. So as to provide a sense of what #snack may look like, it may help to dip into several other social media platforms before using the dataset from Instagram to walk-through this approach. #snack images from Flickr were also considered for this research as a contrast to those from Instagram, but the researcher was unable to extract the necessary images for datasets. A brief note on Flickr is in order. Flickr was founded by Ludicorps in 2004 as a web service for image and video hosting to embed in blogs and social media. It was purchased by Yahoo in 2005. As of March 2013, Flickr had 87 million registered members (Jeffries, 2013). As of June 10, 2015, Flickr had 112 million users in 63 countries; this service featured a set of 10 billion images as of May 7, 2015 and over 3.5 million new photos shared daily (Smith, Aug. 10, 2015). Flickr has over two million groups (public and private) of users with shared interests.

Related Tags Networks on Flickr

In Figure 2, "#snack" is used as a seeding term to find co-occurring tags in Flickr. There are adjectives that describe various snacks ("delicious," "yummy," and "homemade"), references to locations ("china," "japan," "tokyo," and "street,"), time of day ("night,"), context ("travel,"), camera terms ("closeup," "macro," "bokeh," and "canon"), color references ("blue," "orange," yellow," and "red"), types of meals ("breakfast," "lunch," and "dinner"), ingredients ("butter," "cream," "chocolate," and "egg") as well as direct named foods ("candy," "chips," "cake," "pastry," "cookies," "fish," "popcorn," and "sweets").

The same #snack related tags network with static thumbnail imagery from Flickr is available in Figure 3.

Figure 2. #Snack related tags network on Flickr (1 deg.)

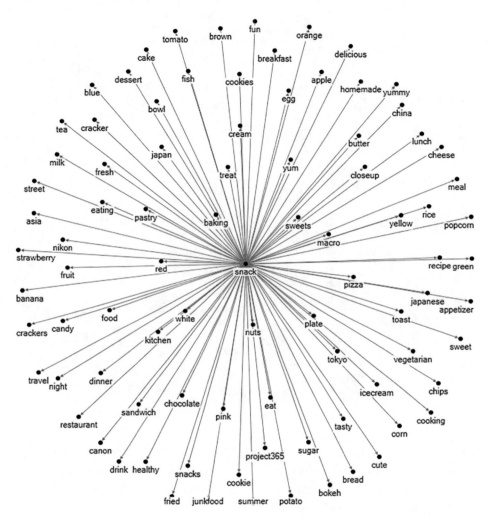

In terms of the graph metrics for the #snack related tags network on Flickr, please refer to Table 1. This related tags network contains 89 vertices (nodes). As with one-degree networks, the edges are all unique connecting dyadic pairs of nodes. The network graph itself is small, with a geodesic distance (graph diameter) of two.

At 1.5 degrees, the #snack related tags network on Flickr contains two clusters or groups (based on the Clauset-Newman-Moore clustering algorithm).

Figure 3. #Snack related tags network on Flickr with thumbnail imagery (1 deg.)

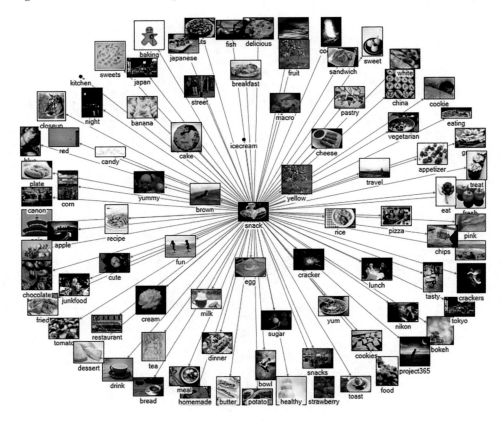

This automated extraction of related tags enables a type of factor analysis. As such, the left group in Figure 4 seems to show direct food, and the right group seems to show more context and photographic details, broadly speaking.

In Figure 5, the 1.5-degree #snack related tags network on Flickr is seen as a network graph with extracted thumbnail imagery at the vertices. This image-rich visualization is more evocative.

The graph metrics for Figures 4 and 5 may be seen in Table 2. This table shows the 89 vertices connected by 2,623 unique edges. This graph has a maximum geodesic distance (graph diameter) of two, and an average geodesic distance of 1.5 hops.

Table 1. Graph metrics for the #snack related tags network on Flickr (1 deg.)

Graph Metric	Value
Graph Type	Directed
Vertices	89
Unique Edges	88
Edges With Duplicates	0
Total Edges	88
Self-Loops	0
Reciprocated Vertex Pair Ratio	0
Reciprocated Edge Ratio	0
Connected Components	1
Single-Vertex Connected Components	0
Maximum Vertices in a Connected Component	89
Maximum Edges in a Connected Component	88
Maximum Geodesic Distance (Diameter)	2
Average Geodesic Distance	1.955309
Graph Density	0.011235955
Modularity	Not Applicable
NodeXL Version	1.0.1.336

Article Networks on Wikipedia

Another way to look at how snacking instantiates on a social media platform is to explore "article networks" on Wikipedia. The English Wikipedia, built on the MediaWiki understructure, has 5,041,907 content articles and a total of 38,098,985 total pages ("Wikipedia:About," Dec. 24, 2015). These article networks are related pages that are hyperlinked on Wikipedia. As such, they work as semantic networks connecting article resources. The Wikipedia standards for creating pages and their work of peer reviewers and peer editors means that these networks tend to be more structured and less haphazard than tagging co-occurrence networks. In this case, "Snack_food" (https://en.wikipedia.org/wiki/Snack_food) is used as the seeding article. The resulting one-degree social graph is viewable in Figure 6.

Figure 4. #Snack related tags network on Flickr (1.5 deg.)

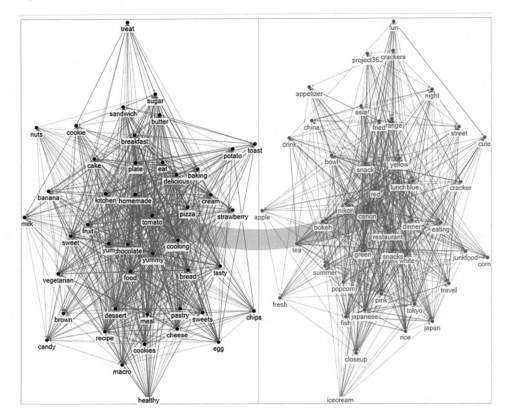

The graph shows direct links to 121 other pages (vertices). These vertices refer to various food types and ingredients as well as some related activities. The graph metrics table for Figure 6 may be seen in Table 3.

At 1.5 degrees, this article network becomes visually unintelligible. This graph has 8,478 nodes and 12,830 unique edges. The maximum geodesic distance (graph diameter) is four. The average geodesic distance between any two nodes is 3.67 hops. There are 37 groups in this network. The specific details of this latter article network may be seen in Table 4.

Another article network extraction was conducted using "List_of_brand_name_snack_foods" from Wikipedia (https://en.wikipedia.org/wiki/List_of_brand_name_snack_foods). This one-degree network shows the direct and defined out-links from the target page. This article-article network graph may be seen in Figure 7.

Figure 5. #Snack related tags network on Flickr with thumbnail imagery (1.5 deg.)

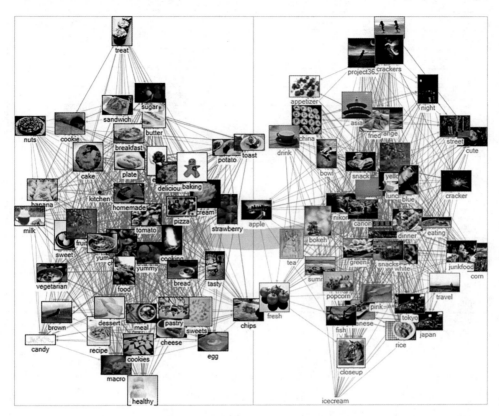

The graph metrics table for Figure 7 may be seen at Table 5. The graph itself has 192 vertices or nodes.

Now that there is a small sense of what #snack may look like on two different social media platforms—Flickr and Wikipedia—it would be helpful to shift to Instagram, which will be the source of the two target image sets.

EXTRACTED IMAGERY FOR OPEN AND INDUCTIVE ANALYSIS AND INITIAL CATEGORIZATION

Understanding what "sorts" of contents are in a social image set is a fundamental first step in harnessing those images for potential research use. As such, starting with something as simple as belongingness to various categories or image subsets is a good way to begin. The work of inducing sets from

Table 2. Graph metrics for the #snack related tags network on Flickr (1.5 deg.)

Graph Type	Directed
Vertices	89
Unique Edges	2623
Edges With Duplicates	0
Total Edges	2623
Self-Loops	0
Reciprocated Vertex Pair Ratio	0.304975124
Reciprocated Edge Ratio	0.467403736
Connected Components	1
Single-Vertex Connected Components	0
Maximum Vertices in a Connected Component	89
Maximum Edges in a Connected Component	2623
Maximum Geodesic Distance (Diameter)	2
Average Geodesic Distance	1.470016
Graph Density	0.334908069
Modularity	Not Applicable
NodeXL Version	1.0.1.336

image collections is not defined in the academic research literature (as far as this author can tell). Researchers have made some headway in defining the work of inducing themes from texts, including informal approaches such as "pawing" and sorting through texts as a scrutiny technique (Ryan & Bernard, 2003, p. 88), as well as "eyeballing" with a practiced eye (p. 101). The method described here involves a rough-cut categorization in order to inductively extract image processing approaches. This approach does not preclude other approaches and is conceptualized as a way to get started.

As noted in the introduction, this work was created to test three hypotheses:

Hypothesis 1: From a sufficient topic-based image set from social media, there will be emergent natural categorical breaklines that may be inductively observable by researchers (without *a priori* reference to theoretical frameworks).

Hypothesis 2: From a sufficient topic-based image set from social media, there will be some research questions that may be inductively and inferentially extracted by researchers.

Figure 6. "Snack_food" article network on Wikipedia (1 deg.)

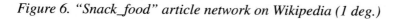

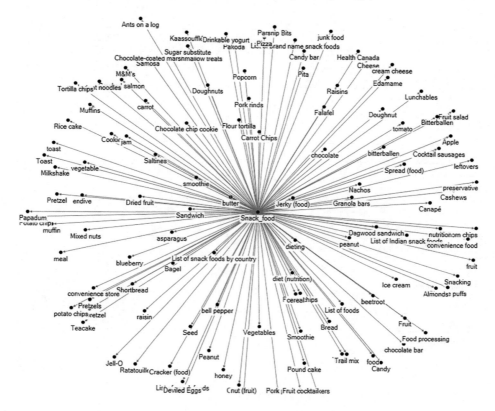

Hypothesis 3: For research analysts using imagery from social media platforms, exploring some of the available imagery through categorization may enhance the work of research design, image coding, and developing a research codebook.

The designed approach was as follows (Figure 8): (1) data extraction plan, (2) data extraction, (3) data cleaning, (4) image categorization, and (5) results (to aid the research). Two main methods for categorizing the images are described. From this approach, researchers are conceptualized as being able to assess some of the types of questions that may be asked of the image data. To see how this would work, some datasets of images were extracted from Instagram.

In late December 2015, a first set of #snack-based imagery was extracted from Instagram (at https://www.instagram.com/explore/tags/snack/). At the

Table 3. Graph metrics for the snack food article network on Wikipedia (1 deg.)

Graph Metric	Value
Graph Type	Directed
Vertices	121
Unique Edges	120
Edges With Duplicates	0
Total Edges	120
Self-Loops	0
Reciprocated Vertex Pair Ratio	0
Reciprocated Edge Ratio	0
Connected Components	1
Single-Vertex Connected Components	0
Maximum Vertices in a Connected Component	121
Maximum Edges in a Connected Component	120
Maximum Geodesic Distance (Diameter)	2
Average Geodesic Distance	1.967079
Graph Density	0.008264463
Modularity	Not Applicable
NodeXL Version	1.0.1.336

time of the extraction, Instagram had 5,860,121 posts with that hashtag. The extraction itself (using the DownThemAll add-in on Firefox browser) was only 694 images, and these were not a de-duplicated set (there were a number of repeat images left in the set that was advertising "Get up to 10,000 followers"). Given the numbers, the 694 / 5,860,141 posts meant that only 0.000118427184602 of the full set was represented. The extracted images were those that were publicly released by the users of Instagram. No special sign-ins or verifications were needed to extract this data. A screenshot of the Instagram #snack page at the time of the first image extraction may be seen in Figure 9.

Three days after the first data extraction, some 922 images were extracted from a total set of 5,869,260 posts tagged with #snack. The base set contained some 9,000 more images than was seen three days earlier. This second set of #snack images represented 0.00015708965 of the full set. Two sets were drawn because such imagery is time-sensitive. While a close count was not done, having a more diverse number of images to begin with might aid in the

Table 4. Graph metrics for the "Snack_food" article network on Wikipedia (1.5 deg.)

Graph Metric	Value
Graph Type	Directed
Vertices	8478
Unique Edges	12830
Edges With Duplicates	0
Total Edges	12830
Self-Loops	1
Reciprocated Vertex Pair Ratio	0.002892433
Reciprocated Edge Ratio	0.005768181
Connected Components	1
Single-Vertex Connected Components	0
Maximum Vertices in a Connected Component	8478
Maximum Edges in a Connected Component	12830
Maximum Geodesic Distance (Diameter)	4
Average Geodesic Distance	3.671246
Graph Density	0.000178508
Modularity	Not Applicable
NodeXL Version	1.0.1.336

hypothesis testing. A screenshot of the #snack landing page on Instagram (at the time of the second data extraction) may be seen in Figure 10.

It is often said that people eat first with their eyes, and from there, appetite follows. If that is so, many of the #snack images would likely spark appetite or even a deep hunger given the rabid "fan sharing" theme and observer empathy. The close-up food images are adoringly rendered (everyone is a "food artist"), with the apparent awareness of the high competition for the human gaze and "likes". If the image is a selfie, the person is often smiling and hand signaling to show enthusiasm (thumbs ups, victory signs); there are happy face buttons and happy emojis and lots of heart overlays to food images. Some express adoration for their own culinary skills. Some are clearly enthusiasts of certain raw and packaged snack foods. For example, there was an image of a girl wearing a big smile and a Bugle (a salty and crunchy corn-based snack) on each of her fingers. Another image showed a young female wearing a backpack that was actually a branded bag of snacks.

In a brief perusal of both image datasets from Instagram (see Figures 11 and 12), some insights became into focus. One observation is that people have

Figure 7. List_of_brand_name_snack_foods article network on Wikipedia (1 deg.)

broad interpretations of #snack, and the #snack itself is not always the focal point of the image. There were some who stayed within the spirit of #snack even as their focus went off-topic, but others were clearly using the popular hashtag to try to drive attention to their paid web-traffic-driving services.

What were some image threads? There were clear differences between raw foods, individually prepared foods, restaurant foods, and packaged foods. Raw foods tended to be portrayed in a natural or peeled form and held in one or two hands (think lichee nuts, chestnuts, an uncooked yellow pepper, and others). Some images portrayed fresh edibles in-the-field at the time of harvest. Individually prepared foods were portrayed either in very tight close-in shots or plated and viewed from an eater point-of-view (POV). The images were taken at any part of the process, from harvesting raw materials for food preparation to purchasing items in stores to preparing and presenting the snacks. Some images were portrayed with some raw ingredients in the background. Others

Table 5. Graph metrics of List_of_brand_name_snack_foods article network on Wikipedia (1 deg.)

Graph Type	Directed
Vertices	192
Unique Edges	191
Edges With Duplicates	0
Total Edges	191
Self-Loops	0
Reciprocated Vertex Pair Ratio	0
Reciprocated Edge Ratio	0
Connected Components	1
Single-Vertex Connected Components	0
Maximum Vertices in a Connected Component	192
Maximum Edges in a Connected Component	191
Maximum Geodesic Distance (Diameter)	2
Average Geodesic Distance	1.979221
Graph Density	0.005208333
Modularity	Not Applicable
NodeXL Version	1.0.1.336

had unique flourishes, such as particular imprints or cutouts in pie shells. There were foods creatively modified, like cream-centered cookies rolled in frosting and sugary cupcake decorations. Restaurant foods were often shown as close-ups, with a selfie, with a dining partner, or in large people groups. Packaged foods often included the snack packaging in the image along with images of the particular snacks. Some packaged food images did not show the food…but rather just the packaging. There was one photo of a young man with a guitar in the background and a bag of snacks in the foreground.

Some personal and commercial objectives could be inferred by the posing of the food images. There were straightforward images of snacks: a fruit and chocolate fondue setup, pigs-in-a-blanket, animal crackers mixed in with other crackers, and foodstuffs posed with flowers. Some were parts of personal stories, such as snack packages with messaging from a wedding.

There were joke images (with food peripherally related to the action)—a man in a Darth Vader mask drinking coffee and reading a newspaper at a table, a guy in a Storm Trooper costume looking at a lot of food on a counter. Another joke image was a baby sitting on a table with lots of opened snack

Figure 8. Basic steps in the inductive social image categorization process

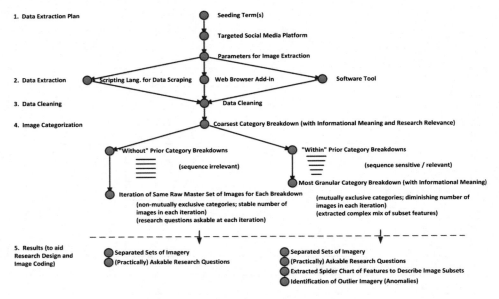

Basic Steps in the Inductive Social Image Categorization Process

Figure 9. A screenshot of the #snack Instagram page at the time of the first data capture

Figure 10. Screenshot of the #snack page on Instagram at the time of the second capture

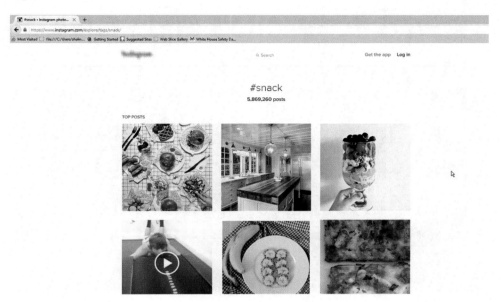

packages spilled around him / her; here is a baby who knows how to eat (badly). There was a clever visual pun, with a cow notepad next to an apple and a coffee; in this image, the cartoonish cow looked like it was eyeing the food.

There were images which consisted of words—from a lit up neon "snack bar" sign to food business signage to just the term "Salapao" ("steamed bun" in Thai) alone.

There were sometimes indications of narratives, of healthy eating (think thick green shakes and fresh fruits) but also of indulgence (doughnuts, deep fried fair food, and red meat). A number of people images showed people in exercise clothes in gyms. One such image had an overlay reading "Resolutions 2016." One image showed a thickly muscled man eating salad out of a bowl. Some labeled images seemed positioned to be memes. One showed a stack of colorful frosted doughnuts with the following message: "Is it too late now to say sorry…cuz I've eaten the equivalent weight of my body." The message was about the futility of suppressing difficult emotions by eating in a message tinted with humor. There were images with their own counter-messaging, such as splurge desserts with accompanying hashtags such as #backtothediet.

Figure 11. Some of the scraped images from #snack on Instagram (first run)

Figure 12. Some of the scraped images from #snack on Instagram (second run)

Some images showed attention to individual portion size, and others included whole meals (multiple sandwiches and drinks), and others showed large spreads of food for groups of eaters.

Occasionally, there were images uploaded in sequence…by the same social media account holder…and the sequences might tell a kind of story. In one, there was a recurring individual who appeared in the snack sequence, and she was pictured with various ice cream desserts. In another case, a gelatin candy was pictured in four consecutive images.

There were quite a few non-human #snack images. For example, there were various animals seen snacking: foxes, chipmunks, squirrels, deer, pelicans, pandas, rabbits, dogs, and hamsters. One image showed a crocodile coming up on a pelican, which might be about to become a "snack." One image was of Ken and Barbie dolls at a plastic snack booth. There were images of people with animals—feeding them snacks, for example. In one, a person and a horse were sharing the same slice of watermelon. In another, a woman wearing brown felt reindeer horns posed kissing an actual raw fish being held by another person (there was not a clear back story or context). If it seems like some of the image sharers are talking to themselves and to a defined narrowcast audience, they are in one sense. Many use Instagram to publicly share imagery through their own microblogging accounts and blogging accounts (with embedded images and embedded short videos).

Some images showed various contexts where foods are sold or served. There were photos of food aisles in grocery stores, vending machines, and various restaurants and eateries. Some were at 30,000 feet, one with a baby eating a snack while sitting in his father's lap in an airplane seat.

There were some short videos as well. One was about pouring syrup over a stack of pancakes. Another showed a baby having a tantrum when his food does not arrive in time. One individual proudly showed him taking a gigantic self-baked chocolate chip cookie out of the oven, writing "just made a big chocolate chip cookie." One video showing a man eating a packaged snack, was, inexplicably, sideways loaded (and uncorrected on the site). Another, inexplicably, was about an animal control officer poking a snake and falling backwards when the snake made a threatening rattle and struck out at him.

In terms of the imagery, there were differing levels of production values. Some images were clearly raw ones taken on-the-fly, such as close-up images of food and selfies with food. Others involved various degrees of food posing, lighting, layout, composition, artfulness, and image reprocessing. There were artificial images, such as one of a man apparently floating to return a milk to a refrigerator. Another photo-edited image showed a man dangling a miniaturized man as a morsel he was about to eat. There were also drawings and posters and composite imagery.

Technically, on the Instagram site, there was not apparently some basic type of machine de-duplication of imagery, given the spam repetition of the spam elicitation for people who might want to acquire 10,000 followers at a price and another "Get free followers!" This may be seen clearly in Figure 11. Also, there were non-snack images: photos of people in soft erotica poses, paper plate packaging, a person smoking, and stylized images of real estate. This would mean that data cleaning is a given before images may be categorized. Another technical observation is that Instagram cleanly manages differing image sizes, especially given the varying widths of the displayed images (while aspect ratio is protected). Also, each of the images have their own serial number based on how Instagram handles uploaded images. In terms of the data extractions, none of the comments were scraped, and none of the other tags were scraped (in this approach). While one could log in, click into each image, copy the comments, record the social media account from which the image was posted…and record the numbers of likes and so on, that was not done in this case.

There seemed to be two main ways to categorize the images. One would be to use an image set holistically and to divide that same set in a number of different ways in various image subsets (Figure 13).

For example, in the #snack image sets, they may be broken down in a variety of stand-alone ways. The various subsets of the images would all be drawn from the total image set, but not every image would necessarily make it into each image subset. A brainstorm of how this might look is available in Table 6.

In other words, a brainstorm of various types of potential subsets (based on different rules of subdivision) may be done without prior category dependencies. Each new categorization set is built from the pristine master set of images. Running the master set through each time enables researchers to ensure that there are as many categories as necessary to include as much of the pristine master set as possible. The real-world image set also may help in determining the coarseness or granularity of the categories. (It is feasible to have a category with only one exemplar if that example image is a highly anomalous one.) All subsets may have an "other" catch-all category.

Figure 13. "Without" category dependencies and standalone askable questions

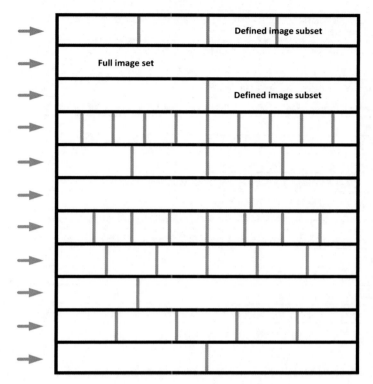

For the stand-alone subsets to work, there will need to be rules that define membership into that partition or grouping. If an image may meet several of the categories within the subset, the subset may need to be better defined to differentiate between the two potential groups (for example, if a snack food is salty, sweet, and sour).

The types of categories brainstormed may suggest certain askable questions. Brainstorming these broadly may enable ways to exploit the #snack imagery. Also, if the questions are unanswerable, at least the asking of the questions may enable tactical ways forward to finding out. If these questions are answered in other ways, the social media image stream may at least provide yet another data channel.

For example, snack food imagery from different brands (the last category in Table 6) may be analyzed with the following questions in mind:

- Based on the shared social imagery, what is the brand strategy for the particular brand, and then for each different type of snack?

Table 6. Some ways to conceptualize stand-alone subsets of #snack imagery

Snack food imagery with differing levels of processing: raw, human-processed (manual and small machine), mass-processed (multi-step and factory production)
Snack food imagery broken down into various food groups
Snack food imagery broken down into various raw base ingredients
Snack food imagery from different regions of the world
Snack food imagery that seems to fit "breakfast," "brunch," "lunch," or "dinner" (if applicable)
Snack food imagery of food served hot vs. that served cold
Snack food imagery with people or with animals or with no other apparent living being
Snack food imagery from vending machines vs. restaurants or eateries
Snack food imagery belonging to the categories of "healthy" or "unhealthy"
Snack food imagery in-process vs. in finished eat-ready form
Snack food imagery with positive portrayal vs. that with negative portrayal (vs. with neutral portrayal)
Snack food imagery that portrays savory flavors, sweet flavors, and sour flavors
Snack food imagery that portrays individual portions vs. group portions
Snack food imagery showing different social contexts
Snack food imagery with mixed people groups, men, with women, with children, and with babies
Snack food imagery depicted for the elderly, adults, for teenagers, for children, for toddlers, and for babies
Snack food imagery from different brands

- What images are apparently from the parent company? What images are from the self-selected fans of the respective snacks? How do these differ? What do these differences suggest about the tactics for both groups? (In terms of fans, what are different subgroups of interest?)
- Who are informal brand ambassadors? What are their interests? Is there a way to befriend them? Empower them?
- What are images that show the various products in positive light? In negative light? In neutral light? How are these communicated?
- In these image sets, what are some unique riffs on the way the snack food is consumed? Are there some new suggested flavors that should be tried?
- Are there regional differences in how the target snack foods are received? What are these apparent differences? Why?
- Is there potential for finding new markets in terms of re-framing the particular snack food? How so? What are flavor combinations to avoid? Why?
- How do the competing #snack brands compare?

- How do the competing #snack products (between the respective brands) compare?
- Are there any snack foods within a company that are in competition with other products within the company? If so, how may that conflict be addressed? (and others)

This takes one subset, "snack food imagery from different brands," and it involves asking questions based on the categorizations within that subset. The reverse may also be done—starting with a research question, downloading an image set, and then setting up subsets to answer that particular question.

Another approach may be seen in Figure 14. In this approach, there are within-set dependencies. The idea here is to start with as broad a categorization

Figure 14. "Within" category dependencies and both standalone and cumulative askable questions

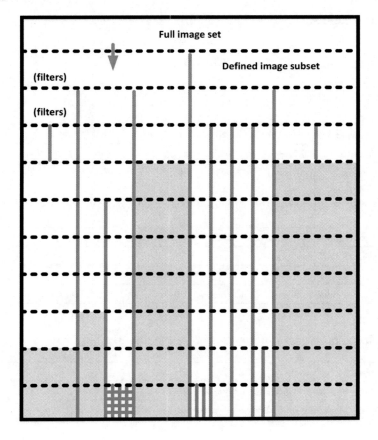

as possible of the full set of images…and then to filter the set from there. In this conceptualization, an image appears is slotted in a best-fit in the table (somewhat like a game of Tetris).

In this scenario, it is much easier to ask questions about which images are outliers (those at the bottoms of each of the columns because those that belong in the main areas of the bell curve of images will have been stopped by the more defined filters as the images are positioned). Conceptually, the idea is to have the most coarse-grained filters at the top. A given is a data cleaning question: "Is the image a valid image in the set or spam?" Because of the dependencies in the subsetting, it is important to be mindful of the sequence of the filtering because that will affect the images captured. Depending on the image set (especially its variety and size), it is possible to have empty cells.

Examples of this approach are available in Tables 7 to 13. These seem to work better with a somewhat *a priori*-defined research question. The idea is to sort and filter imagery in a non-destructive way, which means that data is not lost if one can help it, even if it does not end up selected into the particular image set.

Table 7. Taste profiles for depicted desserts

Identified desserts (vs. all other snacks)
Types of desserts
Main types of taste profiles for the desserts (and especially anomalies)
Messaging around those main taste profiles (as sub-categories)

Table 8. Presentation strategies for identified luxury snack foods

High-end or luxury snack foods (vs. all other snacks)
Types of "high-end" or "luxury" snacks
Hand made vs. processed
Presentation strategies for the communication of high worth in #snack food imagery (as sub-categories)

Table 9. Abstract imagery in the #snack food image set

Abstract imagery (vs. figurative)
Contexts for the uses of abstract imagery in the #snack image set
Imaging strategy in the uses of abstraction (as sub-categories)

Table 10. Food and sociality messaging in the #snack food image set

#snack food imagery with people depicted (vs. those where the people are not in the picture)
Selfies / dyads / groups
Locations depicted
Social contexts depicted
Sociality messaging around #snack foods (as sub-categories)

Table 11. Gendering and snack foods in the #snack food image set

Feminine portrayal of snack food, masculine portrayal of snack food
Analysis of the respective food sets for image patterning (as sub-categories)

Table 12. Appealing and unappealing snack foods in the #snack food image set

Appealing #snack food imagery (vs. unappealing #snack food imagery)
Strategies and tactics for creating appealing snack food imagery
Strategies and tactics for creating unappealing snack food imagery (as sub-categories)

Table 13. Geo-based categorization of the #snack food image set

Categorization by geotagged locations
Snack preferences by regionalisms
Regions represented / regions not represented (as sub-categories)

From the examples, it is pretty clear that these filters may be pretty exclusionary early on and that the filter layers may be fairly flat or shallow. This may be explained in part on probabilities. For example, based on Table 8, it is possible to surface the following probabilities for an image to make it to the fourth tier down.

.5 (luxury vs. non-luxury) * .1 (assuming 10 categories of luxury snacks) * .5 (hand-made vs. processed) * .1 (assuming 10 presentation strategies) = .0025

The probability for such an image to make is .0025 or .25 of one percent or a fourth of a percent. In other words, there are fast diminishing probabilities for an image to make it into a particular set the further down it is in a categorization sequence. Depending on the complexity of the research and the size and diversity of the image set, it is possible to have much deeper sequences, even those were not portrayed here. The general intuition is that there is fast-diminishing probability of an image's membership into a lower category, particularly as the conditional sequence gets deeper.

Once the subsets have been extracted, it is possible to inductively look at the totality of images in each subset to identify patterns and anomalous images. Categorizing into sets may be achieved as a recursive process. Also, it is possible to capture additional image data from other sources (or the same sources at later times) in order to surface additional insights. One question not directly answered in the set includes the following: What is not seen depicted in this set? Is there over-representation of imagery? Under-representation? Whose voices are seen here? Whose voices are not seen here (and why not)?

It is possible to apply these same approaches to sorting imagery to sorting videos although videos are even more complex informational objects.

Another important takeaway is that differing social media platforms attract different parts of the global human population, and they collaborate in somewhat different ways, so the images that are hashtagged similarly on different platforms will result in notably different mixes of imagery, with over emphases of some types of images and less of others. As part of this work, the researcher also attempted to extract #snack image data from Flickr. In Figure 15, a screenshot of the site at the time of the attempted extraction may be seen. Figure 16 shows the "fail" message given a site setting or browser add-in challenge with capturing the images en masse. It may be that another method to extract image data from Flickr, such as by using a built-in application programming interface (API), may work, but that is currently beyond the scope of this chapter. The idea is that broader sampling across social media platforms and the capture of larger image sets would benefit the range of analysis. In an initial perusal of the differing sets of #snack images from Instagram and Flickr, there were no apparent cross-posted images.

DISCUSSION

The conceptualizations in this chapter were lightly addressed with a topic-based image set—as an initial proof-of-concept. More rigorous applications

Figure 15. Some of the scraped images from #snack on Flickr

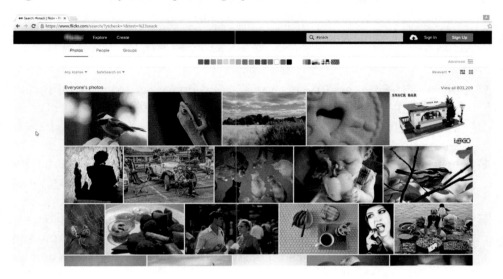

Figure 16. A failure download images from the Flickr content sharing site (using a Web browser add-in)

of these ideas could have been achieved, but the intention of this chapter was to do a fast exploratory walk-through, as a kind of extended thought experiment. So what does this all mean for the initial three hypotheses? They read as follows:

Hypothesis 1: From a sufficient topic-based image set from social media, there will be emergent natural categorical breaklines that may be inductively observable by researchers (without *a priori* reference to theoretical frameworks).

Hypothesis 2: From a sufficient topic-based image set from social media, there will be some research questions that may be inductively and inferentially extracted by researchers.

Hypothesis 3: For research analysts using imagery from social media platforms, exploring some of the available imagery through categorization may enhance the work of research design, image coding, and developing a research codebook.

Using the #snack image sets from Instagram, it was fairly easy to conceptually slice the images into various types, in both stand-alone and prior category dependent ways (Hypothesis 1). This categorizing is done without the express dictates of extant theory or pre-defined taxonomies or ontologies (but these external conceptual structures may be applied if the researcher so chose.) Per Hypothesis 2, the subset structures lent themselves to the creation of research questions, particularly those based on counting and other simple patterns. This approach seems like it may benefit research projects, whether the research includes analyzed social imagery as a small part of a larger research project or whether social imagery is the research project (Hypothesis 3). Using sets may inform research design by suggesting what features to pay attention to in social imagery. Images may be coded based on their membership in particular image sets, and such codes may be informative and insightful in a research codebook.

This approach may seem intuitive but also fairly simplistic. As such, this was designed for a practicable, general-use approach, which does not require high-end technologies or complex skill sets. This does assume some level of expertise with the related topics and issues in an image set (even though the author here is not an expert in #snack foods, just somewhat conversant). Coarse-grained sorting provides users with a "way in" to understanding the image set. The conceptualization of possible "askable questions" extends the potential work of research design and coding plans.

Next steps in terms of coding the imagery would include the identification of themes and sub-themes in the imagery, semantics and narratives in the imagery (and along the same lines as "subtextual messaging," "subimagistic messaging"), research question answering, and other types of analytics.

Summary Features of Social Image Datasets

It is possible, too, to describe features of image sets. One approach, illustrated here, describe an image set based on various informational features. In Figure 17, how this might look is conceptualized in a spider chart with a dozen features: I – geolocation; II – peopled; III - clarity of messaging / call to action; IV - subjectivity: ego, emotion, sentiment; V – novelty / originality; VI – representational / figurative; VII – image resolution; VIII – field of vision; IX – image post-processing; X – color information; XI – metadata, and XII – textual contents. Geolocational information is relevant because it is often included in image EXIF (exchangeable image file format) data, which may be automatically captured in the digital camera or smartphone camera. This may locate a camera person's location to within a foot or less.

Figure 17. Summary informational features of respective social image datasets

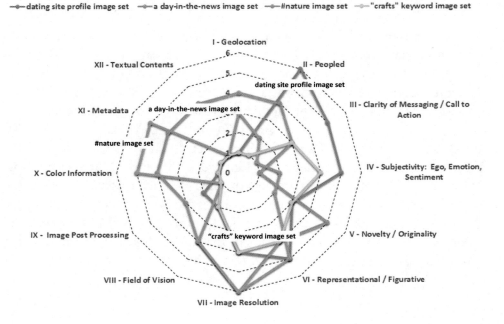

Whether an image is peopled or not may be relevant given the ability to identify people by name based on tagging or by facial recognition tools, or others. The clarity of the messaging has informational value because images are often shared for tactical reasons (whether commercial, public relations, political or other); particularly, whether the image is used as a call to action is critical (especially if the image may spark mass actions). The subjectivity of an image is important. Subjectivity refers to a kind of relationship to an author or ego; subjectivity, computationally, may be represented also as communicated emotion and sentiment (an expressed public message as a communication of an internal or hidden state). The novelty or originality of an image is another aspect of informational value. The more original an image is, in one sense, the more valuable it is for others. Whether an image is representational or figurative (vs. abstract) highlights its informational value. Something that does not have clear form may be less informationally valuable than something that is highly abstract (in most cases). The resolution of an image, the field of vision (whether an image is close-in or zoomed-out), the amount of image post-processing, the color information, the image metadata, and in-image textual contents may all highlight other aspects of informationality in the image. These were conceptualized in a broad sense—not as a comprehensive or closed list, but as a way to get started looking at ways social imagery may be informationally valuable.

A spider chart is used to describe an object (or a set) based on selected features. Each spoke is understood to start with none or 0 at the center (or even as non-applicable or N/A) and increase in informational value up to 6, in this case. Each level is a gradation, with 1 as low, 4 as medium, and 6 as high. Different types of social image collections (or image subsets) may rank differently on the various variables; in some cases, the respective feature variables may not be relevant. In this figure, four synthetic image sets were used: a dating site profile image set, a day-in-the-news image set, a #nature image set, and a "crafts" keyword image set. Such a spider chart may be more useful with social image sets that are within-topic, such as multiple image sets all related to robotic self-driving cars, to better understand the respective social media account holder, the respective social media platforms, the respective state of the technologies in different geographical locales, and so on. There is variable value of each of the spider chart features depending on social image set and the potential research questions asked.

FUTURE RESEARCH DIRECTIONS

One near-term research direction may involve cases in which this approach to openly and inductively categorizing social media images is applied and assessed—by both individual researchers and research teams. If this approach is built into a software tool, how that is instantiated and how well that works for research may also be informative. There may be others' innovations to build on and improve this approach to making use of social media imagery for research.

CONCLUSION

Even though social media platforms enable access to large sets of social images, there are not many (any?) non-theoretical approaches to image analysis, categorization, and coding. This work introduced a systematic, open, and inductive approach to identifying conceptual categories from topic-based image sets from social media in an emergent, bottom-up way. The idea is that this initial categorizing from the extracted real-world image set may benefit the creation of research questions, research design, image coding, and even the development of a research codebook. The initial testing of these hypotheses based on two image sets from Instagram show that the approach may have some merit. Given the widespread availability of imagery from social media platforms on the Web and Internet, researchers would benefit from fresh ways to engage these in open learning approaches.

ACKNOWLEDGMENT

I am thankful to Scott Eugene Velasquez for a conversation a year or two ago that was the initial spark for this chapter. While I never saw the "10-deep" coding structure for your project, Scott, the idea was of sufficient interest that I wanted to explore how coding imagery might work—albeit at a more generic / emergent / grounded level and without the informed direction of any of the following: theory, frameworks, taxonomies, or ontologies. Also, I wanted an approach that would not directly rely on in-depth expertise yet…so I could define something very general and usable by non-experts (amateurs and novices) and experts.

REFERENCES

Ahangama, S. (2014). Use of Twitter stream data for trend detection of various social media sites in real time. LNCS, 8531, 151 – 159.

Amengual, X., Bosch, A., & de la Rosa, J. L. (2015). Review of methods to predict social image interestingness and memorability. *LNCS, 9256*, 64–76.

Anagnostopoulos, A., Kumar, R., & Mahdian, M. (2008). Influence and correlation in social networks. *Proceedings of KDD '08*, 1 – 9. doi:10.1145/1401890.1401897

Bakhshi, S., Shamma, D. A., & Gilbert, E. (2014). Faces engage us: Photos with faces attract more likes and comments on Instagram. *Proceedings of CHI 2014*, 965 – 974.

Bennett, S. (2013, Nov. 19). Social Media Growth Worldwide—2 Billion Users by 2016, Led by India. *Social Times*. Retrieved Dec. 26, 2015, from http://www.adweek.com/socialtimes/social-media-growth-worldwide/493361

Celebrating a Community of 400 Million. (2015, Dec. 26). *Instagram*. Retrieved Dec. 26, 2015, from https://www.instagram.com/press/?hl=en

Derby, K. L. (2013). Social media: Multiple channels to capture multiple audiences. *Proceedings of the SIGUCCS '13*, 159 – 162.

Giannoulakis, S., & Tsapatsoulis, N. (2015). Instagram hashtags as image annotation metadata. IFIP International Federation for Information Processing. doi:10.1007/978-3-319-23868-5_15

Holmberg, C., Chaplin, J. E., Hillman, T., & Berg, C. (2016). Adolescents presentation of food in social media: An explorative study. *Appetite, 99*, 121–129. doi:10.1016/j.appet.2016.01.009 PMID:26792765

Hu, Y., Manikonda, L., & Kambhampati, S. (2014). What we Instagram: A first analysis of Instagram photo content and user types. Association for the Advancement of Artificial Intelligence.

Instagram Demographics. (2015, Aug. 17). Mobile Messaging and Social Media 2015. *Pew Internet*. Retrieved Dec. 26, 2015, from http://www.pewinternet.org/2015/08/19/mobile-messaging-and-social-media-2015/2015-08-19_social-media-update_09/

Jeffries, A. (2013, March 20). The man behind Flickr on making the service 'awesome again': Markus Spiering talks photography, daily habits, and life under Marissa Mayer. *The Verge.* Retrieved Dec. 28, 2015, from http://www. theverge.com/2013/3/20/4121574/flickr-chief-markus-spiering-talks-photos-and-marissa-mayer

Kuo, Y.-H., Chen, Y.-Y., Chen, B.-C., Lee, W.-Y., Wu, C.-C., Lin, C.-H., . . . Hsu, W. (2014). Discovering the city by mining diverse and multimodal data streams. *Proceedings of MM '14,* 201 – 204. doi:10.1145/2647868.2656406

Lavis, A. (2015). Food porn, pro-anorexia and the viscerality of virtual affect: Exploring eating in cyberspace. *Geoforum.* doi:10.1016/j. geoforum.2015.05.014

Lee, C. S., Bakar, N. A. B. A., Dahri, R. B. M., & Sin, S.-C. J. (2015). Instagram this! Sharing photos on Instagram. *LNCS, 9469,* 132–141.

Lim, B. H., Lu, D., Chen, T., & Kan, M.-Y. (2015). #mytweet via Instagram: Exploring user behavior across multiple social networks. *Proceedings of the 2015 IEEE / ACM International Conference on Advances in Social Networks Analysis and Mining (ASONAM '15),* 113 – 120.

Mejova, Y., Haddadi, H., Noulas, A., & Weber, I. (2015). #FoodPorn: Obesity patterns in culinary interactions. *Proceedings of DH '15,* 51 – 58.

Mika, P. (2005). Ontologies are us: A unified model of social networks and semantics. *The Semantic Web,* 1 – 15.

Ryan, G. W., & Bernard, H. R. (2003). Techniques to identify themes. *Field Methods, 15*(1), 85 – 109. Retrieved Jan. 4, 2016, from http://crlte.engin.umich. edu/wp-content/uploads/sites/7/2013/06/Ryan-and-Bernard-Techniques-to-Identify-Themes.pdf

Salie, F. (2013, Dec. 1). Don't take selfies of your food. Sunday Morning. *CBS News.* Retrieved Mar. 6, 2016, from http://www.cbsnews.com/videos/faith-salie-dont-take-selfies-of-your-food/

Sharma, S. S., & De Choudhury, M. (2015). Measuring and characterizing nutritional information of food and ingestion content in Instagram. *Proceedings of WWW 2015,* 115 – 116. doi:10.1145/2740908.2742754

Smith, C. (2015, Aug. 10). By the numbers: 14 interesting Flickr stats. *DMR: Digital Statistics, Gadgets, Fun.* Retrieved Dec. 28, 2015, from http://expandedramblings.com/index.php/flickr-stats/

Social Networking Fact Sheet. (2014, January). Pew Research Center's Internet Project January Omnibus Survey. Retrieved Dec. 26, 2015, from http://www.pewinternet.org/fact-sheets/social-networking-fact-sheet/

Sorokowski, P., Sororkowska, A., Oleszkiewicz, A., Frackowiak, T., Huk, A., & Pisanski, K. (2015). Selfie posting behaviors are associated with narcissism among men. *Personality and Individual Differences*, *85*, 123–127. doi:10.1016/j.paid.2015.05.004

Souza, F., de Las Casas, D., Flores, V., Youn, S. B., Cha, M., Quercia, D., & Almeida, V. (2015). Dawn of the selfie era: The Whos, Wheres, and Hows of Selfies on Instagram. *Proceedings of COSN '15*, 221 – 231.

Van House, N.A. (2007). Flickr and public image-sharing: Distant closeness and photo exhibition. *Proceedings of CHI 2007*, 2717 – 2722.

Wikipedia: About. (2015, Dec. 24). *Wikipedia*. Retrieved Dec. 28, 2015, from https://en.wikipedia.org/wiki/Wikipedia:About

KEY TERMS AND DEFINITIONS

Breakline: "Natural" points of separation or differentiation between image objects.

Broadcast: A message sent to a wide audience.

Flickr: An image- and video-sharing social media site.

Framework: A basic structure.

Image Analysis: Systematic examination of images.

Instagram: An image-sharing social media site.

Interestingness: A measure of attractiveness and attention-holding for a general human audience.

Microcast: A message sent to a targeted and small audience.

Related Tags Network: A network graph consisting of co-occurring tags.

Selfie: A digital self-portrait photograph taken and shared on an online social networking site.

Section 2
Exploring Social Phenomena

Chapter 3

Engaging Technology–Based Manifestos Three Ways:
(1) Manual Method–Based Coding, (2) CAQDAS–Supported Manual Coding, and (3) Machine Reading and Autocoding

ABSTRACT

Researchers today have a variety of ways to engage with their textual research data. Three main approaches include (1) manual method-based coding (with light computational supports), (2) Computer-Assisted Qualitative Data AnalysiS (CAQDAS)-supported manual coding (with data queries), and (3) machine reading and autocoding. To enable deeper understandings of data coding, exploration, and knowing, the above three approaches were applied in the above sequence to a corpus of technology-based manifestos. This work resulted in observations of different types of findable data from the three textual coding approaches, which may be used to inform research design.

INTRODUCTION

Contemporary researchers, almost invariably, will engage with textual data during their work. The text may be a set of formal research articles collected for a review of the literature. The text may be responses to open-ended survey questions, interview questions, focus group prompts, or other elicitations. The

DOI: 10.4018/978-1-5225-2679-7.ch003

text may be various types of data extractions from social media platforms. Regardless of the origin of the texts, researchers have to code the text for understandings—whether through light reading (and note-taking) for decoding or more intensive coding work. Augmentations to human coding of textual data involve data query features in Computer Assisted Qualitative Data AnalysiS (CAQDAS) tools as well as new software features like machine reading and autocoding. To broadly overgeneralize, it is possible to divide coding of textual data into three approaches, with increasing levels of technology application: (1) manual method-based coding (with light computational supports with non-CAQDAS tools), (2) CAQDAS-supported manual coding (with data queries), and (3) machine reading and autocoding (Figure 1). In this conceptualization, manual coding (1) involves the researcher reading the data, coding for important aspects, and even using non-CAQDAS tools for data analytics. Some software tools may include linguistic analysis tools, basic quantitative analytics tools, and spreadsheet software programs. CAQDAS-supported manual coding (2) involves the digitization of the codebook, the coding of the text in the software, and the running of various data queries against both the original source texts and the coding and other mixes (like matrix queries combining both source texts and coding). Machine reading and autocoding (3) involves the use of both supervised and unsupervised machine learning applied to research texts and research data. Researchers who have experiences with these various approaches may project what they gain from each textual coding method, but as with most research work, a project is likely inaccurate and preliminary; researchers have to do the work and see where it actually goes.

In general, the data analytics sequence may start with some "close reading" of the text and manual coding (whether based on *a priori* methods or emergent ones). This early engagement ensures that the researcher has some familiarity (even intimacy) with the data. Then, once that stage is generally complete, researchers may move on to data exploration with the data queries and autocoding capabilities of the CAQDAS tools. (Some researchers, especially those dealing with big data, may work in the complete opposite approach—by exploring the big data with data queries and autocoding—and then spending some time for selective "close reading.")

To simplify the research, this work assumes that there are no frictions over theory, methodological practice, or epistemological approaches. A theoretical purist might suggest that computational and quantitative means do not have a

Figure 1. Coding three ways: From manual to CAQDAS-supported manual coding to machine reading and autocoding

(1) Manual Coding (with light computational supports)	(2) CAQDAS-Supported Manual Coding (with data queries)	(3) Machine Reading and Autocoding

direct place in qualitative research, but in the decades that such software has existed (from the early 1980s to the present), CAQDAS tools have been an integral part of qualitative research work. This chapter essentially explores one hypothesis—that different types of textual coding with different intensities of technology-integration will affect the types of insights extracted.

Hypothesis #1: Different types of textual coding methods [(1) manual method-based coding (with light computational supports), (2) CAQDAS-supported manual coding (with data queries), and (3) machine reading and autocoding] will result in different (non-overlapping) observable types of insights from a text set.

Sub-Hypothesis #1a: The respective strengths of each of the three coding methods may be harnessed to strengthen the coding capabilities of the others.

Sub-Hypothesis #1b: Knowledge of the different types of extractable insights from the three explored coding methods may benefit research design, data coding, and data exploration strategies and tactics in other contexts.

To further operationalize the hypothesis (from the coding angle), the following initial research questions were created:

- What may be learned from the respective types of data coding (with intensifying levels of technology adoption and application):
  - Manual method-based coding (with light computational supports),
  - Computer-Assisted Qualitative Data AnalysiS (CAQDAS)-supported manual coding (with data queries), and
  - Machine reading and autocoding
- What types of insights may be commonly captured using each of the three coding methods as applied to qualitative / mixed methods / multi-methods data? What are some of the strengths and weaknesses of these respective types of coding methods?

- What are insights that are only create-able from a particular type of coding approach? Why is it that those particular insights are only accessible using a particular coding approach?
- What are some strengths and weaknesses of using all three coding methods in a synthesized way?
- Based on the insights from answering the prior questions, when should each coding method be used and to surface what types of insights and from what types of information and what sorts of research contexts? How generalizable are these respective insights?
- Finally, are there ways to strengthen each of the three coding approaches to collect more insights than might be possible in a basic or simplistic approach?
- And as an exploratory research byproduct, what has been learned about technology-based manifestos?

In a typical research sequence, the source data may be attained any number of ways. To simplify the walk-through, pre-existent texts were selected—in this case, technology-based manifestos.

Manifestos are public pronouncements of commitments to particular principles and practices and calls-to-action. The authorship angle of manifestos—by individuals, by groups, by organizational entities, by (anonymized) crowds—makes them inherently analyzable in various ways: voice, tone, point-of-view, factuality, values, and calls-to-action; further, a range of psychometric analyses may be applied to understand the author. Manifestos are often text-heavy, which make them good substance for various types of text analytics (including linguistic analysis, parsing between text and subtext, content analysis, and so on). Because manifestos have origination dates and maybe ascertainable breakout dates, they can be used to run survival analyses. Because these documents spring (organically?) from particular social ecosystems, it is possible to add social context and color in their analysis. (Manifestos may emerge during times of social unrest or in response to particular events.) Because manifestos are the basis for the actions of many—in some cases—they are inherently dramatic and of interest. Technology-based manifestos are a subset of manifestos, and the set selected for this study was ultimately only a collection of 16, and these were the technology manifestos listed on the crowd-sourced (and ultimately crowd-filtered) Wikipedia page "Manifesto." The list includes the following, in the ascending date order: The GNU Manifesto (1985), The Hacker's Manifesto (1986), The Debian Manifesto (1993), A Cypherpunk's Manifesto (1993), Industrial Society and its Future / Unabomber Manifesto (1995), The Third Manifesto (1995), The Cluetrain Manifesto (1999), The Agile Manifesto (2001), Pluginmanifesto "film statement" (2001), The Hacktivismo Declaration (2001), The Mozilla Manifesto (2007), Principles of Programming Languages (2007), You Are Not a Gadget: A Manifesto (2010), The Hardware Hacker Manifesto (2010), The Reactive Manifesto (2014), and The BINC Manifesto (2015).

Before research questions were more seriously formalized about technology-based manifestos, some initial ones included the following:

- What are some of the technology-based manifestos widely available?
- What are the main topics of such manifestos? What technologies do these manifestos address?
- How were these manifestos apparently inspired?
- Who created these manifestos?
  - What does the author (whether individual or group) hand look like?
- What animated the particular manifestos to inspire readers to action? How compelling were (and are) these arguments?
  - What sorts of values were pointed to to inform the manifestos?
  - What idealized visions of the field or the technology or people or the world was/were the manifesto creator(s) pointing to?
  - What sorts of changes were the creators trying to bring about with their manifestos?
- Who are the apparent audiences for these manifestos? Are there latent audiences as well? If so, who are they, and why?
- How popular are the respective manifestos? How can one tell?
  - What might account for the popularity? The lack of popularity? Why?
- Are the manifestos long-lived and enduring? How can one tell? What does it mean that the manifestos are long-lived? (What is a typical time span before manifestos sunset?)
- Are the technology-based manifestos relevant? How can one tell?
- What were some of the observable and measurable impacts of these technology-based manifestos?
  - Any residual effects?
  - Positive or negative (socially)? Positive or negative (technologically)?
- Are the manifestos dated? Why or why not?
  - What are some features that make for a long-lived manifesto?

The main focus of this work is on coding textual data, but a byproduct of this work should be some preliminary insights about technology-based manifestos.

Delimitations

All research has limitations, and it is important to bound the research early on. To test the hypothesis, there are three main elements: the conceptualization of how to code data three ways, the technologies used, and the target text sets.

Three Approaches to Coding Data

The approach of separating three different approaches to coding data—manual, CAQDAS-supported manual coding, and machine reading and autocoding—is somewhat arbitrary. While these data coding approaches may be conceptualized as in competition with other methods, especially given time and researcher preference limitations, these approaches are also mutually complementary and stand to strengthen the respective approaches. There are many other proper ways to conceptualize data coding, particularly informed by research theories, frameworks, models, and other approaches; even with grounded theory and emergent coding, there are ways to approach technology-based manifestos, such as by topic, by time period, by technology, by calls-to-action, by underlying values, and many other potential angles. The particular approach of focusing on deepening uses of technologies was used to try to create generalizable insights, with some transferability into other contexts (without a risk of overfitting to the particular content data in this work).

Also, an apparent underlying assumption about this research is that the three approaches are somehow separate and stand-alone, without much bleedover or overlap. If that is the impression, though, that is not an actual assumption of the researcher. Very little research data is coded purely in a manual way without any technological supports. There are a number of software programs that may be used for various types of data analytics. Machine reading and autocoding also is a part of some state-of-the-art CAQDAS tools. Even in the most machine-supported analytics, the human researcher plays a critical role in analyzing findings and using those findings to understand situations, make decisions, and plan strategies and tactics. In other words, the conceptualization of the three approaches as somewhat stand-alone and clean ways of coding is illusory. Also, the sense of "either-or" is a false limitation and a conceit; after all, many data analytics methods are set up in complementary ways; proper applications of the respective research techniques of each type of approach will stand to benefit the overall work and the work in each respective lane.

Selected Software

Another limitation in this work is that a few commercially available software programs were used to explore the data. The central one used, NVivo 11 Plus, is a proprietary and commercial software, with a pricing structure that may be prohibitive for many researchers. There are competitor software programs to this CAQDAS tool, and there are some free programming languages and natural language processing that may enable some similar analytics. Some linguistics analyses were done using the Linguistic Inquiry and Word Count (LIWC, pronounced "luke"), which is a low-cost software tool, but with this, too, there are other ways to achieve at least some of the linguistic analysis (but not so much the psychometric constructs). Also, SPSS is used for the survival analysis part.

Selection of Technology-Based Manifestos as Research Target

A contemporary topic was selected to seed the research and to extract a text set against which to conduct various types of manual and computer-supported coding. Collecting a text set begins with the search term "technology-based manifestos." In a search on web-based indexes, subscription-based databases, the WWW and Internet, and others, some 207 texts were captured. While plentiful, these files are not likely anywhere close to a full set of possible files for this topic.

An initial read-through of these enabled clearer definitions of the type of text desired. Essentially, the author was conceptualizing technology-based manifestos written to the general public, with potential direct implications to the general public if the manifestos were followed. Of the initial full text set, many were political technology manifestos by a number of political parties in Europe to share party platforms with voting constituencies. Various commercial companies also hosted their own online manifestos of workplace #goals, which were more for their internal publics (employees) and select external publics (customers, stockholders, and potential employees). There were manifesto "stubs," with landing pages for particular manifestos but no actual access to manifesto text. There were also academic and mainstream media articles about various technology-based manifestos and response writings to original manifestos. If these were all included, there would be too much noise in the data, and there would not be the sufficient coherence of a bounded set. The author ultimately decided to go with a list of "Notable manifestos: Technology" from the crowd-sourced Wikipedia page "Manifesto" (at https://en.wikipedia.org/wiki/Manifesto). All the manifestos here were originally written in English. All are widely publicly available on the Internet, which enables reader exploration, the possibility of follow-on research, and broad scale transparency. Most of the manifestos are text-heavy and structured in the following ways: as documents, as articles, as letters, as lists of rules, as websites, as videos, and other formats. There were more complex digital presentations, such as interactive image maps on websites to embody digital messages; one was laid out as a printable digital bookmark, with its main precepts listed in order; one was released as a press release (from Cult of the Dead Cow, no less). Some were illustrated with visualizations, like diagrams for a more intuitive grasp of the concepts or ASCII-text art to illustrate identities and draw attention to contact information. The researcher only had access to broadly public manifestos and none that were *sub rosa* ("under the rose" in Latin) or "secret" manifestos shared among secret organizations with hidden memberships. This work is very much a product of its time and context, with both obvious and non-obvious dependencies. One main concern is that any text set selected will skew findings, but to do a walk-through of the three main text coding methods, a researcher has to start somewhere.

Also, there are *ceteris paribus* (all things being equal) assumptions, which are generally not addressed. For example, there is little here about research designs, data types, data pre-processing / cleaning, varied research contexts, and so on. The hypothesis and its related sub-hypotheses are conceptualized to apply to a research context with all other conditions remaining the same. If any of the other conditions change, then the findings may be more or less robust. Whatever the case is beyond the purview of this work.

REVIEW OF THE LITERATURE

A manifesto is a public statement of goals and commitment to them. The idea is to not only commit the author(s) to a particular direction but to win over followers—based on the compellence of ideas, of vision, of stated values, and of personality and passion. A manifesto is supposed to capture the imagination of others and to recruit others to particular attitudes, beliefs, actions, and commitments. Some are written with a revolutionary flare and militate against aspects of the *status quo*. Others are written as personal commitments and expressions. Regardless, manifestos are seen as history-changing, whether on a personal, group, or society-wide level.

In the crowd-sourced Web-based encyclopedia, Wikipedia, the "Manifesto" article network is linked to 189 nodes, consisting of authors, committees, formal manifestos, statements, and contracts (Figure 2). Behind these words are coalesced expressions of hope and ideals, calls for rebellion and change, with varying levels of practicability and influence. By denotation, a "manifesto" is "a written statement that describes the policies, goals, and opinions of a person or group," and was first used in 1748, according to *Merriam-Webster* ("manifesto," n.d.). According to the "Manifesto" article on Wikipedia, a manifesto is "a published verbal declaration of the intentions, motives, or views of the issuer, be it an individual, group, political party or government" ("Manifesto," July 26, 2016). While it may attest to personal

Figure 2. "Manifesto" article network on Wikipedia (1 deg.)

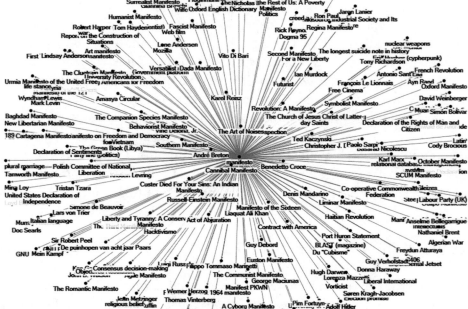

commitments—whether political, professional, social, economic, or other—there is also often a social component. A declaration made to a public often focused on a designated close-in audience as well as the general public; it is both narrowcast and broadcast. A public announcement, for many, is apparently more binding because there are more witnesses to the attestation and more people to hold a person or group accountable. There are efforts to bring on signatories and recruits, whether that audience is a targeted one or the broader public. "Manifesto" is an attention-getting word, and it is often a conversation starter. While the denotative meaning of a manifesto contains a kind of gravitas and sense of purpose, the connotative meaning may evoke a sense of extremism and self-importance, such as from political extremists who were found to have written manifestos in the aftermath of acts of violence (an act of costly signaling in politics).

Given the 268-year history of the use of the term "manifesto," a query was run on the Google Books Ngram Viewer's English Corpus from 1700 to 2000. A run from 1500-2000 shows the usage of "manifesto" even earlier than the 1748 mentioned in *Merriam-Webster*. In this query, there were periods

Figure 3. "Manifesto" search on the Google Books Ngram viewer from 1700 – 2000 (English corpus)

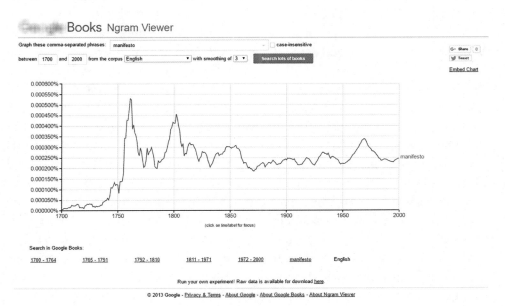

of interest suggested: 1700 – 1764, 1765 – 1791, 1792 – 1810, 1811 – 1971, and 1972 – 2000. This latter line graph shows periods of interest in Google's Web search holdings: 1500 – 1524, 1525, 1526 – 1827, 1828 – 1994, and 1995 – 2000. (See Appendix) Interestingly, the line graphs show bursty periods of high usage of the term "manifesto," but this could be due in part to the fact that there were fewer books in the past against which the counts of "manifesto" have to compete. In the current page, with tens of thousands of books being published in the U.S. alone annually and many more globally, it may well be harder for a term to register against the entire textual corpus. There may also be the effect of the holdings that the Google Books project has given that not all texts have yet been digitized.

While manifestos seem fairly popular as a genre, there is not a lot of formal definition about what it should contain. From the technology-based manifestos reviewed, it does not seem that there are formal definitions of what manifestos should contain or how they should be structured. Rather, it seems that people develop manifestos based on memetic emulation, inspiration, technological affordances, and other factors.

Basic Elements to a Manifesto

The basic elements of a manifesto are fairly scant: a name, a byline, and text, which often include a description of the world (or the problem as the author sees it), motivating values or impetuses (a rationale), and proposed actions. Whether implied or directly stated, there is an idea of an idealized state (of the world) that may be achieved with proper actions. There are implied audiences for the work—or those who may be activated into action. In some cases, the distribution is one-to-many (one author publishing out to the broad public); in other cases, the distribution is many-to-many (such as crowd-sourced writing shared with the even larger crowd). In many manifestos, proposed actions taken are not costless and may have long-term implications, but it's presented as the right thing to do. Often, there are general guidelines or principles for moving forward. There may even be defined redlines not to cross. Some manifestos are written as academic articles and include suggested ways to cite the work. (A search on Google Scholar for "technology manifesto"— with quotation marks—resulted in 88 works.) Online manifestos sometimes include a form field through which site visitors may sign as an expression of support, public commitment to the particular cause as a signatory, or an expression of interest (such as by receiving emails about the progress of the work behind the manifesto). Indeed, manifestos may transfer fairly well locally as well globally depending on the resonance of the particular issue.

Manifestos have varying levels of anticipated effects if they are carried through with the suggested actions. In some cases, manifestos with political implications may spark counter manifestos and competing visions and adversarial points-of-view. In many cases, the release of a manifesto is done to a somewhat prepared audience, in the sense that a portion of the public may be aware that there is a contested issue. In other cases, the audience may be a limited one (such as of technologists with an understanding of a complex or esoteric field). Occasionally, manifestos will emerge in the public consciousness when people take in-world actions based on a manifesto, whether as an adherent or an antagonist.

THE TECHNOLOGY MANIFESTO SPACE

"Technology" has been around since humans have created tools. The term itself has been around since 1859, according to Merriam-Webster. Decades after the launch of the precursor of the Internet and the popularization of the Web, this current age may be the apotheosis of technology manifestos that address such technologies and their deep effects on people's lives.

A light review of technology manifestos shows a wide breadth of topics, points-of-view, technologies, and calls-to-action. There are different apparent audiences for the respective manifestos. On the whole, these seem to be generally prosocial; they are about throwing public conversations among professional practitioners and the larger publics about how to improve software, technology conferences, human-computer interfaces, animal-computer interfaces, and the creation of technologies to improve human lives.

In the technology manifesto space, there is a wide range of approaches. As noted in the Delimitation section, there were many selected out because they were policy pieces based on particular democratic governance contexts or public relations pieces by companies to their internal publics (employees) and external publics, or were incomplete stubs. While an initial search resulted in 207 pieces, many of these did not meet the requirements for the research either. Summarizing some of these may still be valuable, though.

Digital Humanities and Technologies

One cluster of technology-based manifestos dealt with the emerging field of the digital humanities—or the uses of various technological means to enable a wider range of research and scholarly work in the humanities. These manifestos included a student manifesto demanding training in this field and critiquing the digital "immigrants" for being slow to change: "Today, we need collaboration, not lectures; we need to learn concepts, not singular facts; we need networking and socialization, not isolation; we need interactive learning, not to sit back and listen. We need new outcome objectives, not standardized tests" (Bloomsburg U. Undergraduate 'Manifesto' on Digital Humanities," 2010). A faculty member wrote a digital literacy manifesto describing what students must know to be fully digitally literate (Petty, 2013, "Digital Literacy Manifesto"). Several involved stances on how to properly conduct digital humanities work (such as digital curation) as informed by ideologies and principles. There is a lot of attention to this issue, with multiple versions currently of the Digital Humanities Manifesto (v. 1 in 2008, v. 2 in 2009), which originated during a conference and has been evolved multiple times since. These were quite academic and really focused more on an evolving sense of the humanities than on technologies. Participants in a 2010 conference (THATCamp in Paris) created a "Manifesto for the Digital Humanities" (released in 2011, 2012), with a vision of transdisciplinarity to include the social sciences (Manifesto for the Digital Humanities, 2011/2012, THATCamp Paris, p. 1). Then follows a list of declarations for professional practices in the field, including, "We call for the integration of digital culture in the definition of the general culture of the twenty-first century." The New Digital Humanities Manifesto, an online publication with the tagline "perpetually in beta," contains a continually updated space with various ideas on how to evolve the digital humanities. Indeed, authors have observed that the definition of the digital humanities itself is highly contested with many wanting a different mix of technologies and humanities (Porsdam, 2011). "Manifesto of Modernist Digital Humanities" emphasizes the importance of preserving modernist approaches while using digital strategies (Christie, Pilsch, Ross, & Tanigawa, Nov. 13, 2014).

Handling Data

The Denton Declaration (2012) calls for open access to research data and proposes the creation of proper standards for open data sharing (Denton Declaration, 2012). A work which seems to build on data sharing is "A Manifesto for Data Sharing in Social Media Research," which advocates for the interests of researchers exploring social media data and is based on ethical, legal, and methodological factors (Weller & Kinder-Kurlanda, 2016, p. 166). Beyond data sharing, there are works that guide others into how to capture and use data analytically, such as via the Gameplay Visualization Manifesto (Joslin, Brown, & Drennan, 2007) or how to create effective process models (Nichols, Kirwan, & Andelfinger, 2011).

Choosing Ethical Work

Some manifestos attempt to protect the well-being of human workers in a field. The "First Things First" Manifesto by Ken Garland in 1963 addressed the sense of many "creatives" that they were working only for commercial purposes and losing meaning in their work. This early manifesto expressed fatigue with "gimmick merchants, status salesmen and hidden persuaders" and advocating the use of their skills for more "worthwhile purposes" (Garland, et al, 1963 / 1964). "First Things First" Manifesto was revised in 2000 by 33 visual communicators and then in 2014 by Cole Peters. This was revised in 2000 by 33 visual communicators and then in 2014 by Cole Peters. These updates are created periodically in order to engage the changing field of marketing, including big data, "one-hit-wonder apps" and "the lack of diversity in science, technology, and engineering". This reads in part:

We have become part of a professional climate that: prizes venture capital, profit, and scale over usefulness and resonance; demands a debilitating work-life imbalance of its workers; lacks critical diversity in gender, race, and age; claims to solve problems but favours those of a superficial nature; treats consumers' personal information as objects to be monetised instead of as personal property to be supported and protected; and refuses to address the need to reform policies affecting the jurisdiction and ownership of data. ("First Things First 2014: A Manifesto," 2014)

The manifesto goes on to skewer a range of actions taken in the field and how those fall short of political ideals and values, and it lists out "pursuits more worthy of our dedication…such as education, medicine, privacy and digital security, public awareness and social campaigns, journalism, information design, and humanitarian aid" ("First things First 2014: A Manifesto," 2014). The fact that the prior manifesto has survived for over 50 years is remarkable. In a different professional domain—that of services—there is a new manifesto calling for ways to improve cross-field research in services as a science (Chesbrough & Spohrer, July 2006), with the harnessing of technologies to advance this work.

Work Methodologies

Another common category of technology-based manifestos deals with design and development. Some read like "how-to's" to specifically defined audiences: for example, one addresses how to use a text specification language (Cook, Kleppe, Mitchell, Rumpe, Warmer, & Wills, 2002); another manifesto describes how to use "atomicity in system design and execution" (Jones, Lomet, Romanovsky, Weikum, Fekete, Gaudel, Korth, de Lemos, Moss, Rajwar, Ramamritham, Randell, & Rodrigues, March 2005). Two authors have created a seven-point manifesto named "Pervasive Information Architecture: Designing Cross-Channel User Experiences Manifesto" which describes foundational changes to cross-media user experiences and the implications to design (Resmini & Rosati, 2009; 2011).

One manifesto addresses the phenomenon of end-user development (EUD), which is a feature of technologies that enable end users to customize component configurations and program functionalities into the software and / or hardware (Fischer, Giaccardi, Ye, Sutcliffe, & Mehandjiev, 2004, p. 33). This meta-design which enables end users to script within the tool broadens the capabilities of the software tools. Another manifesto argues that those who design computational systems should also consider "incidental users" whose accesses to computerized systems "are less active and often unplanned, yet still meaningful" (Inbar & Tractinsky, 2009, p. 56); here, manifestos are used to speak for those whose voices may not be as directly heard. One publishing team offered a framework for merging models from collaborating individuals in distributed contexts in A Manifesto for Model Merging (Brunet, Chechik, Easterbrook, Nejati, Niu, & Sabetzadeh, 2006, p. 5). The concept of sustainability (social, economic, and environmental) is applied to software creation in the Karlskrona Manifesto for Sustainability Design (Becker, Chitchyan, Duboc, Easterbrook, Penzenstadler, Seyff, & Venters, 2015, p. 467 and 470); this prior manifesto shows the commonality of the cross-fertilization of ideas and practices from various parts of society.

While many manifestos call for change and new ways of doing things, there are some that argue for going back to traditional understandings (because practitioners in a field may have gone astray from important fundamentals). One defines what an "interactive documentary" actually is and suggests that the term has been used too loosely to videos that overuse pictures instead of "moving images" (Almeida & Alvelos, 2010, p. 124).

Deploying Technologies

A number of technology-based manifestos relate to how particular technological tools should be deployed. There are multiple cloud computing manifestos, database management manifestos, computer code manifestos, and others. One advises on cyber publishing (Berghel, 2001). An Internet of Things (IoT) manifesto focuses on do-it-yourselfers (DIYers) who might create smart products ((De Roeck, Slegers, Criel, Godon, Claeys, Kilpi, & Jacobs, 2012, p. 172).

The Task Force on Process Mining has a Process Mining Manifesto, supported by "53 organizations and 77 process mining experts"; this manifesto advocates the use of event logs to mine processes "to discover, monitor and improve real processes (i.e., not assumed processes) by extracting knowledge from event logs readily available in today's (information) systems" (van der Aalst, 2011, p. 45). A "soundiness" manifesto proposes a way to test computer programs' functionality which combines rigor with real-world practical considerations based on common computer language features; as such, this manifesto argues against "soundness" analysis which models and tests software program behaviors that do not occur "in any program execution" (Livshits, Sridharan, Smaragdakis, Lhoták, Amaral, Chang, Guyer, Khedker, Møller, & Vardoulakis, 2015, p. 44). The authors explain: "A *soundy* analysis aims to be as sound as possible without excessively compromising precision and/ or scalability" (2015, p. 45)

Going Punk

In other technology-based fields, there are calls to rebellion, anything but the *status quo*. One work calls for the advent of "Punk HCI" (human-computer interface design). In the abstract, the authors write:

This paper presents two fingers to the HCI establishment. We reject the status quo that defines what language and forms are appropriate 'contributions' for this staid 'community' of quasi-scientific poseurs. We argue that CHI in particular is a tool that serves to reinforce the political and ideological status quo, favouring sell-out researchers wielding arcane verbiage and p-values, all paid for by corporate and government interests that reward the building of systems that distract, subdue and subjugate. We present our manifesto for Punk HCI, which celebrates principles of anarchy and freedom in exploring the impact of technology on human culture, values, social structures and psychology. We encourage research motivated by passion and dissent over patents. (Linehan & Kirman, 2014, p. 741)

The authors actually even provide a song to rally anarchist researchers (Linehan & Kirman, 2014).

Hacking as Empowerment and Self-Actualization

Several manifestos tap into the hacker movement. "The Hacker Manifesto" is famously written from the perspective of a disaffected young hacker who is explaining what it means to him to hack. The FemTechNet group has a manifesto about hacktivism for feminists which unifies global "feminist thinkers, researchers, writers, teachers, artists, professors, librarians, mentors, organizers and activists (who are) sharing resources and engaging in activities that demonstrate connected feminist thinking about technology and innovation" (FemTechNet, 2016); this reads like a general call to empower women working with and in technology.

Being and Doing in New Endeavors

Another manifesto, from 2013, dealt with how to think about and approach massive open online courses (MOOCs) through 23 directives; there was no apparent attributed authorship. There was a maker movement manifesto about the centrality of making in people's lives. This reads, in part, "You must learn to make. You must always seek to learn more about your making. You may become a journeyman or master craftsman, but you will still learn, want to learn, and push yourself to learn new techniques, materials, and processes" (Hatch, 2014).

Social Justice Aims

Another manifesto was written to improve "the inclusion of disabled people in SIGCHI conferences" (Kirkham, Vines, & Olivier, 2015); this work calls out invisible ways that people with disabilities are slighted and not considered in terms of conference practices. This work seemed to be addressed to conference organizers and colleagues in the field. An eloquent manifesto focuses on animal-computer interface design to protect animal well-being (Mancini, 2011). The "South2South Manifesto," as a "living document," was created by "journalists, activists and media development specialists from 14 countries" to discuss ways to promote freedom of expression and information in the Global South. The manifesto starts:

We stand for using digital technologies to foster freedom of expression and information—a fundamental right enshrined in Article 19 of the United Nations Universal Declaration of Human Rights.

Freedom of expression in countries of the Global South is challenged by undemocratic regimes, human rights abuses, inequality, poverty, corruption, surveillance, lack of access to information, poor media literacy and high costs of internet and communication services. However, we believe digital technologies can be used in innovative, ethical, democratic, inclusive and collaborative ways to solve problems and improve people's lives.

We believe that in order to foster freedom of expression and information, individuals, government, media and other organisations should observe the South2South principles when designing, developing and implementing projects using digital technologies.

This is a living document and open for discussion. ("How to use digital technologies to foster freedom of expression and information in the Global South," 2014, p. 1)

Balancing Human Needs and Technological Advances

A recurring grand theme (or meta-story) in some technology-based manifestos is the need to anticipate the affordances of technologies and to ensure that whatever is created does not ultimately cause human harm. There has been some deep theorizing work put into the meshing of organisms and machines, and the effects on human identity and social relationships, such as in the Cyborg Manifesto (Haraway, 2000). One author of multiple works in this direction has been Jaron Lanier [in *You Are Not a Gadget* (2010) and *Who Owns the Future?* (2013)]. Lanier has been warning of an unwitting lock-in of computational systems without sufficient thinking through of their respective effects on people and their interrelationships. He writes (2010) of the allure of computationalism that may result in suspension of critical analysis of effects:

Those who enter into the theater of computationalism are given all the mental solace that is usually associated with traditional religions. These include consolations for metaphysical yearnings, in the form of the race to climb to ever more "meta" or higher-level states of digital representation, and even a colorful eschatology, in the form of the Singularity. And, indeed, through the Singularity a hope of an afterlife is available to the most fervent believers.

Is it conceivable that a new digital humanism could offer romantic visions that are able to compete with this extraordinary spectacle? I have found that humanism provides an even more colorful, heroic, and seductive approach to technology.

This is about aesthetics and emotions, not rational argument. (Lanier, 2010, p. 177)

He worries about the concentration of power in digital networks and the online economic spaces, with people giving up their personal information without remuneration (Lanier, 2013).

In 2014, Tim Berners-Lee, the creator of the Web (and its underlying specifications for HTTP and HTML, among others), is apparently promoting the writing of an Internet Magna Carta (a guarantee of rights and privileges) (Wood, April 20, 2015). One author has suggested that there should be an "onlife" bill of rights for those engaging online:

Critical areas under discussion in the Onlife manifesto include concepts such as hyper-history, the lack of mediation in the online sphere, the erosion of privacy, a loss of context, distributed epistemic responsibility and even the right to digital euthanasia. (Oates, 2015, p. 229)

Not all technology-based manifestos focus on adults as end users of the technologies. There is a "slow tech" manifesto for parents to balance children's uses of technologies against other interests. On the website advocating this approach, it reads: "Slow Tech Parenting is about fostering real, personal connections and interactions in our everyday experience rather than allowing technology to dominate habits and lifestyle" (Hofman, 2013).

Anti-Technology Manifestos

Also, not all manifestos are uncritically pro-technology. While a number of technology-based manifestos deal with how to harness technologies for particular contexts, there were also some anti-technology sorts of manifestos, including a Buddhist-based one (Zahn, Apr. 7, 2016), and of course, the so-called Unabomber Manifesto (which is actually part of the included analyzed manifestos). Ironically, this reads: "We therefore advocate a revolution against the industrial system. This revolution may or may not make use of violence: it may be sudden or it may be a relatively gradual process spanning a few decades. We can't predict any of that…This is not to be a POLITICAL revolution. Its object will be to overthrow not governments but the economic and technological basis of the present society" (Kaczynski, 1995, p. 1).

Reverse Engineering Manifestos

Some organizations, like the Anonymous hacker collective, eschew manifestos as a matter-of-course, but an ideology may be reverse extracted based on their actions and public statements (Hai-Jew, 2013).

THE FINAL 16

The above then refer to the manifestos captured from an initial scan for technology-based manifestos through electronic means on the Web and

Internet and various subscription databases. Ultimately, the researcher went with the 16 technology manifestos listed in the crowd-sourced "Manifesto" article on Wikipedia. The ones that were actually used in the study—coded by manual (1), CAQDAS (2), and machine reading and autocoding methods (3) are the following, listed in the order of their publication: The GNU Manifesto (1985), The Hacker's Manifesto (1986), The Debian Manifesto (1993), A Cypherpunk's Manifesto (1993), Unabomber Manifesto (or "Industrial Society and its Future") (1995), The Third Manifesto (1995), The Cluetrain Manifesto (1999), The Agile Manifesto (2001), Pluginmanifesto (2001), The Hacktivismo Declaration (2001), The Mozilla Manifesto (2007), Principles of Programming Languages (2007), You Are Not a Gadget: A Manifesto (2010), The Hardware Hacker Manifesto (2010), The Reactive Manifesto (2014), and The BINC Manifesto (2015). To avoid redundancy, these were not summarized in the above section except in a few fleeting references.

If there may have been a particular Golden Age, it is possible that some of the time periods mentioned may include those. For this particular work, the focus will be on technology manifestos, with most of these originating between 1985 – 2015 (a 30-year period). By count, 2001 may have been a watershed year with three such manifestos broadly shared (Figure 4).

Figure 4. The modern era of technology-based manifestos: 1985 – 2015

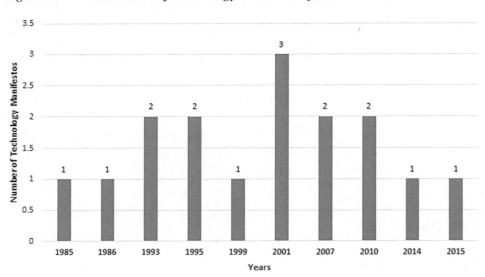

A majority of the 16 technology-based manifestos were written by individual authors, as may be seen in Figure 5.

In this subset of technology-based manifestos, a majority of the works (10) were authored by individual named authors (with three of the names online "handles," but all identified to verified actual persons). Four were written by dyadic authors (teams of two). In terms of the groups, one group was a team of four authors, and the other was a non-profit organization that creates a popular Web browser with crowd input.

ANALYZING TECHNOLOGY-BASED MANIFESTOS THREE WAYS: MANUAL, CAQDAS-BASED, AND MACHINE READING AND AUTOCODING

Each of the selected manifestos is summarized lightly in Table 1.

Per the hypothesis, three coding methods will be explored: (1) manual method-based coding (with light computational support), (2) CAQDAS-supported manual coding (with data queries), and (3) machine reading and autocoding.

Figure 5. Size of author groups for (selected) technology-based manifestos

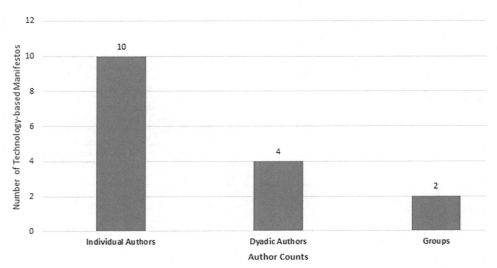

Table 1. A summary of the 16 technology-based manifestos in this study

Technology-Based Manifesto	Year of Origin	Author(s)	A Brief Summary
1. The GNU Manifesto	1985 (1983, updated in 1987)	Richard Stallman	An open call for support for developing the GNU operating system on Linux; "GNU" stands for "Gnu's Not Unix"
2. The Hacker's Manifesto	1986	"The Mentor" (Loyd Blankenship)	An explanation of the motivations of hackers striving to express their talents and to right economic imbalances through their activities
3. The Debian Manifesto	1993	Ian Murdock	A promotion of the development of Debian Linux in a modularized way and distributed in an open and free way
4. A Cypherpunk's Manifesto	1993	Eric Hughes	This manifesto is a call to rally cypherpunks to work together technologically and socially / collectively to protect people's privacy through anonymous transaction systems and encryption and to fight any regulatory restrictions on encryption
5. Industrial Society and its Future (Unabomber Manifesto)	1995	Ted Kaczynski	This manifesto argues that advancing technologies will harm human autonomy and human dignity, lead to worsening social disruptions, cause psychological suffering. and ultimately harm the natural world further; in that light, he is calling for a "revolution against the industrial system" by destroying the economic and technological basis of society (Kaczynski, 1995, p. 1)
6. The Third Manifesto	1995	Christopher J. Date and Hugh Darwen	This is a response manifesto to two earlier manifestos about how to proceed with future database management systems, mainly to replace Structured Query Language (SQL) with a hypothetical D (specifications for a database language)
7. The Cluetrain Manifesto	1999	Rick Levine and Christopher Locke	This manifesto focuses on the Web and Internet as disruptive technologies that enable human sociality and inter-communications that will change how businesses function
8. The Agile Manifesto	2001	Doc Searls and David Weinberger	A call to development software using an approach that…
9. Pluginmanifesto	2001	Ana Kronschnabl	A call to create a new cinema to the specifications of mobile devices and the technological ways that films are delivered to and consumed by audiences
10. The Hacktivismo Declaration	2001	Oxblood Ruffin (Hacktivismo's "foreign minister" and member of cDc or Cult of the Dead Cow)	This declaration argues for the application of the Universal Declaration of Human Rights and the International Covenant on Civil and Political Rights to the Internet—in order to protect human rights, human privacy from spying, and access to information through an uncensored Internet; this work rallies hackers and free speech advocates
11. The Mozilla Manifesto	2007	Mozilla Community	This manifesto provides a vision of a communal, open, and interactive internet in which people collaborate and develop together to "enrich the lives of individual human beings" through being open to people's online experiences and maintaining proper security and privacy online

continued on following page

Table 1. Continued

Technology-Based Manifesto	Year of Origin	Author(s)	A Brief Summary
12. Principles of Programming Languages	2007	Robert Harper	This reads like an accidental manifesto drawn from a course description (15-312 Principles of Programming Languages); this argues the importance of knowing principles because they are foundational to the "design, implementation, and application of programming languages" (Harper, 2015, p. 1; Harper 2007)
13. You Are Not a Gadget: A Manifesto	2010	Jaron Lanier	This work proposes a kind of unintended technological determinism in which technological decisions manifest in human societies, many times to the detriment of people
14. The Hardware Hacker Manifesto	2010	Cody Brocious (Daeken)	An assertion of consumer rights to hack their own hardware to learn more about the product and even to reverse engineer the product software if they so chose (in part based on the fact that people in the past could fix their own products and with an essentialist question: "… once you've purchased something, do you own it?") / jail breaking
15. The Reactive Manifesto	2014	Jonas Bonér, Dave Farley, Roland Kuhn, and Marin Thompson	This manifesto suggests that there should be coherence built into systems architectures (at all levels, even down to constituent parts) to ensure that they are "Responsive, Resilient, Elastic, and Message Driven" (so-called REACTIVE Systems)
16. The BINC Manifesto: A Manifesto for the Emerging Technological and Societal Transition	2015	Lene Andersen and Steen Rasmussen	This manifesto calls on scientists and others to study technology-driven societal transitions to empower citizens to have a voice in how to develop new societies; "BINC" refers to "bio-, info-, nano-, and cogno-" technologies, in reference to biological, informational, nano-technological, and cognitive issues

MANUAL METHOD-BASED CODING (WITH LIGHT COMPUTATIONAL SUPPORTS)

The art of manual coding is a central part of training for researchers. For many, computational methods for data exploration are also important. "Manual" coding generally refers to human-conducted coding, often using light computational supports, using software that is not specifically dedicated to text analysis. One simple method involves counting features of interest. This works fairly well if the textual examples are not too many and if the features counted aren't excessive.

A Feature Count

In terms of manual coding, one of the easier approaches is to define some of the features of the studied texts and then count them. Count data gives a descriptive sense of the studied texts but is not generalizable to the larger set of all such files (unless the sample is randomly selected and of sufficient size to generalize), and files are fairly consistent.

A summary of the count features from the selected technology-based manifestos follows. In terms of authorship, 10 of the manifestos were authored by single authors, four by dyadic teams, and two by groups. This may suggest that the personal framework is an important impetus for the writing of manifestos and maybe also that others understand manifestos through the personal framework. Many of the authors, like Richard Stallman, are stars in their own rights because of how they embody the proposals and how far their ideas have gone. Eighteen (18) of the authors used their own names as bylines on the manifestos, and only four used handles (but their actual names were included or revealed at some point). Only one manifesto did not show authorship, but that was the Mozilla Manifesto written by a number of people. A visit to the "Our 10 Principles" page of The Mozilla Manifesto (https://www.mozilla.org/en-US/about/manifesto/) shows a diverse range of people's faces...to represent everyperson (as authors). How are manifestos titled? Are they titled by the original authors, or are they named by the public? In general, 16 of 16 manifestos showed an author hand in the titling, but one had a public moniker that overshadowed the title chosen by the author (the "Unabomber Manifesto" aka "Industrial Society and its Future." The names of the manifestos were arrived at in different ways—by topic (GNU Manifesto), by author (Unabomber), by identity (hacker, cypherpunk, Internet filmmaker), by technologies (BINC), by count (Third Manifesto), by disambiguated terms ("cluetrain"), by methods (agile), by organization names (Mozilla), by locations, and other means.

Another count approach was to see if the particular manifesto had an abstract or introduction or foreword, as a sign of structural formality of the writing. Seven (Cluetrain, Unabomber, Hardware Hacker, Mozilla, Reactive, Third, and You are Not a Gadget) all had some type of opening, and the remaining ones (Hacker, Principles of Programming Languages, Debian, Cypherpunk, BINC, Hactivismo, GNU, Agile, and Pluginmanifesto) did not. So seven had an artifact of formality, while nine did not. One had a full listing of differences between a prior version of a manifesto than the current one, as if this were a formal publication (The Third Manifesto); this also had formalized definitions of terms, which is also a feature of academic publishing.

Did the manifestos contain described inspirations for the manifestos? On the whole, most did. Some described challenges with the status quo and suggested ways to create improvements. Others anticipated futures based on the world's current tracks and suggested ways to change directions. Several dealt with technological paths to take. Others described idealized and practical versions of being hackers, hacktivists, cypherpunks, and coders. Several described visions for how to best enable the development of the Internet and Web going forward. There were a range of underlying values, too, such as being human rights, information rights, open communications, open-access to data, privacy rights, the freedom of self-expression, and social justice causes (such as ensuring a greater distribution of wealth through economic means).

So what were the expressed stances towards technology—broadly speaking? A majority looked at the promise, and several identified threats (to human privacy, to human society, and to nature, writ large). In this selected set of 16 manifestos, the authors dealt with a range of technologies: hardware, software, operating systems, databases, data, cryptographic methods, Linux, Internet films, hacking, hacktivism, marketing, Web browser development, and others.

The voices of the respective authors differed. Most established their credibility to the issue by either citing clear expertise or claiming a technology-based identity, or both. Several of the manifestos used mixed points of view: Most of the sample set was written in the third-person point-of-view. The Hacker's Manifesto shifts between voices—that of a young hacker and a chorus of the establishment in society decrying the young hacker's approaches to the world. Then, too, in the Cluetrain Manifesto, most of the observations are in the third-person point-of-view, but there are some first-person insights as well. The "Unabomber Manifesto" was written in the first-person plural ("we," "our"). The shorter versions were about a page long while the longer ones ran hundreds of pages. (A word count using LIWC showed a min-max word count of from a pithy 229 words to 65,701 or so. There is a little inaccuracy with the data because of the fact that the respective files capture some extra metadata as downloaded files off the Web, which were not cleaned off. It is best to understand these counts as approximate or ≈.) Several included linked visualizations, like explanatory diagrams or photos. Several had online sign-ups for supporters.

In general, the main audiences seemed to be practitioners and technologists in the field first and then the general public second (although this order was reversed in some works). Calls to action included requests for help developing certain technologies or supporting particular points-of-view. Others requested support, funding, and resources. A majority of the manifestos were in Version 1, and several were in v. 2 or v. 3.

A Questions Brainstorm

Another approach in the manual coding approach is to draw on a disciplined imagination in order to consider what types of information may be relevant (and potentially knowable) from the particular text set. An earlier version of a brainstorm was offered in the Introduction. A more fully developed version follows, with maybe only some parts of the original brainstorm apparent. This ambitious brainstorm gives a way forward for questions to pursue and data to code, even if the full set of insights is not captured in this first round.

PART 1: THEMATIC CONTENTS OF TECHNOLOGY-BASED MANIFESTOS

Themes of Tech-Based Manifestos

What are some main themes across tech-based manifestos? What are these themes about? What has apparently inspired these themes?

- Do the themes show certain stakeholder interests? Which stakeholders are best represented in the respective themes? Why is this so? (Do other stakeholders express their interests in other ways?)
- Are there event-based features of tech-based manifestos?
- Are there personality-based features of tech-based manifestos?
- Are there geographical regionalisms in terms of particular themes?
- How may these themes be understood?
- Are there competing manifestos?
- Are there conceptualizations of an "us" vs. "them"? Is there an enemy conceptualized, or an extreme competitor?
- Are there textual and subtextual meanings? How so?

Extrinsic and Intrinsic Values

Are there extrinsic values in the tech manifestos? Intrinsic ones?

- What are the extrinsically expressed values in the tech manifestos? Where do these values come from?

- Are there intrinsic values in the tech manifestos? Where do these intrinsic values come from?
- What are the philosophical values and ideas underlying tech-based manifestos?

Technology Focus

What technology / technologies was / were the focus of the technology-based manifestos? How technologically savvy are the tech manifestos? (Why? How so?)

- How were the particular technologies or class of technologies selected for discussion in a technology-based manifesto?
- How were the technologies depicted?
- How informed are the creators of technology-based manifestos about technologies?
- Which technologies are of special interests for those who write technology-based manifestos?
- Besides technology, are there apparent blind spots in the tech-based manifestos? If so, what are they? Why might these blind spots exist? Are there logic gaps in the tech-based manifestos? If so, what are these? What is the relevance of such gaps? How are such gaps filled?
- What are some counterfactuals to the arguments in the tech-based manifestos? Why?

PART 2: ADVOCACY ROLES OF TECHNOLOGY-BASED MANIFESTOS

Imagined (Idealized) Futures

Are there imagined futures in the technology-based manifestos?

- If so, are these imagined futures positive or negative?
- What are idealized end states from the tech manifestos? How apparently realistic are these end states?
- What are practical ways to benchmark these? Are methods included in the technology-based manifestos?

Calls to Action / Suggested Changes

Do the technology-based manifestos contain calls to action? Buy-in?

- What sorts of changes are being advocated for across tech-based manifestos? Are there common themes? What are the calls-to-action in the technology-based manifestos?
- What is the behavioral role conceptualized in tech-based manifestos? Who is thought to be the main drivers to enact the respective changes? Why?
- Are there incentives to motivate action? Leverage? Bully pulpit compellence? Coercive measures?
- How can these envisioned and proposed changes be actualized?
- What are some of the likely costs to these proposed changes?
- Are there apparent pros and cons to the respective proposed changes?

Freedom of Interpretation

How much margin is there for interpretation by readers of tech manifestos?

- Are tech manifestos deeply spelled out and precise?
- Are measurable objectives given and used?
- Are the objectives of tech manifestos pretty broad and open to interpretation?
- Would it be obvious to an objective outside observer if a person is following a manifesto or not?

PART 3: ORIGINS AND HISTORIOGRAPHY OF TECHNOLOGY-BASED MANIFESTOS

Original Inspirations

What inspired the creation of tech-based manifestos (based on the manifestos themselves or on accompanying documentation)?

- Where do tech manifestos come from?
  - Are they inspired by events?
  - By philosophies?

- ○ By technological advancements?
- ○ Are the core inspirations identified in the body of the technological manifestos?
- ○ By various mixes?

PART 4: AUTHORSHIP AND STYLE OF TECHNOLOGY-BASED MANIFESTOS

Authorship

Who are the authors / seminal thinkers of tech manifestos? If there are multiple authors, how are they selected or self-selected (opt-in)? If the manifestos are crowd-sourced, how are the respective authors addressed? What is the make-up of the crowd-sourced authoring teams?

- How collaboratively written are they? How can one tell?
- How are tech manifestos written? collated? (Is this information shared?)
- Are there differences between the technology-based manifestos based on single authorship? Small group authorship? Crowd-based authorship?

Style (Writing, Presentational)

What are the styles of technology-based manifestos?

- What are some common style features of technology-based manifestos?
- Are new terms coined in the technology-based manifesto?
- Are these written in multiple voices? Multiple tones? Points-of-view?
- What about the breadth of topics in manifestos? How broad are the topics?
- How are technology manifestos styled in terms of their various appearances?
- What are structural features of tech manifestos? What texts? What imagery? What URLs? What multimedia features?
- What are some linguistic features of technology manifestos?
- In terms of clustering, what general clusters are there in terms of styles of technology manifestos?

PART 5: DISTRIBUTION AND OUTREACH

Distribution

How are the tech-based manifestos distributed?

- How available are tech manifestos? Where are these usually hosted?
- What technologies are used to distribute tech-based manifestos? Why?

Publicity

What features of tech manifestos result in their broad publicity? Their attention-getting?

Targeted Audiences

Who are their apparent targeted audiences? Who are the main targeted audience members vs. peripheral target audience members? Why? Are there latent audience members and stakeholders?

PART 6: POPULAR REACH AND EFFICACY
OF TECHNOLOGY-BASED MANIFESTOS

Popular Reach / Impact and Efficacy of Tech Manifestos

How popular are the respective manifestos? (How can one tell?) How efficacious have the technology-based manifestos been? (How may the efficacy of the tech manifestos be observably and rigorously evaluated? By how much digital ink is spilled? By signers? By donations? By effects on policy? By broad public discussion? By common practices? By public awareness?)

- Is there a common public attentional trajectory for tech manifestos? If so, what might that be? How are tech manifestos received? Why? (Is it clear what some contributing factors may be to how they are received?)
- For those that do not follow this type of trajectory, what are some anomalous trajectories? What gives a tech manifesto second life or third life or greater usage after the first rollout?

- What were some of the observable and measurable impacts of these technology-based manifestos?
    - Any residual effects?
    - Positive or negative (socially)? Positive or negative (technologically)?
- Do the manifestos "age" well over time?
    - Are the manifestos dated? How so? Why or why not?
    - What are some features that make for a long-lived manifesto?
    - Which types of manifestos are updated (vs. those that are left in v. 1 form)?
        - Who carries the mantle to actually update manifestos?

Updating of Tech Manifestos (Survival Analysis)

How often are tech manifestos updated? What is the rationale for the updating of the tech manifestos?

- What percentage of the tech manifestos evaluated are still in version one? Version two? Version three? What seems to be the impetus for updating a tech-based manifesto?
- How long do technology-based manifestos last? Why? How can one tell when a technology-based manifesto is no longer relevant?

A structured brainstorm with some organization to the numbered sections and questions enables a thought-out approach to the research and the data analysis. A brainstorm is never truly comprehensive, and generally, not all the questions brainstormed will be addressed or answered because not all will be directly relevant to a research design. In this case, where the focus is actually on the three textual data coding methods, the particular questions are not the main focus.

A Linguistic Analysis

Using the Linguistic Inquiry and Word Count (LIWC, pronounced "luke") too, a linguistic analysis was run on the 16 technology-based manifestos, and some interesting patterns emerged (Figure 6). The manifestos tended to show high Analytic scores (expressed as $0 - 1$): with a min-max range of 50.76 - 97.84 and a mean of 83.97. A fairly high percentage of words dealt

Figure 6. A linguistic analysis of the technology-based manifesto corpus in LIWC

Filename	Segment	WC	Analytic	Clout	Authentic	Tone	WPS	Sixltr	Dic	function	pronoun	ppron	i	we	you	shehe	they	ipron	article	prep	auxverb	adverb	conj
01The GNU Manifesto - GNU Project - Free Software Founda...	1	4912	79.07	51.63	9.27	76.66	46.34	22.70	83.06	50.18	10.14	3.75	0.96	0.75	0.69	0.26	1.08	6.39	7.70	14.07	9.61	3.77	5.37
02___ Phrack Magazine ___.pdf	1	811	61.53	72.30	18.67	11.43	27.03	12.70	69.17	41.31	15.04	9.99	3.95	2.59	2.22	0.49	0.74	5.06	5.80	8.26	7.15	2.47	3.70
03A Brief History of Debian - The Debian Manifesto.pdf	1	1212	90.99	43.44	12.54	74.88	75.75	25.00	77.64	49.50	8.00	1.40	0.25	0.00	0.17	0.08	0.91	6.60	10.07	14.77	8.66	2.81	5.61
04A Cypherpunk's Manifesto.pdf	1	917	64.58	79.33	13.55	65.04	61.13	25.41	81.13	50.49	12.76	7.74	2.29	3.93	0.44	0.11	0.98	5.02	6.00	13.20	9.05	3.93	6.22
05UnabomberManifesto.pdf	1	35577	84.47	65.73	12.55	30.12	97.74	26.40	82.37	48.91	8.96	3.50	0.03	0.93	0.12	0.84	1.59	5.46	7.84	14.53	8.40	3.79	6.00
06TTM-2013-02-07.pdf	1	8227	90.06	42.90	9.32	57.72	18.83	27.26	72.37	44.29	4.63	0.57	0.16	0.19	0.00	0.00	0.22	4.06	8.78	13.05	9.88	2.87	5.81
07CluetrainasOne.pdf	1	65701	80.98	76.65	28.80	49.36	50.38	22.74	82.46	48.52	11.08	5.54	0.89	1.70	1.41	0.22	1.32	5.53	8.02	13.96	7.39	4.31	5.81
08Principles behind the Agile Manifesto.pdf	1	229	97.84	74.39	17.03	90.56	15.27	37.99	73.80	36.68	3.06	2.18	0.00	0.87	0.00	0.00	1.31	0.87	9.17	13.54	4.37	1.75	5.24
09Plugin Manifesto by Ana Kronachnabl.pdf	1	855	86.73	56.51	20.89	79.17	15.00	21.52	85.50	52.40	8.89	3.51	0.00	1.52	0.58	0.00	1.40	5.38	10.18	14.97	9.82	3.51	6.08
10HacktivisimoDeclaration.pdf	1	1375	96.99	64.21	16.99	34.61	29.26	33.24	73.53	41.38	5.89	2.04	0.00	1.09	0.07	0.22	0.85	3.85	7.85	16.22	5.24	1.02	5.53
11The Mozilla Manifesto in Totality.pdf	1	794	96.91	85.78	5.15	85.32	16.20	36.90	71.03	40.55	6.80	3.02	0.00	2.52	0.13	0.00	0.38	3.78	11.08	12.85	4.16	1.64	5.16
12H1S-312 Principles of Programming Languages.pdf	1	1021	91.83	66.68	9.76	53.38	85.08	33.10	74.05	41.14	5.58	2.25	0.69	0.49	0.20	0.00	0.88	3.33	6.66	14.20	6.07	4.51	5.29
13YouAreNotAGadget-A_Manifesto.pdf	1	65578	88.11	62.56	29.59	50.84	20.50	24.62	81.88	49.94	9.09	3.53	0.97	0.84	0.85	0.23	0.63	5.54	9.15	15.05	8.23	4.43	5.64
14The Hardware Hacker Manifesto – I, Hacker.pdf	1	860	50.76	60.56	44.92	51.91	22.05	16.84	80.23	53.84	19.42	9.19	5.35	1.74	1.63	0.00	0.47	10.23	6.63	12.67	10.00	3.37	5.58
15The Reactive Manifesto.pdf	1	691	90.29	61.40	23.39	15.58	57.58	40.96	69.90	37.05	6.37	1.88	0.00	0.58	0.00	0.00	1.30	4.49	5.50	12.74	4.63	2.32	6.37
16FLInT - The BINC Manifesto.pdf	1	2284	92.44	68.96	23.36	63.12	50.76	30.17	76.49	40.67	5.25	2.10	0.00	1.58	0.04	0.00	0.48	3.15	8.27	12.96	5.52	3.11	7.01

with cognitive processing (8.30 – 16.14 range as a percentage total of the respective documents). These counts are suggestive of the manifesto form, which purports to observe issues and enable their solving through committed individual and collective action.

In terms of the psychological construct of drives—indicators of affiliation, achievement, power, reward, and risk—the manifestos showed that the Cypherpunk Manifesto and Mozilla Manifesto had high drive for affiliation. The Agile Manifesto showed a high focus on achievement. In terms of Power, the Hacker's Manifesto, Unabomber Manifesto, Hacktivisimo Declaration, and Reactive Manifesto were relatively high in this measure, as compared to the other manifestos. For all the manifestos, they ranked fairly low on the pursuit of Reward and the pursuit of Risk. These findings (Figure 7) bolster the idea that some manifesto writers want to reach out to affect the world (a power focus), but the ultimate aims are not necessarily for self-reward or the fulfillment of the excitement of risk. These relative (non-absolute) linguistic features may provide direction for further research.

Another approach involved looking at references to time. In LIWC, there is a measure that enables analyzing whether a text is focused on the past, the present, or the future (labeled as focuspast, focuspresent, or focusfuture). An initial and naïve assumption may be that manifestos are future focused and use that focus to drive actions, but that would be inaccurate. According

Figure 7. An analysis of drive in the language of technology-based manifestos (LIWC)

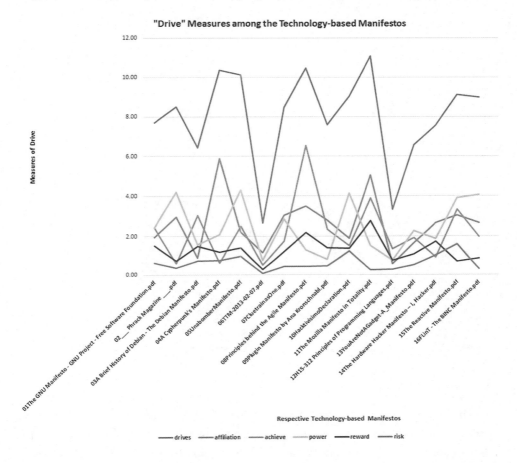

to the LIWC data, the manifestos generally tended to focus mostly on the present and much less on the past or the future. On a linegraph visualization, the focuspresent dominates both the focuspast and focusfuture (Figure 8).

What about informal language use? To be expected, these technology-based manifestos tended more towards formal language than informal. However, in the informal set, netspeak was fairly common as compared to swearing, assent, nonfluencies, and filler terms. Only one of the manifestos ranked fairly high on swear words (Figure 9).

In terms of function words, verbs, prepositions, and pronouns ranked high (Figure 10). Verbs may be indicative of actions. Prepositions are highly used in explanatory writing. Pronouns are used address people.

Figure 8. Relative time references in the technology-based manifestos

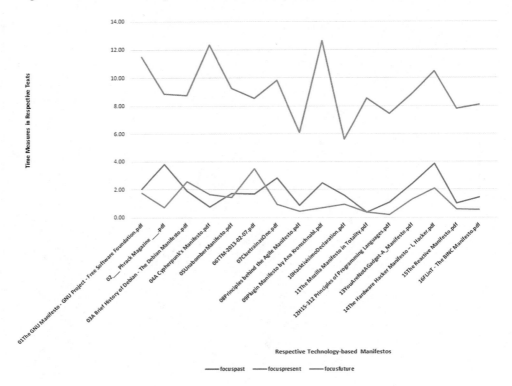

There are other approaches that may be taken as well. It is important to be open to data patterns and anomalies in the set—as a form of discovery. It is also important to have hypotheses and questions that may be pursued using a computational linguistic analysis approach. Observations may be made of the full text set as well as of text clusters and individual texts. In this case, there was not direct clustering although that may be achieved by manifestos with similar time frames of origin, similar topics, and so on.

A Survival Analysis

Classically, a survival analysis is a statistical technique that examines how long a particular person with certain health conditions (and health interventions) is likely to survive, based on empirical information. This approach is built on non-normally distributed outcomes. It treats time as an important independent variable since length of time may affect survivability. Based on the descriptive information, predictive approaches may be created. To run a survival

Figure 9. Informal language counts in the technology-based manifestos

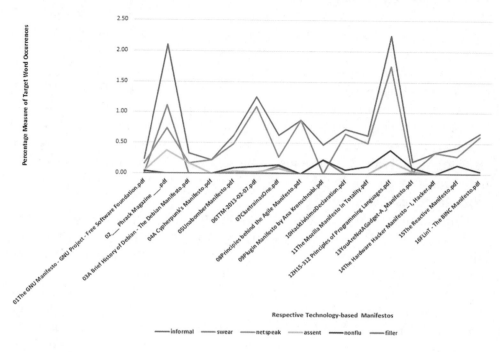

Figure 10. Function words in the technology-based manifestos

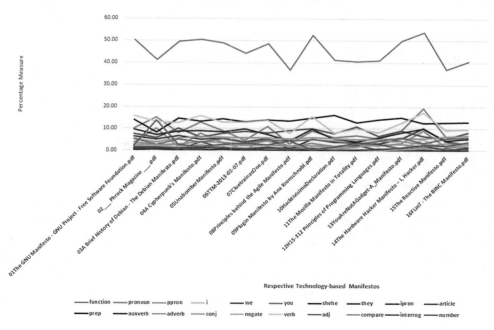

analysis, researchers need to establish a time scale (unit of analysis) and a clear definition of an "event." This statistical approach also includes left- and right-censoring. Data "censoring" refers to unknown information—such as that of individuals who enter a certain state at an unknown time before they started a survival analysis study (left censoring)…and right-censoring which refers to individuals who participate in a study and have not yet experienced the target event by the end of the study (at which point they are not followed by the researchers). Censored data is a data limitation or lost data. A related graph to the survival analysis is the hazard function, which looks at increasing risks to the individuals in the surviving set over time. What is acting on the individuals in the set is the so-called "force of mortality" and potentially other variables and factors.

Outside of a health context, "survival analysis" is known as "time-to-event analysis" or "event history analysis," among others, with the focus on "duration analysis". Here, the random variable is still the time to event, and the associational factors may be any number of variables.

The way this survival analysis was set up, the 16 technology-based manifestos are all considered alive in the "launch" state the moment they are published. The "event" of focus is when these go through a "breakout" and reach a much wider audience than the initial targeted audience of specialists. Each of the manifestos enter this set in a staggered way, but there is no left censoring (because all the data of each manifesto is known from history). Of this set, some percentage in the "at risk" set of manifestos will not survive in the original set and transition to the "breakout" state set based on various hazard factors ("risks" of non-survival in the first set) (Figure 11). Later, some hypothetical "hazards" are addressed.

An important next step is to figure out how to define an "event" based on objective information. One challenge to acquiring a dataset on which to create a survival analysis was on how to find information indicating whether a technology-based manifesto actually broke out of a narrow audience or not. At first, queries were run on the respective technology-based manifesto names on Google Books Ngram Viewer (introduced first in Figure 3) to see if there were clear peak years of term use in the digitized books. Then, queries were run in Google Scholar to see what mentions there were through the lifespan of the respective technology-based manifestos through the present; this web-based tool enables access to research articles, books, citations, and patents. Google Search was not ultimately used because the results were noisy, even when the search box was seeded with the following: "name of technology-based manifesto" and target year. The breadth of the search

Figure 11. A visualization of 'survival analysis' applied to technology-based manifestos

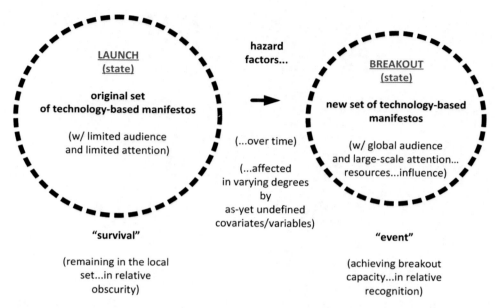

engine means that many contemporary works which reference the historical year is captured, and there was not an apparent way to only find references in a wayback way. Initially, it seemed that combining results from multiple sources (Google ones, all) would result in normalized data, but the Google Books Ngram Viewer data and the Google Scholar data only converged occasionally. In a sense, the Google Books data is partially (fully?) captured in Google Scholar. Ultimately, Google Scholar data was used with the first breakout moment captured to inform the survival analysis, and there was not further data refinement (Figure 12). (This researcher did so many queries on Google Scholar at a sitting that the web-based tool asked multiple times for verification that the user was not a robot but a human—and it required a photo identification verification based on identifying all images with numbered addresses...before the service would continue.)

A glance at annual Google Scholar counts may give a sense of particular points at which a breakout may have occurred because the data may be captured in a time-series way. In Figure 13, the Hacktivisimo Declaration (2001)'s presence in the Google Scholar index is shown in both a linegraph at the top and a bar chart (with a trendline) below. While the general trajectory is up,

Figure 12. Overall popularity of respective technology-based manifestos by Google Scholar counts

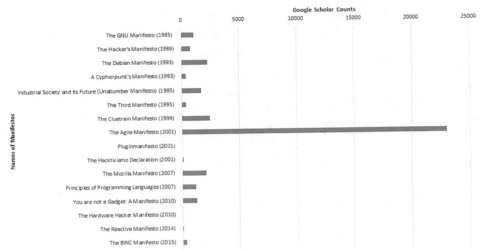

there have been particular years when there have been apparent breakouts of interest, all of which may be used to inform a survival analysis (more on this follows).

A collective linegraph is shown in Figure 14. Each of the 16 selected technology-based manifestos is listed in this linegraph, with differing dates of entry or publication (in a "staggered entry"). This study covered 31 years, from 1985 – 2016. Interestingly, two of the manifestos (the pluginmanifesto and the Hardware Manifesto) did not have any citations in their first year of existence. Neither one has captured much academic attention either, which may be in part due to their messages and the resulting audiences. The pluginmanifesto deals with Internet filmmaking for the small (mobile device) screen. The Hardware Hacker Manifesto deals with consumer rights to take apart and reverse engineer purchased hardware. While both have apparent audiences, these may not be audiences who write for the academic literature. A general Google Search of <pluginmanifesto> results in 3,840 results, "pluginmanifesto" in 2,760 results, <Hardware Hacker Manifesto> in 34,200 results, and "Hardware Hacker Manifesto" in 938 results.

While each manifesto has a start date (time of publication), all are thought to continue but with differing level of human attention. The curves also vary in terms of trajectories and intensities, with some barely registering in Google Scholar, others with gradual inclines up through the present, others with fairly jagged ups and downs (such as with the Hacktivisimo Manifesto in Figure 14), and other linegraph patterns. Some of the included manifestos are so new, originating in 2014 and 2015, for example, that it is hard to even suggest that a pattern is apparent. The general thinking is that manifestos will slowly "sunset" over time unless they are somehow relevant and in people's awareness. Another reasonable direction for manifestos is that their ideas are integrated with other ideas and just become part of the informational ecosystem as residua but are not called out by name or author, and their points of origin may well be ultimately lost to history. While this work includes a "survival analysis," this statistical technique is not used to capture manifesto lifespans but something different: the length of time manifestos remain with a small "local" audience before breakout to a broadcast potentially web-scale audience, as inferred by Google Scholar data. Here, "survival" means remaining in a set of technology manifestos that haven't launched to a broader public; a "hazard" is the risk of making it big to a broader public; an "event" (non-survival in the original set) refers to breakout to a broader audience. In this conceptualization, the hazard is conceived as a net positive. As a simple survival analysis, there are no predictor variables in this case. Table 2 shows the classic setup for survival analysis (using the Kaplan-Meier approach in SPSS).

A Kaplan-Meier analysis in SPSS showed an average (mean) of approximately eight (8) years for breakout, give or take two years. The lower bound of the 95% confidence interval is 3.9 and the upper bound is 11.7 years. The median (midpoint of the data) amount of time-to-event is four (4) years but with a standard error of 4.4 and 0 – 12.6 as the upper and lower bounds of the 95% confidence interval, so the curve skews more towards shorter time-to-event. The findings may be skewed by having a small sample set and also by having a few manifestos that did not break out until some 15 years in.

Of the full set of selected technology-based manifestos, a full fourth of the data were right-censored, which meant that they had not achieved breakout by the end of the study in August 2016. None of the data was left-censored, since all were historical documents with known release dates. A few of the works had known precursor drafts and revisions thereafter (including full versions), but this survival analysis engaged the data in a summary way. Some 75% had achieved breakout in the lifetime of the particular manifesto. The min-max time range for the 12 manifestos that reached breakout was 1 – 19 years. This year range may be seen in Figure 15.

A survival function curve is depicted as a non-increasing curve but with diminishing survival in the original set over time. Here, too, plateaus indicate

Figure 13. The Hacktivisimo Declaration (2001) on Google Scholar

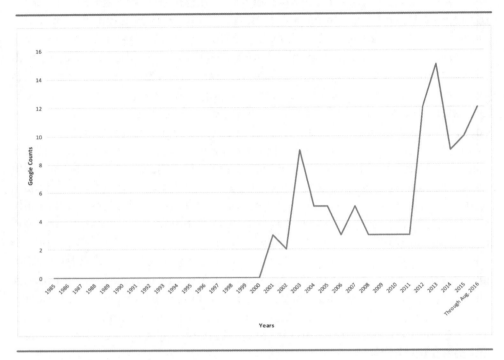

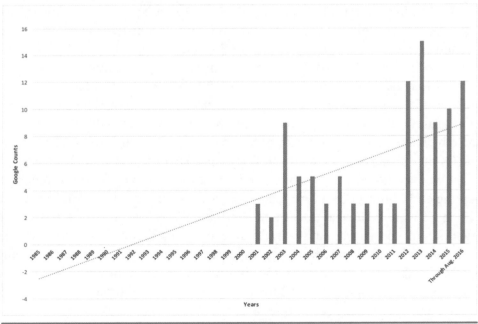

Figure 14. Identification of breakout years of technology-based manifestos through annualized Google Scholar counts (articles, books, citations, and patents)

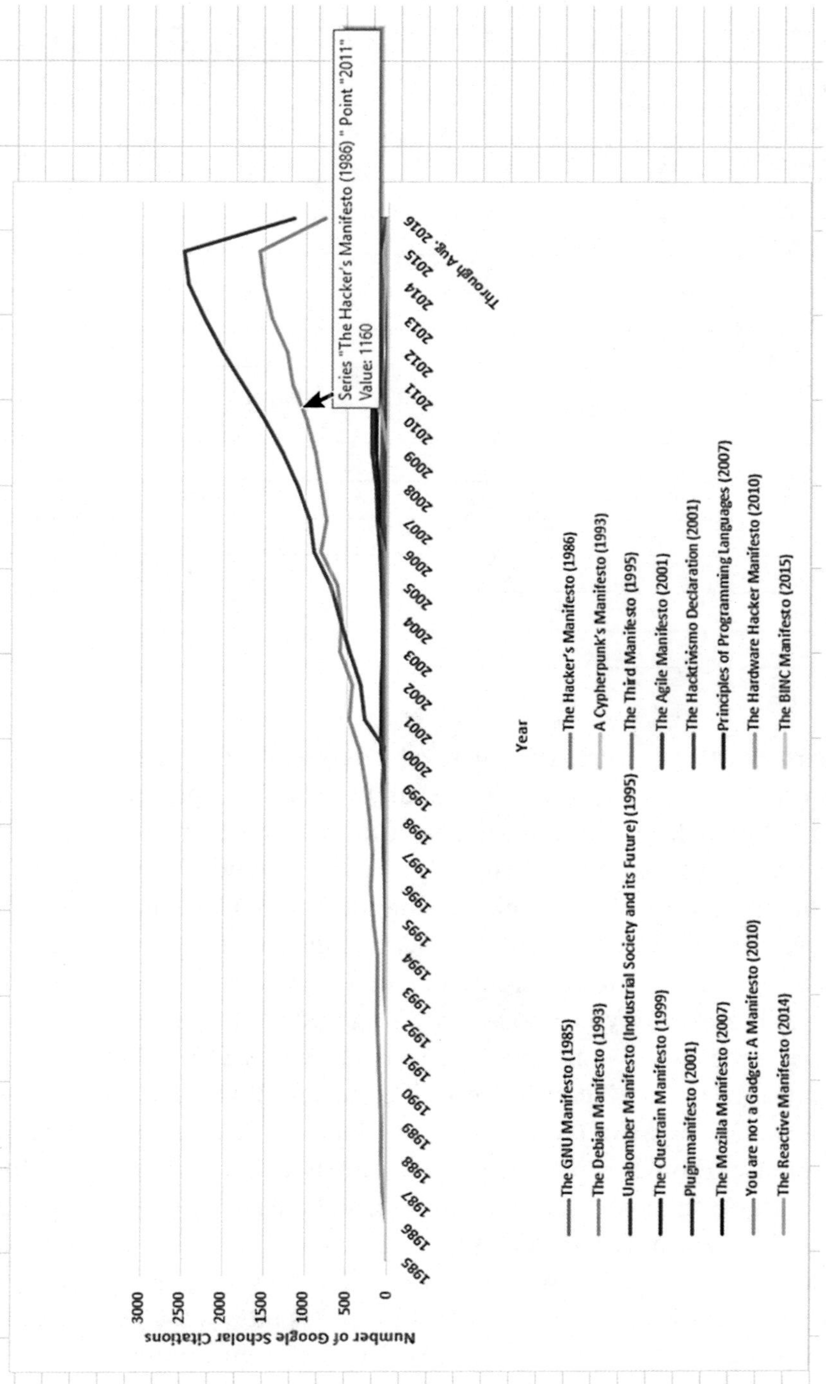

Table 2. Underlying data for the Kaplan-Meier Survival Analysis (SPSS)

ManifNam	TimeUnit	Censored
GNU	9	1
Hacker	4	1
Debian	1	1
Cypherpunk	17	1
Unabomber	19	1
Third	2	1
Cluetrain	8	1
Agile	1	1
Plugin	15	0
Hacktivi	2	1
Mozilla	1	1
PrinProg	1	1
NotGadg	2	1
Hardware	7	0
Reactive	3	0
BINC	2	0

periods of non-decreasing survival, but over the lifetime of the curve, there is ultimate loss. At the top left, the full population is present, but over time, the population diminishes. In survival functions based on mortality, the survival function reaches zero eventually; however, when "survival" is defined as remaining in a set of technology manifestos that have not achieved breakout, it is possible to have residual "surviving" manifestos that never break out (and are represented as right-censored manifestos).

A hazard curve is a non-decreasing curve that shows the risks of hazards over time, with some time periods of increasing hazard and others of a plateaued or non-increasing risk. The hazard function is non-monotonic in its increase because of the periods when the curve plateaus and does not directly increase. From this plot, breakouts seem to occur early on in the lifespan of a manifesto and also in later maturity. Breakouts early on show sparking within the first year or two of release, which may suggest that a manifesto captures ideas in an evocative way. Many of these that spark early seem to continue for long runs of popularity over time. This latter case seems to describe an "overnight sensation" which has actually been around for a few decades before discovery and broader public awareness (Figure 16). Such works may

Figure 15. Survival function for technology-based manifestos over time in the pre-breakout set

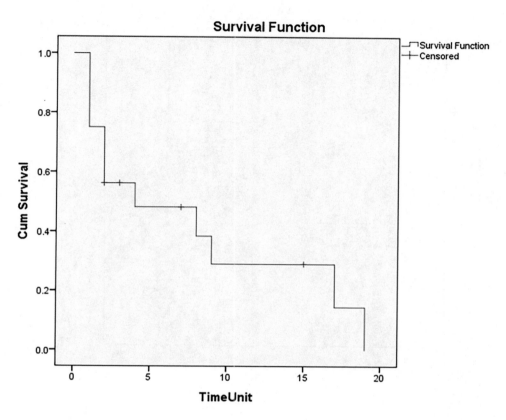

There is a negative association between the hazard rate and the survival rate, namely, a higher hazard rate means a lower rate of survival, and vice versa. As may be seen in Figures 15 and 16, there is a diminishing survival rate of manifestos in the non-breakout set over time, and the "hazard" for

exist within a small group as a staple but not reach broader public awareness unless there is a sparking event or need; it is possible that works that break out later accrete awareness slowly, and when there is a sufficient user base, it achieves breakout. (Technology adoption models do show at least initial resistance to new ideas, technologies, and methods.) The cumulative hazard function does rise over time. (The results of this survival analysis may be skewed in part from the small sample set and also from the sampling based on a listing in a crowd-sourced Wikipedia page entry.)

There is a negative association between the hazard rate and the survival rate, namely, a higher hazard rate means a lower rate of survival, and vice versa. As may be seen in Figures 15 and 16, there is a diminishing survival rate of manifestos in the non-breakout set over time, and the "hazard" for

Figure 16. Hazard function of technology-based manifestos breaking out over time

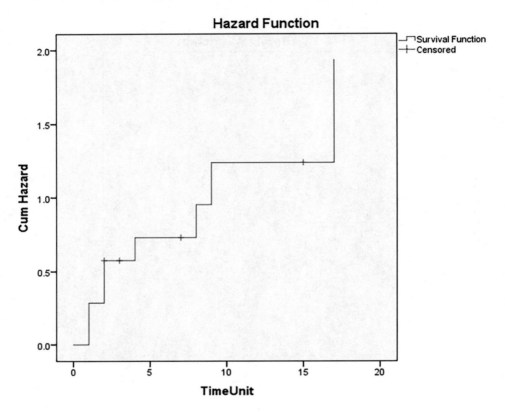

breakout increases with time. The survival function is also non-monotonic (because of the plateaus) but is cumulatively decreasing as a general trend. (A monotonic trend is either entirely increasing or decreasing at any one time.)

What are some "hazards" for technology-based manifestos in terms of breaking out? While the hazard functions and survival functions shed light on time-based patterning of breakout, they do not directly indicate what the particular factors might be that result in some manifestos breaking out and others not. It is possible, though, to hypothesize based on some light readings of the respective manifestos and some light research in this space.

- A manifesto needs sufficient momentum and velocity to break out from a particular sub-population into the larger population.
    - **User Base:** Technology-based manifestos often are focused on a sub-group in a general population who have a stake in the

particular technology or method or ideology (or the mix). For example, there are groups of developers who work in particular fields or hackers whose identity is tied into the activity of hacking. It seems important to have some sort of user base to which a manifesto is linked. These advocates may support the popularization of a manifesto and turn it into a popular and widely-known phenomenon.

- ○ **Link to Events:** Oftentimes, technology-based manifestos are launched from conferences when an individual is inspired or when groups collaborate around solving a particular problem or addressing a perceived social issue. Many manifestos are rolled out at public events also to gain publicity, new followers, and buy-in. Re-versioning of manifestos sometimes happens around events as well. The cachet of events, the leadership, the branding, and the participants, are all important parts of launching technology-based manifestos.
- ○ **Bridging Individuals:** According to social network theory, there may be bridging nodes that connect otherwise-disconnected sub-populations. Such nodes may be charismatic individuals who have credibility among multiple sub-groups and can credibly link different groups.
- ○ **Easy-to-Recall Name:** The technology-based manifestos should have easy-to-remember (and easy-to-pronounce) names, so they are easy to refer to and come to mind easily.
- ○ **Intellectual Traction:** Ideas that catch fire tend to have intellectual traction, and they have to have broad meaning to a lot of people (even if the ideas themselves are ambiguous and interpretable in multiple ways). The core ideas of a technology-based manifesto have to resonate. It helps further if the ideas actually are seen to contribute to and to benefit society.
- ○ **Glamor:** People tend to pay attention to glamorous individuals and concepts. It helps to have a spokesperson and / or spokespeople who are memorable and embody the concepts they extol. People also understand ideas through the so-called "personality frame," and the more salient the personality, the easier it is to remember and possibly follow that personality.

If some of the above may be defined, quantized, and made objectively observable, it may be possible to operationalize these variables ("co-variates" in survival analysis) for further analysis to see if there are actual associational relationships. This would take the survival analysis beyond description and into something that is more predictive. Finally, technology-based manifestos may be fully successful even if they never go broadly public. Some manifestos are written to smaller audiences and apply to more local stakeholders. Others are written to attract the attention of a general public right away (Mozilla Manifesto, You Are Not a Gadget, Industrial Society and its Future / Unabomber Manifesto, the BINC Manifesto, and others). That said, it may also be true that remaining in obscurity is a dominated (losing) strategy.

COMPUTER ASSISTED QUALITATIVE DATA ANALYSIS (CAQDAS)-SUPPORTED MANUAL CODING (WITH DATA QUERIES)

A CAQDAS tool enables users to collect, curate, code, and analyze data in a broad range of ways. This section covers some of the affordances of NVivo 11 Plus, one of the foremost CAQDAS tools in the world.

A Word Frequency Count Query

To understand points of emphasis, researchers may run word frequency counts over the textual data. For this step, the author chose to run the count on the full set of 233 texts and all the coding in an NVivo project file. The idea here is to pack the project sufficiently with relevant texts in order to see how some of the clustering visualizations look in the tool. Here, 1000 most frequent words were extracted and all words on the built-in stopwords list and words less than 3 characters in length were omitted. A resulting word cloud gives a gist of these types of manifestos, with words mentioned more often represented in larger text and along the vertical axis (Figure 17). The same word frequency count data may be represented as a treemap and other hierarchy charts (like sunbursts).

The extracted words from a frequency count may clustered by word similarity…and then visualized as a 2D cluster diagram, a 3D cluster diagram, a dendrogram (horizontal or vertical), or even a ring lattice graph (circle graph). A 3D cluster diagram is visualized in Figure 18.

Figure 17. A word cloud from a word frequency count of the entire project's texts

A Text Search Query

As noted earlier, value-laden words seem to play an important role in the technology-based manifestos. To explore what the role of "conscience" may be in the text set, a Text Search Query was run over all the data. A resulting interactive word tree was created that showed the context of the use of the term in the texts…and enabled access to the underlying text sets by double-clicking on any of the branches (Figure 19).

A Geographical Query

Another capability in this particular CAQDAS tool is the ability to analyze geographical information and to map it. To continue with the theme of

Figure 18. Frequently Occurring Words in a Corpus Clustered by Similarity and Depicted as a 3D Cluster Diagram

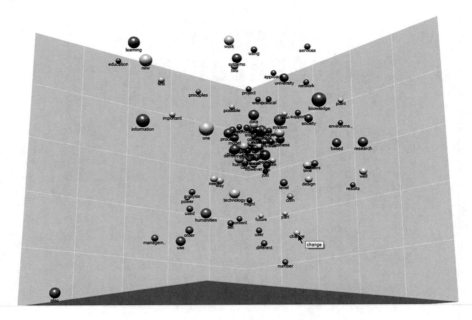

Figure 19. "Conscience" word tree with a branch highlighted

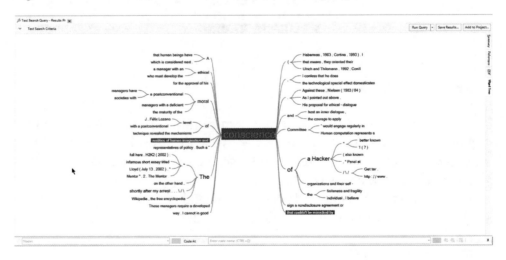

technology-based manifestos, a number of Twitter accounts linked to manifestos were analyzed, but most had dated out or had few microblogging messages. Finally, the researcher settled on McKenzie Wark's Twitter account, which had 19,780 Tweets, 259 following, 9,369 followers, and 3,695 likes (https://twitter.com/mckenziewark). Wark (@mckenziewark) is the author of The Hacker's Manifesto and is an educator. The Tweetstream captured comprised 3,200 messages including retweets. His map, shown in Figure 20, shows a suitably global social network that is actually worldwide.

A Social Network Map

One other type of extraction that may be done from a social media data extraction is that of a social network map (sociogram). Figure 21 captures those whom @mckenziewark follows in an out-degree directional graph (digraph) based on the ego neighborhood of @mckenziewark. If there is interest in trying to understand who the individuals are who are supporting a particular manifesto, it may be possible to not only view public sign-up lists of signatories, but if there are social media accounts supporting particular manifestos, and if the accounts are public and data may be shared from the social media platforms (such as through application programming interfaces), it may be possible to infer some of the members.

Figure 20. Mapping the geographical network of @McKenzieWark's recent Tweetstream on Twitter

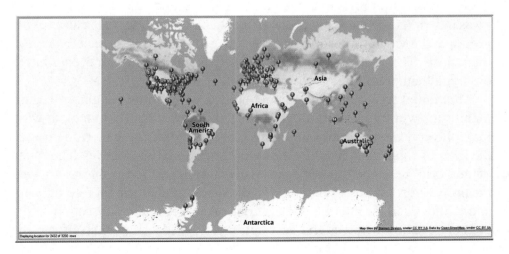

Figure 21. A related Sociogram of @McKenzieWark's recent Tweetstream on Twitter

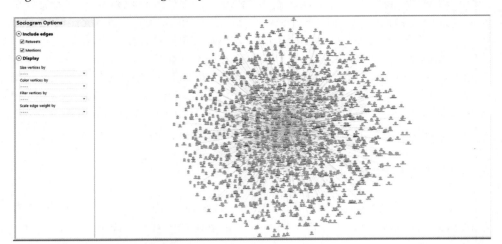

A Codebook Extraction

One of the main strengths of a CAQDAS tool is to capture the unique insights of a human coder in a computational way and then to run various coding and other queries against that conceptual structure. A quick analysis of the 16 technology-based manifestos resulted in four main sections, under which the other concepts could be subsumed: 1StateoftheWorld, 2AnimatingValues, 3StatedGoalsObjectives, and 4Methods. The 1StateoftheWorld explains the manifesto writers' senses of the context in which they are living and being. 2AnimatingValues refer to the ideals, principles, and values that they abide by as individuals and groups. 3StatedGoalsObjectives refer to the aims of the group, and 4Methods describe the various strategies and tactics to achieve those aims. The codes of the codebook were labeled using camel case based on digital data traditions.

This initial rough draft of a codebook surfaced some insights. Because manifestos win followers through their ideas, it was helpful to look at ways that followers may be drawn in. In this sense, the texts could be read through the filter of "appeal"—in both rational and emotional approaches. The "state of the world" described people's senses of reality, identified problems, showed the proposed solutions, and often described possible ideational futures (with and without certain intermediary actions taken). A major subsection of the methods section involves the description of the identities that inform the action, such as "hacker," "hacktivist," or "cypherpunk." Aligned with various flavors of identity were references to words like "conscience" and ethics and fairness. The actualization of an identity linked to a manifesto is apparently a driving motivation for participants. The codebook is suggestive of some themes. One observation is that while some technology-based manifestos point to revolution and law-breaking, others advocate working within the law and in a context of understanding of competing (and not necessarily conflictual) aims, such as the balance of people's need for privacy protections but balanced against government's law enforcement objectives. The manifestos, in other words, were bounded or delimited in different ways, with different redlines about what would or would not be permissible. At the far edge, one mentioning the possibility of violence to achieve aims and in the world, that was backstopped by actual violence and mayhem over a 17-year period ("FBI 100: The Unabomber," Apr. 24, 2008). An exploration of the coded text to each segment may be analyzed for further insights. While coding usually occurs at phrase and sentence levels, this quick exploration involved some coded segments that involved a large number of paragraphs in one mass coding…to speed up the work (Figure 22).

A codebook enables identification of some ideas that interweave across different technology-based manifestos. In this case, the coding surfaced general strategic elements in these manifestos

Figure 22. First run at a rough codebook in an outline format from a CAQDAS Tool

Nodes

Name	Sources	References	Created On	Created By	Modified On	Modified By
1StateoftheWorld	7	19	8/18/2016 1:09 PM	SHJ	8/18/2016 4:51 PM	SHJ
1ExplanationRationale	4	14	8/18/2016 4:18 PM	SHJ	8/18/2016 4:53 PM	SHJ
2IntergenerationalTensions	1	1	8/18/2016 12:36 PM	SHJ	8/18/2016 4:53 PM	SHJ
3ASenseofPrecursorWork	1	1	8/18/2016 3:11 PM	SHJ	8/18/2016 4:53 PM	SHJ
2AnimatingValues	8	13	8/18/2016 12:19 PM	SHJ	8/18/2016 4:51 PM	SHJ
1PrinciplesandSystemsViews	1	1	8/18/2016 1:20 PM	SHJ	8/18/2016 4:53 PM	SHJ
2IdealizedRationales	2	2	8/18/2016 12:26 PM	SHJ	8/18/2016 4:53 PM	SHJ
3AMultivoiceStrategy	2	3	8/18/2016 12:35 PM	SHJ	8/18/2016 4:53 PM	SHJ
4PossibleFutures	2	7	8/18/2016 4:35 PM	SHJ	8/18/2016 4:54 PM	SHJ
3StatedGoalsObjectives	2	3	8/18/2016 12:37 PM	SHJ	8/18/2016 4:51 PM	SHJ
1EnvisionedSolutions	1	2	8/18/2016 12:55 PM	SHJ	8/18/2016 4:54 PM	SHJ
2RationaleofCapabilities	1	1	8/18/2016 12:22 PM	SHJ	8/18/2016 4:55 PM	SHJ
3AlternativesasNon-options	1	2	8/18/2016 1:23 PM	SHJ	8/18/2016 4:54 PM	SHJ
4AuthorPledgeCommitment	1	1	8/18/2016 4:11 PM	SHJ	8/18/2016 4:54 PM	SHJ
5AnticipatedArgumentsAgainst	1	11	8/18/2016 12:27 PM	SHJ	8/18/2016 5:11 PM	SHJ
4Methods	7	7	8/18/2016 12:44 PM	SHJ	8/18/2016 4:52 PM	SHJ
1RationaleofProgress	1	1	8/18/2016 12:22 PM	SHJ	8/18/2016 4:55 PM	SHJ
TechnologiesMentioned	1	2	8/18/2016 12:19 PM	SHJ	8/18/2016 12:21 PM	SHJ
2IdentityandActualization	5	6	8/18/2016 12:36 PM	SHJ	8/18/2016 4:53 PM	SHJ
3CalltoRevolution	1	1	8/18/2016 1:25 PM	SHJ	8/18/2016 4:56 PM	SHJ
4Outreach	1	1	8/18/2016 12:19 PM	SHJ	8/18/2016 4:56 PM	SHJ
1NamedAudience	1	1	8/18/2016 4:23 PM	SHJ	8/18/2016 5:12 PM	SHJ
2RequestsforSupport	1	1	8/18/2016 12:26 PM	SHJ	8/18/2016 5:12 PM	SHJ
3CoordinationforDonations	1	1	8/18/2016 12:26 PM	SHJ	8/18/2016 5:12 PM	SHJ
5DelimitingtheWork	1	1	8/18/2016 1:31 PM	SHJ	8/18/2016 4:57 PM	SHJ
6SenseofLawbreaking	1	1	8/18/2016 12:34 PM	SHJ	8/18/2016 5:13 PM	SHJ
RespectfortheLawasaTheme	1	1	8/18/2016 12:24 PM	SHJ	8/18/2016 12:24 PM	SHJ

A Matrix Coding Query

A matrix coding query enables a researcher to compare coding by using a matrix structure. Here, the author compared the manual coding against the machine-coded themes and subthemes. This resulted in a very sparse matrix. In this particular case, the matrix was quite sparse, showing little overlap. A naïve glance at it might suggest that this matrix is a binary one (only 0s and 1s), but the matrix coding query actually results in intensity matrices (so allowing 0+ numbers to represent the intensity of relationships). What this matrix shows is that there is very little overlap between the human coding of the text set and the machine learning (autocoding by theme and sub-theme) (Figure 23). The pullout at the right in this figure shows the sparseness.

MACHINE READING AND AUTOCODING

Finally, the third approach involves the use of computational means to interpret text sets through "machine reading". There are two general approaches. Unsupervised machine learning does not use human pre-labeled data to run

Figure 23. Overlap between manual coded and autocoded themes

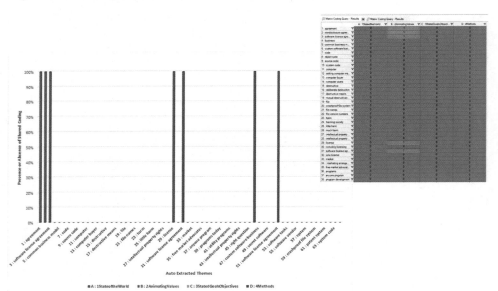

its analyses; supervised machine learning refers to human-labeled data as a basis for the computer autocoding. Ultimately, autocoding here is used to extract meaning from the text sets.

A Sentiment Analysis

A sentiment analysis of the 16 manifestos showed that there were four that engaged sentiment words heavily. They are, in descending order: You Are Not a Gadget, Cluetrain Manifesto, Unabomber Manifesto, and the GNU Project (Figure 24). The pullout image at the right of this figure shows the 16 manifestos and the respective levels of sentiment word instances across the four sentiment categories (very negative, moderately negative, moderately positive, and very positive). The four categories may be collapsed into the two categories representing the polarities of "positive" and "negative" sentiment.

A Theme and Sub-Theme Extraction

Theme and subtheme extraction is based on topic modeling, or the condensed representation of texts based on computationally extracted features. The theme and sub-theme autocoding feature in NVivo 11 Plus extracted 48 themes (in alphabetical order): business, change, community, computer, corporate, data, database, design, development, expression, form, group,

Figure 24. Four of 16 manifestos with relatively high sentiment words (in four categories)

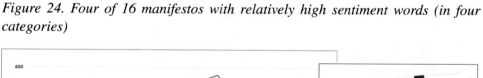
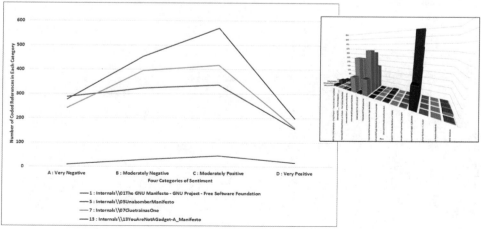

human, idea, individual, industry, information, internet, key, knowledge, language, leftist, man, marketing, music, operator, people, personal, power, process, product, program, public, reality, relation, rights, society, software, system, technological, time, traditional, transaction, type, use, value, work, and world. All of these themes were accepted without change by the author. (In the autocoding theme / subtheme extraction wizard, the software user may uncheck extracted themes / subthemes as desired.) The subthemes tend to be literal occurrences of the particular top-level themes albeit with related terms. For example, the subthemes to data include: "access privat (sic) data, big data, data entry specialist, data forensics, data formats, data streams, enough data, hailstorm data, runtime data, and scalar data type". While one common visualization of the data is in a sparse text-theme matrix, a more visually appealing data visualization is as an interactive treemap (Figure 25).

An autocoded theme extraction shows the main topics in a corpora and enables the analysis also of what each text contributed to the total. From this data, article histograms may be created to show how each manifesto contributes in terms of the main identified themes from the text set. Each text invariably has a unique histogram. Depending on the size of the corpus, some histograms may be wholly sparse, with 0s in every cell, indicating that the article has contributed nothing (in terms of word counts) to the extracted themes. In Figure 26, there is a manifesto histogram for the Cluetrain Manifesto, with the theme/subtheme intensity matrix in the background.

Figure 25. An interactive hierarchical treemap of auto-extracted themes and subthemes from the technology-based manifesto corpus

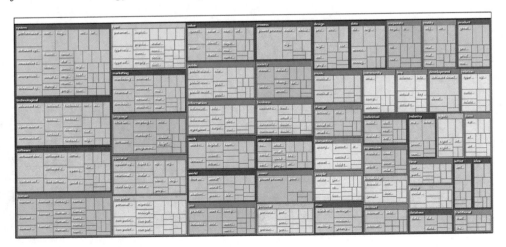

Figure 26. An article histogram of the "Cluetrain Manifesto" with the theme intensity matrix in the background (depicted in excel)

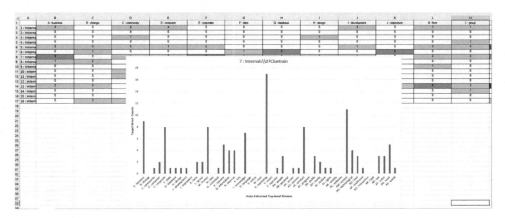

If all the manifestos were combined into one text set and themes / subthemes were extracted from that one file, the top-level themes tend to be more condensed and simpler than if they were extracted from a set of all 16 manifestos as their own stand-alone files. Figure 27 shows the smaller set of top-level extracted themes from a combined set of all 16 technology manifestos. It is important to understand that how data is touched affects the types of information that are extractable through data mining and machine learning practices.

With sufficient and appropriately selected text files, it is possible to map an area or domain to capture the main themes and related subthemes…based on word counts.

Note: To run a theme and sub-theme extraction in NVivo 11 Plus, the PDF files had to be changed to MS Word ones to enable processing. (This is not always the case with data in NVivo 11 Plus, but when there are complex files that include images and annotations, it's better to go with simpler file formats to enable the processing. There were a half-dozen attempts to do the coding using the portable document format files before the author changed to the .docx file format.)

Coding by Existing Pattern

This approach is a human-supervised type of machine learning because the computer is informed by labeled data. To show how the coding by

Figure 27. Main themes from the technology-based manifesto corpus (as a bar chart)

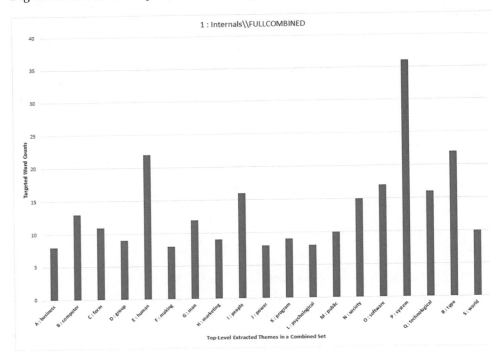

existing pattern works, a messy and uncleaned set of the original manifestos (including some extra copies of the target 16 manifestos) were used…and the coding pattern applied is the one shown earlier with the four top-level sections: 1StateoftheWorld, 2AnimatingValues, 3StatedGoalsObjectives, and 4Methods. The setting was left at the midpoint between "less" and "more" in terms of "how much coding" NVivo would create. The Auto Code Wizard showed varying levels of accuracy in its coding based on the exemplars created (in the suitability analysis), but the author still decided to go through with all the levels of coding even if some of the coding may be machine-coded with a little less confidence. Because of the structure of the text in the manifestos, the autocoding was done at sentence level (vs. paragraph or cell levels respectively).

To be clear, the original (rough) human-coding was done based on the 16 original technology-based manifestos. Those 16 represent only 7% of the full set that was re-coded by NVivo 11 Plus through the "autocoding by existing pattern" tool. Of the 217 from the larger uncleaned text set, 99 were found to have relevant coding to contribute to the four human-coded top-level nodes and related subnodes. A Cohen's Kappa analysis of the comparison between the coding between the person and the computer ranged from 0.5 to 1 (anything less than 100% agreement is treated as 0.5). The capability of applying computational coding efficiencies to a human coding codebook with high accuracy is a powerful feature (Figure 28). Researchers may add other texts over time and apply the human-made coding structure to particular folders. What this tool doesn't do is add new nodes to the original codebook based on what is read using the "autocoding by existing pattern." (To have the machine create wholly new nodes, a researcher may use the "autocoding by sentiment" and the "autocoding by theme," both of which were introduced earlier.)

So how did the machine coding (based on the human-created codebook) turn out? The two main top-level codes that were most popular were 1StateoftheWorld and 4Methods (Figure 29).

"NV," the software, only identified 99 of the 233 technology-based manifestos as contributing some text to the four coded nodes (and all related subnodes). This may reflect some of the messiness of the initial text set. Recall that some of the texts were manifestos written as political party platforms, and others were public relations creations for companies. This may suggest that the original human-created codebook was overfit to the original 16

Figure 28. A coding comparison query between the human coder and "NV" through the autocoding by existing pattern feature

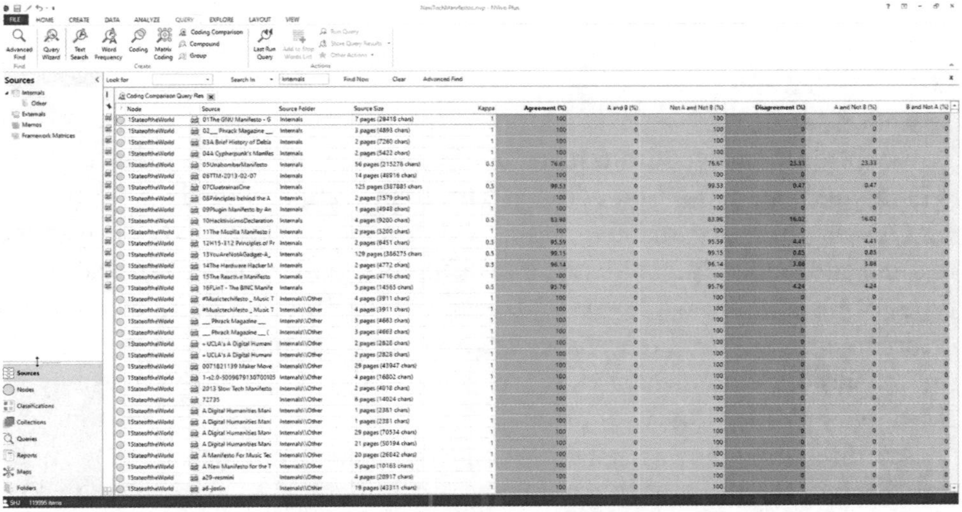

Figure 29. Frequency of coding to the four coding nodes (autocoding by existing patterns based on human created codebook)

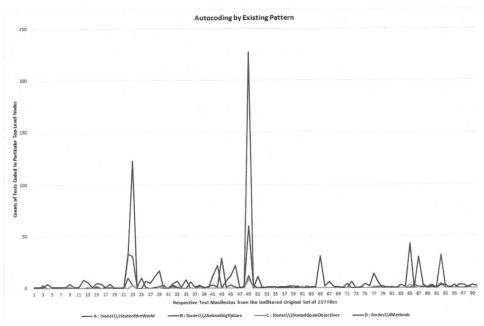

manifestos and so was not as applicable to the full set of 233 texts. All said, the autocoding now enables a human research to approach the texts based on the codebook concepts.

DISCUSSION

To recap, the main hypothesis read: "Different types of textual coding methods [(1) manual method-based coding (with light computational supports), (2) CAQDAS-supported manual coding (with data queries), and (3) machine reading and autocoding] will result in different (non-overlapping) observable types of insights from a text set." To explore this, the author made a serious effort in each of the three phases to discover what may be learnable from the technology-based manifesto text set(s) and to generalize what may be learnable broadly from various texts.

An initial thought was that there could be some way to measure how much time each of the three coding methods took as compared to the insights that each enabled. Very early in the process, it became clear that each of the three approaches require human insight and some intimacy with the data. Each approach requires effort at data collection and data pre-processing. Each requires human oversight and review; after all, no result (however it is arrived at) is uncritically accepted. How much time a process requires for one researcher than another will differ, and the research design and research questions will also affect the required inputs. Each of the three textual coding methods are cognitively challenging, but each also enables various strengths. Also, the work of going through the textual data with different means enabled recursive review of prior findings to see if those are actually valid, and they enabled the discovery of new insights.

A general research approach may be conceptualized as the following semi-recursive sequence (the left column in Table 3), then it is helpful to conceptualize some of the requirements for each of the three approaches: research design <-> data collection <-> data pre-processing / cleaning <-> data queries <-> machine reading <-> autocoding <-> data visualizations <-> data analytics <-> extraction of insights <-> data table exports <-> further analytics.

Table 3. Required processes in the respective three data coding approaches

	(1) Manual Method-Based Coding (With Light Computational Supports)	**(2) CAQDAS-Supported Manual Coding (With Data Queries)**	**(3) Machine Reading and Autocoding**
Research Design (or Open Data Discovery Approach)	x	x	x
Data Collection	x	x	x
Data Pre-Processing / Cleaning		x	x
Data Queries (Exploratory Methods)	x	x	x
Machine Reading		x	x
Autocoding			x
Data Visualizations	x	x	x
Data Analytics	x	x	x
Extraction of Insights	x	x	x
Data Table Exports	x	x	x
Further Analytics	X	X	x

In this chapter, the three coding methods were conducted in the following ways:

1. Manual method-based coding (with light computational supports)
   a. A feature count
   b. A questions brainstorm
   c. A linguistic analysis (LIWC)
   d. A survival analysis (SPSS)
2. CAQDAS-supported manual coding (with data queries)
   a. A word frequency count query
   b. A text search query
   c. A geographical query
   d. A social network map
   e. A codebook extraction
   f. A matrix coding query
3. Machine reading and autocoding
   a. A sentiment analysis
   b. A theme and subtheme extraction
   c. Coding by existing pattern

The initial intuition is that human coding will diverge from computational textual coding in terms of insights, even though one underlying text set will be used. Also, it was thought that there will be some convergence around some ideas and observations, because of the underlying data. To operationalize this, 16 technology-based manifestos named in a Wikipedia article were used for the in-depth research. Several dozen other manifestos were briefly summarized to give a sense of the technology-based manifesto "space." Because the focus is actually on manual and computational coding methods, the analytics related to the tech manifestos is limited and not refined to a higher degree. At core, the idea is that there is a difference between what may be seen by a human coder and computationally-attained insights.

Three basic types of coding were employed to analyze technology-based manifestos: (1) manual method-based coding, (2) Computer Assisted Qualitative Data AnalysiS (CAQDAS)-supported manual coding, and (3) machine reading and autocoding. In the manual coding scenario, the technology-based manifestos were analyzed by hand and through the use of some basic office desktop software programs. In the CAQDAS-supported manual coding, the selected technology-based manifestos were analyzed through manual coding in the CAQDAS tool and through data queries enabled by the software. In the third scenario, the technology manifestos were analyzed using unsupervised machine learning, through the machine reading (using the computer to interpret or decode text) and autocoding features (sentiment analysis, theme and subtheme extraction, and "coding by existing pattern") of the CAQDAS tool. This "three ways" approach was selected to enable analysis of the affordances and constraints of each of the respective analytical methods and to find ways to augment each of the approaches. Table 4 contains some of the affordances and constraints of each of the approaches.

The concept of equifinality suggests that different approaches may each attain the desired end state; in research, this idea is sometimes applied to competing research models, which may result in data convergence. Another analogous approach in research is the comparison of the results from various research and data analytics methods—to assess how much agreement there may be about the same underlying data and to understand biases (leanings) in various methods. New computational models may be tested against human expert coding to assess efficacy and also to tune new systems. This equifinality approach (Do results coalesce around basic insights? Do results ultimately converge?) does not directly apply here because the approaches apparently surface different insights from high-dimensionality textual data. To validate or invalidate particular approaches and findings, a researcher would have to apply unique techniques in each approach for insights. Table 5 highlights some validation methods for the respective three approaches.

While this approach might suggest some clear delineations between the three coding approaches, this is actually somewhat artificial. Most researchers do not take a purely manual coding approach without any use of technologies; many will integrate some light computational capabilities. Also, those who take a CAQDAS-based approach to data analytics may well bring in some aspects of manual coding and some aspects of autocoding. Also, few would use purely automated means to conduct data coding and forgo any form of manual coding. In other words, it is fairly rare to take only one approach exclusively and to exclude others (once researchers have crossed the Rubicon of using CAQDAS tools for more than manual coding). These data coding methods can be highly complementary and mutually enhancing to each other. Further, data analytics methods may be additive and accretive in terms of insights.

In terms of the types of insights captured with each of the three methods, specifically to the particular text sets, manual methods with light computational supports (1) enabled ways to extract features and to count them for some insights into the text set (from close reading). It enabled the brainstorming of a broad range of questions as points-of-entry to understanding the topic (and

Table 4. Affordances and constraints of manual, CAQDAS-supported, and machine reading and autocoding data coding of texts

(1) Manual Method-Based Coding (With Light Computational Support)		(2) CAQDAS-Supported Manual Coding		(3) Machine Reading and Autocoding	
Pros (Affordances)	Cons (Constraints)	Pros (Affordances)	Cons (Constraints)	Pros (Affordances)	Cons (Constraints)
• Encouragement to theorize and apply the imagination and past learning and experiences • Focus on examining patterns from close reading • Pursuit of the "telling detail" to evoke an in-world phenomenon • Engagement of brainstorming for breadth and depth • Emphasis on reflection • Pursuit of customized and local insights • Applications of light computational analysis (such as "survival" or "time-to-event" analysis) • Ability to bring in specific software tools that address particular aspects of the data exploration and coding • Nuanced attention to details, including differentiating between connotative and denotative meanings	• Non-trivial time investment • Sufficient academic and other training often required • Not reproducible by other researchers per se (which aligns with the broad assumptions of qualitative research)	• Ability to handle bigger data • Ability to apply data queries (word frequency count, word search, mapping, social network diagrams) • Ability to code data based on a unique human coding "fist" • Expression of rich data visualizations • Enablement to conduct Cohen's Kappa similarity analysis (dyadically—between two coders) on team coding projects • Ability to export data for analysis in other software tools	• Investment in initial training on the software • Non-trivial cost of proprietary software • Dependency on proprietary software and file types • Data pre-processing / cleaning required • Initial coding required if data queries are run on the manually-created code	• Ability to handle bigger data (but not big data unless the software is hosted off servers and the big data is available) • Higher speeds and efficiencies in data processing • Coding by existing pattern • Autocoding for sentiment analysis (with the ability to review underlying coded text) • Autocoding for theme and sub-theme extraction • Expression of underlying data tables through rich data visualizations • Generalized insights of "inherent" patterns in the textual data based on the original text set • Reproducibility of text analyses through autocoding • Ability to re-apply unique coding "fist" on new data • Ability to export data for analysis in other software tools	• Investment in initial training on the software • Non-trivial cost of software • Requirement for data pre-processing / cleaning • Hidden algorithms in some third-party software tools (and the need to make inferences about what is going on within the software and through the algorithms) • Requirement for textualization of analog and multimedia information (transcoding)
Possible Augmentations to Manual Coding		Possible Augmentations to CAQDAS-Supported Manual Coding		Possible Augmentations to Machine Reading and Autocoding	
• Ways to bring technologies alongside the close reading work o to enhance what may be knowable only through basic human coding o to add some efficiencies in data analytics • Ways to strengthen the human imagination and creativity when it comes to data analytics • Ways to strengthen conceptualization of variables • Ways to expand human capabilities to create new manual data analytics techniques		Ways to balance the CAQDAS technological affordances (manual coding in the software, data queries, data visualizations, statistical analyses for similarity, and others) with the close reading and rumination that may benefit the coding and research work … and the automated unsupervised machine learning autocoding benefits of built-in tools for pattern mining from textual data		• Ways to better understand unsupervised machine learning approaches based on the built-in algorithms (from more documentation from software creators) • Ways to better use human-supervised machine learning (with labeled data) to improve the coding and analysis work • Ways to use data queries to enhance findings from autocoded text sets • Ways to bring human analytics to delve into machine reading and autocoding insights (such as through hypothesizing, theorizing, and analysis)	

Table 5. Validation methods of manual, CAQDAS-supported, and machine reading and autocoding data coding

Validation Methods for Manual Coding (With Light Computational Support With Non-CAQDAS Software)	Validation Methods for CAQDAS-Supported Manual Coding	Validation Methods for Machine Reading and Autocoding
• Peer critique • Built-in validation methods and confidence intervals for survival analysis (based on various models) • Research findings supporting or not supporting hypotheses and predictions	• Reproducibility in other software tools • Repeatability within NVivo 11 Plus (reliability)	• Reproducibility in other software tools • Repeatability within NVivo 11 Plus (reliability) • Linguistic Inquiry and Word Count (LIWC) validity and reliability of constructs

knowing what to code for). It enabled a linguistic analysis to better understand the textual contents if the respective manifestos and overlapping style elements across the various texts. It enabled survival analysis understandings of points at which technology-based manifestos might break out and led to theorizing about what "hazards" might lead to manifesto breakouts. The CAQDAS-supported manual coding (with data queries) (2) highlighted data summaries of the text sets through word clouds from word frequency counts. It enabled deeper understandings of the frequently used words and the similarities between them through cluster analyses. A word search query led to word trees that showed the proxemics contexts of words and their contextual meanings. A geographical query—in this case—highlighted the geographical locations of the @mckenziewark social network on Twitter based on a recent Tweetstream, and that network was also portrayed in a social network map. A more heavy-duty approach involved the creating of a codebook extraction based on a human reader's engagement with the underlying texts and identifying themes from across the text corpus. This codebook was reorganized as an outline, and as a digital codebook, it could be and was applied to an autocoding application. (It could also be shared with other human coders for shared coding duties… or as a hand-off for future researchers.) A matrix coding query was run to compare the human coding and autocoding. Matrix coding queries may be done with all sorts of codes created both manually and automatically. Finally, machine reading and autocoding (3) was done to acquire insights about sentiment. One insight about the data was that there were huge variances between manifestos in their expression of sentiment and then in how much sentiment was in each particular work…and what the underlying text sets showed about what the authors saw as positive and negative. A theme and subtheme extraction highlighted the huge disparity between what a human coder would see as relevant vs. what the algorithms identified as relevant from the respective works individually and from the corpus. Finally, the coding by existing pattern used the human-created codebook in order to identify relevant text from a larger set of source texts, thus amplifying the reach of the human coder and his/her/their insights.

The third initial research question dealt with the strengths and weaknesses of using all three coding methods. As this chapter showed, using all three methods provides a broader overlay of non-similar data from the underlying source text sets, and the respective observations from the various methods can benefit stand-alone methods. Further, the findings from each method can be used to compare and contrast insights from other methods (such as conducting a matrix coding query from both manual and computational coding). In a data exploratory phase, there may be many benefits to attaining a wide range of insights, especially for researchers who are comfortable with informational complexity. There may be benefits to exploring larger text sets with machine reading and then formulating a strategy for selective close reading. In other cases, machine reading may be applied for a data cleaning sequence, in order to decide what to include and what to exclude from the text corpus. That said, the abundance of insights—and these are not the only ones available in the three categories—will require the researcher or research team to have clear objectives and focus. The capabilities have to contribute to answering the research questions; the methods have to capture insights that may be useful in particular analytical and decision-making contexts.

There are potential insights unique to each approach. Close reading seems like a positive way of encouraging researcher intimacy with his / her / their data; this approach can bring in more unique insights that are possible based on complex human backgrounds and thinking capabilities and their power of imagination and analysis. In terms of CAQDAS-supported coding, there are certain types of underlying patterns that be extracted through this method and not others, such as codebook structure, word frequency tables and visualizations, and text searches with unique word trees. The use of CAQDAS software enables unique ways for researchers to engage their data. Third, the machine reading and autocoding approach enables the extraction of yet further patterns in textual data based on sentiment analysis, the extraction of themes and subthemes, and so on. As noted in Table 4, there are various ways to augment the respective research approaches.

This preliminary work is too limited to answer broader questions about when each coding method should be used and to surface what types of insights and in which research contexts. Some general observations have been made which are generalizable, but the degree of that generalizability is not yet fully clear. This work is descriptive, not prescriptive.

Finally, this chapter has highlighted some insights about technology-based manifestos—their general structures, their technological focuses, their apparent break-out patterns, their linguistic contents, and so on. This initial work suggests at the power of ideas to animate people to actions. As a potent example, one of the authors of the manifestos in this selected set is serving eight life sentences in the ADX Florence SuperMax Prison in Colorado for trying to actualize his vision (through violence). In general, the metrics used here are somewhat indirect in regards to the effects of a manifesto. It would be helpful to find ways to tie a manifesto's ideas and calls for action to actual actions, such as tangible code, Internet films, collaborating volunteer work groups, or ambitious social change. It would be interesting to know how much manifestos are in the lives of their authors and co-authors.

FUTURE RESEARCH DIRECTIONS

This work explored whether using different manual-to-high-tech approaches to coding textual data would result in observably different insights from a text set of technology-based manifestos. The thinking was that there would be observable differences and that this knowledge could enhance the work of the respective three textual coding approaches and could be helpful in research design and data exploration. Hypothesis #1 and the two related sub-hypotheses have been borne out. So what comes next?

Richer Manual Coding Approaches

This work highlighted several manual (with light computational supports) coding approaches. One of the statistical methods used was a light version of survival analysis, with all the texts belonging to an initial set of pre-outbreak tech manifestos. This analytical technique may be applied to the same set of manifestos but with different ways to defining the outbreak "event." Or a larger set of manifestos may be analyzed to see if the pattern of either early or much later breakout occurs. If the technology manifestos are represented as a set of features, it is possible to see if there are certain features that may be associated with breakout ("event") or right-censoring ("non-event" during the span of the research observation) or early-breakout or late-breakout, etc.

Even more complex observations may be made with the Cox Proportional Hazards Model, which enables the testing of associations of co-variates to survival / non-survival and how hazards change over time. The time unit used in this work was annual, but it is possible to go to even more granular time, assuming the underlying information is available and "events" may be defined to the month and year, for example. Of interest would be ways to assess what trajectory the respective technology-based manifestos are on. Are they gathering strength over time, or are they undergoing diminishing power? If the manifesto experiences "burstiness" in terms of popularity, what is causing this?

Sequentiality of Data Coding and Analytics

This work contains some potential follow-on working hypotheses, such as that the sequence of deploying the (1) manual method-based coding (with light computational supports), (2) Computer-Assisted Qualitative Data AnalysiS (CAQDAS)-supported manual coding (with data queries), and (3) machine reading and autocoding will also affect the available insights. Technologically intensive exploration of data may result in different insights than if the researcher started with manual analytics (as was done in this case), *ceteris paribus*. To see what some of these other sequences might look like, based on the capabilities of the software tools used in this chapter, Figure 30 provides a sampler. These sequences may represent the full entirety of the data analytics sequence, or they may be a part of a larger multi-part sequence. Note that the arrows are not just forward pointing to represent linearity but are double-headed, which suggests a semi-recursiveness as needed. Data queries and machine learning sequences are often iterative and recursive ones. These technologies should be applied based on researcher agency and not in some sort of deterministic lock-step. And further, each step should be documented closely so that they may be remembered and repeated (as "macros").

Exposure to a machine-based structure of data may unduly affect the researcher's mental conceptualizations and models, whether consciously or subconsciously. The role of the researcher is not to necessarily affirm machine-based findings unthinkingly but to harness the data to discover new insights. The converse is also true—that computationally supported coding is not necessarily set up to affirm human coding, but in cases where there may be coding overlaps, there may be light "checks" on the manual and the computational coding. Observations of computational insights may skew

Figure 30. A small sampler of mixed textual coding sequences starting with computational analyses

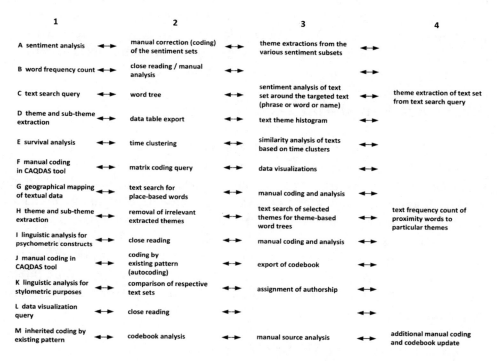

researcher interpretations of the data. In the same way that people cannot "unlearn" something that they've learned, and that learning occurs on both conscious and subconscious and unconscious levels, people cannot "unsee" computer analyzed results nor necessarily erase potential influences of observing computationally extracted insights. This is why having a tactical ordering of researcher observations may be helpful to the work. Researchers may also benefit from being open to seeing familiar data in new ways, which various computational approaches enable.

Designed Pauses in Data Coding and Analytics

Similarly, putting in pauses or time-interruptions between one application to another may benefit the overall data analytics because this allows time for researchers to reflect on the research and data. Sometimes, if multiple methods are applied intensively simultaneously, that will allow one mental effect vs. others that are more delayed and stretched out in time. Any of the approaches described may provide fodder for follow-on efforts.

Another follow-on working hypothesis can be that there is a foundational difference between the resulting codebooks using the three respective textual coding methods. A codebook is a representation of the coding used to extract meaning from textual (and multimedia and analog) data.

Other Case-Based Approaches

This work provided a case-based approach surrounding analysis of technology-based manifestos. For others focusing on different types of data and research, their respective cases may provide fresh insights about what the three approaches may offer and the amount of assertability they can make based on the data coding. It may be that there are some optimal sequences and methods for particular cases in particular domains. It is also possible that people may generalize about coding approaches that work optimally for particular general non-case-based contexts, and insights regarding those would also be helpful. Follow-on works may be more prescriptive whereas this chapter is mostly descriptive.

Integration of Other Technologies

There may be research on various other types of technologies that may be harnessed to actualize the three approaches: (1) manual method-based coding (with light computational supports), (2) Computer-Assisted Qualitative Data AnalysiS (CAQDAS)-supported manual coding (with data queries), and (3) machine reading and autocoding. How would this look with programming languages (like Python and R) and textual analytics packages and command line interfaces? How would this look with different CAQDAS tools? What about actualizing (3) with machine learning approaches as applied to text?

Improving Textual Coding Methods

What are some ways to improve all three textual coding methods—singly and in a synthesized (all three methods) way? Are there ways to improve all three data coding approaches to enable the influence of serendipity and chance inspiration? What are some mistaken approaches and follies in text coding, and how can these be avoided?

A Broader Range of Technology-Based Manifestos for Exploration

As for future research into technology-based manifestos, there are a large number of technology-based manifestos that were not addressed in depth in this work. A fuller set of such manifestos beyond the 16 mentioned in the Wikipedia article could include some of those briefly mentioned here and many others. The target subject could be broadened, with a more formal definition of the more complete text set and even classifications of the various types of technology-based manifestos. By nature, many (all?) technology-based manifestos are global. [As an example, the Agile manifesto is translated into over 65 languages on their website ("Manifesto for Agile Software Development," 2001)]. A rewarding line of inquiry could look at competing and clashing voices around shared issues of interest. It would be intriguing to have researchers map the lingering effects of manifestos, in terms of values, proposed actions, terminology, and mythologies. Do manifestos actually accelerate certain proposed approaches and delay others?

Addressing a Broad Range of Technology-Based Manifesto Research Questions

The question brainstorm offered earlier in this chapter may provide some directions. There may be more direct ways to elicit information about manifesto authors by engaging them directly on social media or phone calls or email, and other means.

There is other follow-on research that may be pursued, which has not been mentioned here. These ideas are a start.

CONCLUSION

Researchers train for many years in order to specialize in their respective fields, and many are capable of finding deep insights in their research data through non-computational means alone. However, that approach is from a prior era and may be woefully limited for the masses and types of textual data that require analysis today. There is something to be said for acquiring the additional computational text analytics skills as yet another researcher capability. Researcher work may benefit from data mining through the uses of CAQDAS tools and machine reading and autocoding. There are benefits to knowing what data analytics software tools are available and to knowing how to wield them strategically and tactically. So much textual data is currently unexplored and unexploited. It is also helpful to consider whether particular steps in a data analytics sequence affect the outcomes. Using technology does not supplant human insights or human agency. The ultimate arbiter of research value is still the researcher and the other stakeholders to the research. Technologies can extend human coding, such as through "coding by existing patterns" to extend the researcher's (or research team's) coding "fist." While it may seem that computational means result in quantitative-based insights and glamorous data visualizations, there are limitations to technological analytics. The optimal approach generally seems to be a "cyborg" one, with both human "manual" and computational means employed. These latter machine learning approaches are not achievable in any other way. [Of course, human coding is not emulable either because of the unique insights of people. One other point: while "big data" is the term *du jour* currently, there are many ways for both people and machines to learn from one example of a thing and extrapolating insights from the one (Winston, 2010, 2014). Discovery is a trained enablement from practiced seeing. While this work is about learning from a set of texts, it is wholly possible to learn a lot from an in-depth reading of one manifesto or one text document or a small text set. Any one exemplar may be informative on its own.]

It may also be said that researchers will use the methods and research tools that they are most comfortable with based on their training, their experiences, and the common practices in their respective fields. The types of research questions asked will define in part what technologies may be harnessed, but the converse is also true—that the technological enablements will inform the types of research questions asked.

The up sides to acquiring computational analytics approaches include the extended ability to benefit from richer augmented and more efficient analytics. There are potential downsides as well, such as turning to computational means as the "go to" and electing to forgo manual coding. Manual analytics is *not* directly replaceable through computational means, and to forgo the manual part may mean unexplored potential nuanced insights, hypotheses, and imaginative interpretations. Research design and data analytics require a complex playbook, which is partially determined by the environmental context. For example, in a context of severe time constraints and the need for some early understandings from dynamic data, it may be that machine learning through machine reading and autocoding is the only reasonable approach—to surge in response to the data. For all the capabilities of machines, it helps to know that it is the human who is animating the issue and that people research and write for each other and each other's betterment, ultimately.

A Note About Technologies: The technologies used in this chapter (in any capacity) include the following: NVivo 11 Plus, IBM's SPSS, Excel, LIWC (Linguistic Inquiry and Word Count), NodeXL (Network Overview, Discovery and Exploration for Excel), Google Books Ngram Viewer, Visio 2016, and Adobe Photoshop.

A Research Note About Manifestos: A recent exploration of the "manifesto" in Google Correlate found that from 2003 to the present (mid-2017) that there have been occasional spikes in the search for this term, in 2007, 2013, and 2014. Usually, these spikes occur when there are real-world events. Based on the time patterns for other searches highly correlated

Figure 31. "Manifesto" searches on Google Search and highly correlated other searches over time from 2003 – mid-2017 in Google Correlate

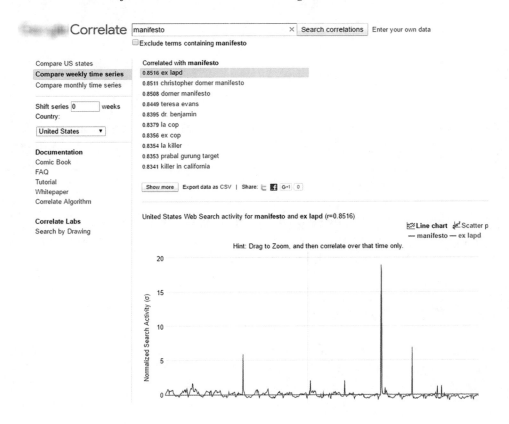

Figure 32. "Manifesto" searches on Google Search and highly correlated other searches over time from 2003 – mid-2017 in Google Correlate compared across the U.S. states

with "manifesto," it seems that most of these are related to violent criminal acts. The line graph below shows the correlation between "manifesto" and "ex lapd" in the Google Search. Google Correlate's data comes from billions of anonymized searches.

Mapped to the U.S. by state, the search terms correlated with "manifesto" change extensively, with more focuses on culture, music, literature, and the arts. The correlations are less crime-based.

REFERENCES

A digital humanities manifesto 1.0. (2008, Dec. 15). Retrieved Aug. 14, 2016, from http://manifesto.humanities.ucla.edu/2008/12/15/digital-humanities-manifesto/

A digital humanities manifesto 2.0. (2009, May 29). Retrieved Aug. 14, 2016, from http://manifesto.humanities.ucla.edu/2009/05/29/the-digital-humanities-manifesto-20/

Almeida, A., & Alvelos, H. (2010). An interactive documentary manifesto. LNCS, 6432, 123 – 128. doi:10.1007/978-3-642-16638-9_16

Becker, C., Chitchyan, R., Duboc, L., Easterbrook, S., Penzenstadler, B., Seyff, N., & Venters, C. C. (2015). Sustainability design and software: The Karlskrona Manifesto. *Proceedings of the 2015 IEEE / ACM 37th IEEE International Conference on Software Engineering*, 467 – 476.

Berghel, H. (2001, March). A cyberpublishing manifesto. Digital Village. *Communications of the ACM*, *44*(3), 17–20. doi:10.1145/365181.365914

Blankenship, L. (1986, Jan. 8). *Hacker Manifesto*. Retrieved Aug. 3, 2016, from https://www.usc.edu/~douglast/202/lecture23/manifesto.html

Bloomsburg, U. Undergraduate 'Manifesto' on Digital Humanities. (2010). *4 Humanities: Advocating for the Humanities*. Retrieved July 25, 2016, from http://4humanities.org/bloomsburg-u-undergraduate-manifesto-on-digital-humanities/

Boehm, B. (2011). Towards richer process principles. *Proceedings of ICSSP'11*, 234. doi:10.1145/1987875.1987918

Bonér, J., Farley, D., Kuhn, R., & Thompson, T. (2014, Sept. 16). *Reactive Manifesto*. Retrieved Aug. 3, 2016, from http://www.reactivemanifesto.org/

Brocious, C. (2010, Sept. 21). The Hardware Hacker Manifesto. *I, Hacker*. Retrieved Aug. 3, 2016, from http://demoseen.com/blog/2010-09-21_The_Hardware_Hacker_Manifesto.html

Brunet, G., Chechik, M., Easterbrook, S., Nejati, S., Niu, N., & Sabetzadeh, M. (2006). A manifesto for model merging. *Proceedings of GaMMa '06*. Retrieved August 1, 2016, from http://www.cultdeadcow.com/cDc_files/declaration.html

Chesbrough, H., & Spohrer, J. (2006, July). A research manifesto for services science. *Communications of the ACM*, *49*(7), 33–40. doi:10.1145/1139922.1139945

Christie, A., Pilsch, A., Ross, S., & Tanigawa, K. (2014, Nov. 13). Manifesto of Modernist Digital Humanities. *dh + lib*. Retrieved Aug. 14, 2016, from http://acrl.ala.org/dh/2014/11/13/resource-manifesto-modernist-digital-humanities/

Cook, S., Kleppe, A., Mitchell, R., Rumpe, B., Warmer, J., & Wills, Alan. (2002). The Amsterdam Manifesto on OCL. *LNCS, 2263,* 115 – 149.

Darwen, H., & Date, C. J. (1995, March). The third manifesto. *SIGMOD Record, 24*(1), 39–49. doi:10.1145/202660.202667

De Roeck, D., Slegers, K., Criel, J., Godon, M., Claeys, L., Kilpi, K., & Jacobs, A. (2012). I would DiYSE for it! A manifesto for do-it-yourself internet-of-things creation. *Proceedings of NordiCHI '12*, 170 – 179.

Denton Declaration. (2012). *Open Access @ UNT*. University of North Texas. Retrieved August 14, 2016, from https://openaccess.unt.edu/denton-declaration

Digital Humanities Manifesto 2.0. (2009, May 29.) Retrieved July 25, 2016, from http://manifesto.humanities.ucla.edu/2009/05/29/the-digital-humanities-manifesto-20/

Durability vs. reproducibility. (n.d.). *The New Digital Humanities Manifesto*. Swarthmore College students. Retrieved July 25, 2016, from http://www.thenewdh.com/durability-vs-reproducibility/

FBI 100: The Unabomber. (2008, Apr. 24). *The U.S. Federal Bureau of Investigations*. Retrieved Aug. 19, 2016, from https://archives.fbi.gov/archives/news/stories/2008/april/unabomber_042408

FemTechNet. (2016). *Manifesto*. Retrieved Aug. 14, 2016, from http://femtechnet.org/publications/manifesto/

First Things First Manifesto 2000. (1999). *Émigré 51. Émigré Essays*. Retrieved July 28, 2016, from http://emigre.com/Editorial.php?sect=1&id=14

Fischer, G., Giaccardi, E., Ye, Y., Sutcliffe, A. G., & Mehandjiev, N. (2004). Meta-design: A manifesto for end-user development. *Communications of the ACM, 47*(9), 33–37. doi:10.1145/1015864.1015884

Garland, K. (1963/1964). *First Things First. Design is History*. Retrieved July 28, 2016, from http://www.designishistory.com/1960/first-things-first/

Hai-Jew, S. (2013). Action Potentials: Extrapolating an Ideology from the Anonymous Hacker Socio-Political Movement (A Qualitative Meta-Analysis). In *Digital Democracy and the Impact of Technology on Governance and Politics: New Globalized Practices* (pp. 51–107). Hershey, PA: IGI-Global. doi:10.4018/978-1-4666-3637-8.ch005

Haraway, D. (2000). A cyborg manifesto: Science, technology and socialist-feminism in the late twentieth century. In D. Bell & B. M. Kennedy (Ed.), The Cybercultures Reader. London: Routledge. doi:10.1007/978-1-137-05194-3_10

Harper, R. (2007). Principles of Programming Languages (2007), by Robert Harper. *Manifesto Portal*. Retrieved Aug. 17, 2016, from http://manifestoindex. blogspot.com/2011/04/principles-of-programming-languages.html

Harper, R. (2015, Dec. 21). *15-312 Principles of Programming Languages*. Retrieved Aug. 17, 2016, from https://www.cs.cmu.edu/~rwh/courses/ppl/ phil.html

Hatch, M. (2014). *The Maker Movement Manifesto: Rules for Innovation in the New World of Crafters, Hackers, and Tinkerers*. New York: McGraw Hill.

Hofman, J. B. (2013). *Slow tech parenting*. Retrieved Aug. 15, 2016, from http://www.janellburleyhofmann.com/slow-tech-manifesto/

How to use digital technologies to foster freedom of expression and information in the Global South: The South2South Manifesto. (2014). Retrieved July 28, 2016, from http://akademie.dw.de/S2Smanifesto

Hughes, E. (1993, Mar. 9). *A Cypherpunk's Manifesto*. Retrieved August 1, 2016, from http://www.activism.net/cypherpunk/manifesto.html

Inbar, O., & Tractinsky, N. (2009, July - August). The incidental user. *Interaction*, 16(4), 56–59. doi:10.1145/1551986.1551998

Jones, C., Lomet, D., Romanovsky, A., Weikum, G., Fekete, A., Gaudel, M.-C., & Rodrigues, L. et al. (2005, March). The Atomic Manifesto: A story in four quarks. *SIGMOD Record*, 34(1), 63–69. doi:10.1145/1058150.1058165

Joslin, S., Brown, R., & Drennan, P. (2007). The gameplay visualization manifesto: A framework for logging and visualization of online gameplay data. *ACM Comput. Entertain.*, 5(3), Article 6. http://doi.acm. org/10.1145/1316511.1316517

Kirkham, R., Vines, J., & Olivier, P. (2015). *Being reasonable: A manifesto for improving the inclusion of disabled people in SIGCHI conferences.* doi:10.1145/2702613.2732497

Kronschnabl, A. (2001). *Plugin Manifesto.* Retrieved Aug. 17, 2016, from http://manifestoindex.blogspot.com/2011/04/plugin-manifesto-by-ana-kronschnabl-web.html

Lanier, J. (2013). *Who Owns the Future?.* New York: Simon & Schuster.

Linehan, C., & Kirman, B. (2014). Never mind the bollocks, I wanna be anarCHI: A manifesto for Punk HCI. *One of a CHInd,* 741 – 748.

Livshits, B., Sridharan, M., Smaragdakis, Y., Lhoták, O., Amaral, J. N., Chang, B.-Y. E., & Vardoulakis, D. et al. (2015, February). In defense of soundiness: A manifesto. Viewpoints. *Communications of the ACM, 58*(2), 44–46. doi:10.1145/2644805

Mancini, C. (2011, July – August). Animal-computer interaction: A manifesto. *Interaction, 18*(4), 69–73. doi:10.1145/1978822.1978836

First Things First 2014: A Manifesto. (2014). Retrieved July 28, 2016, from http://firstthingsfirst2014.org/

Manifesto, G. N. U. (1983, 1985, 1987-2015). Free Software Foundation. Retrieved Aug. 3, 2016, from https://www.gnu.org/gnu/manifesto.en.html

Manifesto. (2016, July 26). In *Wikipedia.* Retrieved July 28, 2016, from https://en.wikipedia.org/wiki/Manifesto

Manifesto for Agile Software Development. (2001). Retrieved on Aug. 18, 2016, from http://agilemanifesto.org/

Manifesto. (n.d.) In *Merriam-Webster.* Retrieved Aug. 11, 2016, from http://www.merriam-webster.com/dictionary/manifesto

Mentor. (1986, Sept. 25). Hacker's Manifesto. *Phrack Magazine.* Retrieved Aug. 3, 2016, from http://phrack.org/issues/7/3.html

Mozilla Manifesto. (2016). Retrieved August 1, 2016, from https://www.mozilla.org/en-US/about/manifesto/details/

Murdock, I. A. (1994, Jan. 6). *A brief history of Debian: Appendix A – The Debian Manifesto.* Retrieved Aug. 3, 2016, from https://www.debian.org/doc/manuals/project-history/ap-manifesto.en.html

Nichols, W. R., Kirwan, P., & Andelfinger, U. (2011). A manifesto for effective process models. *Proceedings of ICSSP '11*, 242 – 244. doi:10.1145/1987875.1987921

Oates, S. (2015). Towards an Online Bill of Rights. In L. Floridi (Ed.), The Onlife Manifesto (pp. 229 – 243). doi:10.1007/978-3-319-04093-6_22

Petty, K. (2013, Jan. 21). Digital literacy manifesto. *Digital Manifesto Archive*. Retrieved July 25, 2016, from https://www.digitalmanifesto.net/manifestos/69/

Porsdam, H. (2011). *Too much 'digital,' too little 'humanities'? An attempt to explain why many humanities scholars are reluctant converts to Digital Humanities.* Retrieved July 25, 2016, from https://www.repository.cam.ac.uk/handle/1810/244642

Resmini, A., & Rosati, L. (2009). Information architecture for ubiquitous ecologies. *Proceedings of MEDES 2009*, 1 – 4. doi:10.1145/1643823.1643859

Resmini, A., & Rosati, L. (2011). *Pervasive Information Architecture: Designing Cross-Channel User Experiences Manifesto*. Retrieved Aug. 15, 2016, from http://pervasiveia.com/manifesto

THATCamp Paris. (2011, 2012). *Manifesto for the Digital Humanities*. Retrieved July 25, 2016, from http://tcp.hypotheses.org/411

Van der Aalst, W. (2011, Dec.). Process mining: Making knowledge discovery process centric. *ACM SIGKDD Explorations Newsletter, 13*(2), 45 – 49. Retrieved Aug. 15, 2016, from http://www.kdd.org/exploration_files/V13-02-07-vanderAalst.pdf

Weller, K., & Kinder-Kurlanda, K. E. (2016). A manifesto for data sharing in social media research. *Proceedings of WebSci '16*, 166 – 172. doi:10.1145/2908131.2908172

Winston, P. H. (2014, Jan. 10). *Lecture 15: Learning: Near Misses, Felicity Conditions*. Artificial Intelligence. Massachusetts Institute of Technology. MIT OpenCourseWare. YouTube. Retrieved Aug. 12, 2016, from https://www.youtube.com/watch?v=sh3EPjhhd40

Wood, I. (2015, Apr. 20). Why we need a global human / technology manifesto. *Wired Magazine*. Retrieved July 27, 2016, from http://www.wired.com/brandlab/2015/04/need-global-humantechnology-manifesto/

Zahn, M. (2016, Apr. 7). Zen and the art of zombie killing: A Buddhist anti-tech manifesto. *Religion Dispatches.* USC Annenberg. University of Southern California.

KEY TERMS AND DEFINITIONS

A Priori **Coding:** A pre-determined coding method, which may be based on theories, frameworks, models, or other influences.

Article Histogram: A bar graph which shows the main themes in an article.

Autocoding: Use of unsupervised or supervised machine learning to code textual data.

Close Reading: Human-based reading of text.

Codebook: The created codes used to process textual data; also known as a "code list" or "code set."

Distant Reading: Use of computational means to decode text.

Emergent Coding: The creation of a codebook based on the underlying coded data (instead of a pre-determined coding structure); an approach roughly based on grounded theory.

Manifesto: A public declaration of commitment to stated aims and intentions.

Manual Coding: Hand-created code set or code book using various tools like pen and paper, and common computer programs.

Word Network: A network graph of interrelated words.

APPENDIX

Figure 33. "Manifesto" in the Google Books Ngram Viewer from 1500 – 2000 (English Corpus)

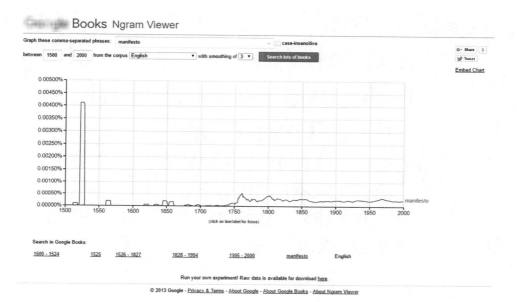

Chapter 4

Exploring "Mass Surveillance" Through Computational Linguistic Analysis of Five Text Corpora:
Academic, Mainstream Journalism, Microblogging Hashtag Conversation, Wikipedia Articles, and Leaked Government Data

ABSTRACT

A lot of digital ink has been spilled on the issue of "mass surveillance," in the aftermath of the Edward Snowden mass data leak of secret government communications intelligence (COMINT) documents in 2013. To explore some of the extant ideas, five text sets were collected: academic articles, mainstream journalistic articles, Twitter microblogging messages from a #surveillance hashtag network, Wikipedia articles in the one-degree "Mass_surveillance" page network, and curated original leaked government documents. These respective text sets were analyzed with Linguistic Inquiry and Word Count (LIWC) (by Pennebaker Conglomerates, Inc.) and NVivo 11 Plus (by QSR International, Inc.). Also, the text sets were analyzed through close (human) reading (except for the government documents that were treated in a non-consumptive way). Using computational text analytics, this author found text patterns within and across the five text sets that shed light on the target topic. There were also discoveries on how textual conventions affect linguistic features and informational contents.

DOI: 10.4018/978-1-5225-2679-7.ch004

INTRODUCTION

Real truth lies, if anywhere, not in facts, but in nuance. -- John le Carré, The Pigeon Tunnel: Stories from my Life

In the past few years, the issue *du jour* has been about the secret "mass surveillance" of citizenry in the U.S. (and other Western democracies and the world) through the collection of various types of electronic information: metadata about phone interactions, recorded phone conversations, locations of mobile phones around the world, social media data, email messaging, communicated imagery, and other electronic contents. "Mass surveillance" is broadly defined as the monitoring of a large percentage of a population, for any number of purposes

These revelations occurred when a contractor with the National Security Agency, Edward Snowden, copied an estimated 1.5 to 1.7 million secret documents and leaked some 58,000 of these to multiple journalists in May – June 2013. These documents included Level 3 documents considered "the Keys to the Kingdom" (Epstein, 2017, p. 75). U.S. federal prosecutors filed a sealed criminal complaint against Snowden on June 14, 2013, charging him with theft of government property and unauthorized communication of classified communications intelligence (COMINT) information to unauthorized persons under the 1917 Espionage Act, and this complaint was released to the public a week later. In June 2015 came word that both Russia and China had accessed the bulk of the encrypted NSA files—which Snowden had said he'd fully "destroyed"—and these revelations led to the pulling out of various Western intelligence agents from both countries for their safety (Kelley, June 13, 2015). The fugitive was given temporary asylum in Moscow, Russia, where he had landed, after a brief stay in Hong Kong, China; up to the present, through September 2016, he remains in Moscow, with an extension of his political asylum.

In the intermediate years, there has been a recognizable mass media cycle: the revelation of a new surveillance method, new outrage, and then efforts by the U.S. government to clarify and explain both the general methods, the limits of those general methods, and the needs for law enforcement. In democratic governance where the "consent of the governed" has to be obtained, even intelligence agencies—for whom it is anathema to share information with the general public—has complied with requests to declassify some of the authorizing documents that enabled the mass surveillance (a month after 9/11) (Subramanian, Dec. 21, 2013). The articles releases have come in increments over years partially in part because of the complexity of the information and the need to bring on experts to understand the details; also, there is an interest for news organizations to spread out the revelations over time to ensure that the story has "legs" or endurance. Hundreds of formerly covert programs have been revealed.

One academic, in 2015, published a five-part taxonomy of the technologies as revealed, including collection programs, processing programs, attack programs, isolation programs, and database ones; there are also programs for which too little information is available. In the summary, Hu identifies bulk telephone metadata collection, uniform resource locator (URL) data, the capture of metadata and communications traveling through fiber-optic cables, hierarchy analysis through social network analysis, exploration of emails and website searches, the ability to redirect web browsers without user knowledge, spyware, programs to target heads of state and their aides, databases with collected data for various periods of time, and others (Hu, 2015, pp. 1693 - 1702). This taxonomy was collected in part to serve as a resource for those who may be exploring the constitutionality of the surveillance.

Along with this information comes a narrative of U.S. government heavy-handedness. For example, Academy Award-winning *Citizenfour* filmmaker Laura Poitras who has sued the U.S. government to find out why she has been stopped at the U.S. border. Heavily redacted government files on her—released through FOIA (Freedom of Information Act) requests—were the subject of a show at the Whitney Museum of American Art in NY (Williams, Feb. 17, 2016). There is a sense that there are hidden redlines to what movie makers may explore (Silverman, July 8, 2013). There is also a sense that the country that various citizens envision may be beyond acceptance for those who manage national security.

The leeriness of the public to any sort of surveillance spilled over to domestic law enforcement. When there was expressed government interest in keeping a national database of where license plates were seen on traffic cameras (and other sources) with automatic license plate readers, and the public disagreed, the proposal was later retracted by the Department of Homeland Security (Friedersdorf, Feb. 19, 2014). For example, the revelation that those in domestic law enforcement and intelligence had a tool (Stingray) to emulate a cell tower to capture device signals trying to connect to a cell tower in order to physically locate individuals caused more consternation. Activists asked, why wouldn't law enforcement be required to get a warrant to operate Stingray when they had to get one to acquire cell phone location records from cell service providers? Surveillance drones have been much more commonly used stateside to deal with issues of manhunts and firefighting. Privacy advocates are finding fewer and fewer places where people may live, work, and breathe unseen, off-the-grid. The sense is that the only way to "hide" is by not coming to the notice of law enforcement.

Historical Precedent

In the heat of the present immediate, it may be easy to forget that there are historical precedents that suggest the present moment. "Surveillance" is a term from the French language (1790-1800) that dealt with the watching over of others, with "*veiller* from the Latin *vigilare* or "to watch". Long before Snowden, there have been concerns about panopticon surveillance conditions (with "panopticon" a term coined by Jeremy Bentham in the late 18th century) that posits a power structure in which a watcher can observe others without their knowledge and enabling "a new mode of obtaining power of mind over mind" (Bentham, 1843).

The insider threat has long been a part of the security research literature. There is even precedence for an "Edward Snowden" writ large. In the past, individuals in the employ of the NSA have also decamped to Russia, such as in the case of cryptologists William Martin and Bernon Mitchell, during the 1960s (Calamur, July 25, 2013).

Prior to the broad popularization of the Internet and Web, Robert Clarke (1988) coined the term "dataveillance" to refer to "the systematic monitoring of people's actions or communications through the application of information technology" (Clarke, 2003). Lawrence Lessig (1999) observed presciently just how much control computer code may exert and how much it may shape people's lives. (Lessig's creation of the Creative Commons licensure is an effort to broaden sharing without contravention of copyright.)

Mass Surveillance Today

Maybe a kind of perfect storm of a lot of factors that brings society to this present reality. Since the advent of Web 2.0 (the Social Web), the popularization of "smart technologies," the Internet of Things (IoT), and wearable computers, people have placed so much more of their personal information in public spaces. With this sharing comes various unintended externalities, including oversharing, advertently and inadvertently. The power of data analytics enables powerful profiling and individual identification, locational placement of people, remote reading of personality, drawing of social networks, and other features). As such, it is not only the government interested in people's data but also private industries. Experts in private industries with access to massive amounts of data have suggested that the capabilities have outstripped the legal capabilities to provide oversight, and companies often have to self-regulate in terms of private data handling and use (Grumbling, 2016, pp. 31 – 38).

The amount of personal data being shared digitally will likely only grow, with the uses of sensors for exercise and health routines and then the Internet of Things (use of the Internet to connect everyday objects to enable broad awareness, connectivity, remote access to various computerized controls, and other elements). The IoT is offered referred to in reference to smart homes and spaces, healthcare monitoring, and other things. For all the concerns about privacy leaks, there are clearly many benefits to be had with Internet connectivity. The question—for all the stakeholders—is how to get the right balance.

Then, too, it is not only the information shared but how it may be captured, analyzed, and cross-referenced with other information to draw often-accurate conclusions. Facial recognition technologies may be broadly applied to identify people on social media and websites. Cutting-edge machine learning (a form of artificial intelligence) may be deployed to find patterns in people's behavior. The advent of cloud-based computing means that querying across complex data is possible in ways not possible in earlier eras because now masses of data are accessible and query-able en masse. The big data architecture is a feature of "big data cybersurveillance methods" and heralds "the dawn of the National Surveillance State" (Hu, 2015, p. 1680).

This recent incarnation of "mass surveillance" concern has enabled various constituencies to suggest *prima facie* unconstitutional government overreach, over-extension of the military-industrial complex, technological determinism, and any number of other large-scale narratives. The meta-narratives themselves are partially informed by risk potentials, informed by some of the best traditions of science fiction, such as George Orwell's *1984* (1949) and Neal Stephenson's *Cryptonomicon* (1999).

The U.S. government has spokespersons who explain the limits of the program and the legality of the programs and the various types of oversights to the accessing of different types of information. All said, this issue has widely captured the public imagination. The issue of "mass surveillance" involves sufficient complexity where all may be "right" to varying degrees.

The general public does have to be aware and protective of their privacy rights; governments may have to capture some types of data in a broad-scale way to try to better protect its citizens, non-citizens within its borders, and its allies' citizens abroad. All have a role in ensuring that the system works as fairly as possible.

The salience of this issue and public access to related texts make this topic a suitable one to "seed" the capture of text corpora for computational linguistic analysis. In this work, five collections of texts were collected: academic articles, mainstream journalism articles, Twitter #hashtag discourse text sets, Wikipedia articles, and a small sample of original leaked government documents (with some redactions).

REVIEW OF THE LITERATURE

If there has been a temporary equilibrium that has arrived with this issue of "mass surveillance," it may be summarized as the following two "camps": the various stakeholder publics and the U.S. government. Barnard-Wills (Fall 2011) summarizes the two discourses as follows:

One is a discourse of appropriate surveillance, which draws upon discourses of crime prevention, counterterrorism, and national security. The second is a discourse of inappropriate surveillance that draws upon discourses of privacy, Big Brother, and personal liberty. (Barnard-Wills, 2011)

This is clearly an over-simplification, but such summary approaches are necessary to enable a general grasp of the arguments.

From Various Publics

The U.S. Government's capturing of our communications and information goes well beyond what is needed to keep the public safe. It is personally intrusive; it is mass scale. Such broad access is open to broad potential abuses. These surveillance programs show a "totalitarian mentality," such as with the capturing of 80% of all audio calls coming into the U.S. (not just metadata) (Loewenstein, July 11, 2014). Where American citizens have protections, that leaves some 94% of the world's peoples without constitutional protections against U.S. surveillance, and then Americans are spied on through the partnerships of "Five Eyes" allies, which means this is a world of people who are targeted for mass surveillance. Cybersecurity activist Bruce Schneier as observed the risks of mass surveillance: "If you're truly worried about attacks coming from anyone anywhere, you need to spy on everyone everywhere. And since no one country can do that alone, it makes sense to share data with other countries" (Schneier, Mar. 2, 2015). He sees an endgame of "a global surveillance network where countries collude to surveil everyone on the planet" (Schneier, Mar. 2, 2015).

Large-scale surveillance is seen as harming the social fabric, and these erode "the integrity of democratic processes and institutions" (Parsons, 2015, p. 1). "Indiscriminate mass surveillance," without rules and without restraint, interferes with the populace's rights to collective self-determination, social relationship-making, beyond harm to individual decision-making (Stahl, March 2016). The author explains:

We can only make sense of such practices when we acknowledge that the collective ability of a group to control who participates in a given social context amounts to control over the form of relationships that become possible in that context and that such control sustains practices and forms of reasoning that are essential for political agency in the public sphere. (Stahl, 2016, p. 39)

If the Web, as a social tool, is about people's empowered self-determination, non-consensual surveillance is also seen as undercutting the emancipatory potential of social media:

The consequence of mass surveillance is the loss of the liberating potential of these tools, the destruction of trust, and the degradation of privacy that weakens civil society and significantly inhibits the development of democracy. (Lange, 2014, p. 63)

It is not only governments that are the villains in terms of access to and control over private information. Mark Andrejevic (June 2002) has observed a shift to private ownership of personal information from individuals to private corporations (p. 243). He gives the example of DotComGuy in the early days of the Web who agreed to be surveilled through the Internet in exchange for goods and the chance for a large payout at end of a year.

Conceived as a form of labor, the work of being watched can be critiqued in terms of power and differential access to both the means of surveillance and the benefits derived from their deployment. The operative question is not whether a particular conception of privacy has been violated but, rather: what are the relations that underwrite entry into a relationship of surveillance, and who profits from the work of being watched? (Andrejevic, 2002, p. 232)

In the above scenario, Andrejevic identified imbalanced power differentials. His observations, though, are echoed in the present moment in which people share their personal information through various forms of social media and whose opinions are harnessed by commercial entities in order to sell goods and services. Private industry is seen not only to hold the keys to accessing private data, but also encrypted private data. In the aftermath of the 2015 San Bernardino attack, which left 14 dead and 22 seriously injured, the FBI and U.S. Justice Department wanted to compel Apple to access messages on one of the attacker's iPhones but was rebuffed not only by Apple but by a number of other high tech companies. The argument by the technology companies was that weakening encryption for government in one case would result in weakening encryption for all and would harm their bottom lines as well as the quality of their product for consumers. Ultimately, U.S. law enforcement was able to access the information they needed by other means, and the high technology companies were able to avoid this particular precedence of having to create a method to decrypt data on one of their smart phones.

Analyses of the leaked documents have shown that there is a capability to track cellphone locations worldwide in order to find co-travelers (whose cell phone signals travel together), or prior unknown associates, people with hidden links to each other (Gellman & Soltani, Dec. 4, 2013); this program apparently involves the collection of five billion cell phone records daily (with the incidental capture of U.S. citizenry's cell phone location records). Historically, computer technologies have been harnessed by despotic governments to find individuals against whom to commit mass genocide (Black, 2001, 2002, 2009, & 2011).

Another example of negative effects of state surveillance comes from the post-WWII Cold War period, the Stasi in East Germany, with surveillance costs to society in unexpected ways:

We find that a higher spy density caused lower self-employment rates, fewer patents per capita, higher unemployment rates and larger population losses throughout the 1990s and 2000s. Overall, our results suggest that the social and economic costs of state surveillance are large and persistent. (Lichter, Löffler, & Siegloch, 2015, p. 1)

State surveillance, in the E. Germany case during the Cold War, was also linked to population declines from mass exoduses (Lichter, Löffler, & Siegloch, July 2015, p. 4) and dropping electoral turnout (p. 19).

The knowledge of large-scale surveillance by government may intimidate a population into silence, with writers unwilling to take the risk of self-expression. After all, something that may have been said in jest may somehow be recalled in the future as evidence of illegality. Can people live free while under mass surveillance? There are risks of an "echo chamber" in which only certain *acceptable* concepts are expressed, "amplifying widely-held opinions and weeding out other perspectives" (Waddell, Apr. 5, 2016). Similarly, surveillance may be seen as protecting the existing power structures and not enabling disenfranchised groups to advocate for their own belonging and rights—without being seen as threats. Technologies have been used as "totalitarian levers" (Clarke, Jan. – Feb., 2001, p. 10) and as "persuasive technology"(ies) to control people's behaviors (Fogg, 2003, as cited by Jespersen, Albrechtslund, Øhrstrøm, Hasle, & Albretsen, 2007). For example, a population may turn to self-policing.

Sadly, we are already beginning to see signs in countries like the UK and the US of surveillance being used as a means of suppressing criticism and political speech. Although it is often claimed that the police record public demonstrations and rallies with a view to detecting and investigating possible criminal and terrorist behavior, the reality is that such tactics are now commonly used at almost every type of protest, ranging from anti-war marches to environmental group protests, often not with the intention of arresting or charging individuals with a crime, but rather in the hope that it will cause them to alter their behavior and become effectively self-policing. Equally, the mass and routine monitoring of electronic communications like email – as revealed in a recent European Court of Human Rights judgment against the UK – may severely affect the ability of individuals to share their views with others or to be willing to criticize the government in their private communications. (Goold, 2010, p. 43)

Or worse, people may turn against each other and report on each other. People would control each other, as in some authoritarian-totalitarian political spaces in the 20th and 21st centuries.

Another concern is that government capture of metadata from people who are not yet charged with a crime undermines the legal principle of the "presumption of innocence" and thus harms the legal due process (Milaj & Bonnici, 2014). Is everyone seen as potentially guilty? Does mass surveillance create a culture of suspicion that causes an imbalance against citizens ultimately charged with crimes? The authors explain:

In conclusion it can be said that the classical understanding and safeguards of the principle of presumption of innocence are challenged in our society by mass surveillance and data retention programmes. These forms of interference with the private life of the individuals do not only question the fundamentals of a democratic society, but also undermine the role of the principle of presumption of innocence at the stages of a criminal process, compromising the very effectiveness of the legal system. We argue that the battle against mass surveillance and data retention programmes in the EU is not just a battle of the protection of the private life of the individuals and of the proportionality of the measures. It is also a battle to protect the standards of a fair process and therefore, of the procedural guarantees that are inherent in the principle of presumption of innocence. (Milaj & Bonnici, 2014, pp. 426 – 427)

Government can turn malign as it has in history and in the present, and these tools enable government to be technologically omniscient and potentially very harmful to the common person. You're using so-called friendly governments to collect on Americans and are using that information, which suspiciously looks like a workaround on the U.S. Constitution and particularly the Fourth Amendment. You have not come clean with the U.S. publics until the data leaks happened. Schneier's critique, informed by a sense of betrayal, resonates among many:

By subverting the internet at every level to make it a vast, multi-layered and robust surveillance platform, the NSA has undermined a fundamental social contract. The companies that build and manage our internet infrastructure, the companies that create and sell us our hardware and software, or the companies that host our data: we can no longer trust them to be ethical internet stewards. (Schneier, 2013)

A sweep of the journalistic and academic literature shows technologists and others working on "secure" encryption methods and training others on ways to use the Web and Internet tools in more secure ways. Some researchers are exploring how to change transnational data routing to avoid using certain technical infrastructures which are tappable or known to be tapped (for "dataveillance"), but with real world limits to transnational routing detours for Internet traffic:

Unfortunately, some of the more prominent surveillance states are also some of the least avoidable countries. Most countries are highly dependent on the United States, a known surveillance state, and not dependent on other countries. Neither Brazil, India, Kenya, or the Netherlands can completely avoid the United States with the country avoidance techniques. With the overlay network, both Brazilian and Netherlands paths avoid the United States about 65% of the time, and the United States is completely unavoidable for about 10% of the paths because it is the only country where the content is hosted. Kenyan traffic can only avoid the United States on about 40% of the paths from Kenya to the top 100 domains. On the other hand, the United States can avoid every other country except for France and the Netherlands, and even then they are avoidable for 99% of the top 100 domains. (Edmundson, Ensafi, Feamster, & Rexford, 2016, p. 568)

Some cloud companies advertise that they keep data in-country as a protection measure against having data skimmed or copied in transit. Some companies offer end-to-end encryption of text messages. Some mobile device makers promise device security and encrypted data storage. A major selling point for modern customer-facing, business-to-business, and business-to-government technologies (b2c, b2b, b2g, and others) is security, understood as general non-hackability in the public mind.

Many activists see a need for mass change at an international or global level, such as through a treaty ensuring data privacy (or "data protection" in the European Union), based on "customary international law" (Zalnieriute, 2015, p. 100). Indeed, a global treaty was suggested by four individuals: Snowden, filmmaker Laura Poitras (*Citizenfour*), David Miranda, and Glenn Greenwald proposed The "International Treaty on the Right to Privacy, Protection Against Improper Surveillance and Protection of Whistleblowers" on Sept. 24, 2015 (Moody, Sept. 25, 2015). The United Nations Human Rights Office of the High Commissioner's office notes that the UN General Assembly adopted Resolution 68/167 in December 2013 which called on "all States to respect and protect the right to privacy" and directly observed "the negative impact that surveillance and interception of communications may have on human rights" ("The Right to Privacy in the Digital Age," n.d.). There is another thought—that with sufficient sousveillant oversight of "the watchers" that some sort of "equiveillance" balance may be achieved (Bakir, 2015, p. 13).

"Sousveillance" is broadly in reference to peer or participant recording of events. If everyone is watching everyone else, the idea is that there will not be destructive excesses or abuses.

These include "sousveillance", variously described as watching from a position of powerless-ness, watching an activity by a peer to that activity, and watching the watchers; and "equiveillance", where a balance, is achieved between surveillant and sousveillant forces.

Accepting the inevitability of surveillance in contemporary societies, Mann and Ferenbok (2013, p. 26) seek to counter-balance surveillance by increasing sousveillant oversight from below (what they term "undersight") facilitated through civic and technology practices. Once this balance is achieved, they suggest that such a society would be "equiveillant".

Some Positives About Government Surveillance

As for one of the rare voices on the other side, David Danks (Winter 2014) suggests that the arguments around mass surveillance may be conceptualized as a moral dilemma, with no single morally acceptable choice, but an issue \ which may be partially solved by borrowing Pascal's Wager in his argument about the existence of God. The argument for mass surveillance may go like this: If people accept mass surveillance and terrorists plan an attack, then it's positive because law enforcement can engage and possible head off the attack. If there is no mass surveillance and terrorists plan an attack, people lose. If people accept mass surveillance and terrorists do not plan an attack, they people lose because of the inconveniences of that surveillance. If there is no mass surveillance and terrorists do not plan to attack, then people continue on with their regular lives, without the actual and opportunity costs of pursuing mass surveillance. (p. 158) Danks portrays the various possibilities in a 2x2 payoff matrix. He notes that one of the assumptions has to be that the mass surveillance has to be at least somewhat effective against terrorism for the assumptions of the Pascal's Wager to work, in the same way that there has to be a benevolent God who rewards faith (Danks, Winter 2014, p. 159). Mass surveillance had better be effective in promoting security, or else its many costs and potential harms will be unjustified.

Another researcher suggests that privacy itself is not a monolithic phenomenon; rather, it is complex, with privacy-privacy tradeoffs: more privacy in one aspect means loss of privacy in another. Privacy can conflict "with itself," including in the case of NSA surveillance. The author provides some examples:

Privacy-privacy tradeoffs come in a variety of flavors. Sometimes they are unexpected and unwanted. When EU citizens began exercising their right to be forgotten last year and flooded Google with "delete me" requests, the deleted links quickly re-appeared - together with the relevant search terms - on a website devoted to documenting Internet censorship. These citizens' bid for online privacy thus seems to have triggered the Streisand effect, "whereby an attempt to suppress a disclosed item of information only draws more attention to it." Other times, privacy- privacy tradeoffs are consciously cultivated and promoted. The Transportation Security Administration's PreCheck program invites travelers to "volunteer personal information in advance" if they wish "to leave on their shoes, belts and light outerwear and keep their laptops in their bags." Enhanced governmental access to your data can be traded for reduced access to your body and belongings. (Pozen, 2016, p. 222)

In the NSA context, "minimizing the network privacy of its own employees and contractors, the NSA can safeguard the communications privacy of everyone else" (Pozen, 2016, pp. 232 - 233). There are efforts that may be taken that may increase oversight of NSA employees in order to ensure that the surveillance is limited and purposive. Certainly, others have argued that "mass surveillance" itself is a misnomer; rather, "the NSA and its partner agencies have been running huge quantities of communications metadata through computer programmes designed to identify extremely small target sets on the basis of very strict criteria" (Inkster, Feb. – Mar. 2014, p. 52).

Another tact involves trying to find less potentially intrusive ways to increase population security. One approach is to encourage stronger communities in order to enable people to be aware of each other and to identify threats to law enforcement (Tryfonas, Carter, Crick, & Andriotis, 2016), something along the "see something say something" campaign in the U.S. The authors suggest that increased transparency would be helpful:

We believe that deployment of intrusive systems on line, where necessary, should be of clear and transparent purpose to the public and accompanied by measures that empower the affected communities to tackle the root causes of concern, e.g. radicalisation, hate speech etc. Drawing on analogies from other surveillance systems we develop the idea of co-creation, in the civic innovation sense of the term, arguing that otherwise Western states risk developing non-transparent and unaccountable structures of power that undermine the fundamental values of their civilisation. (Tryfonas, Carter, Crick, & Andriotis, 2016, p. 176)

Some activists around this issue see the U.S. government's actions as self-serving and their lines of argument inaccurate. They are untrusting about the effectiveness of oversight to the various surveillance programs.

From the U.S. Government

Our mandate is to provide national security through law enforcement, which includes an important intelligence component. If you want us to connect the dots of potential terror attacks or other mayhem, we need all the potential dots, and we need the most cutting-edge capabilities to find potentially relevant patterning. To do this work, we have to "play to the edge" of legal and technological capabilities (Hayden, May 3, 2016, in Houghton, May 3, 2016), with simultaneous defense and offense. The rationale is that government does not know ahead of time what information will be relevant until a later context helps define what is important, so they need to collect everything and retain for a sufficient period of time (or forever) just in case. Data may be mined for patterns and for awareness, but generally, the information is not explored in a personally identifiable way unless necessary for law enforcement or intelligence purposes. Law enforcement strives to know information in time in order to interrupt potential terrorist attacks. As upholders of the law, they work within the constraints of the U.S. Constitution. Their programs have to be legally, legislatively, and executively vetted; they remain under strict legal oversight for their efforts. At the same time, their work is determined by the nature of the environment. In a context of fast-moving information and networked communications infrastructures, law enforcement has to be able to function in that space (with speed, access, and accuracy) and to enforce laws there as well. Multiple officials have suggested that if they had less potentially intrusive ways to acquire the same information for law enforcement, they would consider those. They have argued that there are procedural, technological, and oversight protections in place to ensure that the U.S. Constitution is not contravened. (Interestingly, the leaked government documents do show a lot of processes in place to protect U.S. citizens against accidental collection.) They argue: Security is a basic necessity before any other right. If people are living under threat, how can they exercise their citizenship duties or enjoy their full breadth of democratic rights?

ANALYSIS OF THE RELATED TEXT SETS

To better understand some of the trenchant ideas being shared around "mass surveillance," five text sets were extracted: an academic text set, a mainstream journalistic text set, a Twitter #surveillance hashtag discourse set, a Wikipedia article network text set (seeded with the "Mass_surveillance" page, and some curated leaked secret U.S. government documents. These texts are limited by topic, by general time frame, by language (English), by general region (the West, writ large), and by online availability.

Set 1

The academic articles were collected through multiple subscription databases (JSTOR, SpringerLink, ACM, and others), and these included articles from academic publications like *The Atlantic Monthly* and *The New Yorker.* Many of the works debated the legality of the various signals intelligence and communications intelligence programs revealed in the leaked secret documents. Many took a stance of the need to protect human dignity and privacy, to protect human rights. There were academic works about engineered technologies that could potentially foil various surveillance efforts, such as by cloaking while surfing online, encrypting communications, and others. There have been calls for more sophisticated understandings—between activists and engineers, and vice versa—in order to enable more inclusive problem solving (Kullenberg, 2009). While there are a range of area studies directly concerned with issues like mass surveillance—like surveillance studies, intelligence studies, and journalism studies (Bakir, 2015)—this sample drew even more broadly from various studies, including communications, sociology, computer science, and other fields.

Set 2

The mainstream journalistic article set was extracted from ProQuest and other subscription databases, and these included articles also from *The New York Times, The Washington Post, The Guardian,* and *The Intercept.* The mainstream journalistic set of articles on "mass surveillance" shows the bursty roll-out of stories as various journalists analyzed the leaked government files (some as they became available) and explored their implications, often by talking to technological specialists, government officials, and others. At times, as revelations were made, stakeholders to the particular issues spoke up. Quite a few articles focused on Edward Snowden, in interviews, in retellings of how he managed to abscond with so many secret files, and events in which he took part through web conferencing tools, robot embodiment, and later, even a Hollywood film by Oliver Stone.

Set 3

The Twitter microblogging dataset was extracted using #surveillance as the seeding term for a social network of individuals discussing this topic over a weeklong period in September 2016 (using the NodeXL Basic tool).

Set 4

The Wikipedia articles were extracted from the one-degree article network seeded by the "Mass_surveillance" article (located at https://en.wikipedia.org/wiki/Mass_surveillance). A few of the articles had new titles at the time of download (which was the same day as the mapping of the article network), so it seems that the third-party data importer for MediaWiki files used in NodeXL may have been pulling page names from a different text field than the title. The prior, of course, is a crowd-sourced encyclopedia that has its contents constantly vetted by human and (approved) robot editors. In the Wikipedia articles (pages), there are single or multiple citations in every sentence and plenty of links, particularly in the "See also' section.

Set 5

The fifth part were some curated leaked U.S. government documents that had been the subject of mass media coverage. These were released on the Web with redactions by the Canadian Journalists for Free Expression (CJFE) at https://snowdenarchive.cjfe.org/greenstone/cgi-bin/library.cgi. In this set, there were 552 files, and a little over 500 of these were captured. There was not a way to mass download the respective articles, and many of them were pointed to from various other sources. While a serious effort was made to capture most of it, not all the files were captured, and some were repeated files, which were then deleted out of the initial collected set.

They included a wide variety of file and data types: formal government documents, briefing slides, work-place memos, draft documents, prioritizing lists, slide decks, wiki pages, decision trees, diagrams of data models, glossaries of terms, legal guidance, and others. Many were labeled with "Top Secret//SI// NoFORN" (to indicate that no one without top secret security clearance and especially no foreigners should be given access to the contained information). Some of the documents were redacted but not wiped fully clean of all names. A brief sampling from this sub-sample showed technological capabilities that are boggling for the outsider. In this initial reading, the author decided to treat this text set as a non-consumptive one, without content summaries in the body of the paper and only high level computational linguistic analysis.

What finally decided this author was how public such documents already were, how dated much of the materials are (2009 and 2010 were common years for the shared documents in this set), and also how informative these raw documents might be in terms of linguistic analysis (especially compared to more processed files). This was done in the intelligence spirit of "collect everything," "read everything," and "press every advantage" that came through in the raw files. In the CJFE set, some of the slide visualizations had overlapping images. Some documents looked digitized but very old school in terms of layout and simplicity and visual noise. There were snippets of other articles included. The files themselves had cross-throughs (strike-throughs) and black rectangular redactions (which may / may not have worked with a text analysis that can capture the underlying text). Also, there were a few pieces of post-leak related information, including some articles from NBCNews, for example, and these were included also. While the site had links to the articles, the article set was actually arrived at by different means and did include some of those referred to in the CJFE set. Interestingly, there were no research articles and nothing from the academic literature—as if the agencies made no reference to academia. This "Snowden Surveillance Archive" included direct links to the respective articles (processed data) which referred to the respective documents (raw data). Since the purpose was to examine the linguistic style of the respective documents, only those were captured. Some of the articles had been included in the mainstream journalistic set from other sources. All of the document downloads were in .PDF format, but it was not clear if that was the format of the original sources in the leaked archive or if the CJFE had conducted file conversions. None of the downloaded raw files (some 500) had any applied "SECURED" settings (and only one of the academic articles did); SECURED settings in PDF files disallow note-taking, editing, and re-saves of the PDF file. (A brief visit to the holdings at *The Intercept* showed some different leaked government documents that were contextualized differently. For simplicity's sake, only those from the prior archive were included.)

Initially, the author was going to follow professional writing ethics and practices and avoid using illegally acquired information. However, the 500- or so documents were only a small percentage of the supposedly 1.5 to 1.7 million documents estimated to have been downloaded by Edward Snowden (.000294 of the total set), and these are already widely publicly available on the Web and Internet. The documents were leaked in 2013. Since then, there have been changes to policies, technologies, and government information sharing. In some ways, the inherent damage in the leaked documents has somewhat lessened (hopefully). The author did not include summaries of the documents extracted from close reading but only used machine-reading-based summaries of the captured documents. She used a "non-consumptive" machine reading approach to the texts.

Initial Hypotheses

Once the texts were collected (unread), some initial hypotheses were conceptualized. These hypotheses were informed by the following observations:

- Conventions of non-fiction genre writing for academia, journalism, and the crowd-sourced encyclopedia (from professional ethics, publishing policies, and common practices);
- Conventions of microblogging messages on twitter;
- Conventions of government documents;
- Publishing protocols for academia, journalism, crowd-sourced encyclopedias, microblogging sites, and publicly released government documents;
- Common usages of texts from the respective sources (fresh analyses from academia, basic reportage from journalism, summary information from wikipedia, social opinions and data sharing from twitter, dry policy and legal decisions from government documents), and
- Knowledge of the text processing capabilities of nvivo 11 plus and linguistic inquiry and word count (liwc), the two software programs used to analyze the texts.

The first set of hypotheses were based around the qualities of the respective text sets. The summary of these hypotheses are available in Table 1. The

Table 1. A table of hypotheses re: academic, mainstream journalistic, and wikipedia articles related to "mass surveillance"

Academic Articles	Mainstream Journalistic Articles	Twitter Microblogging / Social Media Set	Wikipedia Articles	Original Leaked U.S. Government Documents (c/o CJFE)
1. Most analytical	Fourth most analytical	Fifth most analytical or least analytical	Third most analytical	Second most analytical
2. Third most advocacy	Most advocacy	Second most advocacy	Fifth most advocacy or least advocacy	Fourth most advocacy
3. Second most emotional	Most emotional	Third most emotional	Least emotional	Fourth most emotional
4. Second most social	Most social	Fourth least social	Third least social	Least social
5. Second most perceptual	Most perceptual	Fourth least perceptual	Third least perceptual	Least perceptual
6. Highest human drives	Second highest human drives	Fourth highest human drives	Third highest human drives	Fifth highest human drives
7. Second highest personal concerns	Most personal concerns	Fourth least personal concerns	Third highest personal concerns (lowest)	Fifth least personal concerns
8. Fourth most informal language	Second informal language	Most informal language	Third most informal language	Fifth most informal language (not very informal)
9. Second highest lifestyle factors	Highest lifestyle factors	Fourth highest lifestyle factors	Third highest lifestyle factors	Fifth highest lifestyle factors (not much re: lifestyle)
10. Highest cognitive processes	Third highest cognitive processes	Fifth highest cognitive processes	Fourth highest cognitive processes	Second highest cognitive processes
11. Third most sentiment	First highest sentiment	Second most sentiment	Fourth most sentiment	Fifth most sentiment
12. Second most divergent themes	Most divergent (somewhat unrelated, broad) themes	Third most divergent themes	Fourth most divergent themes	Fifth most divergent themes (least divergent, most focused)

hypotheses are framed as relational and comparative across the various text sets, which will make these easier to test.

Of addition interest regarding the text sets: What are some of the informational overlaps of the respective text sets (similarity coverage)? Also, what fresh insights are available in the respective text sets that are not as apparent or present at all in the other text sets?

In other words, if there is a lot of sentiment, what is the direction of the sentiments and on what issues? The ultimate ends of this research would be to explore the writings around "mass surveillance" and to answer the following questions through close reading and computational linguistic analyses in order to identify textual patterns that would not otherwise be observable (such as through close reading):

1. **Main Stakeholders:** Who are the main stakeholders to this issue of mass surveillance? Who are the main voices and players in this space?
2. **Animating Ideologies, Values, and Emotions:** What are some expressed ideologies in regards to mass surveillance? What are some appeals to values? Emotions? Lived lives? What are the main themes and subthemes at play?
3. **Foundational Facts:** What are the sets of facts that the main stakeholders are using? Where do these facts come from? How solidly understood are they?
4. **Predictives:** Where does this issue of "mass surveillance" seem to be headed, and why?

Besides this particular "use case," there are other potential practical applications to the insights from this work. For example, insights about the respective public text sets may be applied to future research—based on the types of data that are generally found in the respective text sets. After all, modern societies use publishing as a mechanism through which society has public discussions and come to agreement around controversial and contested issues. Also, the methods to analyzing the texts may inform future works that use computational linguistic analysis. Finally, the insights about "mass surveillance" may be informative to those conducting research on this particular topic as well.

To test the hypotheses, the following steps were taken:

1. The texts were collected for sufficient coverage of the topic.
2. They were processed into file formats that could be processed in the computational linguistic software programs.
3. The texts were run through various linguistic analyses, autocoding, and data queries (using both NVivo 11 Plus and LIWC).
4. The resulting insights were captured and reported.
5. Each of the capture articles and documents went through close reading so that the linguistic analyses would not be applied in a non-consumptive

way. In other words, all the underlying texts were accessible and were accessed, so that summary understandings could be offered in the Review of the Literature section and so the proper insights may be applied to the linguistic analysis findings.

6.   The acquired insights were used to make assertions about the respective text sets as well as make observations about the respective hypotheses.

The non-fiction prose texts (academic and mainline journalistic) were mostly from 2013 through the present, but some existed prior, and many of the Wikipedia articles had existed prior. All the prose works were curated by editors—for publication in academic works, in journalistic publications, and even in Wikipedia. The microblogging messages were only potentially edited by whomever posted the microblogging message. Finally, a set of over 500 documents released by Edward Snowden (and curated by journalists) were analyzed as well. These were created work whatever work-place oversight was in place. Some of the works seemed to be more highly vetted than others, but for an outsider, that is an impression only from inferences.

The files range from raw government documents and uncensored Tweets to crowd-edited Wikipedia articles to processed journalistic and academic articles. By labeling the government documents as "raw," this is not to say that the documents did not themselves go through vetting and processing in-house, but these were written for in-house workplace use and occasional sharing with the U.S. Congress, but they were never created for public mass distribution and would likely not been so broadly shared were it not for the illegal data theft and broad leak.

The data may be conceptualized as "raw" or "processed" on a continuum. "Raw" texts are those with the least editorial oversight and processing for public consumption. "Processed" texts are those that go through an editorial process and are vetted and cleared for public consumption. Those professionals who might engage in such processing include public relations professionals, journalistic editors, peer editors, and so on. These five text corpora may be conceptualized as follows (Figure 1), with the most unprocessed or raw text corpus consisting of the microblogging messages (no actual external editorial oversight). Leaked government documents are considered fairly raw because while the documents have apparently gone through some extensive internal oversight, they were not vetted for public release. Many of the documents are highly technical and for a limited audience. Wikipedia articles go through crowd-sourced editing (and some robot editing). Mainstream journalistic

Figure 1. From raw to processed: Five related text corpora

From Raw to Processed: Five Related Text Corpora

articles go through editorial oversight. Academic articles are vetted by professional editors and peer editors.

None of the captured text sets are comprehensive but contain only a sample of available information. Some summary details of these respective text sets are available in Table 2. The main measures include the number of articles or items in each set, the word count, and the average per-unit word count; page counts were not included because of the high variance in page counts for the same set depending on how the data was handled.

The numbers vary somewhat across the respective text sets. Part of this is explained by the phenomenon of transcoding of text files from one format type to another. Every time text is processed computationally, there may be

Table 2. General features of the text corpora

Text Corpora	Articles / Items	Word Counts	Average Word Count per Unit (as a "Sanity Check")
Academic Articles	130	1,049,527 in LIWC 991,096 in MS Word (difference: 58,431)	8,073 in LIWC 7,624 in MS Word
Mainstream Journalistic Articles	136 (-1 which was Secured)	202,332 in LIWC 198,529 in MS Word (difference: 3,803)	1,488 in LIWC 1,460 in MS Word
Twitter #Hashtag Discourse	2,459 user accounts; 113 groups or clusters (based on the Clauset-Newman-Moore clustering algorithm); 41,708 message interactions	108,039 in LIWC 150,313 in MS Word (not sure how this handles abbreviations) .65 words (difference: 42,274)	44 words per user account in LIWC 61 words per user account in MS Word 2.6 words per message in LIWC 3.6 words per message in MS Word
Wikipedia Articles	236	1,703,038 in LIWC 1,583,645 in MS Word (difference: 119,393)	7,216 in LIWC 6,710 in MS Word
Original Leaked Government Documents	531	955,720 in LIWC 908,478 in MS Word (difference: 47,242)	1800 words in LIWC 1,711 words in MS Word

information loss or gain—which may affect the actual analytical work. To review, the files were mostly captured as .PDF (portable document format) files, and each set was merged into one large .PDF using the "Combine" feature in Adobe Acrobat Pro DC. Initially, those files were saved as .txt, which resulted in extensive text loss. Initially, word counts were not run on the respective sets. When word counts were finally run after multiple computational analytics runs were done, it was found that many of the text sets had much fewer contents than originally captured. This could be seen especially in the parenthetical data—the word counts per unit. .65 words in a Tweet message?! Those counts did not pass a "sanity check," so the original combined files were analyzed for word counts in MS Word.

- **Academic:** 360,454 in LIWC (2,773 words per academic article)
- **Mainstream Journalism:** 26,841 in LIWC (197 words per journalistic article)
- **Twitter Hashtag Discourse:** 27,253 in LIWC (11 words per account, .65 words per message)
- **Wikipedia Articles:** 87,022 in LIWC (369 words per Wikipedia article)
- **Government Documents:** 16,362 (31 words per unit)

The high disparities in word counts led to a different reworking of the text transcoding in order to minimize text lossiness. The more effective approach was to go from .PDF to .docx (MS Word). The word counts of the Word files were much closer to those of the original sets and resulted in more accurate average word counts per unit. When comparing MS Word and LIWC2015 counts of the respective corpora, there was still some variance, but by relatively small amounts (3,803 words to 119,393), given text collections with min-max counts ranging from 108,039 – 1,703,038 words per corpus.

But what can explain these changing word counts. First, the movement from PDF to MS Word means some words in images, logos, and diagrams, are often lost. They are not OCR-ed (run through "optical character recognition") and turned into textual data. The only text remaining from visuals are captions and in-text references to those visuals. Some non-English words may not transfer well, turning instead into computer garble. In a PDF to MS Word transfer, various types of metadata, header data, footer data, and other text were not captured. So what about the word count differences between MS Word counts and LIWC2015 ones? Interestingly, by comparison, LIWC tends to undercount some words in the Twitter messaging set (maybe because of the abbreviations in the Tweetstreams? the lack of punctuation?) and overcount in the other corpora as compared to MS Word. It is not clear which software tool would be most accurate to the underlying data although the typical assumption is that the more text there is to analyze (that is not noise), the better.

Why is transcoding needed in the first place? Generally, it is easier to have files in the types that are easiest for the software and computer to process. Files that are too large, too complex, and too multimedial, tend to be difficult to process and cause hang-ups in the text processing, or are too unwieldy to handle altogether. That said, researchers would do well to be as meticulous as possible at every stage of data handling. With the speed of software changes and sometimes a lack of oversight in terms of interactions between software tools, researchers have to conduct some experiment text runs on smaller sets in order to understand what is going on. After all the text processing was completed, the data was processed using both LIWC and NVivo 11 Plus.

To provide a sense of the size differences in the files, the text counts from within LIWC2015 were used even though there were some discrepancies between the word counts in LIWC2015 and those in MS Word. The largest text set was the Wikipedia one (1,703,038 words), the academic article set (1,049,527 words), leaked government document set (955,720 words), mainstream journalism set (202,332 words), and hashtag discourse data (180,039).

Figure 2. Word counts of five respective related corpora

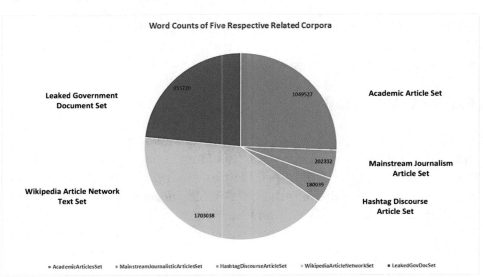

Just Push Play. Not

One other note is needed to describe the experience of computational linguistic analysis. In NVivo 11 Plus, because of some problems with PDF-file coding from web pages, some of the initial auto-coded sentiment analysis and the theme and sub-theme extraction efforts resulted in error messages. At first, the author had combined all the collected files into large text sets in single files and tried to process these using more accessible file formats. This approach did not help. She experimented with different types of character set encoding (going to UTF-8 instead of ANSI, for example). She finally found a method that worked by running the sentiment analysis and theme extraction machine learning features by using the original .PDF files but processing small batches at a time and incrementing the counts to the nodes within NVivo 11 Plus. In this work, she came across multiple files in both the Wikipedia and journalistic article sets that were corrupted and somehow unable to be machine analyzed. At the time of publication, it was still not clear what the underlying challenges may have been that made it impossible to run analytics on a few of the files (some dozen or so). All the coding was run at the sentence level of granularity, not the paragraph level. If researchers assume that computational linguistics is easy work, this chapter will show that this is actually effortful and hard work.

COMPUTATIONAL LINGUISTIC ANALYSIS

While the full range of built-in linguistic analyses tools on LIWC2015 were run, this effort resulted in some salient insights. First, it helps to examine the descriptive aspects of the respective text sets.

Text Set Complexity

Another data point in the LIWC2015 analysis involves the Sixltr variable (literally counts of words larger than "six letter" ones as a general proxy for language complexity). The respective text sets ranked as follows: hashtag discourse (54.78), Wikipedia article set (30.28), academic article set (29.96), mainstream journalism (29.46), and leaked government documents (26.17). The high word length count of the Twitter microblogging messages may be because of the LIWC2015 not understanding how to read Twitter messages. (LIWC2015 read the Twitter set as having sentences on average about 93.92 words long in the WPS or "words per sentence" column). It seems a little ironic that the leaked government documents had the fewest counts of words with greater than six letters given the various codenames like DeityBounce (11 letters), BoundlessInformant (18 letters), and Sandkey (7 letters). That said, the prose text sets are all fairly close in terms of their Sixltr counts. (Note that the percentages and scores are all within set ones.) Without a direct comparison, it would be hard to know what terms are in each of the works that are not represented in the dictionary, but some generally safe assumptions may be proper nouns (names), new technologies, non-English terms, and other terms of art. (Along the same lines, some of the words that are in the dictionary may have utterly different meanings, such as the codenamed "Echelon," "PRISM," "Pinwale," "Mainway," "TrafficThief," or other such projects with borrowed terms to refer to secret data collection by the National Security Agency.)

Percentage of Text Set Found in the LIWC2015 Dictionary (Dic)

The percentage of a text set found in the built-in LIWC2015 dictionary (Dic variable) include the following: mainstream journalism (70.02), academic articles (65.58), Wikipedia articles (58.92), leaked government documents (55.07), and hashtag discourse (23.82). For the hashtag Tweetstream set, over 75% of its language is not represented in the LIWC2015 dictionary. While the LIWC2015 dictionary does have informal and some text related to social media talk, a majority of the Twitter data was not found in the LIWC2015 dictionary, which has implications for extractable linguistic insights. Social media communications, given their dynamism, always offer a moving target. The legalese, high-tech observations, wild codenames, and cryptic references in the government set may explain why some 70% of its text was not represented in the LIWC2015 dictionary. The topic itself is highly technical and changing, and creative codewords are not likely to be found in a generalized dictionary. In four of the five text sets, more than 50% of the words found in each set had representation in the LIWC2015 text set.

Function Words

In terms of function words, sometimes used to establish stylometry (metrics of style), the prose sets seemed to follow similar general trajectories, with low uses of "I" and other personal pronouns but a fair amount of prepositions (Figure 3). The Twitter set ranked low on most function words, maybe in part to save on word use given the 140-character limit. A perusal of microblogging messages show plenty of semantic (meaning-bearing) terms and many abbreviations. Tweets often point to other websites, often minimized to shortened uniform resource locators (URLs). For stylometric analysis, the function words may be more effective at the per-author level, which will likely indicate much more variance and stylometric fingerprinting.

A basic analysis of the punctuation patterns across these five text sets shows that the microblogging messages in terms of having more "OtherP" / other punctuation as compared to the prose text sets (Figure 5). There also were many more periods used in the Wikipedia and academic article sets than in the microblogging set. All five sets showed little use of semicolons, question marks, and exclamation points, as well as parentheses. The Wikipedia articles did not seem to use any recognizable dashes.

Figure 3. Function words across the five text sets

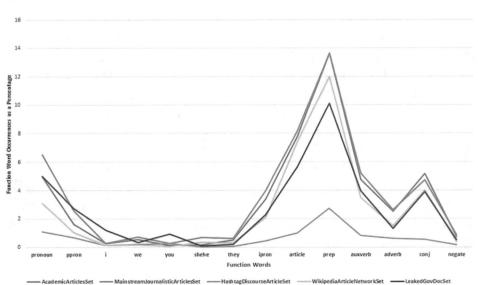

Figure 4. Time-based language focuses for the five text sets

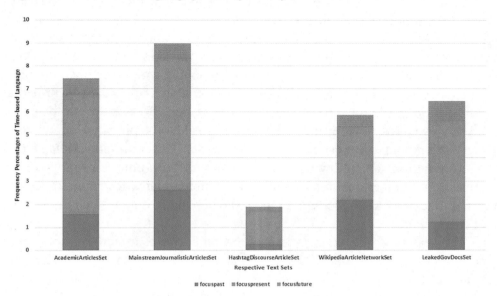

Figure 5. Punctuation patterns across the five text sets

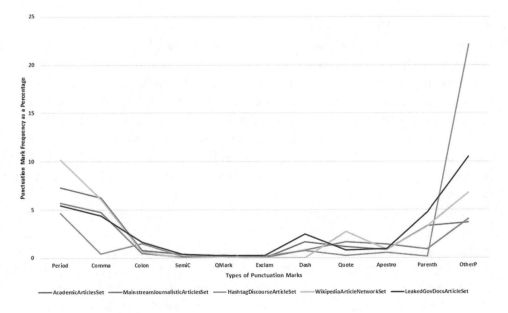

Based on the prior computationally-enabled linguistic analyses, it is clear that the various works in the academic, journalistic, and crowd-sourced encyclopedia set follow the rules of prose writing and therefore share many similarities. Academic articles, by design, tend to be longer and more analytical. Journalistic articles, in general, are about reaching a broad public audience with newsworthy information. Wikipedia articles are required, by Wikimedia Foundation guidelines, to be as objective as possible and to cite original research sources. Twitter messaging is supposed to be pithy and direct, and these often point to websites and other contents. The communications in the microblogging site follow its own conventions, with unique insights about those communications. Government documents related to technologies, to generalize, tend to be focused on the issue at hand, without much in the way of theorizing.

The selectivity of the texts in each of the corpuses affect the scores and counts. As more of the textual contents are collected, there will be some convergence to certain equilibria. It is unclear, though, if these sets have achieved the sufficient threshold amount for that convergence.

Four Summary Language Variables

Some patterns of interest were from the summary language variables, which include four main scores set on a percentile scale of 0 – 100. These five measures include the following: Analytic, Clout, Authentic, and Tone. These are standardized composites based on previously published research, with the scores converted to percentiles (as scaled based on large multi-type text corpora). All five text sets—the academic (95.50), the journalistic (94.48), the Wikipedia articles (97.47), the #hashtag conversations on Twitter (93.97), and the raw leaked government documents (93.79)—ranked high in the Analytic score, all in the 90th percentiles. Interestingly, the most analytic texts were Wikipedia (97.47), academic (95.50), mainstream journalistic (94.48), government docs (93.79), and the hashtag microblogging messages (93.33). Human readers may disagree with the idea that Wikipedia has the most Analytic text, particularly as compared to a large set of academic articles. That said, in terms of a focus on objective writing, the crowd-sourced Wikipedia set may be more "analytical" in that sense. How did these findings compare with the hypothesized ones? The assumed order of the respective text sets was inaccurate, but the hypothesis that the microblogging set would be least analytical was borne out (Hypothesis 1).

The Clout score was highest for the mainstream journalistic set (68.35), #surveillance hashtag Tweetstream set (62.28), the Wikipedia set (61.01), the academic set (58.78), and then the leaked government set (57.89). "Clout" is a measure of language that indicates a "perspective of high expertise" (vs. a humbler style), and as such may be indicative of relatively higher social status or confidence). There are some interesting contrasts between journalistic writing with high Clout and government documents, with the lowest comparative Clout score, by about ten percentage points. This may be a factor of style. It may be a factor of the underlying texts. There may be a lot of reasons for such contrasts.

All five text sets ranked low in "Authentic," which in LIWC2015, is defined as being open. The rankings, in descending order, are as follows: mainstream journalism (14.26), leaked government documents (13.29), academic articles (12.39), Wikipedia articles (12.35), and hashtag discourse (1.00). It may be that Tweets may be too brief to carry much in the way of openness. Intriguingly, the prose text sets were seen as ranking low on authenticity (low in the double digits range) but not as low as Tweets.

Finally, the fourth of the Summary Language Variables deals with Tone, which may be better understood as a sentiment measure. A high Tone indicates positive emotion, and a low Tone score indicates "greater anxiety, sadness, or hostility," according to the LIWC2015 Operator's Manual (Pennebaker, Booth, Boyd, & Francis, 2015, p. 22). At 50, there may be a "lack of emotionality or different levels of ambivalence"; below 50 is negative sentiment or emotion; above 50 is positive emotion. As such, the respective "mass surveillance" text sets ranked as follows in Tone: leaked government documents (44.64), hashtag discourse (44.42), Wikipedia articles (39.88), academic articles (38.08, and mainstream journalism (36.70) (Figure 6). It is important to note that all five sets of texts are in negative sentiment territory. It is unclear why the leaked government documents were seen as most positive (or closest to tonal ambivalence) and the mainstream journalistic ones were least positive based on language use.

As for how "Advocacy"-based a particular text set was (in Hypothesis 2), there was not a direct measure of this in the linguistic analysis. A linguistic indicator of advocacy could be "calls to action" and directives (advisement, requests, and suggestions for actions) to readers. Indirectly, the "drives" variable for "power" and "affiliation" may indirectly indicate advocacy. Power is often alluring and may draw followers who may be interested in the direction of that power. Affiliation is an indicator of language used to encourage relating. In the remote power of writing, affiliative connections

Figure 6. Tone score across the respective five text sets

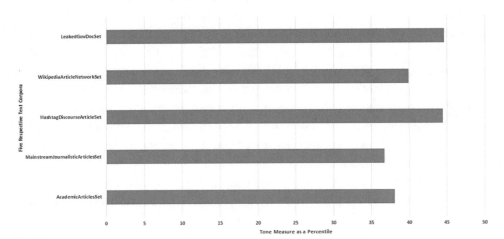

may be a way to create a sense of shared action and remote community. "Futurefocus" may also be a relevant variable since advocating for actions may involve the depiction of a desirable future as a motivation for action. Hypothesis 2 suggests that the text sets would rank in advocacy in the following descending order: mainstream journalistic articles, Twitter, academic articles, leaked documents, and Wikipedia articles.

If "Advocacy" may be conceptualized this way linguistically, as a sum of these three elements—affiliation, power, and focusfuture, then the discovered order is as follows: mainstream journalistic articles, academic articles, Wikipedia articles and leaked government documents (equal), and hashtags set as least Advocacy-based linguistically (Figure 7). Hypothesis 2 was correct in identifying mainstream journalistic articles as most advocacy-based, but the linguistic analysis in LIWC2015 shows that the other guesses were not accurate. Twitter data may be advocacy in some ways, but its data is not the most effectively analyzed using LIWC2015 since only a small percentage of the hashtag data is seen in the built-in dictionary (Dic).

In terms of the expressions of positive and negative emotions (as separate variables from Tone), the most emotional of the text sets are, in descending order: mainstream journalism (3.54: 2.08 posemo, 1.46 negemo), Wikipedia articles (3.23: 2.01 posemo, 1.22 negemo), academic articles (3.21: 1.95 posemo, 1.26 negemo), leaked government documents (2.61: 1.82 posemo, 0.79 negemo), and hashtag discourse (2.32: 1.67 posemo, 1.22 negemo) (Figure 8). In Hypothesis 3, regarding Emotion, the author posited that the listing

Figure 7. A conceptualization of "advocacy" measures

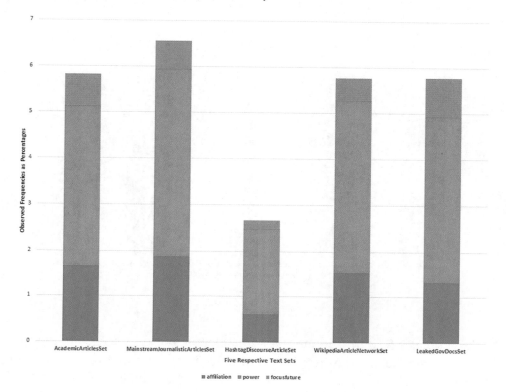

would look as follows: mainstream journalistic articles, academic articles, Twitter, government documents, and then Wikipedia articles. The hypothesis was correct about the mainstream articles as the most emotion laden. The hypothesis that government documents would be fourth in the listing was also correct, but the other hypotheses were incorrect. Emotions may be seen as an appeal to people to take notice and to possibly take particular actions.

The fourth hypothesis posited that in terms of Sociality, the text sets would rank as follows (in descending order): mainstream journalistic articles, academic articles, Wikipedia articles, Twitter hashtag set, and then the leaked government documents. In terms of the "social" aspects in the data, the rankings were as follows: mainstream journalistic articles, academic articles, leaked government documents and Wikipedia article set (equal), and then the hashtag discourse network set. The hypothesized first, second, and third positions were generally correct, but the final two were not (Figure 9).

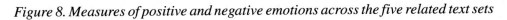

Figure 8. Measures of positive and negative emotions across the five related text sets

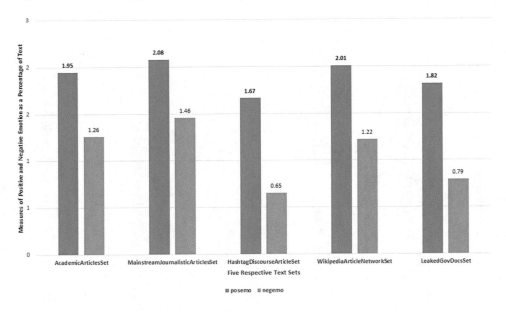

Hypothesis 5 addressed the level of perceptual writing in each of the five text sets, and the rankings were conceptualized as the following: mainstream journalistic articles, academic articles, Wikipedia articles, microblogging set, and the original leaked documents (in descending order). In the actual linguistic-analyzed data, the document sets were ordered as follows: mainstream journalistic articles, academic articles, hashtag discourses, Wikipedia articles, and then the leaked government documents (Figure 10). The first two positions were correct, and the fifth one as well. Seeing and hearing were dominant for the mainstream journalistic article set.

Hypothesis 6 involved the amount of human drive seeable in the respective sets. The hypothesized rank listings were conceptualized as follows: academic articles, mainstream journalistic ones, Wikipedia articles, Twitter microblogging Tweetset, and then the leaked government documents. In the summary data column for drives, the texts ranked as follows: mainstream journalism set (8.30), academic articles (7.53), Wikipedia articles (7.01), leaked government documents (6.81), and then the hashtag Tweet set (3.76). Only the Wikipedia articles were correctly identified in the third position. More nuanced drive data may be seen in Figure 11.

To break human drives down into greater details, it helps to look at words that indicate fundamental human drives—for affiliation, achievement, power,

Figure 9. Measures of sociality in the five related text sets

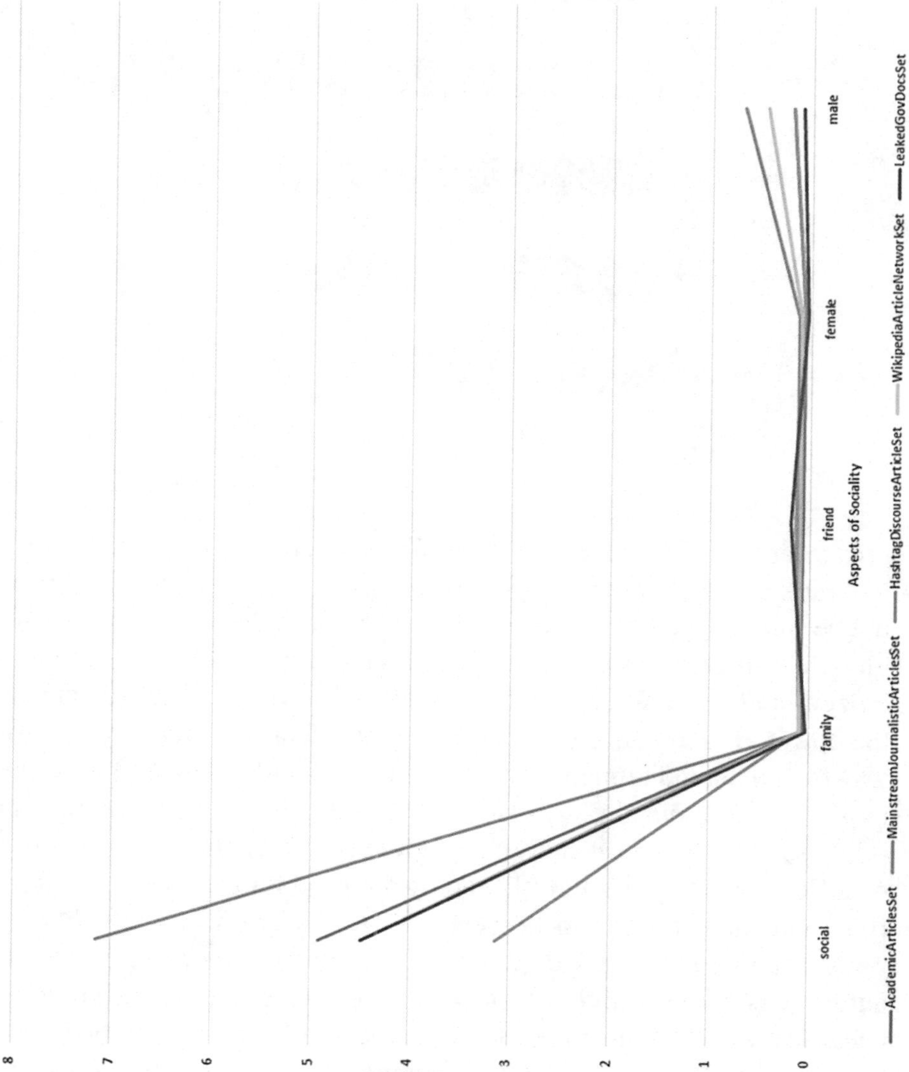

Figure 10. Perception measures in the five text sets

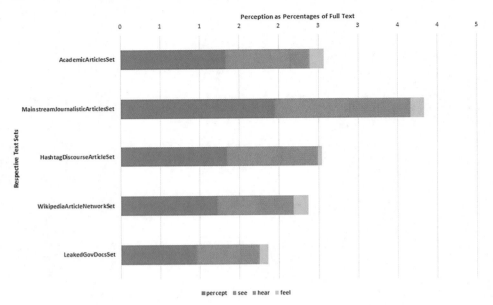

reward, and risk? An analysis of these five text sets in LIWC2015 shows that all five rank relatively high on power (Figure 11). In a sense, this finding should not be surprising. A core reason why "mass surveillance" is so hotly debated globally is that this is an issue of power: government power to surveil its own citizens and non-citizens, people's power of privacy and self-determination, the power of stealth technologies and human data, and other factors. Another way to understand human drives is the idea of authorship and what the texts might reveal about the interests of the collective authors in engaging the issues surrounding mass surveillance. Read this way, the importance of power or influence is important, followed by the need for affiliation, achievement, risk, and then reward (in descending order). The respective lines of the graph may be read individually as well to profile the respective collective author hands. In this light, the leaked government documents are intriguing because they rank high on power and achievement, then affiliation, and fairly low on reward and risk. (A read-through of the documents does show a lot of government oversight and procedures for correct handling of sensitive materials obtained through surveillance, in order not to contravene laws. The texts focus on how to achieve particular aims, but the focuses were on how to do so within boundaries.)

Figure 11. Features of human drives across the five text sets

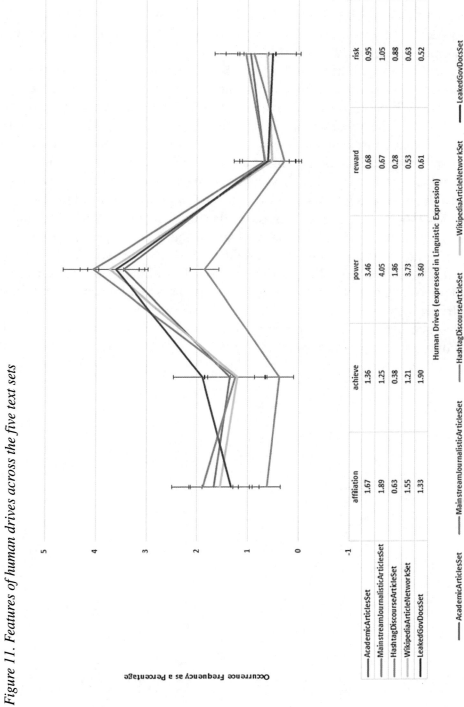

In reviews of the articles, there are some quotes related to power that stand out. Jesselyn Radack, Director of the Government Accountability Project and Snowden advocate, is quoted as commenting: "Information is a currency of power" (Silverman, July 8, 2013).

The seventh hypothesis (of 12) focuses on "personal concerns." These were hypothesized to rank as follows: mainstream journalistic articles, academic articles, Wikipedia articles, Twitter set, and then the leaked government documents. The closest equivalent measure in LIWC2015 is the "bio" measure that counts language expressions related to various aspects of the human biological functions. This is a stretch as "privacy" and "security" are somewhat more abstract than bodily functions. In terms of the actual listings, the findings were as follows: mainstream journalistic articles (0.71), Wikipedia articles (0.66), academic articles (0.62), hashtag discourses (0.61), and leaked government docs (0.51). Note that the y-axis are all percentages of one percent, so these are very small measures, and the differences between the measures are miniscule (Figure 12). The first, the fourth, and the fifth positions were hypothesized correctly, but the gap between "personal concerns" and these metrics (body, health, sexual, and ingest) is a concern as are the very slight differences between the respective variable measures. Note that the "bio" is a summary variable comprised of "body," "health," "sexual," and "ingest."

Figure 12. Biological functions across the five text sets

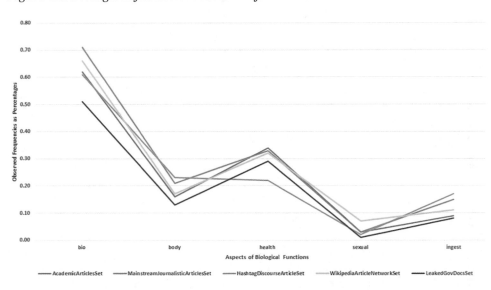

What about language informality? Hypothesis 8 suggested that the respective text sets would rank as follows: Twitter microblogging social media set, mainstream journalistic articles, Wikipedia articles, academic articles, and leaked government data, in descending order. The actual data ranked the five text sets as follows: Twitter hashtag discourse (4.18), leaked government documents (2.40), Wikipedia articles (0.89), academic articles (0.88), and mainstream journalistic articles (0.61). The first and third and fourth positions were correct. On Twitter, the language is informal and youthful; for the leaked government document set, this may be a reflection of the youthful experts in technological fields. (The informality of language would not be a good way to describe the legal documents captured in that text set.) The same pattern was seen in terms of the "netspeak" variable: hashtag discourse set (4.09), leaked government documents (2.26), followed by Wikipedia articles (0.81), academic articles (0.73), and mainstream journalistic articles (0.50). Swear words were low for all the sets (ranging from 0.01 – 0.02 only for the full min-max range).

Hypothesis 9 dealt with "lifestyle factors." As conceptualized in LIWC2015 (under the heading of "personal concerns"), these include the following variables: work, leisure, home, money, relig (religion), and death. This hypothesis suggested that the text sets would rank as follows: mainstream journalistic articles, academic articles, Wikipedia articles, Twitter microblogging set, and then the leaked government text set. As such, the actual ranks were as follows: Wikipedia article set (8.13), mainstream journalistic articles (6.60), academic articles (6.36), leaked government documents (5.38), and the hashtag discourse set (4.20) (Table 13). Not one of the hypothesized positions for this hypothesis worked out.

Hypothesis 10 dealt with the text positions for cognitive processes. This posited the following order: academic articles, leaked government documents, mainstream journalistic articles, Wikipedia articles, and then the Twitter microblogging set. As compared to the actual data, the first, fourth, and fifth positions were correct. In terms of the "cogproc" (cognitive processing) variable, the text sets ranked as follows: academic (9.65), mainstream journalism (9.14), leaked government documents (9.09), Wikipedia articles (6.08), and hashtag discourse (2.12). Interestingly, it looks like the academic, mainstream journalism, and leaked government documents were fairly close in terms of cognitive processing, but in different ways. Academic articles were more tentative than the other text sets. The Wikipedia article set tended to separate from the other text articles. The Twitter hashtag discourse article

Figure 13. Personal concerns across the five text sets

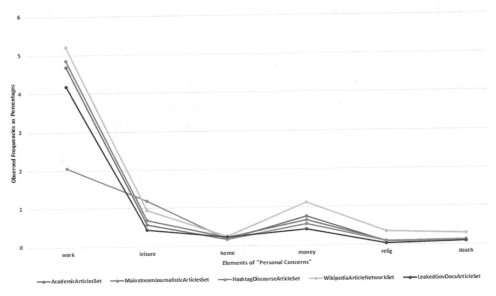

set ranked comparatively lower on all elements of cognitive processing than the other text sets (Figure 14).

Hypothesis 11 suggested that sentiment rankings would place the respective text sets as follows: mainstream journalistic articles, Twitter microblogging text set, academic articles, Wikipedia articles, and leaked government document set. (Based on the posemo and negemo measures, Hypothesis 11 was only correct in the first part of identifying mainstream journalistic articles as having the most in the way of emotion.) In terms of sentiment, though, as identified through NVivo 11 Plus, the respective text sets rank as follows: Wikipedia, academic article set, leaked government documents, mainstream journalism, and then the hashtag set. Note that texts are divided as follows: neutral or sentimental, and if sentimental, then whether very negative, moderately negative, moderately positive, or very positive. The sentiment measure in this case involves adding all the text citations for the four categories for the respective text sets. None of the initial hypotheses were borne out at least not in the analysis using NVivo 11 Plus.

Computationally assigned sentiment has long been understood as a basic polarity—either text coded positive or coded negative, or uncoded as neutral. In NVivo 11 Plus, sentiment may be seen as a polarity, or it may be seen as gradations of sentiment in four classifications: very negative, moderately

Figure 14. Elements of cognitive processing in the five text sets

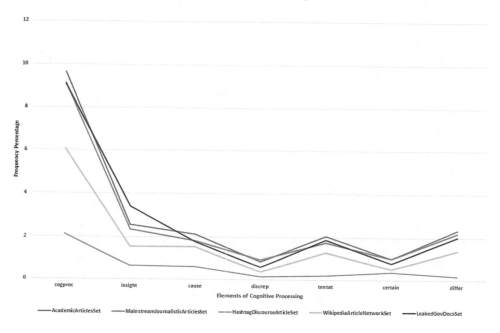

Figure 15. Summary: A comparison of sentiment across five text sets

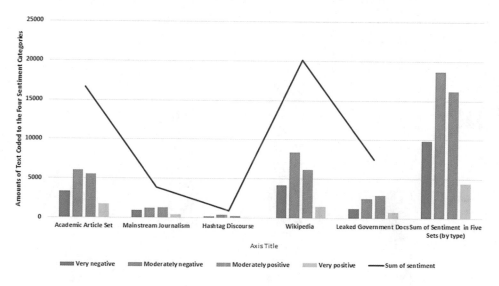

negative, moderately positive, or very positive. In the following section, the sentiment coding of the respective individual five text sets is explored briefly.

In Figure 16, the machine-coded sentiment shows that the academic article set tends to skew towards the mixed middle ground of moderately negative and moderately positive sentiment. In terms of the polarities, there are more citations in the "Very negative" category as compared to the "Very positive."

Interestingly, the sentiment bar chart distribution seems to be somewhat similar for the mainstream journalism article set even though there were fewer coded amounts of text in the journalism set (Figure 17).

In the #surveillance hashtag discourse network from Twitter, the predominant identified sentiment group was "moderately negative" (Figure 18) That said, as noted with LIWC2015, it may be that microblogging messaging may not be captured accurately in the tool. In NVivo 11 Plus's built-in sentiment dictionary, there may not be up-to-date sentiment coding for microblogging.

Further analyses may be conducted on the respective coded text sets in the four categories: very negative, moderately negative, moderately positive, and very positive. One of these types is identifying the top 10 words (generaly unigrams) in each category using the Word Frequency Count data query feature in NVivo. In Table 3, #surveillance is the most common term in each

Figure 16. Sentiment bar chart for the academic article set

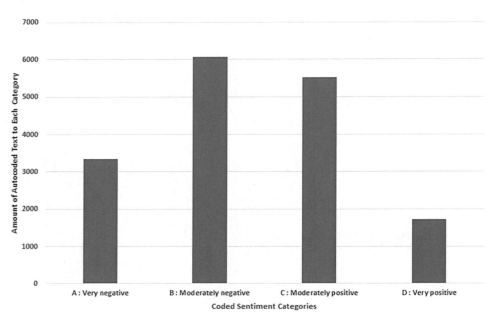

Figure 17. Sentiment bar chart for the mainstream journalism article set

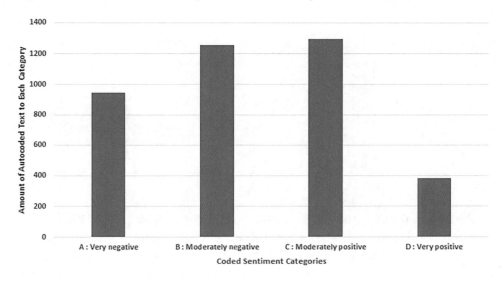

Figure 18. Autocoded sentiment from #surveillance hashtag network from Twitter

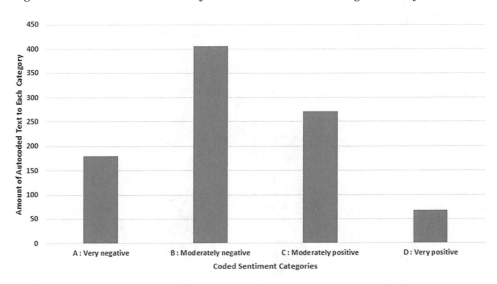

sentiment set Within the tool, it is possible to explore the contexts of the respective terms through a Text Search data query and mapping that data to a word tree (in order to read lead-in words and lead-away words as various branches of this word tree). It is possible to explore URLs to understand the conversations being carried on with other contents on the Web and Internet.

Table 3. Top ten words in each sentiment category of the #surveillance hashtag network on Twitter Tweetstream

Very Negative	Moderately Negative	Moderately Positive	Very Positive
#surveillance	#surveillance	#surveillance	#surveillance
latest	new	read	array
#privacy	generation	robust	catalogue
advance	resist	@blackoakcasino	gear
anonymity	next	hits	leaked
authoritarian	building	jackpot	military
companies	state	#privacy	offered
new	#tor	great	police
regimes	report	amp	reveals
tech	german	new	spy

As for sentiments in the Wikipedia article set, these tend to trend moderately negative, followed by moderately positive. There were more "very negative" coded text than "very positive." From the 233 coded Wikipedia pages, there were thousands of exemplars for three of the four categories and over a thousand instances of coded text even for the smallest "very positive" category (Figure 19).

In the 500+ item leaked government documents set, the sentiment tended towards the middle: moderately negative and moderately positive (Figure 20).

Figure 19. Sentiment bar chart for the Wikipedia article set

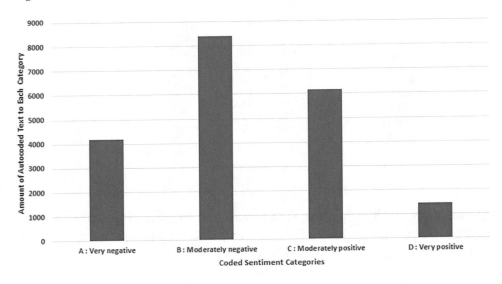

Figure 20. Sentiment bar chart for the leaked government documents text set

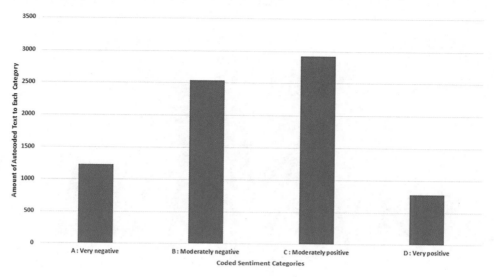

Finally, Hypothesis 12 deals with the phenomenon of automated theme convergence or divergence. Said another way, are the auto-extracted themes in a text set convergent around similar topics or around fairly divergent ones? Do the themes "tell a coherent story" or not? This is a naïve approach. What was found was that the Twitter microblogging set was the most divergent in the sense of "mass surveillance." The other text sets seemed fair convergent around a story about "mass surveillance." For this to work, there has to be auto-extracted theme and sub-theme analysis, using NVivo 11 Plus. For each of the text sets, the autocoding for theme and sub-theme extraction was run on the original articles and the finalized autocoded themes were depicted as treemaps as follows. Also, the most-frequent top-level themes are listed in descending order below. The hypothesis was that the text sets with the most divergent themes would be, in descending order, as follows: mainstream journalistic articles, academic articles, the Twitter microblogging set, Wikipedia articles, and then the leaked government documents. However, for actual rankings, divergence may also be indicated by the number of top-level themes identified by NVivo 11 Plus. Using this approach, the respective text sets rank as follows: Wikipedia, leaked government document set, Twitter hashtag set, journalistic article set, and academic article set, in descending order. Only the third set was in the correct position. A spider chart of these features of the five respective text sets follows in Figure 21.

Figure 21. Five text sets on twelve dimensions (extracted through computational linguistic analysis)

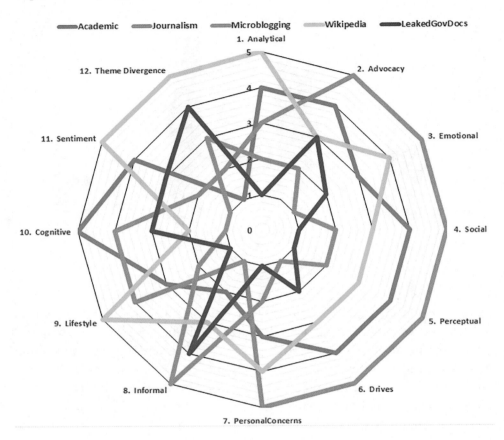

AUTO-EXTRACTED THEMES AND SUB-THEMES

More specific examples about extracted themes follow. To explore whether the texts in the respective corpora represented a convergence or a divergence of themes, "topic modeling" was applied to each set. This procedure extracts the *inherent* themes and subthemes in each set (as defined by the generalist algorithms in the software).

Academic Article Set Themes

The top-level auto-extracted themes from the academic article set, the full list (in descending order), are as follows: surveillance, data, technologies, information, security, communications, state, systems, public, law, political, privacy, use, social, intelligence, individual, internet, mass, user, agencies, government, network, rights, scheme, key, personal, services, service, encryption, media, model, search, system, national, power, human, processing, activity, and programs. In this top-level theme set, there are no bigrams. There are also no proper nouns. Interestingly, the processing of the original .PDF files went without any problems, so it may be that the conversions from Web pages (of Wikipedia articles, of converted leaked government documents, and of journalistic articles from websites) may result in code or something else that snarls the autocoding data processing in NVivo 11 Plus. The full 132 academic articles were accounted for in the automated theme extraction (Figure 22).

Mainstream Journalism Article Set Themes

The mainstream journalistic article set was processed for auto-extracted topics and sub-topics, and three of the articles were unable to be processed. This set included not only unigrams but also bigrams (the only one of the five sets). It also contained some proper nouns (names), also not so common. The entire list of top-level themes follows, from most citations to the least: surveillance, data, intelligence, government, rights, mass, law, collection, privacy, communications, phone, social, media, program, security, internet, agencies, public, records, legal, mass surveillance, technology, system,

Figure 22. Main Auto-extracted Themes and Sub-themes in Academic Article Set

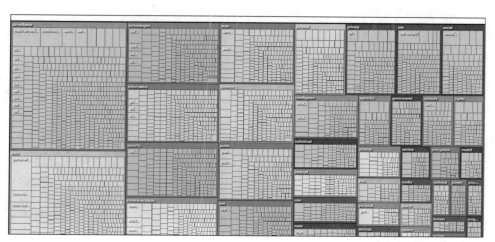

political, programs, forms, state, search, companies, court, police, american, human rights, national, protection, citizens, snowden, retention, conspiracy, cellphone, encryption, information, rules, communities, report, technologies, war, debate, practices, smartphone, software, targets, photos, attack, database, facial recognition, process, warrant, and anti-encryption bill. There were 63 top-level themes listed here (Figure 23).

#Surveillance Hashtag Discourse Network Tweetstream on the Twitter Microblogging Site

The #surveillance hashtag discourse data was captured using NodeXL Basic (Network Overview, Discovery and Exploration for Excel). This dataset consisted of 2,459 Twitter user accounts engaged in the topic of #surveillance (and who labeled their 41,708 exchanged microblogging messages and interactions with that hashtag). Within this network were 113 groups or clusters, 37,777 unique edges and 3,931 edges with duplicates, and 2,271 self-loops. For more details about this network, please refer to Table 4: Graph Metrics Table of the #surveillance Hashtag Network on Twitter.

In order to computationally extract the themes and subthemes effectively, one had to remove "https" and "http" or risk capturing a wide range of URLs only. So, 4,829 "https" and 52 "http" instances were removed from the text set. What resulted were the following high-level themes (in descending order):

Figure 23. Auto-extracted themes and subthemes in mainstream journalistic article set

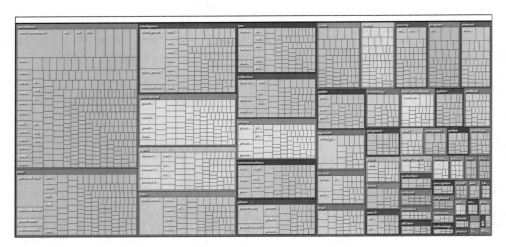

Table 4. Graph metrics table of the #surveillance hashtag network on Twitter

Graph Metric	Value
Graph Type	Directed
Vertices	2459
Unique Edges	37777
Edges With Duplicates	3931
Total Edges	41708
Self-Loops	2271
Reciprocated Vertex Pair Ratio	0.128016758
Reciprocated Edge Ratio	0.226976696
Connected Components	88
Single-Vertex Connected Components	84
Maximum Vertices in a Connected Component	2369
Maximum Edges in a Connected Component	41559
Maximum Geodesic Distance (Diameter)	8
Average Geodesic Distance	2.721003
Graph Density	0.006325545
Modularity	Not Applicable
NodeXL Version	1.0.1.336

#surveillance, new, #homeautomation, #deals, #homephone, #privacy, camera, amp, via, and #security (Figure 24).

A graphed chart showing the extracted top-level topics and their relative popularity may be seen in Figure 25.

This data set showed a wide diversity of conceptualizations of #surveillance. There were varying degrees of personal and impersonal data, semi-private and public data, and narrowcasting and broadcasting. A small group discussed an upcoming lecture on the topic, several on forthcoming papers—all tapping into the site for public attention and recognition. Some messages were about events, such as a casino event with strong surveillance. Some microblogging messages dealt with predictive policing, policies, governance. Several were about new #surveillance technologies to improve security and hack-resistance, and these messages had clear commercial purposes. There were brags about new hacks. Some pointed to news articles, such as: "#Europol plans major integration of #databases and unified #biometrics in Europe - #surveillance https://t.co/XIxgnoKoC2." Quite a few messages were about media: video games, books, movies, interviews, and photos. There were some public

Figure 24. Auto-extracted Themes and Subthemes from the #surveillance Hashtag Network Dialogue from Twitter

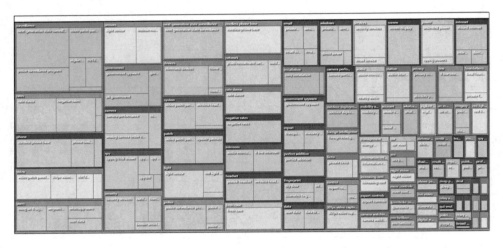

Figure 25. #surveillance Hashtag Discourse Network on Twitter

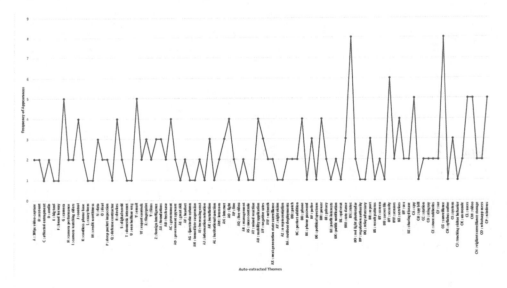

shaming messages, such as messages calling out countries and their industries that sell surveillance tools to authoritarian regimes. Some shared personal insights about power, with one commenting: "RT @culturejedi: At some point I ask myself, why is the state a peeping tom? And then I'm like, duh, power. https://t.co/J9Os2sJpZh#privac…" This set did not only have English-based messages (although a majority were); in a brief glance, there were messages in French, Dutch, and others.

Manually coded insights were captured from the Twitter set as well. The contents of this follow to provide a fuller sense of the diversity of topics. Within each of the coding nodes are a number of Tweets about those issues. Figure 26 provides a summary view as a treemap.

- CommercialIssues
  - BusinessChangeswithMergers
  - CasinoSecurity
  - CreditWorthinessandCorporateSurveillance
  - EventwithHighSurveillance
  - HomeSecuritySystemsExplanation
  - InsuranceSurveillance
  - MediaMonetaryLosswithAdBlockerAdSurveillance
- ConspiracyTheories
  - FaceCoversrealReasonforWaronIslam
- CrimeandSurveillance
  - HackingAttack
  - PredictivePolicing
  - SecuringBorderswithSurveillance
- FutureandPolicyChanges
  - BiometricSurveillanceComing
- HealthSurveillanceandOutbreaks
- Huh?
- Humor
- InternationalIntrigues
- LawEnforcement
  - CopCams
  - JobAnnouncementsLawEnforcement
- NeedforMoreSecurity
  - SchoolSecurity
  - TrafficSurveillance
  - TransportationSecurity
  - VideoCCTVSecurity
  - WaystobeMoreSecure
- NewSurveillanceTechno
  - DroneSurveillance
  - PrivacyProtectionSoftwareorTechno

- ◦ RevealsofHackslikeWifiRouter
- ◦ SmartPhonesandMobileDevices
- ◦ Wearables
- PoliceSurveillanceStateNarrativeandLackofActualSecurity
  - ◦ ExamplesofGovernmentLawEnforcementOverreach
  - ◦ IfYouveDoneNothingWrongArgument
  - ◦ MilitaryIndustrialComplex
  - ◦ StingrayMassSurveillance
- PrivacyPromotionandLegalRights
  - ◦ CautionaryTales
  - ◦ DoNotBuyCubanSurveillance
  - ◦ ProSnowdenDirectly
  - ◦ SocialMediaSurveillance
- ReviewofMediaDealingwithSurveillance
- SelfPromoforPhotoSharingPublicationEvents
- SurveillancePorn
- Terrorism
  - ◦ BlockingiSISAccounts

As may be noted, the Twitter text set contained a wide range of senses of #surveillance.

Figure 26. A Treemap Diagram of the Manually Coded Themes and Subthemes from the Twitter #surveillance Hashtag Discourse

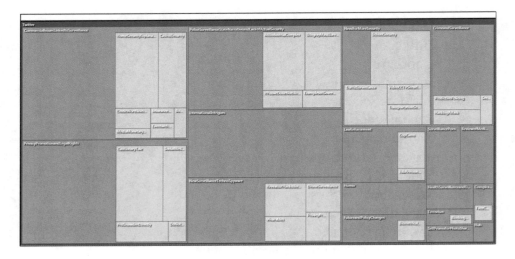

Wikipedia Article Network: As noted earlier, a one-degree article network was extracted from the Wikipedia site, with the main seed article "Mass_surveillance." The article-article graph (a network of articles with direct linkages from the "Mass_surveillance" article on Wikipedia to one degree, may be seen in Figure 27. Note the centrality of the seeding article. Also, a perusal of the one-degree article nodes shows a wide diversity of topics. Researchers can go pretty far afield with only a one-degree network given the richness of Wikipedia data and the interrelatedness of information. A mental conversation beginning with one topic can fast evolve into a wide range of topics based on a crawl of this article-article network.

From the extracted article set of 236 articles, an automated theme and subtheme extraction was run using NVivo 11 Plus, and the extracted themes were coded at the sentence level. Three of the Wikipedia articles were not processable for themes, but all the rest were. While the impression of the

Figure 27. "Mass_surveillance" article network on Wikipedia (1 deg.)

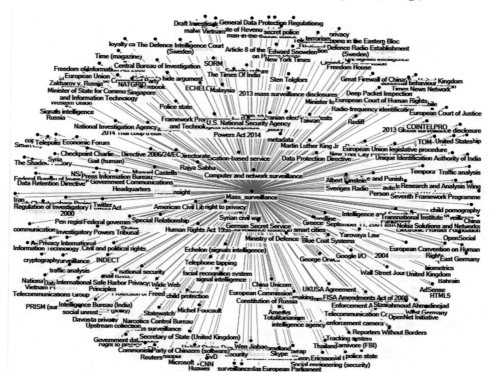

Wikipedia article set by title may seem fairly disparate, the extracted themes (from the textual contents within the articles) actually do seem to "tell a coherent story." The themes, in descending order, are as follows: system, data, government, network, state, public, security, surveillance, information, use, political, law, free encyclopedia, social, national, services, intelligence, internet, agencies, rights, privacy, technology, computer, communications, police, number, official, power, organization, groups, card, traffic, companies, phone, child, program, telephone, personal, service, cameras, economic, identity, communication, military, electronic, greek, operations, relations, human, records, control, issues, media, work, https, video, systems, private, name, process, links, calls, century, foreign, citizens, messages, movement, development, biometric, radio, history, recognition, metadata, content, language, areas, authorities, local, activity, city, party, search, document, terrorism, access, documents, speech, member, software, operators, people, identification, market, mobile, and rule (Figure 28). There were 96 top-level themes here.

Leaked Government Documents Set

In terms of the leaked government documents, the underlying file types were fairly variant, as mentioned earlier. Still, there was a surprising amount of convergence, with the extracted topics telling a coherent story.

Figure 28. Main Auto-extracted Themes and Subthemes in Wikipedia Article Network Set

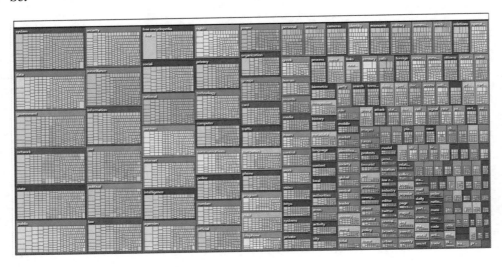

To give a sense of the size of this node matrix, there were 6,535 items (nodes) in this theme/subtheme node matrix. Some of the top-level nodes, from most frequent, are as follows in descending order (based on the exported node list): target, data, information, intelligence, communications, collection, network, metadata, activity, access, content, analytic, security, user, events, source, analysis, system, query, activities, internet, processing, operations, number, systems, specific, support, capability, requirements, key, service, reporting, purposes, capabilities, foreign, sources, email, search, packets, law, mission, http, procedures, name, terrorist, analysts, development, field, cyber, reasonable, servers, address, selector, identifier, application, contact, list, site, value, technology, reports, using, identifier, traffic, process, details, file, direct, session, message, request, tool, person, program, server, call, level, organizations, protocol, target discovery, threat, analytics, foreign intelligence, agencies, legal, results, scores, fingerprint, investigative, software, use, event, messages, sites, management, means, tasking, and term. This listing was limited to the top 100 words.

In terms of time-based language, seen in the stacked bar chart in Figure 29, there are some observable differences between the respective text corpora. Of the five text sets, time in its three incarnations (focuspast, focuspresent, and focusfuture) were most present in the mainstream journalistic, academic, leaked government documents, the Wikipedia set, and then the hashtag set. Proportionally, for all five sets, the main time focus was on focuspresent:

Figure 29. Auto-extracted theme and sub-theme from the leaked government document set

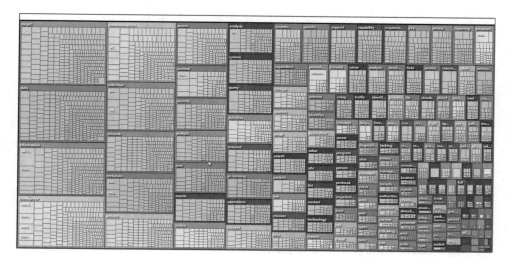

mainstream journalistic set (5.71), academic set (5.15), leaked government data (4.37), Wikipedia article network set (3.15), and hashtag discourse (1.42). Focusfuture garnered the least amount of focus of the three time periods: leaked government documents (0.85), academic (0.69), mainstream journalism (0.62), Wikipedia (0.49), and hashtag set (0.18). The mainstream journalistic article set (2.65) and the Wikipedia article set (2.22) contained the highest levels of focus on the past followed by academic articles (1.62). Journalism tends to be time-aware and time-based because of its fast news cycle, which is considered never-ending in the present age, so it is not surprising that it is ranked first. Also, the microblogging messages may not refer so much to time-based language because it is considered to be so much in-the-now and is so succinct that many communicators may not directly have language referred to focuspast, focuspresent, and focusfuture. Or in its own social lingo, the time references may not be recognized in LIWC2015.

There are some well established computational tools that measure text readability. The Online-Utility.org's Readability Calculator offers a reading including the following indexes: Coleman Liau index, Flesch Kincaid Grade Level (which is also available in Microsoft Word), ARI (Automated Readability Index), and SMOG. These measures indicate the number of years of education required to understand the text easily "on the first reading." Each of the files involve some challenges to readability. Some of the features include the difficulty of the technical materials. Other features include multi-lingual aspects and noise from transcoding from various file types. Also, there are some larger datasets, which also involve processing challenges. It will be important to explore the various computational formulations in more depth to understand how the scores are acquired. For example, some use sentence length as a measure of complexity. The following scores in Table 5: Computational Readability Measures for the Respective Five "Mass Surveillance" Text Sets. were acquired using the Readability Calculator through Online-Utility.org (https://www.online-utility.org/english/readability_test_and_improve.jsp), created by Mladen Adamovic in April 2006. As noted in the table, a few of the sets had to be minimized to about 600 pp. single-spaced of text so as not to overload the web application.

The microblogging text set had very high requirements for readability based on these measures, which is probably attributable to the fact that Tweets are not punctuated in sentence format. For those reasons, those results will not be discussed—because those results are likely spurious.

According to the computational analyses of readability, the academic articles would require 9th grade through the first year or two of university in

Table 5. Computational readability measures for the respective five "mass surveillance" text sets

	Gunning Fog Index	Coleman Liau Index	Flesch Kincaid Grade Level	ARI (Automated Readability Index)	SMOG Readability Formula	Flesch Reading Ease (/100)
Set 1: Academic article text set (partial)	13.20	11.71	10.71	9.29	12.80	43.26
Set 2: Mainstream journalistic text set	14.28	13.88	12.12	12.40	13.75	39.25
Set 3: Twitter microblogging hashtag discourse text set	28.88	32.36	24.40	29.73	21.75	-38.46 (on a 100 point scale)
Set 4: Wikipedia article network text set (partial)	11.09	12.25	9.46	8.31	11.07	44.39
Set 5: Leaked U.S. government text set (partial)	14.65	12.45	12.29	10.89	13.97	36.44

order to read with ease. The mainstream journalistic article set would require freshman to sophomore level reading skills. The Wikipedia set would require 8th grade to a little past high school of education. The leaked government documents would require 11th grade through junior level of university studies in order to read with ease. What these computations show is that the works are eminently understandable with high school and some level of university education (assuming comfort with complex technical and policy issues). According to the Flesch Reading Ease scores, the easiest-to-read text sets were, in descending order: the Wikipedia article networks, the academic articles, mainstream journalistic articles, and the leaked government texts. Again, the Twitter microblogging set is not mentioned because the structure of Tweets is not analogical to that of sentences.

Multiple Linguistic Analysis Runs on the Textual Data

These analyses were run several times because the researcher was working on establishing effective processes and initially thought the text sets were comprehensive and complete when more data was found. For example, the researcher did not originally plan on using any of the government data because it was not officially acquired (it was stolen and leaked broadly), but to leave that out would diminish the work. So she ultimately did decide to capture that data and include it as a fifth text set but to generally treat that as non-consumptive analysis (without accessing the underlying texts for deep close reading or analysis) but going with summary statistics alone. Also, there were multiple runs because there were challenges with partial or lossy text captures of the data during the transcoding process, which was mentioned above.

To summarize then, the various hitches meant that earlier data runs were no longer accurate, and the corrected data had to be re-run, and new insights had to be reported based on the findings. It was a little disconcerting how earlier interpretations of the data had to be discarded, and newer understandings had to be arrived at with analyses of larger amounts of textual data (almost always preferable).

About Internal and External Validation

There are generally two types of validation. Internal validation refers to the strength of a tool to measure what it purports to measure. For example, LIWC2015 was originated in the early-to-mid-1990s, has gone through several iterations, has dictionaries built through a rigorous multi-check process, and has literally decades of research behind it. As a tool, it is a well-documented tool along with alpha levels, which indicate (in)sufficient confidence. QSR International's NVivo 11 Plus has a long track record of quality CAQDAS software, and its newest features of machine reading are state-of-the-art currently.

External validation refers to how well the research findings apply to the world outside of the data set. One validation method involves a close and informed reading of the respective texts by experts; historically, software tools had to compete against human experts and their performance as well as other tools-of-the-same-kind. Other types of validation may involve uses of multiple software tools to measure the same construct to see if there is some convergence or agreement. In this case, there was a human reader (although a non-expert on the target topic) as well as two software tools used to measure some overlapping features of the respective text sets.

DISCUSSION

Mass surveillance is an issue that has a long history of discussion in political philosophy. In its current incarnation, with so many technical means and security incentives for the deployment of surveillance tools on various populaces, this issue is a fraught and complex one. Academic articles wrangle with legal, philosophical, technological, and practical implications of mass surveillance, and many of these pieces are advocacy works. Mainstream journalistic articles offer reportage as various foreign governments and the U.S. government (executive, legislative, and judicial branches) engages these issues. The Tweetstream around the #surveillance hashtag addresses a variety of issues linked to surveillance from a global set of communicators. The Wikipedia articles offer summary details, with highlighted events, personages, URLs, and timely observations. For those who have not seen protected documents before, the leaked "Top Secret//SI//NoFORN" documents may be a letdown; they are dry, technical, and wrapped in bureaucratese—but they do sparkle when technological means and capabilities are discussed. Even more interesting is how these documents may be read in total to understand combined methods and capabilities.

So what was learned in the four areas of direct exploration, as informed by close reading?

1. In terms of the main stakeholders stateside, the most vocal ones seem to be the following: free speech political advocacy groups, leaders of leak sites, some cybersecurity specialists, conspiracy-minded filmmakers, disgruntled former employees of the National Security Agency, and some privacy-advocates in academia. On the other side are U.S. government officials. The picture becomes more complex abroad, with plenty of lawmakers in Europe advocating more extensive privacy protections and more encryption and less (U.S.) government surveillance.

2. What are the animating ideologies, values, and emotions behind this issue of mass surveillance? On the one side are ideas of human rights and privacy, and on the other, are ideas of security within the limits of constitutional protections.

3. The foundational facts do seem to differ depending on the strategic interests of the respective groups. The issues around "mass surveillance" are complex; they entail complex histories, policies, cutting-edge technologies and methods, secrecy, and very real concerns about what the

future may look like. It may suffice to say that people's mental models of the issue are likely far less comprehensive than expert conceptual models, and even the experts all only have a piece of the picture.

4. Finally, in terms of predictives, where is this issue headed? Some observations may be made for the current present and the near-future. In terms of legal changes in the U.S., little has changed. The various SIGINT programs revealed in the leaks have been found to have been put into place legally and been kept under legal and legislative oversight ever since. The National Security Agency is now having commercial companies maintain phone metadata, but the NSA has access to that anytime with an established and legal need. If history is any indication, it is difficult to keep an issue at the forefront of a mass of people for a length of time, and this issue will eventually sunset and be replaced by other issues of the day. For an issue this complex, it has had amazing "legs" (endurance), based on drawn-out reportage and the high public attention that Snowden has received due to various movies and expensive speaking engagements, the work of interest groups, and other factors. With rising terrorist events, the surveillance state has increased in Europe. Likewise, in Russia, there have been increases in surveillance as a way to address security risks and restive populations. How this ultimately resolves in the mid-term and long-term futures is harder to address, but it is hard to imagine that a nation-state would be foolish enough to unilaterally give up security measures in a competitive and often hostile world for the sake of soothing public concerns. The levers in socio-political systems—the various arms of government, the private sector, the fifth estate, and the voting and speaking publics—all have a role.

Based on the personality frame through which many issues are debated in public, Edward Snowden is called a hero by some and a villain by others. In his own narrative, he is a patriot who spoke up for the U.S. Constitution, at great cost to himself. Through legal representation, he has made proffers to the U.S. Government to return from Moscow, where he has been living under political asylum, but only if he does not have to face espionage charges. The American Civil Liberties Union (ACLU)'s Ben Wizner, Director of the ACLU Speech, Privacy, and Technology Project, has petitioned for a presidential pardon on Edward Snowden's behalf. Other organizations supporting this effort include Human Rights Watch and Amnesty International (The Washington Post Editorial Board, Sept. 17, 2016). At the time of this chapter's writing, in the waning days of U.S. President Obama's second and last term in office, there are news reports of Stone's *Snowden* showing the lead character as a "likable patriot." The actor in the role, Joseph Gordon-Levitt, is said to have donated his full actor's fee for the film to the ACLU. As one journalist has observed, "pop culture has a long history of vindicating people" (Merry, Sept. 16, 2016). How the public responds to a public figure depends in part not only on the individual and his messaging but also proxy portrayals (such as through sympathetic actors). A counter narrative about Snowden's likeability suggests that some Snowden fatigue is setting in and that his courting public attention has led to some over-exposure. Some authors have suggested that the "robot-Snowden" is a symbol of his weakness instead of strength and serves as the ever-present embodiment of the fictional Big Brother, "the floating face pervasively reproduced on street posters, staring at passersby and reiterating the catchphrase 'Big Brother is watching you'" (Fuster & Bellanova, May 13, 2014).

If Snowden is somehow not charged, given the seriousness of his actions, the optics may be poor given that all citizens are subject to the laws of the land. Potential future leakers may consider breaking their own oaths in how they handle sensitive data, potentially causing increased insider threats (which tend to be quite high already based on the security literature).

A number of national security officials have shared their sense that Snowden was not only ill-informed but did not follow procedures in his chain-of-command, and he caused immeasurable harm in the U.S. and its interests domestically and abroad. General Hayden, in an interview with the International Spy Museum, observed:

Snowden is effect, not cause. You described a whole bunch of cultural changes. He didn't make those. He's riding that wave. All right, he is reflective of things that are changing. He is flotsam and jetsam on this political and cultural sea that is roiling and shifting, and the tides are moving. Right? And so, if anything, he may—he's got an effect in terms of perhaps accelerating some conversations, distorting some other conversations, and so on, all at great cost.... (Hayden, 2016, in Houghton, 2016)

He argues further that the actual information collection capabilities that Snowden decried have not actually changed much:

We're three years into the Snowden era now, right? What's different? Okay, what's different is NSA doesn't keep the metadata anymore, but they have access to it. Actually, Vince, they have access to more than they did under the old system just because of the way it's been set up. With regard to foreign intelligence collection, we have voluntarily restrained against ourselves from collecting against some foreign leaders comma until we change our mind and decide to start again. And so when you really look at all the huffing and puffing, fundamentally, not a whole lot has changed post-Snowden in terms of what American espionage is allowed to do. (Hayden, 2016, in Houghton, 2016)

An intelligence panel examining the Snowden leak has released a 36-page classified report with 230 footnotes to lawmakers (Nakashima, Sept. 15, 2016). A professional post-mortem on the data leak will not likely be publicly shared for decades, if then. The intelligence panel looking into the Snowden leak reportedly asserted that "Snowden failed basic annual training for NSA employees on a key provision of the Foreign Intelligence Surveillance Act, which included explanations of the privacy protections related to PRISM — another program whose details were revealed as a result of Snowden's leaks" (Nakashima, Sept. 15, 2016). The U.S. House of Representatives Permanent Select Committee on Intelligence sent an open letter to President Barack Obama urging him not to pardon Edward Snowden, "who perpetrated the largest and most damaging public disclosure of classified information in our nation's history". The bipartisan signatories suggest that the U.S. government must hold him accountable for his actions if he returns stateside. In the letter, the group pointedly denies Snowden's claims of patriotism and whistleblower status but rather suggest starkly: "He is a criminal." They write, further, that Snowden's actions do not show a focus on American privacy but "pertain to military, defense, and intelligence programs of great interest to America's enemies. In the course of doing so, he infringed on the privacy of thousands of his friends, colleagues, and fellow citizens by obtaining security credentials through misleading means, abusing his access as a systems administrator, and removing personally identifiable information." They note that the intelligence activities criticized by Snowden were "authorized and overseen by all three branches of government" and that he "took the material to China and Russia-two regimes that routinely violate their citizens, privacy and civil liberties. The information released to the public is also available to hostile intelligence services, terrorists, and many others who wish to do us harm" (U.S. House of Representatives Permanent Select Committee on Intelligence, Sept. 15, 2016). The costs of the Snowden disclosures have been estimated to be hundreds of millions of dollars for the U.S. alone and in the billions for

Silicon Valley firms (particularly those that provide cloud services, social media platforms, and those that create various mobile technologies) (Miller, March 21, 2014). The losses stemmed in part from consumer loss of confidence when information leaked that the NSA has access through "special source operations" to communications and stored data from the servers of nine IT companies to target non-U.S. users. To protect their interests, a number of U.S. researchers in information security have raised awareness of the risks of mass surveillance to "privacy, democracy, and the US technology sector" ("An Open Letter from US Researchers in Cryptography and Information Security," Jan. 24, 2014), available at http://MassSurviellance.info.

The Washington Post Editorial Board published a statement echoing the concerns of Snowden's going well beyond an American privacy platform. They write:

The complication is that Mr. Snowden did more than that. He also pilfered, and leaked, information about a separate overseas NSA Internet-monitoring program, PRISM, that was both clearly legal and not clearly threatening to privacy. (It was also not permanent; the law authorizing it expires next year.) Worse—far worse—he also leaked details of basically defensible international intelligence operations: cooperation with Scandinavian services against Russia; spying on the wife of an Osama bin Laden associate; and certain offensive cyber operations in China. No specific harm, actual or attempted, to any individual American was ever shown to have resulted from the NSA telephone metadata program Mr. Snowden brought to light. In contrast, his revelations about the agency's international operations disrupted lawful intelligence-gathering, causing possibly "tremendous damage" to national security, according to a unanimous, bipartisan report by the House Permanent Select Committee on Intelligence. What higher cause did that serve? (The Washington Post Editorial Board, 2016)

They conclude that Snowden should return to the U.S. and "hash out all of this before a jury of his peers" or seek "a bargain in which Mr. Snowden accepts a measure of criminal responsibility for his excesses and the U.S. government offers a measure of leniency in recognition of his contributions…An outright pardon, meanwhile, would strike the wrong balance" (The Washington Post Editorial Board, Sept. 17, 2016). How this settles out depends on too many factors to predict.

Globally, the outcry against mass surveillance has been trumped by events. Increasing surveillance in Europe is the current trend given the rising terror threat from both its internal populations and those from outside the EU and multiple successful terrorist spectaculars (mass shootings at music venues, the weaponizing of a truck to mow down people observing Bastille Day in Nice in 2016, and others). The security environment plays an important role in informing law enforcement practices. At such moments, practical concerns trump theory and philosophy and ideal-based storytelling.

Twelve Hypotheses of Text Set Characteristics

Of the 12 hypotheses about how the various text sets would rank, ten (Hypotheses 1 – 8, 10 and 12) were partially correct, and two (Hypotheses 9 and 11) were incorrect on all five estimates of text set rankings. There were no hypotheses that were correct on all five rankings of the five text sets on any one of the twelve dimensions: analytic, advocacy, emotion, sociality, perceptual, drives, personal concerns, informal, lifestyle, cognition, sentiment, and theme divergence. These results show the difficulty of predicting text features, particularly across five sets of previously unread texts. This also shows that the software interpretations may be difficult to guess without deeper knowledge of the respective software tools. In this work, both computational and human analytics were applied to the respective text sets, and both are seen to enhance the capabilities of the other. Content analyses would be the weaker if either were not used.

Strengths of the Respective Text Sets

So based on the four main areas of exploration, which of the text sets were most helpful for each area? In terms of identifying stakeholders, the academic article- and journalistic article sets were most informative. In terms of animating ideologies, values, and emotions, the academic articles were the most helpful and analytical; the journalistic pieces often took on the color and hue of the respective communicators, and many of the foremost journalists took on advocacy roles. In terms of foundational facts, the leaked government data, academic articles, and selected journalistic pieces were most informative. Finally, which text sets were most helpful for predictivity? The academic articles offered longer term perspectives and more historical sensibility, broadly speaking, than the other text sets. From this angle, neither of the two "social media" text sets were particularly helpful. The Wikipedia articles were mostly summary works referencing academic and journalistic and documentary texts; the Twitter microblogging messages were used mostly to drive traffic and pointed to substantive works, but the short messaging was not particularly helpful for analytical insights. (Ironically, of the five text sets, the social media and mainstream journalism pieces are the public facing ones. A majority of the public will not delve into either the academic research literature or the raw leaked government documents.) Another way to conceptualize "predictivity" is in a modeling sense. Are there any descriptive features of texts from the five text sets that could predict unlabeled articles? In these cases—for both LIWC2015 and NVivo 11 Plus, there do not seem to be sufficiently clear differentiations between the various text sets to separate out new uncoded manuscripts though computational means.

Overlaps of the Respective Text Sets?

Were there overlaps of information among the respective text sets? Certainly. The core seeding topic of mass surveillance and the confluence of various events around the leaked U.S. government documents meant that there were interesting observable relationships between the text sets. Some observations follow.

- The leaked government documents were a common denominator across the text sets because of the convergence of interest on the human interest story of Edward Snowden but also the tensions and dilemmas facing the U.S. in light of these devastating leaks of secret documents.
- Mainstream journalism articles and Twitter microblogging messages were often at the cutting edge of breaking news, but Wikipedia also had very timely information (with often updating of related articles shortly after news broke).
- Authors in academia and mainstream journalists used Twitter to share information about their publications and events.
- Some academic publications cited mainstream journalistic pieces, and some (fewer) journalistic pieces cited academic works.
- The leaked government documents were often interpreted by technology and policy experts. The hard work of making the issues relevant to and understandable by common readers was taken on by journalists, many of them top-flight ones at respected news publications (like *The Washington Post*).
- Sometimes, Twitter "events" made mainline news, such as a sidebar in which Edward Snowden was thought to have died (in August 2016)

because of a cryptic 64-digit Tweet from his Twitter account and follow-on trumped-up stories in the Russian media.

These interrelationships show something about the informational ecology and how information moves. While there are some overlaps between the respective text sets, each are quite different as shown earlier. The informational overlaps are on the margins.

This work, though, may provide a sense of where researchers may look for particular types of information. It seems advisable to cast a wide and varied net for textual data. Machine reading technologies may be helpful to delimit which particular texts should be read closely, such as through the creation of article theme histograms through theme and sub-theme extraction (Hai-Jew, Fall 2016 / Winter 2017).

Ways to Improve the Research

For every research project, there are always ways to improve. It would help to more carefully vet all texts in each set to ensure that every document is accurately placed. Close reading should happen first before any textual data are run for the various types of computational linguistic analysis and autocoding for sentiment and autocoding for theme and sub-theme extraction. Also, given the speeds of computational analyses, there is sometimes the temptation to skim-read, which is a bad idea. It helps to immerse in a subject area to avoid giving it short shrift, and it probably has helped that the issue has been a point-of-focus for at least three years regarding the Snowden leaks and then for a number of years even prior.

FUTURE RESEARCH DIRECTIONS

What are some types of follow-on research that may be conducted? One approach that builds easily to the processes described here would be to conduct a long tail analysis based on a Word Frequency Count…but focusing on the least frequent terms found in a text set. The "long tail" may show unique and rare mentions of outlier concepts, names, and phenomena.

Also, data collected in the respective sets all include imagery. Content analysis of the related imagery may be helpful, along with the URLs, multimedia, videos, and other digital data.

This research focused on the collection of five textual datasets seeded around the topic of "mass surveillance": academic articles, mainstream journalistic articles, #hashtag discourse, Wikipedia articles, and some original leaked U.S. government documents. Many more samples may be collected of each of these types of textual data. There are a range of other text types that may be tapped for this same topic, such as gray literature, commercial press releases, non-Western based texts, and personal notes and memoirs, and others.

CONCLUSION

Mass surveillance is a cause célèbre for the current age, and even three years out, there has not really been sufficient time or distance to gain sufficient perspective for a clear way forward. For the general public, it is hard to accurately gauge the amount of risk from terrorism or nation-state attacks; if truth be told, it seems to be a challenge even for those in intelligence, with privy information. In John le Carré's memoir, he critiques "the British public's collective submission to wholesale surveillance of dubious legality" and suggests that they are "the envy of every spook in the free and unfree world" (le Carré, 2016, p. 19). Indeed, across the pond, U.S. citizens are not simply accepting government arguments that they must trade away privacy for security.

There are various stakeholder groups that have come forward who want a remedy to "mass surveillance" through lawsuits, policy-making, mixes of technologies, and other efforts. Researchers have been exploring the salient laws in Europe and the U.S. regarding electronic surveillance (Fura & Klamberg, 2012). Others point to the burden of costs for private companies and organizations to have to retain data by EU telecoms and electronic communications service providers to comply with the Data Retention Directive (Maras, April 2012).

This chapter engaged computational linguistic analysis to shed light on larger-scale textual data in order to better understand language patterns in various text corpora. The topic used to seed this exploration is a contemporaneously vivid topic, "mass surveillance," which enabled the extraction of topical academic articles, mainstream journalistic articles, Twitter microblogging messaging, Wikipedia articles, and leaked U.S. government documents. While the present incarnation of this conversation stemmed from the actions of Edward Snowden and revelations that came to light from the documents he stole and leaked, the idea of mass surveillance has been around for hundreds of years.

In the highly complex national security and law enforcement environment, with evolving threats, surveillance is a critical tool, which has to be wielded within the strictures of constitutionality, legal oversight, government oversight, human rights and liberties, and volatile public opinion. People engage in an environment in which technologists are engaged in a "tech arms race," and to the winners go plenty of spoils and the loss of privacy and often the lessening of security. In this sense, democratic governments have to get their first to protect people, citizens and non-citizens, but they work in an environment in which there is a clash of cultures and gaps in knowledge. In this battlespace, those working toward national security and the rule of law have to make their case more convincingly than has been achieved so far.

ACKNOWLEDGMENT

This work would not have been possible without the various respective sources of the texts: academic publishers, journalists and their news organizations, Twitter, the Wikimedia Foundation, and the Snowden Surveillance Archive. I am sincerely grateful for their resources.

Competition between peoples is informed by the capabilities of the age, and the capabilities to be aware and to surveil accurately and lawfully (and constitutionally) are necessary for government and law enforcement.

An early version of this presentation was made at "Aesthesia," at the Marianna Kistler Beach Museum of Art (at Kansas State University), on March 2, 2017. A related slideshow from that event is available on SlideShare at http://www.slideshare.net/ShalinHaiJew/mass-surveillance-through-distant-reading. I am grateful to the organizers for including this presentation at their event.

REFERENCES

Adamovic, M. (2006, Apr.). *Online-Utility.org*. Accessed Oct. 22, 2016, from https://www.online-utility.org/about_us.jsp

An Open Letter from US Researchers in Cryptography and Information Security. (2014, Jan. 24). Retrieved Sept. 9, 2016, from http://MassSurveillance.info

Andrejevic, M. (2002, June). The work of being watched: Interactive media and the exploitation of self-disclosure. *Critical Studies in Media Communication, 19*(2), 230 – 248. DOI: 10.1080/07393180216561

Bakir, V. (2015). "Veillant Panoptic Assemblage": Mutual watching and resistance to mass surveillance after Snowden. Media and Communication, 3(3), 12 – 25.

Barnard-Willis, D. (2011, Fall). UK news media discourses of surveillance. *The Sociological Quarterly, 52*(4), 548–567. doi:10.1111/j.1533-8525.2011.01219.x

Bentham, J. (1843d). Panopticon, Constitution, Colonies, Codification, Liberty fund. *The Works, 4.*

Black, E. (2001, 2002, 2009, 2011). IBM and the Holocaust. Washington, DC: Dialog Press.

Calamur, K. (2013, July 25). For American defectors to Russia, an unhappy history. *National Public Radio*. Retrieved Sept. 20, 2016, from http://www.npr.org/sections/parallels/2013/07/24/205121529/for-american-defectors-to-russia-an-unhappy-history

Clarke, R. (2001, January – February). While you were sleeping… surveillance technologies arrived. *The Australian Quarterly, 73*(1), 10–14. doi:10.2307/20637967

Clarke, R. (2003). *Dataveillance – 15 years on*. Retrieved Sept. 12, 2016, from http://www.rogerclarke.com/DV/DVNZ03.html

Danks, D. (2014, Winter). A modern Pascals Wager for mass electronic surveillance. *Telos, 169*(169), 155–161. doi:10.3817/1214169155

Edmundson, A., Ensafi, R., Feamster, N., & Rexford, J. (2016). A first look into transnational routing detours. *SIGCOMM '16*, 567 – 568. doi:10.1145/2934872.2959081

Epstein, E. J. (2017). *How American Lost its Secrets: Edward Snowden, the Man and the Theft*. New York: Alfred A. Knopf.

Friedersdorf, C. (2014, Feb. 19). Mass surveillance of all car trips is nearly upon us. *The Atlantic*. Retrieved Sept. 8, 2016, from http://www.theatlantic.com/politics/archive/2014/02/mass-surveillance-of-all-car-trips-is-nearly-upon-us/283922/

Fura, E., & Klamberg, M. (2012, Oct. 23). The chilling effect of counter-terrorism measures: A comparative analysis of electronic surveillance laws in Europe and the U.S.A. In J. Casadevall, E. Myjer, & M. O'Boyle (Eds.), *Freedom of Expression—Essays in Honour of Nicolas Bratza, President of the European Court of Human Rights.* Oisterwijk: Wolf Legal Publishers. Retrieved Sept. 11, 2016, from http://papers.ssrn.com/sol3/papers.cfm?abstract_id=2169894

Fuster, G. G., & Bellanova, R. (2014, May 13). Edward Snowden: the last Big Brother? *openDemocracy.* Retrieved Sept. 13, 2016, from https://www.opendemocracy.net/can-europe-make-it/gloria-gonz%C3%A1lez-fuster-rocco-bellanova/edward-snowden-last-big-brother

Gellman, B., & Soltani, A. (2013, Dec. 4). NSA tracking cellphone locations worldwide, Snowden documents show. *The Washington Post.* Retrieved from http://wapo.st/IIaYWp

Goold, B. J. (2010). How Much Surveillance is Too Much? Some Thoughts on Surveillance, Democracy, and the Political Value of Privacy In D. W. Schartum (Ed.), *Overvåkning i en rettsstat - Surveillance in a constitutional government.* Fagbokforlaget, 2010. Available at SSRN: http://ssrn.com/abstract=1876069

Grumbling, E. (2016). *Privacy research and best practices: Summary of a workshop for the intelligence community.* Washington, DC: The National Academies Press; doi:10.17226/21879

Hai-Jew, S. (2016). Creating article theme histograms to map a topic. *C2C Digital Magazine.* Retrieved Sept. 17, 2016, from http://scalar.usc.edu/works/c2c-digital-magazine-fall-2016--winter-2017/creating-article-theme-histograms-to-map-a-topic

Houghton, V. (2016, May 3). *Playing to the Edge: An Interview with Gen. Michael Hayden.* Spycast. International Spy Museum. Retrieved Sept. 8, 2016, from http://www.spymuseum.org/multimedia/spycast/episode/playing-to-the-edge-an-interview-with-gen-michael-hayden/

Hu, M. (2015). Taxonomy of the Snowden disclosures. *Washington and Lee Law Review, 72*(4), 1679 – 1767. Retrieved Sept. 8, 2016, from http://scholarlycommons.law.wlu.edu/wlulr/vol72/iss4/4/

Inkster, N. (2014). The Snowden revelations: Myths and misapprehensions. *Survival—Global Politics and Strategy, 56*(1), 51 – 60. Retrieved Sept. 11, 2016, from.10.1080/00396338.2014.882151

Jespersen, J. L., Albrechtslund, A., Øhrstrøm, P., Hasle, P., & Albretsen, J. (2007). Surveillance, persuasion, and panopticon. In Y. de Kort (Eds.), *Persuasive 2007. LNCS 4744.* Heidelberg, Germany: Springer-Verlag. doi:10.1007/978-3-540-77006-0_15

Kelley, M. B. (2015, June 13). Snowden may have some clarifying to do after bombshell reports that Russia and China accessed NSA files. *Business Insider.* Retrieved Sept. 20, 2016, from http://www.businessinsider.com/snowden-russia-china-and-nsa-files-2015-6

Kirn, W. (2015, Nov.) If you're not paranoid, you're crazy. *The Atlantic.* Retrieved Sept. 8, 2016, from http://www.theatlantic.com/magazine/archive/2015/11/if-youre-not-paranoid-youre-crazy/407833/

Kullenberg, C. (2009). The social impact of IT: Surveillance and resistance in present-day conflicts: How can activists and engineers work together? *FIfF-Kommunikation, 1/09,* 37–40.

Lange, S. (2014, Winter). The end of social media revolutions. *The Fletcher Forum of World Affairs, 38*(I), 47–68.

le Carré, J. (2016). *The Pigeon Tunnel: Stories from My Life.* New York: Penguin Random House.

Lessig, L. (1999). *Code and Other Laws of Cyberspace.* New York: Basic Books.

Lichter, A., Löffler, M., & Siegloch, S. (2015, July). *The economic costs of mass surveillance: Insights from Stasi spying in East Germany.* Discussion Paper No. 9245. Forschunginstitut zur Zukunft der Arbeit Institute for the Study of Labor. IZA.

Loewenstein, A. (2014, July 11). The ultimate goal of the NSA is total population control: At least 80% of all audio calls, not just metadata, are recorded and stored in the U.S., says whistleblower William Binney—that's a 'totalitarian mentality'. *The Guardian.* Retrieved Sept. 13, 2016, from https://www.theguardian.com/commentisfree/2014/jul/11/the-ultimate-goal-of-the-nsa-is-total-population-control

Maras, M.-H. (2012, April). The economic costs and consequences of mass communications data retention: Is the data retention directive a proportionate measure?. *European Journal of Law and Economics, 33*(2), 447–472. doi:10.1007/s10657-011-9245-8

Merry, S. (2016, Sept. 15). Can Oliver Stone's 'Snowden' convince the world that its subject is not a traitor?. *The Washington Post.* Retrieved Sept. 16, 2016, from https://www.washingtonpost.com/lifestyle/style/can-oliver-stones-snowden-convince-the-world-that-its-subject-is-not-a-traitor/2016/09/14/61e88768-79b4-11e6-bd86-b7bbd53d2b5d_story.html

Milaj, J., & Bonnici, J. P. M. (2014). Unwitting subjects of surveillance and the presumption of innocence. *Computer Law & Security Report, 30*(4), 419–428. doi:10.1016/j.clsr.2014.05.009

Miller, C. C. (2014, Mar. 21). Revelations of N.S.A. spying cost U.S. tech companies. *The New York Times.* Retrieved Sept. 18, 2016, from http://www.nytimes.com/2014/03/22/business/fallout-from-snowden-hurting-bottom-line-of-tech-companies.html?_r=0

Moody, G. (2015, Sept. 25). 'Snowden Treaty' proposed to curtail mass surveillance and protect whistleblowers: It's a nice idea, but will it actually achieve anything?. *Ars Technica.* Retrieved Sept. 19, 2016, from http://arstechnica.com/tech-policy/2015/09/snowden-treaty-proposed-to-curtail-mass-surveillance-and-protect-whistleblowers/

Nakashima, E. (2016, Sept. 15). House Intelligence Committee urges no pardon for Edward Snowden. *The Washington Post.* Retrieved Sept. 16, 2016, from https://www.washingtonpost.com/world/national-security/house-intelligence-committe-urges-no-pardon-for-edward-snowden/2016/09/15/f647a6f4-7b86-11e6-beac-57a4a412e93a_story.html?hpid=hp_no-name_snowdenmovie-830pm-1%3Ahomepage%2Fstory

Parsons, C. (2015). Beyond privacy: Articulating the broader harms of pervasive mass surveillance. Media and Communication, 3(3), 1 – 11.

Pennebaker, J. W., Booth, R. J., Boyd, R. L., & Francis, M. E. (2015). *Linguistic Inquiry and Word Count: LIWC2015.* Austin, TX: Pennebaker Conglomerates. Retrieved Sept. 6, 2016, from https://s3-us-west-2.amazonaws.com/downloads.liwc.net/LIWC2015_OperatorManual.pdf

Pozen, D. E. (2016). Privacy-privacy tradeoffs. *The University of Chicago Law Review. University of Chicago. Law School*, *83*(1), 221–247. Retrieved from http://www.jstor.org/stable/43741598

Schneier, B. (2013, Apr. 5). The U.S. government has betrayed the Internet. We need to take it back. *Guardian UK*. Retrieved Sept. 13, 2016, from https://www.theguardian.com/commentisfree/2013/sep/05/government-betrayed-internet-nsa-spying

Schneier, B. (2015, Mar. 2). What's next in government surveillance. *The Atlantic*. Retrieved Sept. 8, 2016, from http://www.theatlantic.com/international/archive/2015/03/whats-next-in-government-surveillance/385667/

Silverman, J. (2013, July 8). Data, secrets, and the surveillance state. *The New Yorker*. Retrieved Sept. 8, 2016, from http://www.newyorker.com/tech/elements/data-secrets-and-the-surveillance-state

Stahl, T. (2016, March). Indiscriminate mass surveillance and the public sphere. *Ethics and Information Technology*, *18*(1), 33–39. doi:10.1007/s10676-016-9392-2

Subramanian, C. (2013, Dec. 21). U.S. officials declassify documents on NSA surveillance program's origins. *Time, Inc.* Retrieved Sept. 13, 2016, from http://nation.time.com/2013/12/21/u-s-officials-declassify-documents-on-nsa-surveillance-programs-origins/

(The) Washington Post Editorial Board. (2016, Sept. 17). The Post's View: No pardon for Edward Snowden. *The Washington Post*. Retrieved Sept. 19, 2016, from https://www.washingtonpost.com/opinions/edward-snowden-doesnt-deserve-a-pardon/2016/09/17/ec04d448-7c2e-11e6-ac8e-cf8e0dd91dc7_story.html?utm_term=.e962f40bb890

Tryfonas, T., Carter, M., Crick, T., & Andriotis, P. (2016). Mass surveillance in cyberspace and the lost art of keeping a secret: Policy lessons for government after the Snowden leaks. LNCS, 9750, 174 – 185. DOI: 16 doi:10.1007/978-3-319-39381-0

United Nations Human Rights Office of the High Commissioner. (n.d.). *The right to privacy in the digital age*. Retrieved Sept. 19, 2016, from http://www.ohchr.org/EN/Issues/DigitalAge/Pages/DigitalAgeIndex.aspx

U.S. House of Representatives Permanent Select Committee on Intelligence. (2016, Sept. 15). *Letter to The Honorable Barack Obama*. Retrieved Sept. 16, 2016, from http://intelligence.house.gov/uploadedfiles/hpsci_members_letter_to_potus_re_snowden-15_sep_16.pdf

Waddell, K. (2016, Apr. 5). How surveillance stifles dissent on the Internet. *The Atlantic*. Retrieved Sept. 8, 2016, from http://www.theatlantic.com/technology/archive/2016/04/how-surveillance-mutes-dissent-on-the-internet/476955/

Williams, J. (2016, Feb. 17). Laura Poitras' FOIA documents part of new surveillance show at the Whitney Museum. *Electronic Frontier Foundation: Defending your Rights in the Digital World*. Retrieved Sept. 21, 2016, from https://www.eff.org/deeplinks/2016/02/laura-poitras-foia-documents-part-new-surveillance-show-whitney-museum

Zalnieriute, M. (2015, March). An international constitutional moment for data privacy in the times of mass-surveillance. *International Journal of Law and Information Technology*, *23*(2), 99–133. doi:10.1093/ijlit/eav005

ADDITIONAL READING

Hai-Jew, S. (2016, May 5). LIWC-ing at Texts for Insights from Linguistic Patterns. SlideShare. Retrieved Sept. 6, 2016, from http://www.slideshare.net/ShalinHaiJew/liwcing-at-texts-for-insights-from-linguistic-patterns

Pennebaker, J. W., Booth, R. J., Boyd, R. L., & Francis, M. E. (2015). Linguistic Inquiry and Word Count: LIWC2015. Austin, TX: Pennebaker Conglomerates (www.LIWC.net). Retrieved Sept. 6, 2016, from https://s3-us-west-2.amazonaws.com/downloads.liwc.net/LIWC2015_OperatorManual.pdf

KEY TERMS AND DEFINITIONS

Article-Article Network (on Wikipedia): A listing of outgoing hyperlinks from a target article page on Wikipedia, a crowd-sourced encyclopedia.

Autocoding: Automated machine coding of text, which may be performed in a human-supervised or an unsupervised way.

Computational Linguistic Analysis: The use of computer programs to describe and analyze various features of texts and text sets (corpora).

Construct: A human created conceptualization of an empirically observed phenomenon.

Consumptive Linguistic Analysis: The language-based analysis of text or text sets with direct access to the underlying selected texts.

Content Analysis: A method of learning and critique that explores various types of multimedial human communications.

Crowd-Sourced: Created and maintained through volunteer contributions such as through online methods.

External Validation: The uses of external from-world information to evaluate the accuracy or inaccuracy of a model or research instrument.

Hashtag Network: The group of social media user accounts and their messaging around a particular #hashtag, with the data captured within a certain continuous time period.

Hierarchy Chart: A data visualization, which communicates information with ranked or gradation information.

Internal Validation: The evaluation of a research instrument to assess whether it is effective and accurate in identifying certain constructs in a consistent way.

Linguistics: The formal study of language.

LIWC (Linguistic Inquiry and Word Count): A software tool that enables the extraction of over 90 language variables.

Mass Surveillance: The capture of broad-scale information about people to enable monitoring and intervention.

NVivo 11 Plus: A computer assisted qualitative data analysis (CAQDAS) software tool.

Non-Consumptive Linguistic Analysis: The language-based analysis of text or text sets with no direct access to the underlying selected texts (such as in the Google Books Ngram Viewer).

Reliability: The ability of a research instrument to yield the same results on repeated research trials.

Sentiment Analysis: The extraction of observed positive or negative sentiment from text sets.

Sunburst Diagram: A hierarchy chart, which captures main topical terms in the center and sub-terms in the periphery.

Theme: A main idea or topic.

Topic modeling: The capturing of the main themes and subthemes in a text document or text set through computational means to provide a meaningful summary representation of a textual work or textual set.

Treemap Diagram: A hierarchy chart, which shows selected word frequencies, with larger clusters to the left and smaller clusters to the right (by convention).

Chapter 5

See Ya!

Exploring American Renunciation of Citizenship Through Targeted and Sparse Social Media Data Sets and a Custom Spatial–Based Linguistic Analysis Dictionary

ABSTRACT

The renunciation of U.S. citizenship is a non-trivial action, with far-reaching implications, for the individual, his / her social group, and even for the nation. While several U.S. government agencies collect information about this phenomenon, little actual data are publicly shared and mostly only through the U.S. Internal Revenue Service. Social media platforms—Twitter, Facebook, Flickr, Wikipedia, and Reddit (among others)—offer some insights about American renunciation of citizenship. From this targeted data, it is possible to design and collate a custom-made spatial-based dictionary (to run on LIWC2015) in order to automate the analysis of textual data about this phenomenon. This paper describes this process of creating a custom spatial-based dictionary, methods for pilot-testing the dictionary's efficacy (with "test" social media data sets, with experts, and with discovered insights about the target phenomenon), fresh space-based insights about American renunciation of citizenship, and future research directions.

DOI: 10.4018/978-1-5225-2679-7.ch005

INTRODUCTION

Human migrations occur for a range of reasons. Some may be disasters, like natural disasters, human warfare, politics, persecution, and the slave trade, and others. There may be economic downturns that lead to out-migration. Some migrations are forced, and others are volitional. In addition to large-scale patterns, there are localized ones: people moving to study, people moving to be with family, people exploring ancestral locations (and their own identities), people exploring different lifestyles, people in pursuit of careers and adventure, and people in retirement. After life traumas, people sometimes move in order to have fresh starts. Such migrations are not barrier-free. There are real-world costs and regulations, bureaucracies on every side of every border, and opportunity costs (moving to one location for some opportunities will close doors on other options). Even more demanding are citizenship requirements, when these are even available. For many countries, they require years of residency, and also proof of health, law abidance, language requirements, and oaths of loyalty.

At any one time, there may be three to eight million Americans living overseas, or even up to nine million non-military U.S. citizens living abroad. These individuals are known as being part of the "American diaspora" ("American diaspora," Dec. 13, 2016). Their living abroad does not mean that this will be a permanent state or that the U.S. expatriates will eventually renounce citizenship. As a matter of fact, the numbers of those renouncing citizenship are vanishingly small.

There may be any number of reasons why people may pursue renunciation or relinquishment of their U.S. citizenship. In the first case, the individual has to file for a Certificate of Loss of Nationality and then square matters with the tax authorities. In the latter case, those filing for relinquishment file a Statement of Voluntary Relinquishment of U.S. Citizenship under Section 349 (a)(1) of the INA" (Immigration and Naturalization Act), and here, the loss of U.S. citizenship is a byproduct of prior actions taking on another nationality and another citizenship. These latter actions may include taking an oath of allegiance to another country, naturalized in a foreign country, served in the armed forces of a foreign state (with non-hostile relations with the U.S.), taken on non-policy level employment with a foreign government, or other actions. In 2015, there are varying estimates for the numbers of former U.S. citizens who chose to renounce their citizenship. One author puts this number 4,250 in 2015, an 18-fold increase from the approximately 250 expatriate renunciators in 2008 (Jamison, Nov. 10, 2016); he named some of the destination countries: Costa Rica, Singapore, and the Bahamas. This author cites sources suggesting that there may be even higher rates of U.S. citizenship renunciation.

In fact, possibly correlated to the election of a new president that year, or even to the start of the great financial crisis, the number of Americans renouncing their U.S. citizenship spiked from a low of roughly 250 expatriates in 2008 by a factor of 18 by 2015. And based on statistics gathered earlier this year by the Federal Register, 2016 promises to generate the highest number of renouncers yet. (Jamison, 2016)

[Side Note: It may be important to note that "expats" or people who live abroad from their countries of citizenship do not necessarily renounce their original citizenship. Living abroad is not a necessary precursor to renouncing citizenship, as some renounce and leave "cold" without having lived abroad. Experiences traveling and living abroad may provide a path to a location of interest for living abroad for some. The inclusion of "expat" studies is that is does have some relationship to the renunciation of citizenship but a very small one. For some, renunciation of citizenship is a thought-through and planned process; for others, it may be impulsive.]

This renunciation of citizenship by Americans is occurring in a time when local trends related to interstate migration declining 25 to 50 percent (based on National Bureau of Economic Research statistics) has been trending downward because of a somewhat inactive jobs market and economy (Leefeldt, Nov. 29, 2016).

According to a writer for *Forbes*, these numbers of former Americans who've renounced their citizenship are even higher (6,545 people) even though the costs for citizenship renunciation and relinquishment have gone up four-fold in order to cover the actual costs to process the paperwork. The U.S. has the world's highest fee to renounce citizenship, according to MoveHub. One author notes: "And the $2,350 fee is more than twenty times the average level in other high-income countries" (Wood, Oct. 23, 2015).

The State Department estimates the number of applications for a Certificate of Loss of Nationality. For 2015, the State Department estimates it separately for renunciations (5,986) and relinquishment (559). The distinction is technical, with the latter qualifying for a reduced fee until recently. Now, the filing fee *to leave the U.S. is $2,345, a whopping increase in fees of 422%. In any case, this would make the State Department tally a total of 6,545. (Wood, 2015)*

The highest costs for formalizing renunciation of citizenship are, in descending order, USA ($2,350), Jamaica ($1,010), Egypt ($800), Sierra Leone ($663), and Poland ($404). The least expensive countries are, in descending order: Taiwan ($30), Germany ($28), Singapore ($27), South Korea ($20), Malaysia ($4), and Chile, Ireland, Japan, South Africa, and Sweden (free) (Cann, Nov. 9, 2016).

Even if the number of former U.S. citizens who've renounced citizenship is 6,545, out of a population of 325 million citizens and counting (according to the U.S. Census Bureau's "U.S. and World Population Clock"), that is only .00002 of the population or 2/100,000. Americans "of means" who have a net worth higher than $2 million or an average annual net income tax for the five previous years of $160,000 or more have to pay an exit tax. Those who sold properties at the time of leaving have a capital gains exemption of $680,000 (Wood, Oct. 23, 2015). The "deemed disposition exit tax" costs apply to those who have green cards as well:

Longterm (sic) residents giving up a Green Card can be required to pay the tax too. No one wants to pay an exit tax if they can avoid it. Sometimes planning and valuations can reduce or even eliminate the tax. But taxed or not, many still seem to be headed for the exits. Some groups are especially vocal about their tax plight. Last year, dual citizens in Canada trying to shed their U.S. citizenship created a backlog at the U.S. consulate in Toronto. President Obama has joked about his birth certificate, but accidental American status is no joke. Many end up in untenable financial situations.

There are other government offices that are keeping count. Besides the U.S. State Department, the U.S. Treasury Department's Internal Revenue Service (IRS) publishes a quarterly listing of individuals who have "chosen to expatriate" permanently ("Quarterly publication of individuals..." Nov. 11, 2016). The U.S. Department of Justice's Federal Bureau of Investigations (FBI) maintains records of former Americans who have renounced or otherwise lost citizenship in order to enforce a "no-buy list" for firearms. There were reportedly 23,807 individuals on this no-buy list as of December 31, 2013 (Wood, Sept. 21, 2015).

No matter what the exact count, it is likely that the reported numbers are short, given that many renounce and relinquish U.S. citizenship in a *de facto* way by going abroad and not maintaining any ties to the U.S. These counts are for those who officially formalize their "divorce" from a nation (by filing under 349(a)(5) of the Immigration and Naturalization Act) and those who are observed by law enforcement. When high-profile citizens relinquish U.S. citizenship, such as Tina Turner's signing of her "Statement of Voluntary Relinquishment of U.S. Citizenship under Section 349 (a)(1) of the INA" (Immigration and Naturalization Act), it may make headlines (Kamen, Nov. 12, 2013), but for the majority, such issues are generally handled fairly quietly.

Citizenship renunciation is not a topic that is commonly in the public awareness. A search in the Google Books Ngram Viewer shows that the term itself ("citizenship renunciation" as a bigram or two words in a particular defined order) did not spark until the early 1960s—a time of social change (or some might say "turmoil") in the U.S. and rising through the 1970s and 1980s, and then dropping in popularity for some years and rising again in 2000 onwards. The Google Books Ngram Viewer points to the following as critical years for this topic of "citizenship renunciation": 1800 – 1970, 1971 – 1978, 1979, 1980 – 1998, and 1999 – 2000. One helpful research track may include research on what occurred during these time periods that may have brought the issue to the forefront of the public mind in terms of research and book publishing.

While citizenship renunciation may seem to be a fairly simple issue of filing some forms and leaving the country, it is actually quite a bit more complicated. In Figure 1, there is a summary of some of the personal and regulatory reasons why people have renounced American citizenship based on both a review of the academic literature and of select social media data streams. The figure suggests that people have various life circumstances in which it may make sense to "renounce" or "relinquish" American citizenship (with the first being more active than the latter). These circumstances may involve issues of adventure-seeking, lifestyle changes, travel, family situations and relationships, children or family citizenship issues, employment opportunities, and others. Regulatory issues may include the rights and responsibilities of citizenship, such as taxation and legal issues, among others. (Historically, a military draft was a reason for moving abroad and taking on other citizenship, but this is not a current issue.) While there may be a variety of personal and regulatory reasons that may encourage Americans to settle abroad permanently, this diagram also shows some barriers to citizenship renunciation: social pressures, costs, logistics, and legal requirements.

In terms of social pressures, citizenship is a feature of identity that is foundational and can feel sacred. It is literally a birthright for many, based

Figure 1. "Citizenship Renunciation" linegraph in the Google Books Ngram Viewer

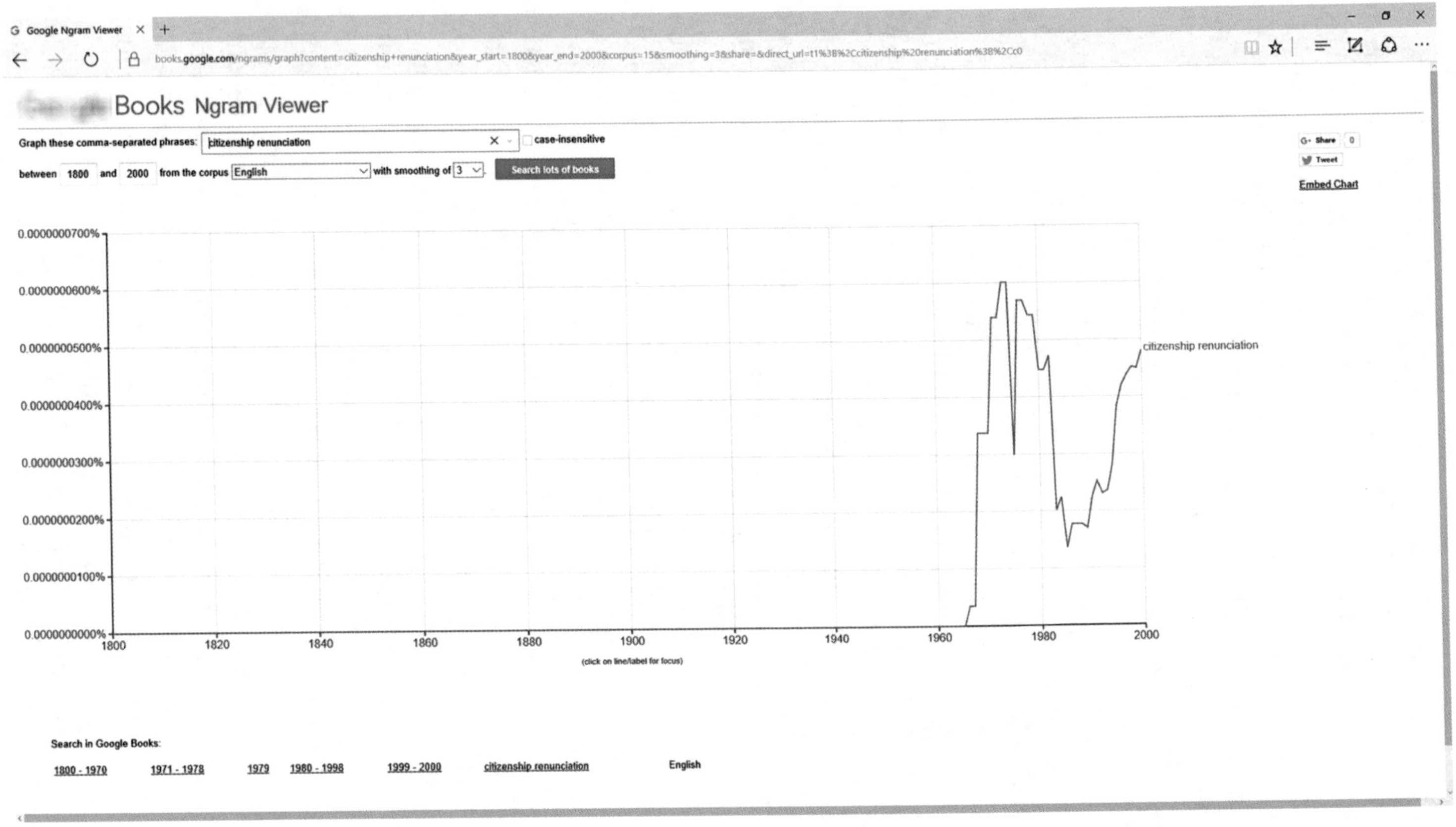

on *jus sanguinis* and by *jus soli*, citizenship by blood (parents' nationality) and by soil (birth within the borders of the U.S.). For many others, there is Americanization based on naturalization—the attaining of a "green card" and then going through the citizenship process as an original foreign national. Suffice it to say that American citizenship is prized in the world because of the high living standards, high education and work opportunities, high baskets of social goods provided by government, and liberal-democratic "live-and-let-live" attitudes. U.S. citizenship often entails national pride. As a document, a U.S. passport enables wide travel.

Exploring the Issue via Social Media Platforms

Since there are not many formal government channels to access for deeper understandings of American renunciation of citizenship, it was thought that social media may offer a way to better understand this phenomenon. The underlying intuition is that while many make such a momentous decision quietly, others do so with public sharing and fanfare, particularly through social media channels. And still others are interested in maintaining relationships with other expats and renouncers and with friends stateside. Also, for practical reasons, people who are interested in renouncing their U.S. citizenship or who already have renounced U.S. citizenship go to social media in order to elicit

Figure 2. Some expressed reasons for renunciation of U.S. citizenship in the literature

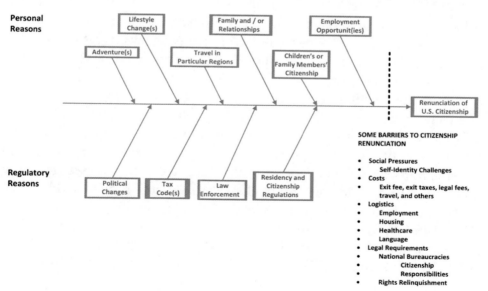

information and advice, and to meet some social needs, including supporting others with similar interests or with similar senses of nationhood. The social media data may show in-world manifestations of this phenomenon given that this cannot be directly emulated in a test or lab environment. It is assumed that there are private underground channels (and Hidden Web businesses linked to human migrations), too, for such information exchange, but that is beyond the purview of this work. For many social media networks, they have some public or semi-public presence that leaks information that may be exploited with manual and computational analytical means. Some early work on the use of social media to learn more about the American renunciation of citizenship was done by this author (Hai-Jew, 2015, 2017).

This follow-on work uses social media to explore the role of physical space related to this topic. What can geolocational information from social media contents reveal about the phenomenon of American emigration abroad? What are some favored locations, and why? How is spatiality conceptualized by American "expats" and "emigrants" abroad? Further, what do these data sets reveal about American renunciation of citizenship? (This does assume that emigration may be a mid-step between the decision to renounce citizenship and move abroad permanently.) What types of geolocational information may be found in various types of social media data (a microblogging site, a social networking site, an image- and video-sharing site, a crowd-sourced encyclopedia, and a news sharing and discussion board site)? How can this information be used to inform the creation of a geo-spatial based dictionary in LIWC2015? What were the methods used to process this information? What are some insights about place and national identity? (After all, there is so much meaning to place-based labels of identity, whether it is "American" or "Britisher" or "Hong Kong Chinese"? Also, are there expressed emotions related to place by those considering renouncing U.S. citizenship or those who have fully renounced U.S. citizenship?

In this work, the data was sampled by extracting a subset of related information based on a topic seed under the general idea "American renunciation of citizenship," American emigration or out-migration, and American expatriate experiences. In this case, the data captured generally involved only one limited non-random data extraction of a small subset of available information. The methods for data sampling and extraction clearly affect what is captured and how accurately the in-world phenomena are represented (De Choudhury, Lin, Sundaram, Candan, Xie, & Kelliher, 2010). Naïve measures will result in less accurate data collection. The type of sampling method to use depends on the research questions, the hypotheses, the types of data needed, the social media platforms, and other factors.

Physical Locations and Renunciation of U.S. Citizenship

Physical locations and mental models of locations are central parts of the dynamic in the renunciation of citizenship from the U.S. In every case of renunciation or relinquishment of citizenship, the individual or family or group has to leave the country and may then only return with a proper U.S. visa and documentation of citizenship from another nation-state. Those who go abroad may not leave forwarding addresses, except possibly to some government offices and to close family and friends; certainly, these are not directly publicly available (and not in the public realm). While social media usage is popular and broad, and mobile devices with locative technologies have been credited for enabling accurate locational data captures, the Internet and mobile devices have been contributors to a sense of "placelessness"; the virtual realm displaces people from their geographical spaces. Hamilton (2009) writes:

Several theorists have argued that we are in danger of losing our sense of place (Poster, 2005). This emerging "placelessness" is not just attributable to the Internet. Rowen Wilken (2005) argues that mobile phones also "insulate their users from the geographical place they are actually in" (p. 4) and others argue that it is a symptom of modern cities in general, which they describe as "nonplaces" (Poster, 2005). Nonetheless, online applications shape our understanding of community, and they are often disconnected from a sense of place. (p. 393)

A more recent understanding is that "locative media" (coined by Karlis Kalnins in 2004), with the labeling of geospatial lat-long coordinates, enables a re-situating of people in space and association with others in space (Hamilton, 2009, pp. 394 and 396). Social media data contains ambient geospatial information and enable the mapping of geographic footprints to enable "a unique opportunity to gain valuable insight on information flow and social networking within a society, and may even support a greater mapping and understanding of the human landscape and its evolution over time" (Stefanidis, Crooks, & Radzikowski, 2011, p. 2). As others have observed, everything happens in space-time, and that data may be evocative of various in-world phenomena:

- People sharing space-time co-movement (co-traveling) may be a group that knows each other walking or otherwise moving together (with their mobile devices on) (Gellman & Soltani, Dec. 4, 2013, Fan, Zhang, Wu, & Tan, 2016).
- People who live in a community may share a general lifestyle, set of values, spending habits, and other predictable features. For examples, people's zip codes can be highly revealing of lifestyles and spending habits (LaFrance, Oct. 14, 2014).
- People who work within a certain proximity (50 feet) in a company are more likely to collaborate than if they are even just a little farther apart (Toker & Gray, 2008).
- It is possible to infer, with fairly high accuracy, the locations of communicators on social media by the types of contents they are creating, based in part on their social networks (Jurgens, 2013, p. 273). The words that people use on social media may be indicative of their lifestyles, levels of education, and other factors, including their sense of happiness in particular geographical locations (Mitchell, Frank, Harris, Dodds, & Danford, 2013).

In other words, there are interaction effects between space and place and a range of human experiences and ways of being. There are rich types of knowledge attainable about people based on observed place-based interactions. So, too, for the issue of American renunciation of citizenship. From the initial research, two hypotheses related to spatiality were created:

Hypothesis 1: Central "Beaten Paths" With Some Outlier Paths

There are identifiable "beaten paths" that Americans who renounce citizenship take to known destinations, based on family, tourism, travel abroad, locational language(s), and cultural features. Also, it is assumed that there are moderating businesses (law firms, moving companies), governments, religious organizations, political organizations, and other entities that facilitate American resettlement in other locales. Also, in contrast to the beaten paths, there will be some anomalous and unique paths for those renouncing citizenship. These outlier paths may be informed by the unique trajectories of some people's lives.

For example, there is the saying, "You can take boy / girl out of the country, but you can't take the country out of the boy / girl." This suggests that a person's experiences growing up will inform their taste for location in the future. In this sense, people prefer the familiar. Of course, there is also the saying, "You can't go home again," which suggests that even if there is a longing for the familiar, the particulars can be impossible to recreate. Hypothesis 2 may be understood both collectively and individually.

Hypothesis 2: Identifiable Attractive and Aversive Forces Related to ("Sending" and "Receiving") Places

Individuals on social media who assert that they have renounced U.S. citizenship have combinations of spatial-based "attractive" and "aversive" forces that drive the decision. In other words, people decide to renounce U.S. citizenship in order to leave places with negative associations (both perceived and real) and to go to places with positive associations (both perceived and real). [This is informed by expectancy theory.] Further, these attractive and aversive forces are determined in part by the regulatory environment (regulations and practices) around formal migrations, and these laws and practices are mostly in the governmental domain. On a macro level, geographical spaces and places are linked to collectively lived human experiences. These places are governed by government rules and policies and practices. These are mediated by global news and social media. Generally, geographical spaces and places may be seen as positive or negative for citizens during particular time periods, and these may result in larger citizenship actions and movements beyond individual decisions.

Creating a custom spatial-based linguistic analysis dictionary for this topic would enable more efficient analyses of this social phenomenon of Americans leaving the borders of the country and finding permanent succor elsewhere. After all, a central aspect of renouncing citizenship involves moving elsewhere because a person who is no longer American no longer has rights to remain on American soil and must apply for a visa to enter U.S. borders. Location is by definition one important aspect of migration. Locational proximity has been used as an indicator of shared language, lifestyle, culture, politics, social lives, and shared values—with data analytics organizations able to profile individuals based on their zip codes alone. Certainly, it is useful to understand people's mental models of their respective spaces as well because people can live disparate lives even when they inhabit the same general physical neighborhood. This draft dictionary is referred to simply as "SeeYa!" (a Custom Spatial-based Dictionary for the Study of US Expatriation and US

Citizenship Renunciation). This does not fit as a classic acronym setup, but it's sufficiently snappy and somewhat memorable.

Limits to Social Media Data

Social media data, though, is not without its limits; they are widely thought to be incomplete, attracting often the sociodemographic elites in a society (Johnson, Sengupta, Schöning, & Hecht, 2016, p. 517). With such sampling bias, social data may only capture limited voices, without full population representation. This is even more of a concern regarding geosocial data:

Haklay (2012) has argued previously, sources of big geosocial data are inherently biased toward 'outliers'. In other words, no matter how many geocoded tweets one is able to collect and analyze, they remain limited in their explanatory value for many purposes, as the number of geocoded tweets is but a small fraction of all tweets, and Twitter is used by only a small subset of all internet users, a group which itself represents only around one-third of global population. (Graham, 2012, as cited by Crampton et al., 2013, p. 132)

In terms of user-generated data, those sharing tend to be those from the "more wealthy, more educated, more Western, more white and more male demographic" (Crampton, Graham, Poorthuis, Shelton, Stephens, Wilson, & Zook, 2013, p. 132). This means that only some voices are included in the data. Of these, only some by personality will share their insights and questions broadly with the public—for social performance, personality, and other needs. Many with elite ties will have the wherewithal to capture necessary advice and information through formal channels instead of social media ones. There are regional disparities in terms of microblogging. For example, one researcher found that "the amount of information generated from regional cities is significantly smaller than that from metropolitan cities" (Ishida, 2015), which suggests that microblogging messages lean towards better representing larger cities than smaller ones.

User-generated data shared on social media platforms also tend towards being "noisy," inclusive of extraneous and unrelated information, and tagged informally and maybe amateurishly. In natural language, classic ambiguity includes "lexical, syntactic, semantic, and pragmatic ambiguity" (Ireson & Ciravegna, 2010, p. 376), and efforts to use contextual information may help disambiguate some social media-based geolocational information, even as "each individual piece of content tends to contain low levels of information" (p. 370). Place names may be inherently ambiguous:

Wacholder et al. identified multiple levels of place name ambiguity: The first type of ambiguity is structural ambiguity, where the structure of the words constituting the name of the text are ambiguous (e.g. "North Dakota" – is the word "North" part of the place name?). Semantic ambiguity is the next level, where the type of entity being referred to is ambiguous (e.g. "Washington" – is it a place name or a person?). Referent ambiguity is the last level of ambiguity, where the specific entity being referred to is ambiguous (e.g. "Cambridge" – is it Cambridge, UK, or Cambridge, Massachusetts? (Overell, 2011, p. 12)

Location information shared on the Internet and created by users tends to be idiosyncratic with place understood "in a general sense, the way an average person might" (Hockenberry & Selker, 2006, p. 853). The authors write:

Part of this is that people's considerations of what is important in the world reflect how they organize spatial information. These different agendas in politics, commerce, and industry have shaped the how and why or how spatial information is organized. (Hockenberry & Selker, 2006, p. 852)

Also, for such a specific and emotional topic, only some of the social media platforms may have data on the particular subject (and data availability may depend on whether a topic is perceived as relevant or not at the particular time).

The respective social media platforms' application programming interfaces (APIs) of the social media platforms will also affect what data may be extracted at any particular time, with varying levels of confidence about the completeness and relevance of the data. The way the data is structured in the social media platforms affects how they may be accessed. In most cases, the data captured is only a sample of what is available, and the collected sample is non-random (although it is impossible to infer what criteria may be used to describe what was collected). [The Wikipedia data was not captured through an API and offers the most complete data set, with the closest to N=all based on the seeding data.] It is possible to parse social media data based on the type of data, such as a machine-extracted locational column vs. a profile-based location vs. a message on the account mentioning location, which range from structured to semi-structured data…and to assign varying levels of confidence for the space-based information. In this context, though, the general level of information vetting will be light, and in many cases, the texts will be considered somewhat equivalent.

That said, the nature of mobile devices and mobile apps has meant that there is more accurate locational data available on social media sharing sites. It is said that 80% of digital data generated today includes geospatial referencing (MacEachren & Kraak, 2001, as cited by Sigala, 2011, p. 117). Even if imagery are not geo-labeled, locational data may be applied *ex post facto*. There are efforts to georeference all shared images and video on the Web. T. Thielmann (2010) writes:

Dan Catt, senior engineer for Flickr, who says about himself that he introduced geotagging into the Web sphere in March 2005, announced at the 2008 Where 2.0 Conference that Flickr will georeference their complete image stock (a sample is visualized in Crandell et al. 2009); thus in the near future one will probably not find any picture and any video on the Web that is not georeferenced. At the same year, Google announced a fundamental change in their product policy: the change from "Google and Maps" to "Google on Maps" (Ron 2008), which means that Google Maps and Google Earth are to become the platform or basic layer for any kind of information we are looking for. Maps may thus become a dominant way of interacting with networks. (Thielmann, 2010, p. 8)

With so much shared imagery and video and the advancements in computer vision, computational means to re-identify an image's location may not be far off, particularly for locations that have been photographed frequently and for which there are samples shared in the Social Web. For the image-sharing photographers and videographers themselves, it may be harder to de-place an image or video (say, by turning off apps and any locational feature on a device…and avoiding any recognizable landmarks…and controlling for images of addresses or place names in the background) than to slip or leak location and place. The world is a big place, but its spaces are ultimately finite. Sensors that harness social media accounts to share information do so from actual locations (such as sensors sampling air quality and broadcasting that data). Astronauts from the International Space Station may share messages from beyond Planet Earth, but they are communicating from a known place.

"Robots" that create digital contents by harnessing others' works may lack "place," but usurped imagery and other contents may be analyzed for place (such as by reverse image search).

To create this dictionary, five social media data sets were geoparsed, with spatial language in the sets recognized and extracted. "Geoparsing" is also referred to as "*geotagging, georecognition,* and *toponym recognition*" (Leidner & Lieberman, July 2011, p. 5). The custom external dictionary would consist of word, numeric, and alphanumeric-based constructs that may be indicative of locational dimensions, and these constructs may be analyzed based on frequency counts that might indicate that a particular textual set of data may include more discussions of certain locations over others...or certain mental places over others...in their discussions of renunciation of American citizenship. This custom dictionary would be informed by data extracted from five social media platforms shown to have relevant contents: Twitter Tweetstreams (microblogging site); Facebook post streams (social networking site); Flickr image sets (image- and video-sharing site); Wikipedia articles from article networks (crowd-sourced encyclopedia); and Reddit (news sharing site and discussion board). The types of data collected include textual and imagery data. The textual data may include words, spatial degree coordinates, symbols, equations, emoticons, emojis, numbers, hashtags, key words, phrases, proper nouns, nicknames, abbreviations, punctuation, formulas, and other information that may be candidates for the dictionary entries. Place references may be built on a wide range of data: place names and toponyms, zip codes, geo coordinates, time stamps (and time zones with geographical equivalents), geographical coordinates, addresses, and others. The dictionary may be constantly updated based on new lingo and #hashtags, based on the fast-changing aspects of social media communications.

This work is conceptualized as comprising eight basic steps: a broad literature review of the topic (1), research design and hypothesizing (2), extraction of targeted data sets from five social media platforms (Twitter, Facebook, Flickr, Wikipedia, and Reddit) (3), manual and computational analyses of datasets (4), draft of the custom spatial-based dictionary (5), pilot-testing the dictionary in LIWC2015 based on other social media data, with experts in geography and political science and sociology, and against extractable (spatial) insights about the target phenomenon, and via other means (6), revising the custom spatial-based dictionary from findings (7), and publication and sharing (8). (Figure 3)

Figure 3. Building a customized spatial-based dictionary re: American renunciation of citizenship (work sequence)

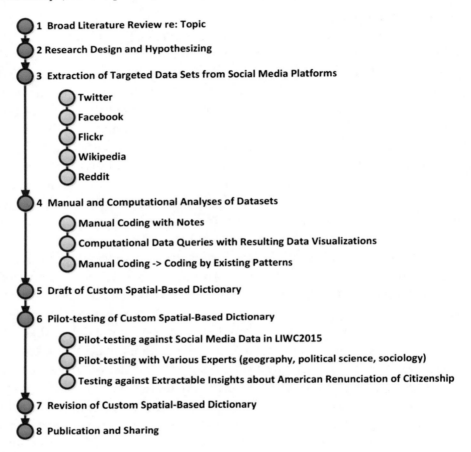

Related Technologies

To actualize this work, a number of technologies were used. To extract the various social media data, NCapture (web browser add-on) of NVivo 11 Plus were used for Twitter Tweetstreams and Facebook post streams. Flickr Downloadr (by brain.no, to differentiate this from other apps with similar and closely similar names) was used to extract images from Flickr. NodeXL

Basic was used to create article networks on Wikipedia, and manual means were employed to capture each of the related article pages. NodeXL stands for Network Overview, Discovery and Exploration for Excel. NVivo 11 Plus and LIWC2015 were used for some computational analyses. Also, the custom dictionary was created using Microsoft Word 2016 and Notepad. For the visualizations, Microsoft Visio and Adobe Photoshop were used. LIWC2015 was used for running the custom dictionary for analyses (Hai-Jew, May 15, 2016).

REVIEW OF THE LITERATURE

Social media data may be informative of location based on textual contents, tags, blog posts, and place names (Fink, Piatko, Mayfield, Finin, & Martineau, 2009) and by social networks (those who interact with a particular social media account) (Jurgens, 2013). However, the challenge is how to verify the interpretation of locational ties. Researchers have explored how often "localness assumption" of volunteered geographic information (VGI)—captured via apps and mobile devices and resulting in data that is so specific that it can be located to an actual specific place on Earth—is actually accurate on a social media platform. The authors first explain the concept of the "localness" assumption in VGI:

Under this assumption, which is almost always adopted implicitly, a unit of social media VGI always represents the perspective or experience of a person who is local to the region of the corresponding geotag. Put more simply, the localness assumption presumes that social media users can be considered locals from everywhere they post geotagged content. For example, adopting the localness assumption, one can assume that a person who posts a geotagged tweet about a political candidate is doing so from her or his home voting district, thereby affording applications like election forecasting and political preference monitoring. (Johnson, Sengupta, Schöning, & Hecht, 2016, p. 515)

So placing communicators in the locations from which they're communicating is only accurate about three-fourths of the time:

Johnson, et al. found that the localness assumption only held in about 75% of the cases in their analysis of datasets from Twitter, Flickr, and Swarm. With the proliferation of mobile devices and people's mobility, the nature of VGI itself has changed to a kind of "transient localness" with people communicating from a variety of locations. (Johnson, Sengupta, Schöning, & Hecht, 2016, pp. 515, 519)

People are peripatetic and travel broadly. They communicate from a number of locations.

MAPPING THE SPACES OF "EXPATS" AND RENOUNCERS OF U.S. CITIZENSHIP

The found words and images from social media accounts may shed light on the roles of geospatial locations and places in the phenomenon of U.S. expat experiences and U.S. citizenship renunciation. This research building on social media will explore two basic hypotheses:

Hypothesis 1: Central "Beaten Paths" With Some Outlier Paths

There are identifiable "beaten paths" that Americans who renounce citizenship take to known destinations, based on family, tourism, travel abroad, locational language(s), and cultural features. Also, it is assumed that there are moderating businesses (law firms, moving companies), governments, religious organizations, political organizations, and other entities that facilitate American resettlement in other locales. Also, in contrast to the beaten paths, there will be some anomalous and unique paths for those renouncing citizenship. These outlier paths may be informed by the unique trajectories of some people's lives.

Hypothesis 2: Identifiable Attractive and Aversive Forces Related to ("Sending" and "Receiving") Places

Individuals on social media who assert that they have renounced U.S. citizenship have combinations of spatial-based "attractive" and "aversive" forces that drive the decision. In other words, people decide to renounce U.S. citizenship in order to leave places with negative associations (both perceived and real) and to go to places with positive associations (both perceived and real). [This is informed by expectancy theory.] Further, these attractive and aversive forces are determined in part by the regulatory environment (regulations and practices) around formal migrations, and these laws and practices are mostly in the governmental domain. On a macro level, geographical spaces and places are linked to collectively lived human experiences. These places are governed by government rules and policies and practices. These are mediated by global news and social media. Generally, geographical spaces and places may be seen as positive or negative for citizens during particular time periods, and these may result in larger citizenship actions and "self-organizing" and emergent movements beyond individual decisions.

RESEARCH IN THE SOCIAL MEDIA SETS

At the time of the data capture, Twitter had 317 users, with 1.3 billion registered users. The average number of monthly visitors that do not log in to this microblogging site are 500 million. Twitter has a hundred million daily active users (Smith, Nov. 17, 2016, "170 amazing Twitter statistics…"). In terms of how #hashtags move through Twitter, researchers have found that there are clear spatio-temporal dynamics. A study of two billion (with a "b") geo-tagged Tweets found that physical distance between communicators constrained the adoption of Tweets. They write:

Based on this study, we find that although hashtags are a global phenomenon, the physical distance between locations is a strong constraint on the adoption of hashtags, both in terms of the hashtags shared between locations and in the timing of when these hashtags are adopted. We find both spatial and temporal locality as most hashtags spread over small geographical areas but at high speeds. We also find that hashtags are mostly a local phenomenon with long-tailed life spans. (Kamath, Caverlee, Lee, & Cheng, 2013, p. 1)

These researchers found that hashtags start locally. They are disseminated through what the authors call a "spray-and-diffuse" pattern, "where initially a small number of locations 'champion' a hashtag, make it popular, and the spread it to other locations. After this initial spread, hashtag popularity drops and only locations that championed it originally continue to post it" (Kamath, Caverlee, Lee, & Cheng, 2013, p. 2).

Facebook, the social networking site, was labeled "the largest social network in the world with over a billion and a half monthly active users and over a billion daily active users." Facebook has 1.8 billion monthly active users and 1.2 billion daily active users. Canada was the country with the most active Facebook users in 2013 (Smith, Nov. 17, 2016, "400 amazing Facebook statistics…").

Flickr, the image- and video-sharing site, had 122 million users and was present in 63 countries; it featured 10 billion images and two million groups (Smith, Nov. 14, 2016). In terms of geotagging of photos on Flickr, male users were more likely to geotag than females, and "the geo-tagged photos of male users have wider geographic coverage than those of females" (O'Hare & Murdock, 2012, p. 33).

At the time of this research, Wikipedia, the crowd-sourced encyclopedia, had close to 41 million pages and 5.3 million articles; it had 29.7 million users and 126,400 active users ("Wikipedia:Statistics," Nov. 30, 2016).

Reddit, the news sharing and discussion board site, had 234 million unique users as of early November 2016. It had some 853,824 subreddits based on different topics as of June 2015. It has 11,464 active communities. Users of Reddit come from 217 different countries. Each month, Reddit provides over 8 billion pageviews (Smith, Nov. 17, 2016, "60 amazing Reddit statistics…").

SOURCE: TWITTER

A dozen different microblogging sites were identified as related to "expat" interests. These Twitter data sets provided both large-scale aggregate knowledge about the phenomenon but also account-level close-in lived human senses of expatriation and the renunciation of citizenship. From the messaging, some online social networks seem tied in close to physical communities in geo-proximity. For example, the @aaro organization seems based out of Paris, France, and there are physical meetups for lunch, tax seminars, weeklong events to celebrate overseas Americans, and hosted talks; further, there are online events, such as surveys and various types of information sharing. Apparently, this organization hosts a tax committee, and their membership page identifies its issues of interest: taxation, voting, lobbying, Medicare, Social Security, banking, representation, FATCA, citizenship, and business & trade. A mapping of the members of the various social networks @ AmericanExpatsUK's Tweetstream show presences in quite a few continents of the world (Figure 4).

In this Twitter Tweetstream, various locations (with varying units of analysis) were named. By frequency count and in descending order, they are as follows: Cyprus, London, Countries, Spain, France, England, Europe, Paris, Dubai, Australia, Singapore, China, Germany, London, York, Canada, Iran, Italy, Singapore, Washington, Russia, Switzerland, Asia, Portugal, and

Figure 4. Locations of the social network of the @AmericanExpatsUK Tweetstream

Scotland. On a few, the hashtag was removed. Regular title case was used for each of these.

In terms of top-level themes, there is a conspicuous absence of place-based references, with main themes as follows: expat, tax, today, stories, and american (in descending order).

A word frequency count of the combined expat accounts shows some listing of locations. (Figure 6)

In Figure 7, the word tree shows various conversations around the renunciation of citizenship. The highlighted branch shows a discussion of citizenship renunciation as a possible aspect of retirement planning. [According to the U.S. Social Security Administration, "just under 400,000 American retirees are living abroad," and they most often live in "Canada, Japan, Mexico, German, and the United Kingdom" (Associated Press, "More Americans are retiring..." Dec. 27, 2016).]

In Figure 8, the various Twitter accounts are clustered based on word similarities in the messaging. To read a horizontal dendrogram, it helps to start with the most granular leaves at the right and examine the clusters as they become larger. Word similarity in messaging may suggest co-communication around similar issues, shared interests, or possibly even a closer shared worldview.

Figure 5. Auto-extracted themes from the dozen combined expat account Tweetstreams

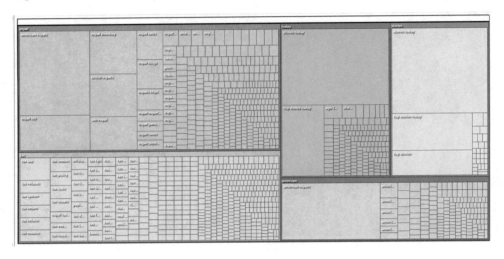

Figure 6. A frequency word count from the mixed Twitter expat sets

See Ya!

Figure 7. One tweet addressing citizenship renunciation as part of retirement planning

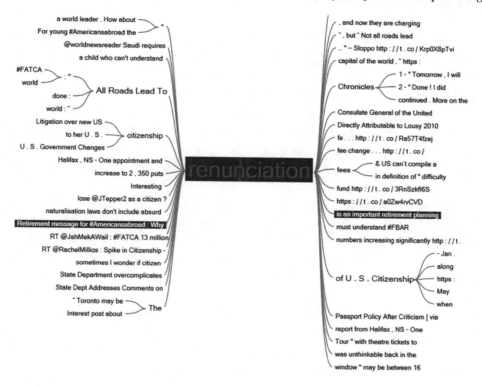

Figure 8. Twitter account sources clustered by word similarity

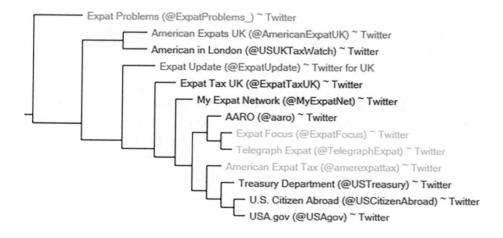

SOURCE: FACEBOOK

It is not by accident that social media data are widely known as subjective and opinion-heavy. The point of social media, without the typical controls of editorial oversight, means that people can post anything. In other cases, editorial oversight by social media account owners means that they can control not only membership and joining but also the messages that are shared through the site. It can be difficult to find an objective information source on social media about a particular topic, so the options are various social media accounts and sites that shade an issue from different angles and so provide some insights.

Several Facebook accounts were analyzed. The first is the American Expatriates Public Group (https://www.facebook.com/groups/AmericanExpatriates/), with 55509 post stream records captured. Theirs is a global community based on the map of locations of respective accounts in this group. A message that is shared with site visitors explains the group's stance:

The American Expatriates group's mission is to inform, educate, & provide current information regarding United States government policies: FATCA, CBT, US citizenship law, passport revocation, and any law DIRECTLY impacting Americans living overseas, Green Card holders living overseas, Accidental Americans, & associated populations. It is extremely important to mitigate the misconceptions about Americans living outside the US vis-à-vis the public at large.

This group does NOT advocate US tax compliance but a change from the exceptional US practice of Citizenship Based Taxation to the rest of the world's practice of Residency Based Taxation.

As such, one of its main constituencies seems to be people who perceive themselves as "accidental Americans" who just happened to be born in the U.S. and who are thus on-the-hook for U.S. taxes, even if they live abroad and do not consider themselves Americans per se and do not feel like they are benefitting from their citizenship or their tax dollars. They are frustrated at citizenship-based taxation and militate against certain government expenditures.

A computational sentiment analysis of the post stream shows that much of the messaging is neutral, but the language with sentiment does fall across

Figure 9. Word frequency counts from the American expatriates public group site on Facebook

all categories: very negative, moderately negative, moderately positive, and very positive, instead of leaning towards the negative or positive polarities.

Sometimes, it may be insightful to explore the text coded to "very negative." This may be seen in Figure 11. The themes and sub-themes in the "very negative" category shows information not about spatiality or place but about policies applied to citizens. Three of the four top level terms have to do with money (tax, account, and bank), and then in the remaining top-level topics is the dyadic contrast between "American" and "foreign." In a sense, then, space and place are defined by the rules of engagement at the respective locations.

In addition, four other Facebook sites were identified with some links to "emigration." Two seem to be based out of Ireland, one out of Punjab, and one out of France. Various related social media accounts may have differing levels of sentiment expressed (Figure 12).

Figure 10. Auto-coded sentiments from the American expatriates public group site on Facebook

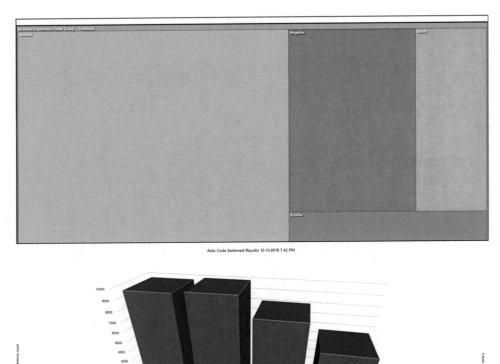

Autocoded Sentiments for the American Expatriates Public Group on Facebook (55,509 messages)

At the top level, the autocoded topics from all four Facebook sites' post streams were as follows (in descending order): trail, tax, public, American, easement, association, non-partisan association, Irish, emigrant, bank, account, use, rights, community, issues, emigrant trail, government, (and) property. These were coded by cell (vs. by sentence or by paragraph). The separate post streams will show different patterns.

Figure 11. Auto-coded themes from the "very negative" coded text set from the American expatriates public group site on Facebook

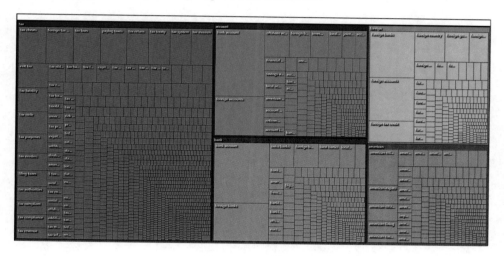

Figure 12. A comparative analysis of autocoded sentiment categories across four "emigrant"-based Facebook post streams

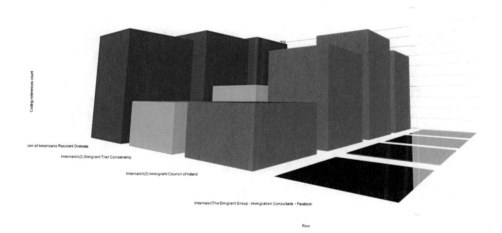

It is possible to compare each of the four post streams across the main topics, as may be seen in the linegraph in Figure 14.

These post streams do not show a lot of terms that are specifically space-based, at least at the level of topic. Only "trail" is a reference to a physical

Figure 13. A comparative analysis of autocoded theme and sub-theme categories across four "emigrant"-based Facebook Post streams in a hierarchical treemap diagram

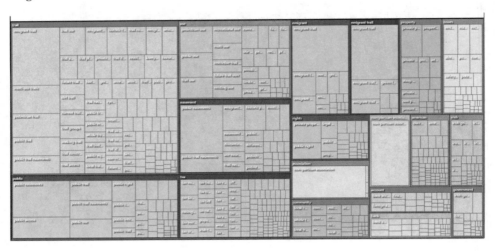

Figure 14. A comparative analysis of autocoded theme and sub-theme categories across four "emigrant"-based Facebook post streams in a linegraph

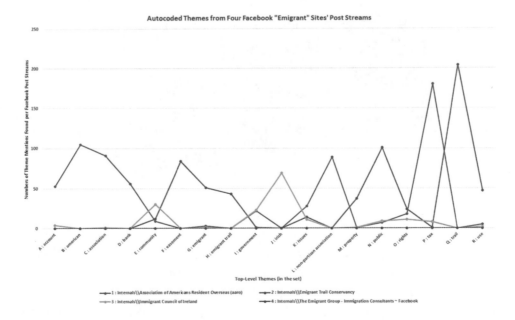

space, and that seems to link to a particular social networking account with trails. The other topics all seem to be generic labels.

It is helpful to explore how particular phenomena are discussed by using text searches and showing the findings in a word tree, to see every instance of the target seed term…and to draw out the context by reading lead-up and lead-away terms in the respective branches. A drill-down of the specific concepts are helpful. In Figure 15, the branch relating to tax evasion is highlighted in the lead-up text.

Figure 15. A "taxes"-seeded word tree from the four "emigrant"-based Facebook post streams

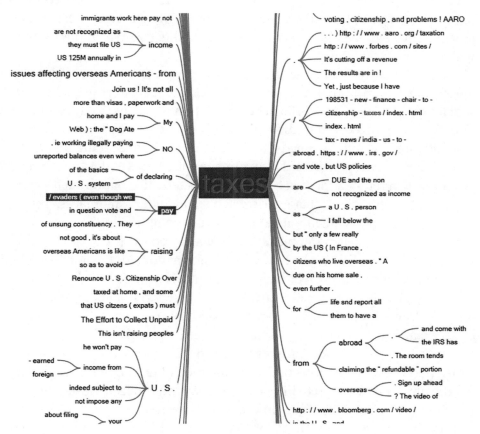

SOURCE: FLICKR

The essential question is how to effectively approach analyzing social imagery. One simple way is to collect summary statistics of each type of image, but that is limited because the data scrape of the images is nowhere near N = all, and the selection of imagery is non-random (with a focus on recency and relevance but also dependent on parameters for the data extraction, the app used, the time-of-day of the data extraction, and the API of the image-sharing site, among other factors). While the tendency may be to get greedy on image scraping, without computational means to analyze the imagery, the social image set fast becomes unwieldy. A visual summary is another approach. In image sets, there are themes that emerge even from seeding words that may not suggest visual themes. For example, when "nation" is used to seed in image set from Flickr, there are a plethora of food images, custom dress, location images, flags, and maps. T15ere are collective evocations of images which signify a "nation."

Content-sharing social media sites enable users to share a broad range of unstructured, unrestricted, and unedited contents, which range in quality. While social image-sharing sites offer access to billions of shared images, the sheer size of such sets make them "difficult to understand, search and navigate" and unwieldy for research (Kennedy, Naaman, Ahern, Nair, & Rattenbury, 2007, p. 631). Researchers have used Flickr image collections to develop computer programs to infer location types based on selected information such as visual features. Geographical characteristics may include "landmarks, regional phenomena, or global phenomena" and various combinations of observations may lead to a "latent geographic feature" such as "coast" (Sengstock & Gertz, 2012, p. 149). The idea is to find which informational indicators have high value in revealing the correct latent geographical label.

In this case, human visual analysis was applied to Flickr contents, which were explored three ways: (1) "expat" related tags networks, (2) "expatriate" imagery, and (3) Flickr groups around the term "expatriate".

A related tags network captures the words that most commonly co-occur with a particular tag in terms of folk application of tags to the shared images. (At the time of this research, Flickr had already introduced auto-tagging, too, which may have had an effect on the respective related tags network. Also the threshold of co-occurrences for a collection of images as big as those on Flickr will generally mean that the related tags are general and abstract, not unusual or outlier-ly.) In a 1.5 degree related tags network around the term "expat," there were the following findings: regional locations (Asia), country references (China, Japan, and Korea), city locations (Hong Kong, Beijing, Shanghai, and Seoul), and generic place terms like "road" and "street" and "bar." The co-occurring tags were necessarily brief and somewhat informal. If there was a geographic center of gravity for "expat," it would be Asia. The resulting related tags network with the three clusters and the highlighted place terms may be seen in Figure 16.

Figure 16. "Expat": Highlighted location-based terms from a 1.5 degree related tags network on Flickr

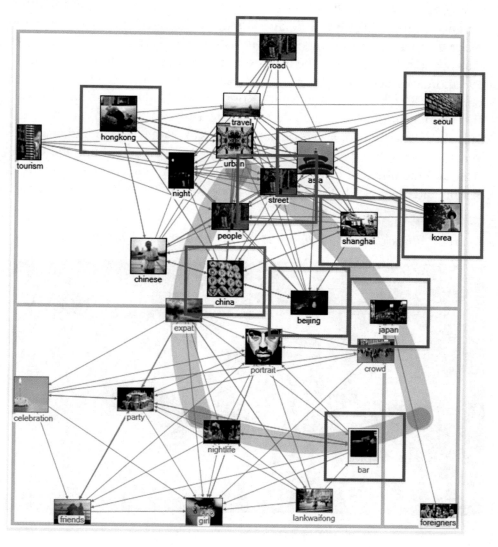

In terms of imagery extracted from Flickr's collections, "expatriate" was used as the seeding term, and the tool used for the extraction was the free web app tool Flickr Downloadr (by brain.no). The parameters of the search involved "Creative Commons" tagging and "Relevance" to the search term. The Creative Commons requirement enables the usage of the image in this chapter, and the "Relevance" enables some shifting. The resulting images show up on a "digital proof sheet" of sorts and may be downloaded as a collection (Figure 17).

A total of 1462 "expatriate" images were collected from Flickr. While this app enabled exploring image names inside the app, when the photos were downloaded at full size, they bore the name of the alphanumeric code identifier assigned to the image but little age: no alt-texting, no EXIF (exchangeable image format) data, no tags, no original image names, no photographer names, and so on. As a set, the images seem to come from all over the world. By landmarks and signage and languages, it is possible to tease out some locales: U.S., China, Britain, South Korea, South Sudan, and the Maldives. The languages observed included English, Chinese, Korean, Arabic, and Dhivehi. The only people whose nationalities are suggested included a male wearing a self-identifying Canadian hat, a young woman holding the Union Jack, and members of a world-renowned rock band with its members from Britain and the U.S. On the whole, the images seem to be of a type. They are

Figure 17. Flickr Downloadr app with images related to "expatriate" on Flickr

from all over the world. There is fascination with landmarks and statues and sightseeing locales; there are many images of nature; the photographers are captivated by native clothes and native performances. The photographers' eyes are drawn to icons like McDonald's and taxi cabs in a city scape and airports and skyscapers. The eyes are also drawn to people—some who seem familiar to the photographer and others who seem to be strangers (a traffic policeman, for example). Indeed, selfies are very popular, with photos of the self, couples, and groups. There are some artistic selfies as shadows of posed selves. There is an appreciation for the novel: a circular bookcase filled with books all the way around, a macro image of a leaf with some sort of blight, a roasted pig with its snout close to the camera, a lush night fruit and vegetable market, and a luxury display of mannequins. There are photos of performances: rock bands, dances, races, fireworks displays, and a rodeo. The photographers experiment with artistic effects: stretched images, tinted b/w photos, blue-filtered imagery, a 360-degree panoramic image, the play of lights at night, and the sketching of imagery over a photo. There are quite a few misfocused photos uploaded—maybe accidentally—as part of a batch. Several of the photos make comments about "expatriate" lives—with posters asking people to "repatriate" instead of "expatriate" and an "America Love It or Leave it" note on the side of an old-style leather suitcase. There is a photo of a building marked with graffiti and a note in the window reading: "Foreigners, please don't leave us alone with the Danes!" There are close-ups of food alongside an image of garbage in shallow water. A few commercial photography outfits advertise their services. One photo shows an old style wall telephone. The images alone do not clearly indicate whether expats are describing themselves or others.

The third approach with Flickr involved exploring groups linked to the idea of "expatriate." What was found was that there were 50 "expatriate" Flickr groups, of which only four were still active:

"Expat in China," "European Expats Worldwide," "Made in Maldives," and "Montreal by her Expatriots" (sic). Some of the messages were about encouraging tourism. The respective groups did not seem that active especially for a global community. This was what was found within the limits of Flickr Downloadr. However, a direct visit to the Flickr site revealed many more groups (98 linked to "expatriate" interests, with 50 if the inactive ones were removed). That said, many of these groups were apparently backed by business interests. The collection of images in the Groups were much fewer but also similar to those in the general Flickr set around "expat" and "expatriate."

SOURCE: WIKIPEDIA

In terms of selecting information from Wikipedia, a one-degree article network was derived from the article "Emigration_from_the_United_States" (https://en.wikipedia.org/wiki/Emigration_from_the_United_States). This article network shows outlinks from the seeding article to other related articles on Wikipedia, which is a crowd-sourced encyclopedia. The English Wikipedia has 4.9 million articles, with contents overseen by editors and approved robots (often to correct spelling and other formatting issues).

Some of the collected information here highlights a somewhat fresh angle—that of forcible revocation of passports and the government right to de-naturalize former citizens ""List_of_denaturalized_former_citizens_of_the_United_States"

(https://en.wikipedia.org/wiki/List_of_denaturalized_former_citizens_of_the_United_States). Some historical reasons for the stripping of U.S. citizenship include the following: "Hiding World War II crimes or association with Nazis" and "Serious crimes, suspicion of spying for the communists, or association with terrorists" ("List of denaturalized former citizens of the United States," Dec. 15, 2016).

In terms of spatial information, it is possible to extract the HTML table by viewing the page source, capturing the textual data and representing with UTF-8 coding (not ANSI), and capturing the various locales where the respective individuals moved, at least initially. The challenge though is that these are unique individual cases occurring in a historical context. These listings provide targeted insights instead of broadly generalizable ones in terms of a broadscale phenomenon like American expatriation to other countries and like American renunciation of citizenship. On some issues, the data are rich and informative, and on others, generally silent. [Outside readings would provide more information about historical movements of people groups based on government policies that favor in-migration of certain groups, but that is beyond the purview of this social-media-based work.]

One informative spatial example involves various locations mentioned in the social media sets. The identified locations from the custom dictionary do not really align with the identified regions with significant populations of Americans abroad from other research sources. The so-called "American diaspora" has gone to the various countries in descending order: Mexico, Canada, Philippines, Israel, United Kingdom, Costa Rica, South Korea, Germany, France, China, Brazil, Columbia, Hong Kong, India, Australia,

Japan, Italy, United Arab Emirates, Haiti, Saudi Arabia, Argentina, Norway, Bahamas, Lebanon, Panama, El Salvador, New Zealand, Honduras, Chile, Taiwan, Austria, Bermuda, Kuwait, Guatemala, Nicaragua, Cuba, and Monaco, with a max-min range of 1,000,000 to 430 ("American diaspora," Dec. 13, 2016). This pattern is non-existent in the social media data extractions likely partially because of the sampling bias from those who go to social media, and of data sparsity, as mentioned earlier. It is important to know what is learnable from which social media platforms and when.

SOURCE: REDDIT

The first subreddit which appears when seeking topics dealing with the "renunciation of citizenship" is the "iwantout" one. This was started in October 2016, and the full list of 988 main text discussion thread headers were captured on December 10. While many Redditors are Americans, the thread itself dealt more generally with issues of international migration. A few of the threads dealt with U.S. renunciation of citizenship and frustrations with the election. (For example, one thread reads: "USA ->Anywhere that isn't a totalitarian dystopia." In general, Redditors would share basic information about their age and background and their desired situations and would elicit general advice. Given the ability to engage wholly anonymously, some would only reveal some information—such as a need to avoid extradition to a home country for prosecution for pedophilia…or wanting to avoid mandatory military service…or some other challenges. Some asked about business laws and practices. Others wanted to make sure that their healthcare would be covered. Some students were looking for greener pastures in Europe where their tuition could be covered by the respective receiving governments: "Questions from two students sick of paying American tuition, and curious about opportunities for low-cost European education." Virtually all seemed to be operating with some barter system, as if they had to have something to offer: youth, education, work experience, and / or a willingness to do volunteer work. Others are negotiating from a down position, with threads reading "On getting out with no education and little money" and "30M broke American with MBA and pet(s) > EU". One of the most active sub-threads in this subreddit reads: "WARNING: U.S. citizens 'escaping' the Greatest Nation on Earth will never escape the IRS, until death. This is really key to understand. You will need to file a federal tax return every single year…" (This one garnered some 158 comments.)

Also, this thread brought out the issue of both expatriate experiences and renunciation of citizenship not only as a lagging indicator but in some cases with the various communicators engaging in the decision-making and planning in real time to their postings. The Redditors who started the respective threads often elicited information. They were looking for the best contexts for their situations, whether they were looking for jobs, housing, education (free tuition preferred), certain climates, and certain lifestyles. In the headings, there were often defined "from" and "to" locations: Italy to Detroit; UK to USA; Australia to UK; Germany to Omaha, Nebraska; ? to Sweden; New Zealand to USA; Russia to Canada or Australia or elsewhere?; U.S. to Europe, ideally Germany; America to Denmark; Macedonia to UK/USA/Aus/NZ/Netherlands/France/Bulgaria, and so on. One Redditor wrote: "Which countries are most receptive to taking in American immigrants?" Some suggested the following: Canada, Germany, Finland, and Panama. Another replied icily: "No country has a yank only route to citizenship."

Figure 18 shows a word frequency count of the top level headers (with all the following structured parts of the messaging included in the stopwords list: comments, share, hours, months, and others. This data visualization shows particular locations both as points-of-origin and as desired or actual destination points. Other words show the issues under discussion: passports, immigration, visas, jobs, work, permits, college, and so on.

At the level of regions, the manual coding process supported by computational emulative coding resulted in a capture of both regions and countries (Figure 19). This may have been in part because the posters to the discussion threads mixed all manner of units of analysis: region, country, state / province, city, and so on.

Manual coding of the subreddit headers was done for mentioned countries, and then, using NVivo 11 Plus, the "coding by existing pattern" was applied to the full data. For this particular list, the trails seem to be from among the "Five Eyes" countries (FVEY): Australia, Canada, New Zealand, the United Kingdom, and the US...and some places in Europe, like Germany (Figure 20).

In terms of identified states, those may be seen in Figure 21. There is again some leakage across types with initial clean manual coding of a percentage of the messages and then the computer program's "coding by existing pattern" standing in for the rest of the coding of the full set.

In Figure 22, coded cities were identified through manual coding and then enhanced with machine autocoding. The cities were much less mentioned. The cities were from Prague, Italy, the U.S., and Canada. This word cloud gives the sense that maybe those who are sharing information are not those

Figure 18. A Word frequency count of the main discussion board headings in the /r/iwantout/ subreddit thread

with the wherewithal to acquire the necessary information through consulates and support organizations and so are going to the general public for help. This suggests that social media may provide insights about individual and outlier narratives but maybe not capture the full gist of large-scale transnational migration trends (unless one can achieve an N=all in terms of information collection, and unless all or a majority who are moving are sharing on social media—and that would include any moving from any location to any location). In other words, even in theory, social media will not be sufficient means alone to represent the totality of ground truth in terms of large-scale (or even small-scale) American renunciation of citizenship.

Interestingly, while many have suggested that the presidential election will result in a mass exodus from the States, in these threads, the 2016 presidential election was just a small subset of the conversations. Only four of the nearly 1,000 messages mentioned "election," as may be seen in Figure 23. There are multiple ways to refer to the election, though. One wrote: "M/36,

Figure 19. Manually and computationally coded regions of interest in the /r/iwantout/ subreddit thread

Denmark > US, Need post-Trump advice," and interestingly, this is about a person going stateside. Another writes, "My family and I fled the violence in Mexico have been living in the US since 2000. We overstayed our visas and have been living here ever since. We now fear of what's to come and want to know our options…" Another wrote, "Everything changed in a day. 26, gay, and frightened for my future." These messages represent groups that fear persecution stateside. This is to say that the following figure may be a little misleading in only identifying four sentences. A search for "Trump" from the same set only resulted in six messages, with at least one of them denying

Figure 20. Manually and computationally coded countries of interest in the /r/ iwantout/ subreddit thread

that the thread had any political meaning or any relation to president-elect Donald Trump.

A broader approach involves using "u.s." to seed a word tree from the subreddit thread. Figure 24 shows some of the issues discussed in the 11 headings mentioning the U.S.

In Figure 25, some top-level themes were extracted from the 988 message headers, coded at sentence level. These include the following (in descending order): visa, citizenship, country, work, job, citizen, permit, questions, rule, degree, passport, and moving. A close read of these messages show a majority of the messages seeking advice and support, and there were also some clearly

Figure 21. Most common states mentioned in Reddit iwantout

Figure 22. Manually and Computationally Coded Cities in the /r/iwantout/ subreddit Thread

Figure 23. "Election" to Seed a Word Tree in the /r/iwantout/ subreddit thread

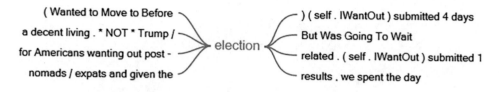

Figure 24. "U.S."-seeded word tree from the subreddit thread

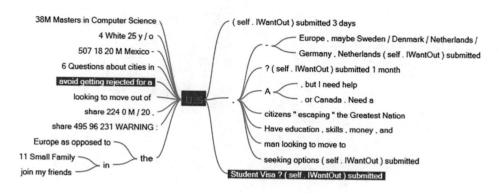

commercial types of messages by outfits that seemed a combination of dream merchants and various local fixers. Some messages read as personal trades, with some apparently offering themselves for marriage for visa and immigration purposes.

Finally, what were the sentiments seen in these messages in this subreddit? A majority of the headings were neutral, without language tied to sentiment. The identified sentiments tended to fall in the middle—in the "moderately negative" and the "moderately positive" categories. These sentiments were coded at the more granular "sentence" level rather than "paragraph" level.

In terms of the language (as analyzed in LIWC2015), the focuses were mostly on the present and a little bit on the past but with little language about the future (which seems ironic) (Figure 27). In terms of time spans, the defined time ranges were from months to years (with some mentioning a three- to five-year plan).

Also, the focuses were not on tourism atmospherics and that dreamscape but much more on the practical and the mundane, filling in the blanks of understandings, and analyzing for which places would best meet the interests

Figure 25. Auto-extracted themes from the /r/iwantout subreddit (in an interactive sunburst hierarchical chart)

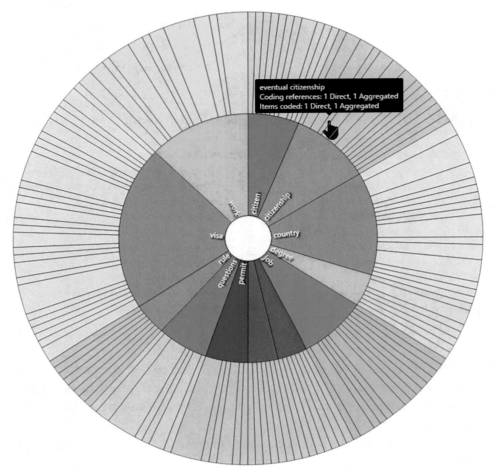

of the individuals looking to move. Theirs is a cool calculus of interests, which, even if not purely rational, does consider some rational features, and so it should be, for the best fit. Of course, anonymous signaling on a public communications space leans more towards "cheap talk" than "costly signaling." In the first, there is nothing at-risk or expensive on-the-line, and posters can always disavow their anonymous postings. "Costly signaling" would be more in the realm of actual payments made and life-impacting actions taken. In social media messaging, for the information to have more value, private and public narratives have to align; people's levels of candor would have to be

Figure 26. Sentiment analysis from the /r/iwantout subreddit [in a treemap diagram (above) and a bar chart (below)]

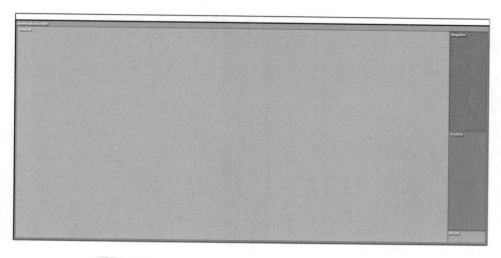

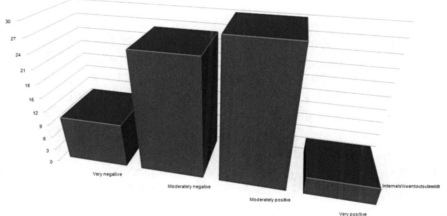

high; plans would have to be actionable and followed-through-on. The prior requirements are not likely in many if not most cases.

In various cases, the sub-reddit communicators indicated locations with particular desired features. Some indicated a desire for a "warm and exotic" place while others indicated that they wanted a location that was cooler. One wanted a beach city. Several indicated interest in locales with career opportunities, such as a "country which values science highest." One wanted a place to "Save Money"; another identified as an economic migrant and wanted to find a place where to make a better living; several asked for

Figure 27. "iwantout" subreddit from Oct. – Dec. 2016 and time focus

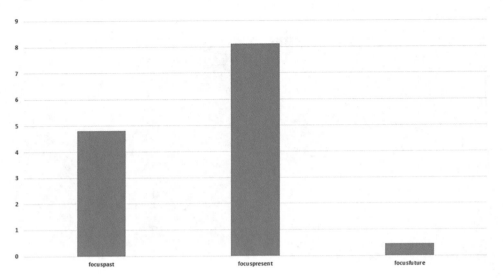

"business friendly" contexts. A number wanted a free ride, whether it was a free education or something else: "I want to spend a year in the US, (without working), can I do it?" A number of would-be expats wanted places which could accommodate their disabilities, their lack of education, their lack of work experience, and other perceived (and maybe real) deficits. Some suggested locations by language—such as indicating desire for a French speaking country in N. Africa or any Spanish-speaking country.

The "here" for the "anywhere but here" category for one communicator turned out to be Iraq: "Iraqi in need of a way out ASAP to US/Canada." Several mentioned locations that they did not want, such as indicating that they wanted to be outside the European Union ("Non-EU" and "Not European Union").

One of the themes in the discussion section /r/iwantout/ was that international migration is actually difficult. For example, one respondent mentioned how incomplete a baccalaureate degree is and the challenges to working menial jobs in a new country because of a lack of main language fluency. Another alluded to this awareness with a thread reading: "Moving to Europe, dream or the nearest possibility?"

For some, the world is a hostile place, and they are looking for "safe haven". The various self-identified groups include the following: "mixed people," those who are gay, those who are trans, those who are bisexual, and others. One wrote: "Bisexual from Pakistan, f stuck in m's body, want to find a new home and transition completely! Advice, help, even two words of 'stay strong' will be helpful! (x-post from lgbt)." One wrote about having family members involved in organized crime and suggesting that he or she did not want blowback from such relationships. There is leeriness about immigrant-receiving locations as well: "Will I face discrimination for my views?"

Some of the messages are about political change. One thread dealt with Donetsk, the contested so-called Donetsk People's Republic (DPR or DNR / Donétskaya Naródnaya Respúblika), which is labeled by the Ukrainian government as "temporarily occupied territories". Another political endeavor involves efforts to try to create space for the "freedom of movement" between the "UK, Canada, NZ and Australia."

In terms of competitive advantage, the various posters were apparently even willing to part with personal hair in order to be more possibly appealing: "Do beards, long hair or any other facial hair impact the picture used to apply for Dv us lottery ?" The Diversity Visa lottery is apparently a program of the U.S. to enable people to apply for green cards enable the holders to reside in the U.S. and to be employed stateside.

Some are clearly thinking and planning ahead over a number of years. One asked: "What is the safest, most stable country in Francophone Africa (especially in regards to the security of property and land)?" Another wrote: "Renouncing US citizenship while pregnant?" Some of the messages on this thread read like a dating site, with one thread's author asking for a co-travel partner.

Participants in social media often keep up with the shared news. In terms of some business ventures, some who started threads in /r/iwantout/ directly targeted Americans with messages such as: "Any American PhD-Holder Expats?" and "An escape guide for Americans." This might indicate a move to start a brain drain, particularly in the applied sciences. Another one wrote: "In anticipation of the questions: This I show an American could move to New Zealand." Another one suggested those with German ancestors would find welcome in Germany: "[Post from /r/LifeProTips] Americans, if your relatives fled Germany between 1933 and 1945 to escape the Nazis, you are eligible for German citizenship today!" Because of how certain messages might be read, several who posted with questions were quick to add that their questions were "not political" or "apolitical" and "*NOT* Trump/election related." In the two-month time span of this subreddit, there were some anticipatory threads. One read: "Could we apply for political refugeeship to any other country should Donald Trump ever get elected President?" While some might see the incoming president-elect as harming their lifestyles and sense of well-being, others worried that his policies might hinder those who want to come stateside: "Will Trump lower my chances of going to the U.S.?"

BUILDING A CUSTOM SPATIAL-BASED EXTERNAL DICTIONARY TO RUN IN LIWC2015

A wide range of insights may be possible to attain from social media data to inform a custom spatial-based dictionary to explore the renunciation of U.S. citizenship. In this work, a range of spatialized data is of interest. The following then inform the initial constructs in the custom dictionary built during this project.

1. **Origin and Destination Regions:** Is it possible to identify origin and destination regions that receive U.S. citizenship renouncers? (broad level of location)
   a. In terms of actual geographic degree coordinates, which are the most popular places, and why?
   b. In terms of folk place references, which are the most popular places, and why?
   c. In terms of shared imagery, what are the most popular places, and why? (What do these images show about how the image taker perceives the place? What sorts of human activities are depicted? What is shown about the social aspects of the individuals' lives?)
2. **Origin and Destination Countries:** Is it possible to identify origin and destination countries that receive U.S. citizenship renouncers? (broad level of location)
   a. In terms of actual geographic degree coordinates, which are the most popular places, and why?
   b. In terms of folk place references, which are the most popular places, and why?
   c. In terms of shared imagery, what are the most popular places, and why? (What do these images show about how the image taker perceives the place? What sorts of human activities are depicted? What is shown about the social aspects of the individuals' lives?)
3. **Origin and Destination States (Provinces):** Is it possible to identify origin and destination states or provinces that receive U.S. citizenship renouncers? (broad level of location)

4. **Origin and Destination Cities:** Is it possible to identify origin and destination cities that receive U.S. citizenship renouncers? (deeper granularity of specific location)
   a. In terms of actual geographic degree coordinates, which are the most popular places, and why?
   b. In terms of folk place references, which are the most popular places, and why?
   c. In terms of shared imagery, what are the most popular places, and why? (What do these images show about how the image taker perceives the place? What sorts of human activities are depicted? What is shown about the social aspects of the individuals' lives?)
5. **Locational Features of Note:** Are there particular geographical amenities and features that are attractive to former Americans?
6. **Personal Experienced Senses of Places:** What are personal experienced senses of place described by former Americans?
   a. What narratives are predominant?
   b. What individual stories are shared?
7. **Relation of Emotions to Spaces and Places:** Are there certain emotions linked to places, and why?

The creation of this spatial-based migration dictionary, informed by social media, is being created in a somewhat *ad hoc* way. The formula described for how the built-in LIWC2015 dictionary is made is highly complex and designed for high-level validated research. In this case, a bottom-up coding approach is used to construct an initial dictionary draft. It draws from five unique types of social media (microblogging site, a social networking site, an image- and video-sharing site, a crowd-sourced encyclopedia, and a news sharing and discussion board site) for a breadth of information types, with data sets seeded with terms like "citizenship renunciation" and "expatriate."

The terms extracted had to include spatial and place-based elements. Initially, this draft dictionary was started with formal spaces—at a broad level: regions of the world based on World Bank labels and found labels from the social media sets. Then, countries (and territories), states, and cities were created as categories. The idea is that there would be links to real-world spaces, even though these would only be general labels. Next, a section was made to capture "Locational Features of Note." These would be the spatial features and rules that are either attractive or aversive to immigrants. The inspiration for this concept comes from work by a research team that found that geographical "check-ins" tended to cluster in particular areas of a city with attractive amenities, which attracted people from great distances and which also resulted in happier tweets from the locale (Gallegos, Lerman, Huang, & Garcia, 2016, p. 570). Destination countries for emigres may be analogically feature-full and attractive to non-residents. Next would be captures of "Personal Senses of Places," with the most common dynamic that of the person's sense of originating country vs. destination country, for example. Other dichotomies are possible: home vs. non-home, the "here" vs. the "there," and so on. The idea is that places are partially informed by people's imaginations, which add color to place. And finally, there was a section of "Personal Emotions and Spatiality." The last section was informed by Robert Plutchik's Wheel of Emotions, and more specifically, the second concentric tier from the center.

The intuition for this last category is that people have lived experiences in a location and anticipation (and maybe lived) experiences in a destination location. While this mentions "emotion," the idea is that a lived experience may evoke any range of human cognitions and perceptions, and that may be captured in social media data. To summarize, the seven areas in the draft dictionary are as follows:

1. Regions of the World
2. Countries (and Territories) of the World
3. Origin and Destination States (and Provinces)
4. Origin and Destination Cities
5. Locational Features of Note
6. Personal Experienced Senses of Places
7. Relation of Personal Emotions to Spaces and Places

It would seem that #s 5 – 7 would be the ones that may be most uniquely informative of this phenomenon of renunciation of U.S. citizenship. As for how information is coded in each category, the information had to be from two sources:

1. Common colloquial phrasing that would fit the particular source
2. Examples from the social media data sets

In this early stage, any words or terms that may be relevant was included. Omitting words may come at a later phrase. (For the LIWC2015 dictionary, constructs or dimensions were removed if they were deemed by a judging team to not fit, if there were low base rates in the counts, if there was low internal reliability for the construct, and if the construct had low frequency of use by researchers. While these were applied to constructs, the same ideas could apply to words within certain constructs.)

There are formatting issues for building a dictionary for running in LIWC2015 as well. Essentially, the various dimensions (constructs) are listed at the top, with each on their own line. These have to be written as one word but can be concatenated words indicated with camel case capitalization (RegionsoftheWorld) or separated with underscores (Regions_of_the_World). The dimensions of the issue are numbered. An unusual character is used to separate the dimensions from the indicator words. The indicator words are capitalized and alphabetized. To be comprehensive, it may be good to either include dictionary words as "misspellings" and "errors" to catch as many of the references as possible. It may help to use core terms with the wildcard asterisk (*), to enable all versions of a word form. Or stemmed words may be included literally, for counts of each one by type, with prefixes and suffixes, singulars and plurals, and verb tense versions. The respective words have to be separated by spaces or tabs. Multi-word phrases may be included, and if so, within LIWC2015, the words in phrases will be counted as parts of phrases and not counted as disaggregated separate pieces.

Following each word on the line is a number, which indicates which construct it goes to. The dictionary is an ASCII text file, which is not saved as a .txt but as a .dic file. In LIWC2015, the dictionary is run against a processor, which increments counts for found words to each dimension or construct, so what is provided is a raw summative count of the respective dimensions based on the found words and the percentage representation of those words as a percentage of the whole file. The words may be phrases, so the dictionary can accommodate unigrams, bigrams or two-grams, three-grams, four-grams, and so on. All the elements of the dictionary have to be pre-defined *a priori*, though. The custom dictionaries are easy to update, involving opening the .dic file, making changes, adding new words, saving the file, and then re-uploading into LIWC2015 and running that revised dictionary against the collected text set(s). In general, though, the process is a "bag of words" approach and does not capture word proximity information or reflect any understanding of writing sequences. The dimensions have to be as comprehensive as possible to fully represent the dimensionalities of the target issue, and the dimensions should be as mutually exclusive as possible, so that there is not multi-collinearity. While raw counts may seem rough-cut, there are available insights from such approaches. In theory, a spatial-based dictionary may shed light on frequent location mentions, counts on particular phenomena, and other insights, especially if the texts and text sets are carefully curated.

In the literature, there are different ways to format a dictionary to run in LIWC2015. The one that this author found makes the most sense and is most clearly human-readable is as follows. There are two sections. At the top are the dimensions or various constructs. At the bottom are the words, which serve as indicators of the respective constructs. The words themselves should be alphabetized. The number of the dimension or construct sets that the words indicate should be listed in ascending order from left to right next to the words themselves. To be as inclusive as possible, the asterisk * to enable wildcard reading was used, and the variants of a term were deleted. For human-readable clarity it helps to have the words listed on their own lines instead of run together in a continuous string (as some of the shared custom dictionaries are, with tab or space separators). Along these lines, too, it is always better for people to see what a technology tool is doing instead of having to rely on a researcher's word.

%
1 Dimensiona
2 Dimensionb
3 Dimensionc
%
Word 1
Word 1 2 3
Word 1
Word 2
Word 2 3

To reiterate, the dimensions then are locations (at varying units of analysis), phenomena linked to locations, personal experiences in places, and emotions and places. This custom external dictionary may indicate what spatial language is related to the phenomenon of moving abroad to be expats and somewhat with the phenomenon of renunciation of U.S. citizenship (as a special case). It may be possible to infer some locational facts around renunciation of U.S. citizenship.

To summarize, the SeeYa! Custom dictionary is comprised of seven sections. The seven sections were organized in the following ways. "1. Regions of the World," "2. Countries (and Territories) of the World," "3. Origin and Destination States (and Provinces," and "4. Origin and Destination Cities" were organized by alphabetical order. The "regions" section had the regions as indicated by the World Bank in alphabetical order, and then the found regions from the social media sets following also in alphabetical order. The more human-created constructs, "5. Locational Features of Note" and "6. Personal Senses of Places" were also alphabetized. Finally, the "7. Personal Emotions and Spatiality," based on Plutchik's Model of Emotions, was listed in clockwise order (of the second concentric tier) based on a visualization of this model. While 1 – 4 are classic references to locations in a colloquial sense, 5 – 7 are more about latent spatial semantics, based on lived experiences, a sense of home and "away," and motivating ideas and feelings. With data from the respective social media data sets, 222 constructs or dimensions were created, and to actualize these constructs, there were 892 words and phrases.

Initial Coding for the Spatial-Based Dictionary

As noted in some of the prior data visualizations, both manual and computational means were used to extract terms from the various social media data sets.

Figure 28. Frequencies of constructs per section of the "See Ya!" dictionary

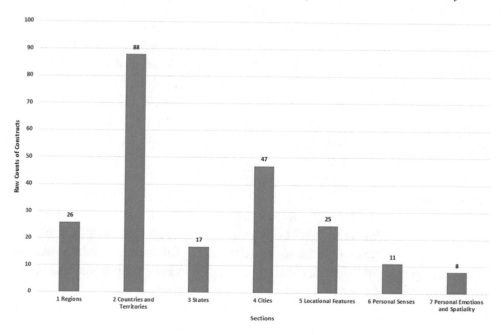

Close readings were done in many of the subreddit threads as well as the messaging from Facebook and Twitter and Wikipedia.

Some light lessons from the initial coding of the spatial-based dictionary follow. First, it makes sense to apply a light hand to the dictionary's initial structure. While the seven basic sections held, the labels were re-phrased multiple times. It helps to not limit the constructs in each category. Originally, it was thought that these would work best if they were limited to the top dozen or so co-occurring constructs. Later, it seemed that just having a very open approach to any possible code initially—as in a brainstorm—would work best so as not to prematurely limit data. Initially, there were attempts to maybe limit word uses to one use in one construct, that soon became too restrictive because words are polysemous, and to deny the coding use of a term for other categories doesn't make sense. Including words in multiple constructs (dictionary sections) might err on the side of "noise" that might muddy the "signal," but it would protect against non-capture of potentially relevant data. Very little data, if any, is unalloyed. Said another way, there would be less precision but higher recall (based on the f-measure). The custom dictionary itself is not inherently disambiguated, and similar terms are used across different contexts and with different meanings. The risk of double- and triple-counting (across spatial-based constructs) seems worth the risk.

Another lesson was that "place" and "space" could instantiate in unexpected ways. One example of conceptual "place" was "anywhere but here," a negative, a non-present non-space-time concept of pure "other," however that might instantiate. Another concept of "place" was of welcome—that other locales would be welcoming of the émigré's youthfulness, talent, and skills—which was then debunked from actual experiences shared on the respective social media platforms. Some Redditors asked for "safe haven," generally defined as a place where they could find protection and succor. In another example, people were looking to move "anywhere warm."

There are surprising examples related to spatiality as well. For example, some communicators referred to countries by the Internet country top domain level codes. [Think "DE" (or actually the ".de" country suffix for Germany and "SA" (or actually the ".sa" country suffix for Saudi Arabia.] Others use the first three letters of the country like "IRE" for Ireland. Others use the European System of Social Indicators list of country abbreviations, like "IRL" for Ireland. It turns out that "space" can be a non-space, such as "non-EU" or "outside the EU" or "not the Northern Hemisphere"; these can describe where people are or where they want to be or something else altogether. Of course, common usage terms also proliferate, such as "Deutschland" for

"Germany." Several used sounds to spell out locations; for example, one used "Oz" for "Aus" or "Australia." Also, there are references to places that are not recognized in terms of the redrawing of boundaries, such as the issue with the self-proclaimed Donetsk People's Republic (DPR or DNR for "*Donétskaya Naródnaya Respúblika*").

Emotions (optimally tied to space) were also tapped. The intuition here is that is a set of texts are edited down to those related to space, then the emotion coding (based on part of Plutchik's Model of Emotions) would be helpful for the researcher. (This is an insight about how LIWC2015 is used, with some finesse required to break out textual data into different sets.)

Each of the different social media platforms and collected data sets offered different insights, and there were many areas of non-overlap. This non-overlap could be because the different platforms attract different demographic slices of the population. Also, it could be that the different platforms contain different types of digital media, and those may lend themselves to different information and communications. (Some messages may be more efficiently communicated by image than by text, for example.) That said, collating all the insights from the various sets…to the point of saturation…is one way to address these challenges.

Another insight was that it is a good idea to go with a lightly structured table of data for building the custom dictionary. Pre-numbering is not a good idea because it might suggest limiting constructs unnecessarily. In an emergent coding approach, it helps to be open. Also, each section would likely be organized wholly differently than numbering. Place names may be alphabetized. They may be clustered to regional areas. They may be clustered by political understandings. In most cases, based on conventions, there are inherent and logical ways to organize the information. To keep the open brainstorming during the information collection and coding stages, it was helpful to not even think about organizing constructs within the seven sections. The seven parts to the initial table were seeded with formal labels initially, and these were augmented by less formal and more colloquially used natural language labels. Ultimately, the sections contained both formal and informal language. A top-down spatial coding approach results in "an administrative view on places, using only official place names" (Keßler, Maué, Heuer, & Bartoschek, 2009, p. 83); a bottom-up emergent one results in a more directly colloquial and natural language approach.

Insights about the ambiguity of geographical terms were true. In natural language, "many non-locations share names with locations" (Leidner &

Lieberman, July 2011, p. 5). One has to address word ambiguity in order to geo parse. The authors describe a range of geographical references:

Perhaps the most obvious type of references are geopolitical entities, such as countries (e.g. "Spain") and administrative divisions ("Brooklyn"; "Midlothian"), as well as populated places such as cities and towns ("Zurich"). Other types of region locations can include postal codes ("CB2 1RD"; "D-76887") and municipal areas. At a smaller scale, various hyperlocal locations could be considered, such as streets ("Einstein Drive"), street addresses ("Sofienstraße 7"), street intersections ("51st St and Lexington Ave"), city centers ("downtown Seattle"), and buildings ("US Supreme Court"). In some applications, natural geographic features would be locations of interest, such as parks ("Hyde Park"), rivers ("Potomac"), and mountains ("Snowdon"). In contrast to formal place name gazetteers, which contain features named on maps, volunteered geographic information [7], which comprises an ever growing part of the Web, frequently also includes vernacular descriptions of locations, as well as references to imprecise areas ("east coast"; "southern France"; "downtown Washington"). Each of these location types affords different kinds of context that enable readers to understand that a location is being referred to. Some or all of these may be considered in the geoparsing task, depending on the application's requirements or utility. Note that we can further distinguish between recognizing simple names referring to locations (e.g. "London") and recognizing complex geographic phrases (e.g. "30 miles North of Austin"; "Washington, DC, USA"). The former refer to locations directly, whereas the latter can be analyzed compositionally, i.e., the meaning or reference of the expression is a function of the meaning of the parts and the way they are combined. (Leidner & Lieberman, 2011, p. 6)

Once the relevant word and other information has been collected from observed sources, it is important to add some anticipated other words. For example, synonyms of the found words may be helpful to add. A fast look at word dictionaries online may be helpful. The point is to extend the custom dictionary in a way so that it is extendable beyond what was observed in the respective data sets. There has to be some comfortable balance between the literal observed words and those that are anticipated.

It made sense to capture words in their various forms first and then to add hashtag, @, and keyword versions of these terms with the proper annotations. The content words are informative of meaning, and the #hashtags, @at symbols, and other elements are annotations on those contents.

An unexpected decision arose when it was clear that there would be quite a few constructs, with a large listing of words. Should there be several related dictionaries, or should all the constructs be harnessed into one? The initial idea was that having one multi-dimensional dictionary might be most effective for a collective list of interrelated contents. The various elements may well be separated out post information-capture. The down side might be that there would be too much complexity, but the up side is that the related constructs would be captured in one dictionary, with both spatial and place-based elements. The challenge though is that the numbering can be quite limiting…and while a few extra empty slots may be included in each section for flexibility, there may be hidden upper limits to how many constructs may be included. At this current point, the SeeYa! Dictionary is one entity and seems to work very well as such.

PILOT TESTING THE SPATIAL BASED DICTIONARY

There were three conceptualized general efforts to pilot-test the spatial-based dictionary.

- First, how did the dictionary perform against related social media data about the renunciation of American citizenship? This is an applied approach.
- Second, what do experts in geography and political science and sociology observe about this dictionary? What do they see as its strengths and weaknesses?
- Third, what extractable (spatial) insights are possible about the target phenomenon as compared to other means? How do the data compare?

This next step will not be taken until the dictionary has been evolved further.

DISCUSSION

Some early use of this custom spatial-based dictionary suggested some required strategy for collecting text corpora for analysis and for comparisons. There are numerous ways to slice text sets: by time, by social media platforms, by threaded topics, and others, in order to make comparisons. Right now, there is not yet any sort of textual baseline set for this topic based on the custom dictionary.

So what were some fresh spatial-based insights about the American renunciation of citizenship from social media data and the *building* of a spatial-based dictionary? Note that this is the learning accrued in the creation of the custom dictionary tool. This includes close-readings of the extracted social data, not just running the data against the custom dictionary.

- Citizenship (its acceptance, its changes, and its renunciation) is a dynamic issue, with any number of issues affecting people's senses of their own interests and sparking people's decision-making.
- Physical spatiality and place are factors, but the central issues are not geographical space and place in a separate isolated sense but rather about the rules and practices and lifestyles in various places. Social connections are also a factor. Resources—both of the individuals and provided by government entities and non-government entities—are relevant.
- Spaces and places are not separate from the lived experiences of American citizens, whether they are living stateside or living abroad. Spaces and places can be a part of people's identities. These inform people's cultural expectations, their language fluencies, and their expectations of the world. Adjusting to new realities can result in "culture shock."
- Those who look to migrate transnationally seem well aware of the marketplace and their need to barter—with their youth, their education, their career prospects, their language capabilities, their relative wealth, and other factors. Even as people are moving towards a basket of goods, they themselves have to offer something.
- Social media offer narrative snippets of people's experiences, but these are only slivers of selected information provided by people behind non-personally-identifiable handles and anonymized social media accounts (oftentimes).
- Many mediators—lawyers, international movers, religious groups— enable transnational migration and the renunciation of U.S. citizenship. There are market and other interests surrounding this socio-political issue. There is a large component of "selling" ideas of escapism and the promise of new locales.

- In terms of social media, social media provide some insights by some demographic slices of individuals. These are limited and are not really generalizable to the larger population of citizenship renunciators. Many social media accounts related to the issue are fairly parochial and local vs. global.
- In terms of data extraction from social media, it is critical to use a number of tacts to capture information. Sometimes, web browser-based apps will delimit results in a way that can be misleading. Using a browser-based search engine directly may result in many more helpful results than through a free app. This requires a fair amount of experimentation, but that experimentation is necessary before assertions may be made with even some light confidence. Every technology and method has its limits.

In terms of large-scale narrative themes in the perspective of the discussants, there were narratives of survival (those inside the lifeboat vs. those outside, survival strategies), of adventure (exploration, high-intensity experience, observations of and appreciations for differences), of identity and becoming (finding a place to fully actualize and self-express), adjustment (culture shock, surprises, complaints, and cost-of-living), and of romance (finding love of place). Broadly generalizing, the textual data dealt with "survival," "adventure," "identity and becoming," "adjustment," and the image data tended towards "adventure" and "romance". This is across the multi-medial social media platforms, including Twitter, Facebook, Flickr, Wikipedia, and Reddit.

Another insight is a qualifying one: that the space-based data from social media platforms seem somewhat locally bound to the respective social media platforms and the demographic slices of people using that platform. The respective platforms have affordances and attract certain sorts of information. The place-based data from text seems quite different than that from social imagery. In many ways, these data sets are not particularly helpful at indicating a broad level of ground truth in the way formal collectors of information may be (such as government agencies and news organizations). Social media data sets may show some local color and give a taste of the issue but does not seem sufficient to define the outside limits of this issue. These data sets are not comparable to ground truth and do not seem to evoke it. In many ways, social media data about the renunciation of American citizenship seems muted and idiosyncratic.

Two Hypotheses

There were two spatial-based hypotheses posited in this work.

Broadly, one idea (Hypothesis 1) was that there would be identifiable "beaten paths" for Americans who renounce citizenship and that they would head to known destinations based on family, tourism, travel abroad, locational languages, and cultural features…and based on moderating entities like religious organizations and churches, government organizations, non-profit activist organizations, and others. They would head to world cities with amenities if they had the wherewithal—financial, skills-wise, and otherwise—or they would head to wherever they had connections and resources. It turns out that there are a wide range of locations mentioned, and many who have commercial motives create websites about citizenship renunciation to drive traffic to various locales (like, say, the Dominican Republic, which is apparently interested in attracting foreign capital from immigration).

Recent news coverage has described a more recent phenomenon known as "citizenship by investment" or even "passports for cash." These setups require people of means to invest hundreds of thousands of dollars into a developing country's economy in order to acquire passports, which enable its holders to travel with ease that may not have been available with their own originating countries.

It's called citizenship by investment and it's become a $2 billion industry built around people looking for a change of scenery or a change of passport, a new life or maybe a new identity, a getaway from the rat race, or perhaps an escape from an ex-spouse or Interpol. In any event, it's brought in huge amounts of revenue for the sellers and attracted among the buyers a rogue's gallery of scoundrels, fugitives, tax cheats, and possibly much worse. (Kroft, 2017)

A perusal of some websites and social media user accounts provide some glimpses of this shadow economy in passports.

The second hypothesis suggested that there would be "attractive" and "aversive" forces related to both "sending" and "receiving" places especially regarding the issue of renunciation of American citizenship, and that was generally supported, particularly in the Reddit subreddit /r/iwantout/ thread, which showed clear forethought and planning for moves and the weighing of pros and cons related to various locales. The Facebook site "American

Expatriates Public Group" articulated frustration at the encumbrance of tax responsibilities on "accidental Americans" thus articulating an "aversive" force apparently driving some U.S. citizens to renounce citizenship. Based on the trajectories of the respective discussion threads, it might be possible to lightly project some possible decision-making of the various individuals and groups, but the limited data and the complexities of such decision-making would likely make such predictions fairly inaccurate.

Eight Steps to Creating a Spatial-Based Dictionary

In terms of the eight-step sequence for creating a spatial-based dictionary [in Figure 3 or "Building a Customized Spatial-Based Dictionary re: American Renunciation of Citizenship (work sequence)"], the general steps bore fruit.

While all of the social media data sets contributed constructs, dictionary terms, and issue-based insights, the most helpful sources were as follows (in descending order): Reddit, Wikipedia, Twitter, Facebook and Flickr. Reddit offered wide-ranging discussions of related issues in a visceral and present way. Wikipedia offered access to summary details collated in a crowd-sourced way and edited by both people and robots. Twitter offered a rich range of organizations with various interests, and their rich data sets enabled data extractions that were not possible with other data extractions. These include maps of the locations of user accounts (based on their profiles) and sociograms. A locational column captured actual coordinate degree data mappable to specific locations on Earth. (This work did not directly explore Tweeting locations and the tie to the topics of U.S. expatriation and U.S. citizen renunciation of citizenship.) Facebook's groups seemed, interestingly, somewhat provincial and not as wide-ranging as the Twitter sets. This may have been a factor of the social media accounts found by the author. And finally, Flickr offered related imagery that was unwieldy to code and not particularly clear in terms of either messaging or locations.

The geographical information though here tends not to be spatially specific, or the regions pointed to are general times at the levels of regions, countries, states or provinces, and cities. Other places mentioned, such as "Engadin Valley" and the "St. Moritz Resort" are left out with this current instantiation of the dictionary. In the same way that locations are kept general, individuals themselves are treated as small parts of a whole. This research approach loses incidentals. For examples, people's origin- and destination- sites are not captured at the individual level, and the various narratives linked to spaces and places are also not captured. In other words, this custom dictionary is underpowered for the desired tasks.

While these steps made sense for this particular project, there may well be much more efficient and thoughtful ways to approach the work. Or, it could be that parts of this approach are effective, and other parts less so.

For example, the author did also find that it would make sense to have multiple information streams to enhance the geoweb data. Four of the five sets involved mostly textual information, and one involved shared imagery. In the current state of the art, most analytics are done with text as the lowest common denominator. With the information capture methods related to Flickr imagery, only the images were captured—without titles, without annotations, without direct tagging. These other channels may contain relevant place information that was not addressed here.

Others who have conducted research using georeferenced data have suggested that there are ways to enhance the online "geoweb" data by complementing the spatial data with additional information channels:

More specifically, we propose five extensions to the typical practice of mapping georeferenced data that we call going 'beyond the geotag': (1) going beyond social media that is explicitly geographic; (2) going beyond spatialities of the 'here and now'; (3) going beyond the proximate; (4) going beyond the human to data produced by bots and automated systems, and (5) going beyond the geoweb itself, by leveraging these sources against ancillary data, such as news reports and census data. We see these extensions of existing methodologies as providing the potential for overcoming existing limitations on the analysis of the geoweb. (Crampton et al., 2013, p. 130)

The sparsity of data from Twitter, Facebook, Flickr, Wikipedia, and Reddit for this topic meant that additional data streams would be helpful to bolster the spatial-based constructs and spatial-based terminology in the dictionary. It would also help to bring in some other types of social media platforms (tagging sites, blogging sites, website networks, multimedia-sharing sites, video-sharing sites, and others) and maybe multiple exemplars of microblogging, social networking, image- and video-sharing, crowd-sourced dictionary, and news sharing and discussion board sites. Also, it may help to explore additional scraping methods to capture social media data. While feedback effects are to be expected with social media informing formal media and vice versa, and messages moving across social media platforms with speed, there are still benefits to coding to saturation. That level of attention has not been achieved here with this particular work yet. There is still much out there to be explored.) Additional rich dictionary features would likely enhance the dictionary's validity in place-based analysis.

Even if all relevant data were coded, the dictionary would only be fully relevant if it were not "overfit" to the social data and therefore more transferable to a variety of contexts. This means that using other sources—like full geographical place name sets for regions, countries, states (and provinces and territories), and cities, and districts…would be helpful for a full set of spatial and place data. The dictionary itself is trivial to update; all it requires is opening the file and adding in the proper data…saving it…and reloading into LIWC2015 to run. (Using automated methods to collect relevant data and to update the custom dictionary would seem like a more sensible approach.)

FUTURE RESEARCH DIRECTIONS

Truths about modern people's lives—that they are global citizens, that they travel broadly, that people are not tethered to place, and that people communicate through a variety of channels (many of them private)—make it harder to use social media to understand a phenomenon about permanent leaving of a country and a movement to elsewhere. Further work in this area would do well to consider such contexts.

In this endeavor to create a spatial-based linguistic analysis dictionary to capture social data about the renunciation of American citizenship, this effort does show that semantic-based verbal mapping of spaces and places is possible and may surface insights about this phenomenon (to scale and with computational speeds). The success depends on capturing sufficient social media data sets and curating proper sets for the respective questions that may be asked.

About the Computational Analysis Dictionary

So what is knowable from the respective counts of the constructs in the spatial-based dictionary? Why do certain locations predominate and not others? Why are certain constructs (of "personal senses of place" and of "personal emotions and spatiality") observed in some social media platform contexts and not others?

About Spaces and Places

In terms of the locational aspects of the spatial-based dictionary, there were some clear challenges. One problem is that if it is not in the dictionary, it is not seen computationally. It may be better to use an all-geographical dictionary (doesn't seem to exist in LIWC2015 yet) first, so that any reference to a known location is capturable…and to enhance that dictionary with social-media-based references to location. After all, there are multiple ways to reference different locales and many different spellings and abbreviations as well.

About Precision

Also, the locational aspects of this work were imprecise. It would help to bring in deeper layers of spatiality, so there can be meaningful placement of location markers on maps at various levels of zoom. The ideal would seem to be a sufficiently formal one, maybe in the standard of so-called gazeteers (geographical dictionaries)—with triples "N, F, T" corresponding to place name (N), geographic footprint (F), and type (T).

About Renunciation as an Observable Event

If renunciation of U.S. citizenship is an event, is it possible to detect that life-changing event through social media? If they are so inclined, how would people share that knowledge socially? If there are certain times when such decisions are made and followed-through-on, such as at year-end, are there ways to pick up on this data and to learn from it?

The topic of renunciation of U.S. citizenship is a controversial one, and based on various geopolitical and legal issues, there may be surprises and issues that "blow up" over time. This issue may recur in a "bursty" way. To that end, it would be important to maintain an official version of this dictionary that is as up-to-date as possible. While there is low overhead "cost" to having extra constructs that are not relevant or not particularly insightful, to keep the tool as sharp as possible, it may be helpful to edit out extraneous information. If one were to model after the makers of LIWC2015, there would be a standard and multi-layered way to vet the dictionary contents.

This custom-dictionary will be going through light initial pilot-testing, involving testing on social media data, perusal by experts from geography and political science and sociology, and against extractable spatial insights about the target phenomenon. Additional and more rigorous testing and constructive critique would benefit the work. It is hoped that the dictionary would continue to evolve over time. Maybe in the future, it would also help to formalize the dictionary with professional annotations based on those trained in geography and human migrations. If the information captured is more specific—such as with specific locational coordinates—it may be possible to have direct mapping of locations. There may be other ways to apply this dictionary for other uses, beyond the study of the renunciation of U.S. citizenship.

There are ways to "salt" social media for deeper insights about the target topic. For example, a stub may be created in Wikipedia, and with sufficient attention, crowds may enhance knowledge. It is possible to identify individuals who reveal their identities on social media platforms and to contact them directly to understand their experiences with renunciation of U.S. citizenship. On news sites and discussion boards, it is possible to start threads to elicit information.

CONCLUSION

The title of this work, "See Ya!..." suggests something jaunty and moving on to something better and maybe leaving something difficult behind. This description may apply to some who leave behind a country and adopt another (or are adopted by another). This work, though, shows that the actual moves are not without challenges and do require complex decision-making and even sufficient planning. Based on multiple social media data sets, a custom dictionary was created to capture glimmers of this phenomenon of renunciation of U.S. citizenship.

Finally, this work involved the building of a spatial-based dictionary to run in LIWC2015 to better understand the American renunciation of citizenship based on data extractions from five social media platforms (Twitter, Facebook, Flickr, Wikipedia, and Reddit). This draft dictionary went through initial light testing. The steps in this work were documented. Four hypotheses were tested and initial findings captured. This work is an early one, and there are many ways to build on this work. The renunciation of U.S. citizenship is, for many, a private issue, but it also has public aspects that are relevant.

For those who are interested in this topic, a query on Google Correlate for "citizenship" in the U.S. shows moments of jagged variability over time in terms of Google Searches from 2003 – present. The time-series correlations for Google Searches, in descending order, are as follows: american citizenship,

Figure 29. "Citizenship" and "American citizenship" Google Search Activity Correlations over Extended Time (Google Correlate)

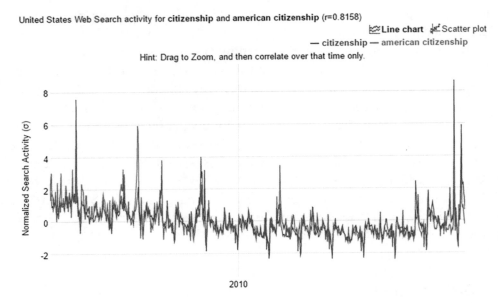

United States Web Search activity for **citizenship** and **american citizenship** (r=0.8158)

becoming a citizen, dual citizenship, work visa, states, united states citizen, immigrating, california population, secretary, elected officials, us citizenship, immigration requirements, california senators, moving to ireland, united states, government positions, county population, republican news, united states president, and president us. These seem to suggest an ongoing interest in "moving to ireland" in connection with citizenship queries in the U.S.

ACKNOWLEDGMENT

This work was the basis for a presentation at the You Are Here conference at Creighton University in Omaha, Nebraska, from March 23 – 25, 2017. Thanks to the organizers of that conference for their hospitality. A slideshow based on this work is available on SlideShare at http://www.slideshare.net/ShalinHaiJew/see-ya-creating-a-custom-spatialbased-linguistic-analysis-dictionary-from-social-media-data-sets-to-explore-american-renunction-of-citizenship. The title is "See Ya! Creating a Custom Spatial-based Linguistic Analysis Dictionary from Social Media Data Sets to Explore American Renunciation of Citizenship."

REFERENCES

American diaspora. (2016, Dec. 13). In *Wikipedia*. Retrieved Dec. 16, 2016, from https://en.wikipedia.org/wiki/American_diaspora

Associated Press. (2016, Dec. 27). More Americans are retiring outside the U.S. *CBS News*. Retrieved Dec. 27, 2016, from http://www.cbsnews.com/news/more-americans-are-retiring-outside-the-u-s/

Boyd, R. L. (n.d.). *00 – EXAMPLE DICTIONARY – READ FIRST*. User Dictionaries. LIWC.net. Retrieved Dec. 16, 2016, from http://dictionaries.liwc.net/index.php/liwcdic/9

Cann, H. (2016, Nov. 9). MAP: Dual citizenship around the world. *MoveHub*. Retrieved Nov. 27, 2016, from.

Crampton, J. W., Graham, M., Poorthuis, A., Shelton, T., Stephens, M., Wilson, M. W., & Zook, M. (2013). Beyond the geotag: Situating big data and leveraging the potential of the geoweb. *Cartography and Geographic Information Science*, *40*(2), 130–139. doi:10.1080/15230406.2013.777137

Data Source: Google Correlate. (n.d.). Google, Inc. Retrieved May 25, 2017, from http://www.google.com/trends/correlate

De Choudhury, M., Lin, Y.-R., Sundaram, H., Candan, K. S., Xie, L., & Kelliher, A. (2010). How does the data sampling strategy impact the discovery of information diffusion in social media?. *Proceedings of the Fourth International AAAI conference on Weblogs and Social Media*, 34 – 41.

Fan, Q., Zhang, D., Wu, H., & Tan, K.-L. (2016). General and parallel platform for mining co-movement patterns over large-scale trajectories. *Proceedings of the VLDB Endowment*, *10*(4), 1–12. doi:10.14778/3025111.3025114

Fink, C., Piatko, C., Mayfield, J., Finin, T., & Martineau, J. (2009). Geolocating blogs from their textual content. Association for the Advancement of Artificial Intelligence.

Gallegos, L., Lerman, K., Huang, A., & Garcia, D. (2016). Geography of emotion: Where in a city are people happier?. *WWW'16 Companion*, 569–574.

Gellman, B., & Soltani, A. (2013, Dec. 4). Online Story: NSA tracking cellphone locations worldwide, Snowden documents show. *The Washington Post*. Retrieved Dec. 20, 2016, from http://www.pulitzer.org/files/2014/public-service/washpost/16washpostnsa2014.pdf

See Ya!

Hai-Jew, S. (2015, Mar. 25). Exploring Public Perceptions of Native-Born American Emigration Abroad and the Renunciation of American Citizenship... through Social Media. *SlideShare*. Retrieved Nov. 18, 2016, from http://www.slideshare.net/ShalinHaiJew/native-emigration-from-the-us

Hai-Jew, S. (2016, May 15). LIWC-ing at Texts for Insights from Linguistic Patterns. *Summer Institute on Distance Learning and Instructional Technology (SIDLIT 2016)*. Retrieved Nov. 18, 2016, from SlideShare at http://www.slideshare.net/ShalinHaiJew/liwcing-at-texts-for-insights-from-linguistic-patterns

Hai-Jew, S. (2017). Exploring Public Perceptions of Native-Born American Emigration Abroad and Renunciation of American Citizenship through Social Media. In N. Raghavendra Rao (Ed.), *Exploring Public Perceptions of Native-Born American Emigration Abroad and Renunciation of American Citizenship through Social Media*. Hershey, PA: IGI-Global. Retrieved from http://www.igi-global.com/chapter/exploring-public-perceptions-of-native-born-american-emigration-abroad-and-renunciation-of-american-citizenship-through-social-media/166455

Hamilton, J. G. (2009, November). Ourplace: The convergence of locative media and online participatory culture. *The Proceedings of OZCHI, 2009*, 23–27.

Hockenberry, M., & Selker, T. (2006). A sense of spatial semantics. *CHI 2006*, 851 – 856. doi:10.1145/1125451.1125618

Ireson, N., & Ciravegna, F. (2010). Toponym resolution in Social Media. *Proceedings of the 9th International Semantic Web Conference on the Semantic Web*, 370 – 385. Retrieved Nov. 29, 2016, from http://iswc2010.semanticweb.org/pdf/209.pdf

Ishida, K. (2015). Estimation of user location and local topics based on geo-tagged text data on social media. *2015 IIAI 4th International Congress on Advanced Applied Informatics*, 14 – 17. doi:10.1109/IIAI-AAI.2015.203

Jamison, B. C. (2016, Nov. 10). Contemplating renouncing U.S. citizenship to avoid Trump's presidency? Not so fast. *Forbes*. Retrieved Dec. 12, 2016, from http://www.forbes.com/sites/binghamjamison/2016/11/10/contemplating-renouncing-your-u-s-citizenship-to-avoid-a-donald-trump-presidency-not-so-fast/print/

Johnson, I. L., Sengupta, S., Schöning, J., & Hecht, B. (2016). The geography and importance of localness in geotagged social media. *#chi4good, CHI 2016*, 515 – 526. doi:10.1145/2858036.2858122

Jurgens, D. (2013). That's what friends are for: Inferring location in online social media platforms based on social relationships. *Proceedings of the Seventh International AAAI Conference on Weblogs and Social Media*, 273 – 282.

Kamath, K. Y., Caverlee, J., Lee, K., & Cheng, Z. (2013). Spatio-temporal dynamics of online memes: A study of geo-tagged Tweets. *International World Wide Web Conference Committee (IW3C2)*, 1 – 11. doi:10.1145/2488388.2488447

Kamen, A. (2013, Nov. 12). In the Loop: Tina Turner formally 'relinquishes' U.S. citizenship. *The Washington Post*. Retrieved Dec. 9, 2016, from https://www.washingtonpost.com/blogs/in-the-loop/wp/2013/11/12/tina-turner-formally-relinquishes-u-s-citizenship/?utm_term=.f78a1d850c54

Kennedy, L., Naaman, M., Ahern, S., Nair, R., & Rattenbury, T. (2007). How Flickr helps us make sense of the world: Context and content in community-contributed media collections. *MM '07*, 631 – 640.

Keßler, C., Mau, P., Heuer, J. T., & Bartoschek, T. (2009). Bottom-up gazetteers: Learning from the implicit semantics of geotags. In *GeoS '09: Proc. Third International Conference on GeoSpatial Semantics*. Springer.

Kroft, S. (2017, Jan. 1). Passports for sale. 60 Minutes. *CBS*. Retrieved Jan. 1, 2017, from http://www.cbsnews.com/news/60-minutes-citizenship-passport-international-industry/

LaFrance, A. (2014, Oct. 14). Big data can guess who you are based on your zip code. *The Atlantic*. Retrieved Dec. 18, 2016, from http://www.theatlantic.com/technology/archive/2014/10/big-data-can-guess-who-you-are-based-on-your-zip-code/381414/

Leefeldt, E. (2016, Nov. 29). Saying put: Why Americans aren't moving. *CBS News*. Retrieved Nov. 29, 2016, from http://www.cbsnews.com/news/staying-put-why-americans-arent-moving/

Leidner, J. L., & Lieberman, M. D. (2011, July). Detecting geographical references in the form of place names and associated spatial natural language. *SIGSPATIAL Special*, 3(2), 5 – 11. doi:10.1145/2047296.2047298

List of denatured former citizens of the United States. (2016, Dec. 15). In *Wikipedia*. Retrieved Dec. 16, 2016, from https://en.wikipedia.org/wiki/List_of_denaturalized_former_citizens_of_the_United_States

List of former United States citizens who relinquished their nationality. (2016, Dec. 12). In *Wikipedia*. Retrieved Dec. 16, 2016, from https://en.wikipedia.org/wiki/List_of_former_United_States_citizens_who_relinquished_their_nationality

Mitchell, L., Frank, M. R., Harris, K. D., Dodds, P. S., & Danford, C. M. (2013). The geography of happiness: Connecting Twitter sentiment and expression, demographics, and objective characteristics of place. *PLoS ONE*, *8*(5), 1–15. doi:10.1371/journal.pone.0064417 PMID:23734200

O'Hare, N., & Murdock, V. (2012). Gender-based models of location from Flickr. GeoMM'12, 33 – 38. doi:10.1145/2390790.2390802

Overell, S. (2011, July). The problem of place name ambiguity. SIGSPATIAL Special, 3(2), 12 – 15. doi:10.1145/2047296.2047299

Quarterly publication of individuals who have chosen to expatriate. (2016, Nov. 11). In *Wikipedia*. Retrieved Dec. 13, 2016, from https://en.wikipedia.org/wiki/Quarterly_Publication_of_Individuals_Who_Have_Chosen_to_Expatriate

Sengstock, C., & Gertz, M. (2012). Latent geographic feature extraction from social media. *ACM SIGSPATIAL GIS '12*, 149 – 158. doi:10.1145/2424321.2424342

Sigala, M. (2011). Exploiting geocollaborative portals for designing collaborative e-learning pedagogies: A model, applications and trends. In B. White (Eds.), *Social Media Tools and Platforms in Learning Environments*. doi:10.1007/978-3-642-20392-3_7

Smith, C. (2016, Nov. 17). *60 amazing Reddit statistics (November 2016)*. DMR Stats | Gadgets. Retrieved Dec. 13, 2016, from http://expandedramblings.com/index.php/reddit-stats/

Smith, C. (2016, Nov. 17). *170 amazing Twitter statistics and facts (November 2016)*. DMR Stats | Gadgets. Retrieved Dec. 13, 2016, from http://expandedramblings.com/index.php/march-2013-by-the-numbers-a-few-amazing-twitter-stats/

Smith, C. (2016, Nov. 17). *400 amazing Facebook statistics and facts (November 2016).* Retrieved Dec. 13, 2016, from http://expandedramblings.com/index.php/by-the-numbers-17-amazing-facebook-stats/

Smith, C. (2016, Nov. 14). *Flickr stats (November 2016).* DMR Stats | Gadgets.

Stefanidis, A., Crooks, A., & Radzikowski, J. (2011). Harvesting ambient geospatial information from social media feeds. GeoJournal, 1 – 20.

Thielmann, T. (2010). Locative media and mediated localities: An introduction to media geography. *AETHER: The Journal of Media Geography,* 1 – 17.

Toker, U., & Gray, D. O. (2008). Innovation spaces: Workspace planning and innovation in U.S. university research centers. *Research Policy, 37*(2), 309–329. doi:10.1016/j.respol.2007.09.006

U.S. and World Population Clock. (2016, Dec. 11). U.S. Census Bureau. Retrieved Dec. 11, 2016, from https://www.census.gov/popclock/

Wikipedia: Statistics. (2016, Nov. 30). In *Wikipedia.* Retrieved Dec. 13, 2016, from https://en.wikipedia.org/wiki/Wikipedia:Statistics

Wood, R. W. (2015, Sept. 21). IRS and FBI track Americans who renounce citizenship. Why is FBI list longer?. *Forbes.* Retrieved Nov. 27, 2016, from http://www.forbes.com/sites/robertwood/2015/09/21/irs-and-fbi-track-americans-who-renounce-citizenship-why-is-fbi-list-longer/#54f1a16b2f84

Wood, R. W. (2015, Oct. 23). U.S. has world's highest fee to renounce citizenship. *Forbes.* Retrieved Nov. 27, 2016, from http://www.forbes.com/sites/robertwood/2015/10/23/u-s-has-worlds-highest-fee-to-renounce-citizenship/#4ac7bfd66568

KEY TERMS AND DEFINITIONS

Citizenship: The state of being an official member of a country with all the related rights and responsibilities.

Computational Linguistic Analysis: The study of natural language using a computer program.

Construct: An element of a theory or theoretical framework, an idea or concept.

External Dictionary (in LIWC2015): A dictionary that is not natively built-into LIWC2015, an external .dic file that may be run using the LIWC2015 processor to analyze texts.

Gazetteer: Geographical dictionary.

Geographical Degree Coordinates: Alphanumeric information that indicates a specific location in two-dimensions on Planet Earth.

Geoparsing: Identifying spatial language in text.

Geotag: An electrical tag indicating a location linked to a particular online digital resource.

"Localness Assumption": The idea that.

Jus Sanguinis:: "Right of blood" (in Latin), citizenship conferred by having one or both parents who hold state citizenship.

Jus soli: "Right of the soil" (in Latin), birthright citizenship, the practice of conferring automatic citizenship on those born in a particular region (within a country's borders).

Manual Coding: The application of codes to information through human close-reading (as contrasted with machine-coding).

Post Stream: A collection of short messages linked to a particular individual or group social identity.

Renunciation: Rejecting a formal status, the formal document indicating rejection.

Social Networking Site: An Internet site that enables people to create self-profiles, communicate with others, and share digital contents—among other capabilities.

Tagging: Attaching a label to a particular online resource.

Toponym: A place name.

Tweetstream: A collection of microblogging messages linked to a particular individual or group social identity.

APPENDIX A: SEEYA! A CUSTOMIZED SPATIAL-BASED DICTIONARY FOR COMPUTATIONAL LINGUISTIC ANALYSIS AROUND THE ISSUE OF AMERICAN RENUNCIATION OF CITIZENSHIP

Table 1.

Constructs	Related Terms (to the constructs)
1. Origin and Destination Regions of the World (according to the World Bank)	
Africa (1)	Africa, North Africa, South Africa, East Africa, West Africa,
EastAsiaandPacific (2)	East Asia, Pacific, E. Asia,
Europe (3)	Europe, European Union, EU,
LatinAmericaandCaribbean (4)	Latin America, Caribbean, Virgin Islands,
MiddleEastandNorthAfrica (5)	Middle East, North Africa, MENA, MENA region,
SouthAsia (6)	South Asia, S. Asia,
UnitedStates (7)	United States, U.S., US, America, US of A,
Anywhere (8)	Anywhere, Anywhere Else, Anywhere Cheap, Anywhere Civilized, Anywhere In, Somewhere Else, Anywhere Really, Somewhere to Save Money, Anywhere in the World, I Want to Disappear, Open to Living Anywhere, Not Here, Get Me Out,
Balkans (9)	Balkans,
CanadianArctic (10)	Canadian Arctic,
CentralAmerica (11)	Central America,
EasternEurope (12)	Eastern Europe, E. Europe, E Europe
FirstWorld (13)	First World, 1st World, Global North, Developed World, Developed Countries,
Francophone Africa (14)	Francophone Africa,
NonEU (15)	Non-EU, Not European Union, Outside EU, Outside European Union
NorthAmerica (16)	North America, N. America, El Norte, N America,
NorthernEurope (17)	Northern Europe, N. Europe, N Europe,
Oceania (18)	Oceania, Asia,
OECD (19)	OECD, Organisation for Economic Co-operation and Development,
Scandinavia (20)	Scandinavia, Scandinavian Country,
SouthAmerica (21)	South America, S. America, S America,
SoutheastAsia (22)	Southeast Asia, S.E. Asia, SE Asia,
ThirdWorld (23)	Third World, 3rd World, Undeveloped Country, Global South
WestCoast (24)	West Coast,
WesternCanada (25)	Western Canada, W. Canada, W Canada
WesternEurope (26)	Western Europe, W. Europe,

continued on following page

Table 1. Continued

2. Origin and Destination Countries (and Territories) of the World	
Albania (27)	Albania
Argentina (28)	Argentina,
AtlanticCanada (29)	Atlantic Canada,
Australia (30)	Australia, AUS, Down Under, Oz,
Austria (31)	Austria,
Bahamas (32)	Bahamas,
Bahrain (33)	Bahrain,
Belarus (34)	Belarus,
Belgium (35)	Belgium, BE,
Bermuda (36)	Bermuda,
Bosnia (37)	Bosnia,
Brazil (38)	Brazil,
Bulgaria (39)	Bulgaria,
Canada (40)	Canada, CAN,
China (41)	China, CN, CHN,
Chile (42)	Chile,
Colombia (43)	Colombia, Columbia,
Costa Rica (44)	Costa Rica,
Croatia (45)	Croatia,
Cuba (46)	Cuba,
Czechia (47)	Czechia, Czech Republic,
Donetsk (48)	Donetsk,
Denmark (49)	Denmark,
DominicanRepublic (50)	Dominican Republic,
Dubai (51)	Dubai,
Ecuador (52)	Ecuador,
Egypt (53)	Egypt,
ElSalvador (54)	El Salvador,
England (55)	England
Estonia (56)	Estonia,
Finland (57)	Finland,
France (58)	France, .fr, FR,
Germany (59)	Germany, .de, DE, GER, Deutschland,
Guam (60)	Guam,
Guatemala (61)	Guatemala,

continued on following page

Table 1. Continued

Haiti (62)	Haiti,
Honduras (63)	Honduras,
HongKong (64)	Hong Kong, HK,
Hungary (65)	Hungary,
Iceland (66)	Iceland,
India (67)	India,
Indonesia (68)	Indonesia,
Iraq (69)	Iraq,
Ireland (70)	Ireland, IRE, IE, IRL,
Israel (71)	Israel,
Japan (72)	Japan,
Jordan (73)	Jordan,
Kuwait (74)	Kuwait,
Latvia (75)	Latvia,
Lebanon (76)	Lebanon,
Lithuania (77)	Lithuania,
Macedonia (78)	Macedonia,
Malaysia (79)	Malaysia, Malay,
Mexico (80)	Mexico,
Monaco (81)	Monaco,
Morocco (82)	Morocco,
Netherlands (83)	Netherlands, NED, .nl, NL,
Nicaragua (84)	Nicaragua,
NewZealand (85)	New Zealand, NZ,
Norway (86)	Norway,
Pakistan (87)	Pakistan,
Panama (88)	Panama,
Peru (89)	Peru,
Philippines (90)	Philippines,
Poland (91)	Poland,
Portugal (92)	Portugal,
Qatar (93)	Qatar,
Romania (94)	Romania,
Russia (95)	Russia,
SaudiArabia (96)	Saudi Arabia,
Scotland (97)	Scotland,

continued on following page

Table 1. Continued

Serbia (98)	Serbia,
Slovakia (99)	Slovakia,
SouthAfrica (100)	South Africa, SA,
SouthKorea (101)	South Korea, SK, S Korea, Korea
Sweden (102)	Sweden, Swe,
Switzerland (103)	Switzerland,
Taiwan (104)	Taiwan,
Tanzania (105)	Tanzania,
Thailand (106)	Thailand,
Turkey (107)	Turkey,
UnitedArabEmirates (108)	United Arab Emirates, UAE, Emirates,
UnitedKingdom (109)	United Kingdom, UK, U.K.,
United States (110)	United States, U.S., US, USA, America, US of A,
Uruguay (111)	Uruguay,
Venezuela (112)	Venezuela,
Vietnam (113)	Vietnam,
VirginIslandsUS (114)	Virgin Islands,
3. Origin and Destination States (and Provinces) (according to the social media data sets)	
Alabama (115)	Alabama, AL,
Arizona (116)	Arizona, AZ,
BritishColumbia (117)	British Columbia, BC
California (118)	California, CA,
Colorado (119)	Colorado, CO,
Florida (120)	Florida, FL,
Illinois (121)	Illinois, IL,
Maryland (122)	Maryland, MD,
Massachusetts (123)	Massachusetts, MA,
Michigan (124)	Michigan, MI,
Nebraska (125)	Nebraska, NE,
Ohio (126)	Ohio, OH,
Oklahoma (127)	Oklahoma, OK,
SouthCarolina (128)	South Carolina, S. Carolina, SC,
Tennessee (129)	Tennessee, TN,
Texas (130)	Texas, TX,
Wisconsin (131)	Wisconsin, WI,

continued on following page

Table 1. Continued

4. Origin and Destination Cities (according to the social media data sets)	
Amsterdam (132)	Amsterdam,
Austin (133)	Austin, Texas
Bangkok (134)	Bangkok,
Belfast (135)	Belfast,
Boston (136)	Boston,
Berlin (137)	Berlin,
Brisbane (138)	Brisbane,
BuenosAires (139)	Bueno Aires,
Capetown (140)	Capetown
CotedAzur (141)	Cote d'Azur
Detroit (142)	Detroit,
DublinIreland (143)	Dublin, Ireland
Edinburgh (144)	Edinburgh,
Fife (145)	Fife,
Frankfurt (146)	Frankfurt,
Glasgow (147)	Glasgow,
Jacksonville (148)	Jacksonville,
Johannesburg (149)	Johannesburg,
Ljubljana (150)	Ljubljana, Slovenia
London (151)	London,
LosAngeles (152)	Los Angeles, L.A., LA,
Luton (153)	Luton, England
Melbourne (154)	Melbourne,
Milan (155)	Milan,
Montreal (156)	Montreal,
NewJersey (157)	New Jersey,
NewYorkCity (158)	New York City, NY, NYC,
Omaha (159)	Omaha,
Oregon (160)	Oregon,
Paris (161)	Paris,
PortlandOregon (162)	Portland, Oregon;
PortlandMaine (163)	Portland, Maine;
Prague (164)	Prague, Praha
Quebec (165)	Quebec,

continued on following page

Table 1. Continued

Rome (166)	Rome,
SaltLakeCity (167)	Salt Lake City, UT,
SanDiego (168)	San Diego,
Shanghai (169)	Shanghai,
Stockholm (170)	Stockholm,
Stuttgart (171)	Stuttgart,
Sydney (172)	Sydney,
Tirana (173)	Tirana, Albania; Tirana;
Toronto (174)	Toronto,
Vancouver (175)	Vancouver,
Vienna (176)	Vienna,
WashingtonDC (177)	Washington, DC; DC; District of Columbia
Wellington (178)	Wellington,
5. Locational Features of Note (according to the social media data sets)	
Budget (179)	Budget, Unemployment Benefits, Wages, Budget, Banking, Funding, Decent Living, Royalties, Paycheck, Bills,
CitizenshipStatus (180)	Citizenship, Dual Citizenship, U.S. Citizenship, US Citizenship, Dual Nationality, Dual Residency, EU Citizenship, Naturalization, Green Card, Non-Citizenship, Placelessness, Sponsorship, Renunciation, Renouncement, Birth, Blood, Permanent Resident, Residency, Descent, Family, Father, Mother, Parents, Grandparents, Family Reunification, Citizenship Status,
CivicDuties (181)	Civic Duties, Voting, Taxes, IRS, Internal Revenue Service, Department of Treasury, US Treasury, Treasury Dept, Tax Man, Uncle Sam,
Climate (182)	Climate, Weather, Sun, Health, Warm Weather, Year-Round Weather Data, Preferably Somewhere Warm, Somewhere Warm, Someplace More Chilly than Hot,
CostofLiving (183)	COL, Cost of Living, How Much, Need to Save, Outflow, Somewhere Cheap, Bills, Expenses, Groceries, Rent, Housing Medical Care,
Crime (184)	Crime, Criminal, Theft, Organized Crime, Rape, Pedophilia, Security, Personal Safety,
Destination (185)	Destination, International City, Warm Weather, Somewhere to Save Money, Anywhere, Anywhere Else, Anywhere Cheap, Anywhere Civilized, Anywhere In, Somewhere Else, Anywhere Really, Somewhere to Save Money, Anywhere in the World, Dream Destination, Luxury Resort,
Education (186)	Education, Tuition, Books, Free Tuition, International Students, Masters, Bachelors, Baccalaureate, Education Requirements, MBA, University, College, Uni, Studies, Study, Course of Study, Degree, Masters, Doctorate, Course, Graduate Student, Undergraduate Student, Senior in College, International Student, High School Senior, BSc, MSc, PhD, Certificate, Diploma, College Dropout, Residence Program, Tertiary Education, Free PhD Programs, Grad School, Graduate School,

continued on following page

Table 1. Continued

Employment (187)	Employment, Job*, Work*, Career*, Work Permit, Immigrant Job Situation, Industry, Computer Science, Pharma, Chemical, Salary Range, Accounting, CPA, ACCA, Registered Nurse, Retirement, Retiring, Online Business, Travel Vlogger, Unemployment, Employment, Military, Swiss Watchmaking Career, Sponsorship, Consultation, Pay, Summer Job, Job Option, Transfer, Work at Home, Wages, Self-Employed, Self-Employed at Home, Writer, Editor, TEFL, EFL, Leave of Absence, Leave, Income, CPA, IELTS, English Language Test, Job Market, Chef, Radiographer, Dental Hygienist, Math Instructor, Web Developer, Meteorology, Dev / Linux Sys Admin, Dev, Linux, Criminal Justice, Public Policy, Freelancer, Tech Job, Engineering, Resume, CV, Curriculum Vitae, Vitae, Stellar Resume, Professional, Computer Science Degree, Working Remotely, Entry Level Data Analysis, Admin Support, In Demand, Profession, Trade, Researcher, Writer, Game Developer, Electrician, Biology, Labor Shortages, Computer Sciences, Game Design, Small Animal Veterinarian, Employer, Clinic, Physical Sciences, Project, Unskilled, Skilled, Experienced, Digital Nomad, IT Worker, Food Technologist, Chemical Engineer, Second Nationality, Philosophy Degree, Finance Professional, Actress, Secondary Maths Teacher, Teacher, Translator, English-to-Italian Translator, Software Engineer, Market Researcher, Architectural Technologist, Job Seeker, Internship, Army, Commerce, Business, Notary, Apostille, Notary Public, Nanotechnology, Manager, Commerce Manager, Teaching Sponsorship, Intern, Firefighter, Barber, Immigrant Job Situation, Salary Range, Registered Nurse, RN, Business Owner, Watchmaking, Tier 1, Tier 2, Tier 3, Tier 4, Unemployment Benefits, Vacation Benefits, Health Benefits, Content Creator, Work History,
Family (188)	Marriage, Civil Union, Wife, Husband, Spouse, Girlfriend, Boyfriend, Family, Children, Fiancé, Fiancée, Knocked Up, Engage, Engagement, Married, Significant Other, SO, Soon-to-be-Husband, Bae, Soon-to-be-Wife, Maternity Leave, LDR, Long Distance Relationship, Civil Union,
Fees (189)	Fee*, Cost*, Budget*, Broke, Poor Man's Expat, Somewhere Cheap, ROI, Return on Investment, Buy Permanent Residency, Free PhD Programs,
GTFO (190)	GTFO, Get the Fuck Out, Get the Hell Out, Get Out, Anywhere But Here,
Healthcare (191)	Health*, Healthcare, Insurance Card, Health, Preexisting Condition, Autistic/ Aspergers Adults, Autistic, Aspergers, Maternity Leave, Special Needs, Clinic, Hospital, Medicard, Travel Insurance, Mental Illness, Service Dog, Service Animal, PTSD,
Home (192)	I'm Going Home, Home*, Return Stateside,
Housing (193)	Housing, Apartment, Room And Board, Work For Housing, Hostel, Hotel, Airbnb, Real Estate, Temporary Stay, Visit,
LawEnforcement (194)	Law Enforcement, Crackdown, Police, Immigration, Enforcement, Crime*, Crimin*, Court System, Judge, Punishment,
Lifestyle (195)	Lifestyle, Vlogger, Backpacker, Personal Life Issues, Personal Life, Vegan, Nomad, Tropical, Relaxed Location,
Move (196)	Move, Transition, Moving, Transport, Run, Get Out, Free Movement, Change, >, ->, --->, Transfer, Flying, Transition, International Movers, Relocating, Relocate, Ways to Leave, Shipping, Shipping Electronics, Moving Furniture, Relocation, Relocation Packages, Making the Move, GTFO, Get the Fuck Out,
Passport (197)	Passport, Secondary Passport, Green Card, Citizenship, Documentation, Papers,
Politics (198)	Politics, Brexit, Election, Political Migrant, Human Rights, Liberal Values, Trans Rights, Accidental American,

continued on following page

Table 1. Continued

Records (199)	Records, American Records of Naturalization, Birth Certificate, Notary, Apostille, Notary Public, Passport, Certificate, Degree,
Security (200)	Security, Property, Land, Law Enforcement, Police, Polizei, Safety, Securi*, Restive, Terrorism, Insecurity, Risk*, Danger*, Public Security, Riot,
Taxes (201)	Taxes, FATCA, Tax Related, Taxation, Exit Tax, Deemed Disposition Exit Tax, Property Taxes, Income Taxes, State Taxes, Property Tax, Income Tax, State Tax, Capital Gains Tax, Write-off, Tax Man, Uncle Sam,
Visa (202)	Visa, Working Holiday Visa, WHV, DV Lottery, Overstay*, Holiday Visa, Refugeeship, Refugee, Migrant, Immigration, Emigration, Interview, Re-applying, Reapplication, Ancestry Visa, K1, Spousal Visa, Income Requirement, Schengen Visa, Competence and Talent Visa, H2b, H2a, Emigrating, Legit Options, Immigration Law, Emigration Law, J1 Visa, Biometric Residence Permit, DS-160, Biometrics, Forms, Apply, Bureaucracy, Government, Investor Visa, Guest-Worker Program, Sectors, Five-Year Visas, Maternity Leave, Blue Card, Silver Fern Work Search Visa, Holiday Visa, Temporary NAFTA Visa, Express Entry, TN Status, TN Visa, Dual Citizenship, Naturalized Citizen, L-1B Visa, Sponsorship, Jobseeker Visa, Internship, Diversity, Notary, Apostille, Notary Public, Certificate, Highly Skilled Migrant Permit, Highly Skilled, Highly Skilled Migrant, Permit, Long Term Visa, Direct Consular Filing, Consul General, Officer, Consular Officer, Residence Permit, Residence, Visa Conversion, Conversion, VITEM 1, Exchange Student, Scientific Research / Exchange Student Visa, Visa Express, Ambassador Passport, Visa Services, Naturalization, Denaturalization, Passport Revocation,
Volunteerism (203)	Volunteerism, Volunteer Work, NGOs, Non-Profits, Nongovernmental Organizations,
6. Personal Experienced Senses of Places **(mental overlays to physical spaces)**	
Abroad (204)	Abroad, Overseas,
MyCountry (205)	MyCountry, Nation-State, My Country, My Birthplace, Where My Heart Is,
DevCountry (206)	Developing Country, 3rd World, Third World, Global South, Undeveloped Country,
Food (207)	Food, Local Food,
Foreign (208)	Foreign, Non-native,
Home (209)	Home*, Domestic, Stateside,
Nation (210)	Nation,
NearAbroad (211)	Near Abroad, Nearby, On the Border, Close, Proximity,
Neighborhood (212)	Neighborhood,
Overseas (213)	Overseas, Abroad,
Vacation (214)	Vacation, Resort, Holiday, Break, Trip, Relaxation,
8. Relation of Personal Emotions to Spaces and Places **(informed by Plutchik's Model of Emotions, specifically the second concentric tier)**	
Joy (215)	Happy, Joyful, Joyous, Smiles,
Trust (216)	Feel Safe, Trust, Believe,
Fear (217)	Fear, Terror, Afraid, Scared, Escape, A Few Hiccups, Nervous, Concerned,
Surprise (218)	Surprise, Shock,

continued on following page

Table 1. Continued

Sadness (219)	Sadness, Sad, Mournful, Mourning, Depressed, Regret, Homesick, Lonely, Loneliness, Missing, Missing Home, Absent, Moody, Mood, Loneliest,
Disgust (220)	Disgust, Sickened, Sick, Frustration, Frustrated, Ire,
Anger (221)	Anger, Angry, Mad,
Anticipation (222)	Anticipation, Hope, Expect, Expectation, Hopefulness, Hopeful, Curious, Interested, Eager,

APPENDIX B: THE .DIC FILE TO RUN IN LIWC2015

%
1 Africa
2 EastAsiaandPacific
3 Europe
4 LatinAmericaandCaribbean
5 MiddleEastandNorthAfrica
6 SouthAsia
7 UnitedStates
8 Anywhere
9 Balkans
10 CanadianArctic
11 CentralAmerica
12 EasternEurope
13 FirstWorld
14 Francophone Africa
15 NonEU
16 NorthAmerica
17 NorthernEurope
18 Oceania
19 OECD
20 Scandinavia
21 SouthAmerica
22 SoutheastAsia
23 ThirdWorld
24 WestCoast
25 WesternCanada
26 WesternEurope
27 Albania

28 Argentina
29 AtlanticCanada
30 Australia
31 Austria
32 Bahamas
33 Bahrain
34 Belarus
35 Belgium
36 Bermuda
37 Bosnia
38 Brazil
39 Bulgaria
40 Canada
41 China
42 Chile
43 Colombia
44 Costa Rica
45 Croatia
46 Cuba
47 Czechia
48 Donetsk
49 Denmark
50 DominicanRepublic
51 Dubai
52 Ecuador
53 Egypt
54 ElSalvador
55 England
56 Estonia
57 Finland
58 France
59 Germany
60 Guam
61 Guatemala
62 Haiti
63 Honduras
64 HongKong
65 Hungary
66 Iceland

67 India
68 Indonesia
69 Iraq
70 Ireland
71 Israel
72 Japan
73 Jordan
74 Kuwait
75 Latvia
76 Lebanon
77 Lithuania
78 Macedonia
79 Malaysia
80 Mexico
81 Monaco
82 Morocco
83 Netherlands
84 Nicaragua
85 NewZealand
86 Norway
87 Pakistan
88 Panama
89 Peru
90 Philippines
91 Poland
92 Portugal
93 Qatar
94 Romania
95 Russia
96 SaudiArabia
97 Scotland
98 Serbia
99 Slovakia
100 SouthAfrica
101 SouthKorea
102 Sweden
103 Switzerland
104 Taiwan
105 Tanzania

106 Thailand
107 Turkey
108 UnitedArabEmirates
109 UnitedKingdom
110 UnitedStates
111 Uruguay
112 Venezuela
113 Vietnam
114 VirginIslandsUS
115 Alabama
116 Arizona
117 BritishColumbia
118 California
119 Colorado
120 Florida
121 Illinois
122 Maryland
123 Massachusetts
124 Michigan
125 Nebraska
126 Ohio
127 Oklahoma
128 SouthCarolina
129 Tennessee
130 Texas
131 Wisconsin
132 Amsterdam
133 Austin
134 Bangkok
135 Belfast
136 Boston
137 Berlin
138 Brisbane
139 BuenosAires
140 Capetown
141 CotedAzur
142 Detroit
143 DublinIreland
144 Edinburgh

184 Crime
185 Destination
186 Education
187 Employment
188 Family
189 Fees
190 GTFO
191 Healthcare
192 Home
193 Housing
194 LawEnforcement
195 Lifestyle
196 Move
197 Passport
198 Politics
199 Records
200 Security
201 Taxes
202 Visa
203 Volunteerism
204 Abroad
205 MyCountry
206 DevCountry
207 Food
208 Foreign
209 Home
210 Nation
211 NearAbroad
212 Neighborhood
213 Overseas
214 Vacation
215 Joy
216 Trust
217 Fear
218 Surprise
219 Sadness
220 Disgust
221 Anger
222 Anticipation

See Ya!

Section 3
Image and Multimedia Coding in Academia

Chapter 6

Coding Online Learner Image and Multimedia Submissions for Assignment Fulfillment:
An Early Assessment Rubric

ABSTRACT

In K12 and higher education, instructors have been eliciting student work in a variety of digital forms: text, audio, image, slideshow, video, and various combinations thereof. These files are uploaded to learning management systems, online training systems, online research suites (online survey systems), and learning applications; they are shared on content-sharing social media sites (with varying degrees of public access). Some are created on presentation sites, which enable the collation of the various media formats into coherent wholes (whether as voicethreads or slideshows or digital publications). While assignments are becoming richer, in many cases, the assessment tools for the work have not changed to accommodate the changes in modality. This chapter provides a light review of the literature, then a decomposition of how to create assessment rubrics for a variety of assignments involving submitted imagery and multimedia. The proposed draft assessment rubric provides a start for instructors, who are encouraged to define customizable parts of the rubric and to add unique requirements based on their local contexts and the requirements of the respective assignments.

DOI: 10.4018/978-1-5225-2679-7.ch006

INTRODUCTION

In the raft of new features for learning management systems and online survey systems is a "file upload" capability, which enables individuals to upload digital imagery (screenshots, photographs, drawings, maps, data visualizations, mash-ups, and others), audio, video, slideshows, small simulations, and other digital file types. In K12 and higher education, instructors are requiring learners to submit multimodal work—well beyond "old school" writing. Today, there are assignments in which learners are required to participate in events or fieldtrips and to take a "selfie" to prove their participation or to highlight some aspect of their experience or learning. Students are required to create data tables and data visualizations, oftentimes in a reproducible research code—so others may run data analytics on their data and see if they can find the same results. Learners explore 3D immersive virtual worlds to experience simulations and to interact with other human-embodied avatars; they are asked to create screenshots and machine-cinema (*machinima*) to capture some of their virtual experiences. The use of Second Life in higher education brings complexity because the virtual space involves what Warburton (2009) calls the "physical layer," the "communication layer," and the "status layer" (p. 420). Learners map both real physical spaces and virtual ones and represent their work in diagrams. Budding strategists draw out game trees to convey both strategy and tactics, with the power coming from the ideas as much as for the depiction. While the submitted works may seem simple, many of the assigned projects involve a fair amount of technological savvy and a half-dozen multimedia authoring tools and social media systems.

While multimedia assignment submissions involve more multisensory dimensionality (including auditory, visual, and symbolic reasoning channels), 4th dimensionality (time added to 3D; sequentiality), interactivity, and other features, oftentimes, the assessment instruments for the multimedia work is a rehash of the assessment for the text-based assignment. A text-based proxy assessment for multimedia-based work is often not a very effective fit to the work, and this leaves many features of the multimedia work unaddressed and unassessed. In other cases, instructors do not define their terms of assessment. One version of this is a pass-fail approach, with a given pass as long as a person has met the basic requirements of the assignment. The thinking sometimes is that the required modality or form itself is so demanding that completion of the work is grounds for full credit. While instructors may view the submitted work with a sophisticated eye—understanding likely inputs that learners made in order to create particular works, and drawing conclusions about learner competence, knowledge, creativity, and intellect—much of what is observed is not codified in an assessment instrument. Said another way, instructors often take an intuitive "know it when I see it" or "wing-it" approach. Another variation is to allow the multimedia learners themselves to assess their own work or their peers (or professionals in a field) to assess the work.

A better way may be to create an assessment instrument for both guiding the creation of the respective works and then assessing them based on shared standards. Having a defined approach will benefit learners, so they know the standards that they are building to. Instructors themselves can have a fairer and more legally defensible grading method. In this chapter, a rubric is the selected assessment tool format; a rubric is a table that describes the criteria for a work on row headers and criteria for the assessment on the column headers.

Rubrics may be focused on the particular assigned work, but they may also be built on competence hierarchies. In this latter case, the rubrics are used to assess the learner's apparent capabilities based on his or her work and his / her knowledge ("grasp degree") and as such. This focus on competence is a step out from assessing the work itself to assessing the author hand behind the work, and this is based on inductive logic and inference. In this latter case, assessors are making inferences of the creator's competence from the work submitted. As part of the feedback to learners, instructors will need to achieve three steps: "1) Identification and definition of competences. 2) Design of course activities that conforms the assessment. 3) Make competences and the level acquisition, as clear as possible for learners" (Mor, Guerrero-Roldán, Hettiarachchi, & Huertas, 2014, p. 85).

To this end, this chapter contains a light review of the literature. Both deductive and inductive methods are applied to the creation of a starter rubric that considers legal considerations, quality features of various digital object modes, and other features, with the idea that parts and pieces may be added or removed to customize the modularize-able rubric for effective use. Also,

Table 1. A basic structure of an assessment rubric

	Excellent (A)	Good, Above Average (B)	Sufficient (C)	Insufficient (D)	Poor (F)
Criteria #1					
Criteria #2					
Criteria #3					

the various point values can be easily changed up so that what is important to the instructor and the learning may be weighted more heavily than some other features. The idea is to articulate some of the expectations in order to encourage (1) improved learner work and (2) improved instructor assessment but not imposing a formalism or structure. Some of these same ends may be achieved with checklists. Both rubrics and checklists can be integrated into LMS grading and combined with creative means of feedback including reply videos, reply audio, textual responses, and group critiques.

The basic conceptualization may be seen in Figure 1, "A Conceptualization of the Online Teaching and Learning Process using Imagery and Multimedia". The assignment is based on defined learning objectives and observable learning outcomes. The learning objectives inform the full design of the assignment: the informational contents, the technologies used, the tasks required, and the final deliverables. In the learning context, learners will have access to support for their multimedia work, such as access to technology tools and access to support expertise. The work is created and then shared with the instructor, within the course with peers, with professionals, and possibly even with the broader world (even crowd-sourcing feedback). Additional learning opportunities may be designed in this sharing—through the sparking of analyses, conversations, and constructive critiques. The work is assessed formally, and the learner receives feedback and encouragement. In this cycle, the rubric plays an important role when the work is assigned, and it also plays an important role during assessment. There can be some extra loops through the cycle if revisions are encouraged for extended learning. Also, in this conceptualization, the rubric is informed by both instructor expectations and also the work created by the learners…so the rubric is not a static and non-changing instrument. It is conceptualized as an adaptive instrument, with high flexibility in terms of adding or removing pieces. As new authoring capabilities become available, those environmental changes will also affect what may be expected of learner multimedia works. With some instructors going to automated means to assess multimedia work (particularly in massive open online courses or "MOOCs"), an assessment rubric can offer a blueprint for computational means for assessment, especially given the advancements in machine vision and artificial intelligence. Automated computational assessment systems are also deployed in various learning systems that automatically generate reports of results and provide "immediate feedback for learners and educators" (Pirnay-Drummer & Ifenthaler, 2010, p. 77).

Figure 1. A conceptualization of the online teaching and learning process using imagery and multimedia

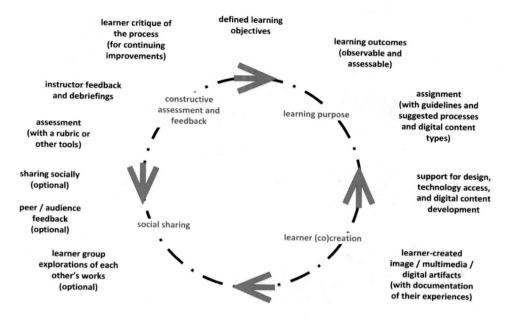

Are there some simple ways to summarize the purposes of assigned imagery and multimedia work, and what types of assignments fit under these respective assignments?

The listing in Table 2 gives a sense of some of the purposes of assigning multimedia-based assignments and some of the related ranges of assignment types. These are a small sampling and are by no means comprehensive. The headings for Table 2 come from observations of assignment types that involve imagery and multimedia.

REVIEW OF THE SCANT LITERATURE

In the academic literature, there are examples of case-based usages of imagery and multimedia-based assignments. For example, in physics learning, naïve students were found to use mental imagery to make sense of the physical world. Visual representations help instantiate elusive concepts, abstractions, and theories.

Table 2. A listing of imagery and multimedia assignment purposes and some related assignments

	Purposes						
Documentary, Description, or Record-Keeping Purposes	Identification, Differentiation, Diagnosis	Theorizing, Conceptualizing, and Imagining	Simulation Purposes	Self-Expression, Interpretation, and Artistry Purposes	Design Purposes (Problem-Solving)	Research and Data Analytics Purposes	Other
Types of Related Assignments							
• Technological setup or software installation • Display, exhibit • Virtual world screen capture • A sequence or process or procedure • Completion of an automated tutorial • Recording of a structured experiment • Recording of an interview • Recording of a panel session	• Image capture of particular flora and fauna, with proper labels • Identification of particular disease manifestations on tissue	• Representation of models and relationships • Counterfactual scenarios • Illustration of abstractions	• Role plays • Case studies Historical re-creations, re-enactments • Machinima captures • Immersive virtual world experiences (such as language immersion, cultural immersion, hostile-environment recreations, and others)	• A multimedia essay • A multimedia review	• A design plan for a particular space (to meet particular objectives) • A game tree to solve a strategic and tactical issue	• Mapping • Representation of a space • Data visualizations • Documentation of a research quest • Description of a data analytics process • A video research journal	…

400

We show that naive students use imagery in making sense of the physical phenomena; that modes of naive students' imagery resemble, on several levels cognitive mechanisms identified in physicists' imagery strategies; and that the product of imagery, pictorial representations, mirror processes of changes in conceptual understanding. (Botzer & Reiner, 2005, p. 147)

Along with thought experiments, mental imagery is used to innovate in physics (Botzer & Reiner, 2005, p. 149). Researchers and learners benefit not only from accurate learning of current ideas but also from the flexibility of seeing beyond current paradigms into unexplored possibilities, re-conceptualizations, and counterfactuals. The authors identified three main modes of visual representation in the history of physics: sensory-based representations (what the researcher observed or otherwise perceived), purely imaginary representations, and "formalism-based representations" (based on physics laws) (Botzer & Reiner, 2005, p. 154).

Since the early days of manual and analog data visualizations (think hand-drawn imagery), advancements in authoring tools have meant enriched ways not only to draw but to create multimedia. Online services provide a range of ways to integrate digital contents, such as digital voice threads mixing imagery, voice, and interactivity, in middle school work (Wood, Stover & Kissel, 2013). These more complex objects require tailored assessment practices that take the respective digital multi-modal aspects into consideration:

Adopting new assessment practices for multimodal compositions becomes problematic if educators and students use ——frameworks and processes of one medium to assign value and to interpret work in a different medium (Yancey 2004, p 90, as cited by Aranguiz, 2015, pp. 5-6). One suggested initial good practice to evaluating multimodal work is to define learning outcomes with "clear criteria" and "statements of the various levels of achievement" (Gray, Thompson, Sheard, Clerehan, & Hamilton, 2010, p. 113). A helpful example of a multimedia-based rubric is derived from "visual and film art" to inform learners' senses of media literacy as well as improve their work (Ostenson, 2012, p. 167). In Ostenson's "Assessment Rubric for Images," his higher level categories include the following: emphasis, lighting, angle, and color (2012, pp. 175); his "Assessment Rubric for Organization" includes the following: sequencing and transitions (p. 176); his "Assessment Rubric for Audio" includes the following: quality and appropriateness (p. 177). Each of the rubrics have much more detail in each of the rubric cells, aligned with quality measures.

Table 3. A draft column header with word and numeric measures

Assessed Feature	Exemplary Submission (9-10)	Exceeds Requirements (7-8)	Meets All Basic Requirements (5-6)	Fails to Meet Some Requirements (3-4)	Does Not Meet Minimum Requirements (0-2)	N/A (for Various Reasons)	Textual Comments

In terms of measures, some use words and numbers, words alone, or numbers alone, or some mix. One sequence may be as follows: exemplary submission, exceeds requirements, meets all basic requirements, fails to meet some requirements, does not meet minimum requires, N/A, and then "text responses".

An early rubric could include layers of criteria based on different categories. At the foundation would be necessary requirements, and as one moves up the layers, there are more granular and complex requirements. At the top are "Other(s)" as a catchall for the particular local context. As noted early on, it is possible to add or remove layers and features. This is not one-size-fits-all.

To explore Table 4 in more depth, the bottom layer focuses on "Level 1: Basic assignment requirements." Unless particular requirements are suspended (such as for accessibility mitigations or special other circumstances), it is assumed that all learners would have to meet the basic requirements.

Next are "Level 2: Legal considerations," including intellectual property protections, privacy protections, and so on. All works on the Web are assumed to be copyrighted unless the clear owner has released rights on a reputable site and in a reputable way (such as through Creative Commons licensure). On the Web, for all the talk of mash-ups, it is not acceptable to appropriate other's work as one's own, and the rules of fair play suggest that learners only use what is released for their use and what they create themselves. Legal considerations are important because for students, very little stops at the classroom door. Students will use their creations to apply for scholarships, grants, apprenticeships, and jobs. They will host their hypermedia (non-linear, interactive digital objects) creations on their own websites or contribute works to a lifelong professional e-portfolio; they will enter competitions for prize money and recognition; they will publish broadly; they will share their works on social media. Since the Internet and Web are "forever," their contributions will be out in the world—and their names will be their brands. Being a high school or university student is a precursor step to professional status for many. If a work does not meet legal requirements, it cannot be used in any way outside of a classroom environment, which will limit learner options. (It is

Table 4. Rubric layers from foundational to more complex (with * indicating specific local requirements for the assignment)

Level 11: Other(s)*:

Level 10: Originality:
    creativity
    innovation
    unique author hand
    discovery, and other aspects

Level 9: Stand-alone value: informative resource with learning value (in informal learning contexts)
Level 8: Focal purpose(s) (of assignment)*:   the point(s) of the assignment

Level 7: Messaging:
    coherence of messaging
    consistency of messaging
    representations of referred-to meanings in the real environment
    visual style, and others

Level 6: Labeling:
    in-image annotations
    metadata
    geolocational information
    folk tagging
    descriptive text with the file uploads, and others

Level 5: Technological functionality:
    designed interactivity
    technological interoperability
    reproducible research
    future-proofing
    portability between technology systems, and others

Level 4: Multimedia forms and their respective defined conventions for quality:
    when zoomed in: non-pixelation, text legibility, line smoothness (vs. line aliasing)
    proper aspect ratio, proper object sizing, non-distorted imagery
    true colors, white balance
    clear audio
    user controls on simulations, and others

Level 3: Accessibility standards:
    accurate alt-texting for imagery
    accurate transcription for audio and video
    proper use of color for informational purposes
    labeled data tables, and others

Level 2: Legal considerations:
    intellectual property protections
    privacy protections, and others

Level 1: Basic assignment requirements: deadlines, originality, fit-to-assignment, technological modalities, supporting raw files, and others

a powerful lesson for learners to know what professional legal requirements are for their work.) While legal intellectual property guidelines may seem onerous, these same rules provide learners with protection for their own work. Knowing the rules of legal fair play is part of the authenticity in the learning. (Also, with the power of text and reverse imagery search online, it is often trivial to trace back objects to actual original sources. IBM Watson and Google and other companies have computational capabilities (machine vision and AI) to identify objects in imagery and video. Google's YouTube checks all uploaded videos against known patterns of copyrighted works—in stills, in audio, and in video—in order to protect copyrighted materials from intentional or unintentional re-use and re-distribution.)

The next layer focuses on "Level 3: Accessibility standards." These are also based on legal requirements, but these focus on ensuring multi-channel delivery of the information, so that users with sensory perception and symbolic processing limitations may still experience and engage the work.

The next level up refers to "Level 4: Multimedia forms and their respective defined conventions for quality." If learners are creating particular modalities of work, they need to strive for the best quality possible based on defined quality conventions, real-world practices, and practical possibilities based on the contexts. For example, digital photos used in a documentary way need to be white-color balanced, properly sized, high-resolution, effectively cropped, and so on.

In the next level up, "Level 5: Technological functionality" points to the need for simulations and games and such to function as required for effective user use. There are a variety of general technology standards, including the following:

interoperability, content portability, device independence (device independence refers to the ability to write content once and display it in many different devices such as cell phones, PDAs, laptops, and desktop systems), internationalization, tool and content longevity, and many other benefits are also achieved (WAI, http://www.w3.org/WAI/EO/Drafts/bcase/). (Treviranus & Roberts, 2006, p. 471)

Within object types, there are more granular standards, too, to ensure proper functioning. For example, touch or haptic interfaces require certain types of 3D image creation to convey information (Treviranus & Roberts, 2006, p. 484). It is beyond the purview of this work to include those features here.

The "Level 6: Labeling" layer requires that the digital objects have appropriate annotations.

"Level 7: Messaging," the next layer up, refers to how coherently a message is shared based on the style (look and feel), words, imagery, multimedia.

Specifically, what is communicated, what is not communicated, and what is mis-communicated (if anything)?

The "Level 8: Focal purpose(s) (of assignment)*" enables weighting the particular purpose of the assignment more heavily. For example, a marketing piece needs to be persuasive to a particular target audience. A photo album from a field trip will require high-fidelity images focused on particular phenomenon-of-interest. A diagram needs to accurately describe the functions of a system. A visual depiction of a model may need to be memorable and serve as a visual mnemonic. A "selfie" may need to trigger viral interest. A slideshow describing a process should have clear sequential order and sufficiently explanatory text and related imagery. This layer is labeled with an asterisk (*) to show that this is especially included to allow for localizing the rubric.

The next level is "Level 9: Stand-alone value." The concept here is that anything shared on the Web will have second- and third-order distributions beyond the local learning context and will be harnessed for usage and appreciation in others' contexts. A work that is well designed will have value as a stand-alone object even unmoored from its original context. Online sharing means that learning spaces are "permeable," and those that engage in informal learning will potentially stand to benefit from the digital object. One author describes feral learners:

The feral learner is unconstrained by the boundaries of curriculum, school hours, academic discipline, or assessment criteria. Feral learners learn, primarily, for learning's sake. Feral learning is to academic study what pure research is to product development. It is about discovering what might be 'out there' rather than reaching pre-defined targets. Understanding the feral learner starts with acknowledging that learning (as compared to being taught) is a natural, instinctual human activity. (Hall, 2008, p. 110)

The next layer, "Level 10: Originality," is often extraneous to the learner work. This "originality" refers to a high level of innovation and discovery. This standard may be instantaneously recognized as fresh and non-existent elsewhere—and relevantly so… or it may require long periods of time before a work is recognized for its actual value. (People's judgments in contemporaneous time have been shown to be often misjudging.) In the long term, substance tends to trump style; concept tends to trump execution; actual contribution tends to trump renown.

Finally, the "Level 11: Other(s)*" enables add-on layers beyond the foundation that may help capture unique goals of the particular digital imagery and multimedia assignments.

Of course, instructors can receive works that are so insightful and powerful and mind-blowing that they exist outside the bounds of the assignment and render the assignment rubric irrelevant. Such works are by definition rare, but instructors need to be open to such works and eventualities.

Certainly, for complex projects, learners do well to maintain their own research journals, so they have a record of their own learning and can preserve their insights for future work. These journals may be required by the instructor, along with raw support files (the unedited video, the b-roll, the imagery, the storyboards, the scripts, and so on) and other elements that may shed light on the student work. These may be housed in labeled folders and zipped for transfer to the instructor.

The next step is to integrate the measures with the draft rubric, which at heart, is still not defined. This may be seen in Table 5. To complete this rubric, the individual cells have to be filled with the features that describe the work. The top row may be switched out for the grades in Table 1.

Narrow to Broad Sharing of Digital Student-Created Contents

For the media-rich assignment, there can be a number of ways that the resulting files are shared. A student can share the results with himself or herself and debrief what he or she sees and share the debriefing with the faculty member. There are assignments that instructors never see and never collect, as part of the design. A learner may share his / her work with the instructor, with resulting two-way conversations about the work. The student may share with the instructor and other peers; the instructor and domain field professionals and peer learners; and with the instructor, peer learners, and the world.

The Social Web is a common destination point for such works, whether the learner is narrow-casting to a private group of fellow learners or broadcasting to the whole world. (As a side note, learners cannot be required to publish to the world to learn and to earn course credit. Learners may be offered substitute assignments if they are unwilling to publish to the world—at least in the U.S. higher education context.) As a matter of course, a number of learning-based images and multimedia are shared on content-sharing sites,

Table 5. An integrated imagery and multimedia assessment rubric (draft)

Assessed Feature	Exemplary Submission (9-10)	Exceeds Requirements (7-8)	Meets All Basic Requirements (5-6)	Fails to Meet Some Requirements (3-4)	Does Not Meet Minimum Requirements (0-2)	N/A (for Various Reasons)	Textual Comments
(11) Others(s)*							
(10) Originality							
(9) Stand-alone value							
(8) Focal purpose(s) (of assignment)							
(7) Messaging							
(6) Labeling							
(5) Technological functionality							
(4) Multimedia forms and their respective defined conventions for quality							
(3) Accessibility standards							
(2) Legal considerations							
(1) Basic assignment requirements							

wikis, blogs, and microblogs. Instructors go to social media because the accounts are often free, and the respective sites have features that enable the showcasing of the uploaded work and methods for learner interactivity. There is also the sense that going broadly social highlights the "authenticity" of the work: the engagements of learners with other practitioners in the world, the broad publishing to reach a wide audience (with the potential of crowd-sourced feedback), the harnessing and use of real-world social media, and the engagement of the larger social ecosystem in shared problem-solving. By publishing, learners automatically become Web 2.0 authors, and they often become part of a community of practice—with amateurs (non-professionals who engage in particular work for entertainment, amusement, or other personal reasons—but not to become a professional ultimately), novices (new learners who aspire to expertise), and experts. As such, learners may leave their works for others' reference and leave behind something to possibly advance the field. There is much accessing of Web 2.0 for contents for teaching and learning in higher education (Franklin & Harmelen, 2007).

Harnessing crowd-sourced insights is no easy feat. It can be highly difficult to get others interested and to encourage them to invest time and expertise to engage with learners. Many of the case studies of applied usage of Web 2.0 shows a distinct lack of engagement with those outside the particular classroom. A perusal of some of the harnessing of crowd-intelligence, such as for labeling Library of Congress image resources, shows some successes. In other contexts, crowd-sourced individuals taking on various tagging roles in coding museum collections were found to be of a number of types ("hobbyists, experts, specialists, geocoders, proofers, uniformists, promoters, remixers, narrators, and oddities") but only some of them with constructive and pro-social contributions (Earle, 2014). In such cases, the "folk" tagging introduces plenty of noise along with "signal." Lesser-known projects such as image-content sharing "for education" shows generic image collections and little group engagement over time.

EVOLVING A DRAFT ASSESSMENT RUBRIC FOR DIGITAL IMAGERY AND MULTIMEDIA

In Figure 2, "A Semi-emergent Image and Multimedia Coding Sequence," this work is conceptualized from the instructor view. Here, the instructor defines the terms of the assignment and maybe provides some examples for learners to use to gauge instructor expectations and grading judgment. The learner submits the work…and there is a basic check done to ensure that basic requirements are met—such as that the work is original, submitted within deadline, and generally fitting of the general assignment requirements. The next step then involves the application of standards to engaging and assessing the work. Part of this assessment depends on a structure based on Bloom's Taxonomy of Learning, with creativity at the apex. This taxonomy is helpful because it hints at foundational requirements and knowledge underlying learner work. Such complex knowledge and skill interdependencies are helpful to promote the learning. To the right are some features of the data visualizations and multimedia that may be assessed.

If the above is the sequential view from the instructor side, it is possible also to conceptualize the work from the learner side. In Figure 3, the timeline

Figure 2. A semi-emergent image and multimedia coding sequence

sequence is maybe a little formalistic, but parts may be dropped, revised, moved, and so on. The importance of this is that it provides an empathetic view of what a learner may experience in responding to an assignment with digital imagery and multimedia. To further the empathy, instructors should be attentive to how much actual effort and time each part of the sequence takes and to be flexible with deadlines since unexpected challenges may arise with complex projects and technologies. Group work adds even more potential for challenges and coordination.

Figure 3. A learner experiential timeline in creating assignment-based imagery and multimedia objects / sets

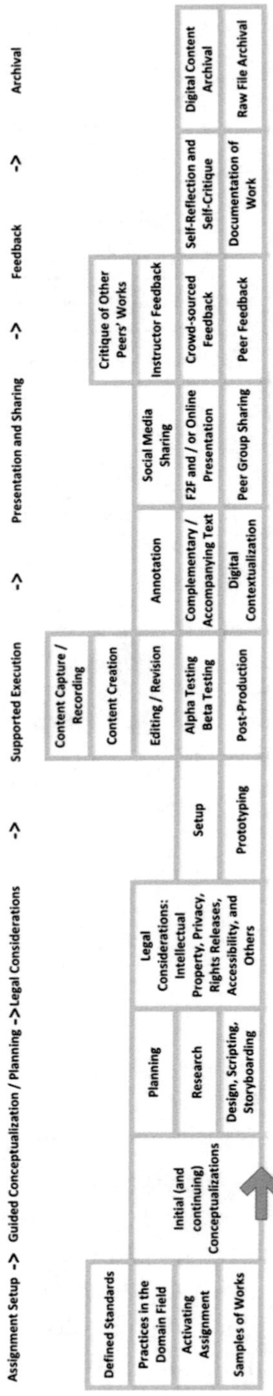

Understanding the complexity of the multimodal pedagogy at play may encourage more efforts to provide direction, resources, professional support, and encouragement to the learners and the learning teams.

FUTURE RESEARCH DIRECTIONS

In this chapter, the importance of formalizing some aspects of assessment of digital imagery and multimedia was emphasized. A draft rubric with general categories, a layered hierarchy, and proposed features within the layers were suggested. This work is highly preliminary, and a logical next step would be finalizing the rubric and putting it out to pilot test in various contexts. It would help to see what variations of this rubric may be used in various contexts.

CONCLUSION

Learners create digital imagery and multimedia objects as part of many learning sequences. Such works offer rich ways of self-expression and also rich facets for assessment. Using thought-out and structured methods to assess the imagery and multimedia not only enhances the learning but also simplifies the work for the creators of the assignments or the instructors. This approach of defining standards for such assignments also applies to feral contexts where individuals learn in the wild and without complex standards. In self-learning, having some light goals to structure the design and development work can be important supports to the learning.

REFERENCES

Aranguiz, A. (2015). *Waiting for the gift of sound and vision: Learning to assess multimodal compositions* (Masters of Science thesis). University of Edinburgh.

Botzer, G., & Reiner, M. (2005). Imagery in physics learning – from physicists' practice to naïve students' understanding. In *Visualization in Science Education*. Berlin: Springer. doi:10.1007/1-4020-3613-2_9

Earle, E. F. (2014). *Crowdsourcing metadata for library and museum collections using a taxonomy of Flickr user behavior* (Master's Thesis). Cornell University.

Franklin, T. & van Harmelen, M. (2007, May 28). *Web 2.0 for content for learning and teaching in higher education*. Academic Press.

Gray, K., Thompson, C., Sheard, J., Clerehan, R., & Hamilton, M. (2010). Students as Web 2.0 authors: Implications for assessment design and conduct. *Australasian Journal of Educational Technology, 26*(1), 105–122. doi:10.14742/ajet.1105

Hall, M. (2008). Getting to know the feral learner. In *Learners in a Changing Landscape* (pp. 109–133). Berlin: Springer. doi:10.1007/978-1-4020-8299-3_6

Mor, E., Guerrero-Roldán, Hettiarachchi, E., & Huertas, M.A. (2014). Designing learning tools: The case of a competence assessment tool. LNCS, 8523, 83 – 94.

Ostenson, J. W. (2012). Connecting assessment and instruction to help students become more critical producers of multimedia. *Journal of Media Literacy Education, 4*(2), 167–178.

Pirnay-Dummer, P., & Ifenthaler, D. (2010). Automated knowledge visualization and assessment. In D. Ifenthaler (Eds.), *Computer-Based Diagnostics and Systematic Analysis of Knowledge* (pp. 77–115). Berlin: Springer; doi:10.1007/978-1-4419-5662-0_6

Treviranus, J., & Roberts, V. (2006). Inclusive E-learning. In J. Weiss (Eds.), *The International Handbook of Virtual Learning Environments*. Berlin: Springer. doi:10.1007/978-1-4020-3803-7_19

Warburton, S. (2009). Second Life in higher education: Assessing the potential for and the barriers to deploying virtual worlds in learning and teaching. *British Journal of Educational Technology, 40*(3), 414–426. doi:10.1111/j.1467-8535.2009.00952.x

Wood, K. D., Stover, K., & Kissel, B. (2013). Using digital VoiceThreads to promote 21st century learning. *Middle School Journal, 44*(4), 58–64. doi:10.1080/00940771.2013.11461865

KEY TERMS AND DEFINITIONS

2D: Two dimensions, lying along the x- and y- axes.

3D: Three dimensions, lying along the x-, y-, and z-axes.

4D: Four dimensions, lying along the x-, y-, and z-axes and including motion.

Crowd-Sourcing: Sharing contents on the Social Web through various platforms in order to elicit feedback from the online "crowd."

Data Visualization: The depiction of raw data or processed information in a figure or image.

Feral Learning: Learning "in the wild," outside the usual formal education and school spaces.

Hypermedia: A form of multimedia that includes text, hyperlinks, imagery, audio, video, and other elements, presented in a non-linear or user-driven interactive way; a term coined by Ted Nelson in 1965.

Immersive Virtual World: An online and persistent virtual space that enables human interactivity through avatars and through simulated worlds (with visual and auditory interfaces).

Interactivity: The feature of enabling people to engage.

Machine Processing: The use of a computer to analyze information

Metadata: Data about data.

Multimedia: Digital and multimodal information, understood as more than text alone.

Post-Production: After audio or video recordings are captured, the work of processing the recordings to a polished final state for delivery.

Raw Files: Unprocessed (unedited) recordings, uncleaned datasets.

Recursive: Non-linear, going forwards and backwards in time, including repetition.

Reproducible Research: Research data that may be re-analyzed with the same results (reproducibility) as found earlier, sometimes termed "repeatability."

Rubric: An instrument (usually in a table format) used to assess and measure a work on various dimensions.

Screenshot: A screen capture, a still recording of the image on a computer screen.

Social Media Platform: An online space that enables people to socialize and interact with each other around dedicated interests (dating, professional interests, commerce, publishing, digital content sharing, and others); these site types include the following: social networking sites, wikis, blogs, microblogs, and others.

Chapter 7

Coding Digital Learning Objects for Adoption for Online Teaching and Learning

ABSTRACT

A general observation is that 20% of reusable learning objects (RLOs) are adopted at least for a time, but a majority of LOs are created (probably for local purposes), placed online, and not used at all by others. This work explores how digital learning objects (DLOs) may be coded for desirable features for local adoption and usage. This then explores how DLOs are actually designed with varying weights applied to the desirable DLO features of users. Finally, there is a gaps analysis between what inheritors of DLOs are looking for and what design and development teams and instructional designers actually create. If digital learning objects are to be more widely shared, having instructional designers and developers close the gap in LO work may be an important step. A main challenge involves a fundamental imbalance in incentives in the LO economy as currently practiced.

INTRODUCTION

The reuse of learning resources is the raison d'être of Learning Object technologies. -- Xavier Ochoa and Erik Duval in "Measuring Learning Object Reuse" (2008)

DOI: 10.4018/978-1-5225-2679-7.ch007

Digital goods have long been conceptualized as products that can be non-rivalrously used and re-used without much (any?) additional cost once the initial production cost was covered (Benkler, 2006). Digital goods are not consumed or destroyed by use, and the same contents may be used simultaneously. This concept extends to (digital) learning objects (DLOs), defined as "any digital resource that can be reused to support learning" and "educational materials designed and created in small chunks for the purpose of maximizing the number of learning situations in which the resource can be utilized" (Wiley, 2002, p. 1). Another defined a learning object as *"a digital file (image, movie, etc.) intended to be used for pedagogical purposes, which includes, either internally or via association, suggestions on the appropriate context within which to utilize the object"* (Sosteric & Hesemeier, 2002, n.p.). Yet another definition is a freeform one: "Instructional content becomes a learning object when it is *used* as a learning object" (Parrish, 2004, p. 52). In this latter case, how something is used defines its label. In practice, there are various "objects" that fit the definition:

Examples of smaller reusable digital resources include images or photos, live data feeds (like stock tickers), live or prerecorded video or audio snippets, small bits of text, animations, and smaller web-delivered applications, like a Java calculator. Examples of larger reusable digital resources include entire web pages that combine text, images and other media or applications to deliver complete experiences, such as a complete instructional event. (Wiley, 2000, p. 34)

While many learning objects (LOs) have been created, their quality has varied, and there has not yet been "firm evidence that RLOs provide educational benefit" (Sinclair, Joy, Yau, & Hagan, 2013, p. 177). A core requirement of modern learning objects is that they have to be reusable, based on factors such as interoperability, "flexibility in terms of pedagogic situations," and "modifiability to suit a particular teacher's or student's needs" (McCormick, Scrimshaw, Li, & Clifford, 2004, pp. 137 - 138, as cited by Kurilovas, Serikoviene, & Vuorikari, 2014, p. 526).

In the early dream of a learning object economy, professional teams (including content experts) would develop shareable digital learning objects (DLOs) that would be distributed online. An early proponent, Advanced Distributed Learning originated the Sharable Content Object Reference Model in 2000 ("SCORM Overview," 2015). If learning objects could be designed to particular shared standards, a number of "ilities" would be possible, such as accessibility, interoperability, durability, and reusability. In other words, content

- May be "located and accessed from multiple locations and delivered to other locations" (for "accessibility"),
- May operate "across a wide variety of hardware, software, operating systems, and web browsers regardless of the tools used to create it and the platform on which it was initially delivered" (for interoperability"),
- May operate without modification even as "versions of software systems and platforms are changed or upgraded" (for "durability"), and
- May stand alone "independent of learning context" for use by different learners in different training situations (for "usability") (SCORM 2004 4th Edition, Version 8, Sept. 15, 2011).

Over the years, other "ilities" and requirements have been added. Some desirable properties of LOs include "independence, granularity, reusability, assemblability (sic), contextualizity (sic), interoperability, flexibility" (Allen & Mugisa, 2010, pp. 64 – 66). "Adaptability" refers to "the ability to tailor instruction to individual and organizational needs," and "affordability" refers to "the ability to increase efficiency and productivity by reducing the time and costs involved in delivering instruction" (Rustici, Jan. 6, 2009). R. McGreal apparently added other abilities to learning objects, including: assessability, discoverability, interchangeability, manageability, reliability, and retrieveability (sic). In other words, learning objects would be evaluate-able based on "pedagogical effectiveness, price, and usability"; findable based on search terms; substituted on in terms of various components; able to be handled with ease; able to be "counted on to work when needed," and retrievable "when and where you want it" (McGreal, 2004, Introduction, n.p.).

In the intervening years, while all sorts of digital contents have been shared online, it seems that only almost a fifth of reusable learning objects have been actually re-used (Ochoa & Duval, 2008, Measuring…). Recent research works still point to major gaps in learning sequences that are not represented by digital learning objects. If "critical mass" was a goal for the learning object economy, that level has not yet been reached except maybe in particular aspects of a learning sequence.

The current diversity of shared digital contents may have made the term "digital learning object" somewhat archaic and even obsolete. After all, an "LO" is not thought to encompass immersive virtual worlds and virtual games and parts of massive open online course (MOOC) sequences. "LO" may or may not include "courseware," or learning materials instantiated in software or code. Many of these techs and practices did not exist when the idea of learning object was first initially shared. What is not at issue is the fact that sequences of online-based learning are expensive and non-trivial to create, and there are challenges to incentivizing sharing.

Learning Object Referatories and Repositories

By the mid-1990s, learning object repositories (LORs) or digital libraries of LOs were being created on the Web and Internet (Yalcinalp & Emiroglu, 2012, p. 476). As of 2012, one research team identified over a dozen learning object repositories—some funded by institutions of higher education (in cooperative endeavors) and others by national government entities (Yalcinalp & Emiroglu, 2012, pp. 480 - 482). Those who wanted to identify possible users of their DLOs did well to place them on reputable repositories to ensure that their work would be discoverable, usable, and citable. (Most repositories have exclusivity clauses, in order to enable "single sourcing" of resources—so that these would not be in multiple online locations simultaneously.) Likewise, those who maintained learning object repositories benefitted from reputable authors and quality learning objects.

Since the early days of learning object repositories, of course, there have been various types of hosting and delivery systems for LOs beyond repositories. Referatories, like MERLOT (Multimedia Educational Resource for Learning and Online Teaching), point to contents hosted on the Web and Internet. These serve as indexers but also offer other functions—like peer review of learning objects, virtual community support features, and others. There are open courseware systems when enable access to learning experiences of various lengths. There are institutional repositories (IRs), which host research but also often learning objects. There are open learning management systems with a range of automated learning, based on massive open online course (MOOC) principles.

How the LORs originate, evolve, and function depends a lot on the communities that use them (Margaryan & Littlejohn, 2008, p. 334). The dimensions of such communities include the shared goals, the intercommunications among members, their respective roles, rules for engagement, and the "predominant teaching and learning approaches used in the community" (Margaryan & Littlejohn, 2008, p. 334). There are conscious efforts to build social networks around learning object repositories to encourage further usage of the learning objects (Minguillón, Rodríguez, & Conesa, 2010).

A resource-based learning environment (RBLE) offers a range of tools for resource searching, tools for cognitive processing (such as productivity tools to represent the learning), manipulating (the ability to "test beliefs/theories"), and communicating (exchanging ideas with others) (Hill & Hannafin, 2001, p. 44). There are tools to help scaffold the learning, including access to accessing support from expert consultants (Hill & Hannafin, 2001, p. 45). While some suggest that RBLEs are "pedagogically neutral" (Hill & Hannafin, 2001, p. 42), there may be something of the "theory of learning objects" here and also an "information processing" approach. The Theory of Learning Objects is a synthetic theory that combines various conceptualizations into a set of descriptive features, but which decouples the object oriented programming features from LOs. Nash (2005) explains the object oriented aspect of LOs, "which suggests that ideal way to build a computer program or anything digital is to assemble it from standardized, small, interchangeable chunks of code" (Nash, 2005, p. 217). The reasoning:

Object orientation is an important factor in our estimation, as it is the main basis upon which one can reasonably anticipate achieving reusability and interoperability from objectifying e-learning content. The entities often regarded as learning objects by the vast majority of models are not able to make use of the features of object orientation intended to produce reusability and interoperability (sic) such as inheritance, polymorphism and instantiation, because they are not objects in the sense of object orientation. (Allen & Mugisa, 2010, p. 60)

The information processing theory suggests an approach to learning in which the human learner's mind is a computer that responds to sensory information from the environment. RBLEs seem like spaces that would be beneficial for self-regulated learners who can learn in a self-driven way in the "feral" wilds of the Internet and Web. Self-regulated learners "are characterized by their ability to initiate metacognitive, cognitive, affective, motivational, and behavioral processes in order to take actions to achieve their learning goals and persevere until they succeed" (Kizilcec, Pérez-Sanagustín, & Maldonado, 2017, p. 19).

In 2000, reusable learning objects (RLOs) became popularized as objects that may be broadly shared and save people development costs. In 2001, Lawrence Lessig originated the Creative Commons licensure, which enables people to share what they create with nuanced levels of rights. At about the same time, the "sharing economy" become predominant, with people enabling others to access what they legally own through rents and rights releases. This licensure has enabled the ability to conduct Creative Commons searches for licensed contents that enable broader use (https://search.creativecommons.org/). The advent of Web 2.0 or the Social Web also meant that people were sharing their photos, selfies, songs, audio podcasts, videos, and ideas—on various social media platforms. There happens to be learning value in "everyday objects." They were also sharing slideshows, e-books, and reviews broadly on the Web and Internet.

One important feature of learning objects is to provide a sense of "motivational relevance to students" (McCormick, Scrimshaw, Li, & Clifford, 2004, p. 150), for these and other learners. Learning objects may be harnessed to deliver adaptive learning to individual learners based on need and should be "adaptable to many instructional contexts" (Parrish, 2004, p. 52). In massive open online courses, learners with stronger self-regulated learning skills "were more likely to revisit previously studied course materials, especially course assessments" (Kizilcec, Pérez-Sanagustín, & Maldonado, 2017, p. 18).

Another vision for the uses of digital learning objects sees them as a necessary step not only in developing e-learning but as necessary pieces to a future Semantic Web (or "Web 3.0" in Tim Berners-Lee's vision) in which contents are machine-recognizable and machine-collectable for human purposes (Berners-Lee, Hendler, & Lassila, May 17, 2001). In this vision, data can be "shared and reused across application, enterprise, and community boundaries" ("W3C Semantic Web Activity," June 19, 2013). For learning objects to be usable in a federated sense (across hosted collections) and also for them to be usable on the Semantic Web, there must be both "structural and semantic interoperability" (Kiu & Lee, 2006, p. 27). With so many learning objects "in the wild," some teams are considering ways to evaluate LOs in an automated way based on content data and metadata.

The actual abundance of resources inside repositories (Ochoa & Duval, 2009) and the availability of contextual evaluations in some of them have opened the possibility of seeking for intrinsic metrics of learning objects that could be used as indicators of quality. This means to say that learning objects could be "mined" and quantitative measures of good and not-good resources could be compared in order to discover intrinsic attributes associated with quality, thus allowing the creation of statistical profiles of good and poor resources that could serve as the basis for quality prediction. (Cechinel, Sánchez-Alonso, & García-Barriocanal, 2011, p. 1255)

Learning Object Metadata (LO Metadata)

While there are a number of learning object metadata schemas, it may well be impossible to create ones that apply to "all methodologies and all learning theories"(Parrish, 2004, p. 60). The space itself is too diverse and complex.

Even when creators of DLOs add metadata, theirs are often informal "folk" tagging done by content experts who often do not have expertise in formal labeling. In their analysis of the metadata used to label digital learning objects, one research team identified general error types, including missing data elements, incorrect use of metadata editors, "correct, but incomplete information," "impossible to track the information" (sorts of errors), incorrect information or "wrong classification," and "unexpected information," among others (Cechinel, Sánchez-Alonso, & Sicilia, 2009, p. 63). The researchers attribute the mistakes in part to the IEEE LOM standard and also to the human annotators (Cechinel, Sánchez-Alonso, & Sicilia, 2009, p. 69). In many cases, hiring "professional indexers" to catalog the learning resources for repositories is infeasible "due to scalability issues and the costs involved" (Ochoa & Duval, 2009, pp. 67 - 68). Some researchers suggest that automatic metadata generation may be a solution to the challenge of LO metadata quality, but the textual contents have to be defined first before automated means may be effective. There are efforts to evaluate learning objects and to use that information to help those searching for relevant LOs, such as by ranking them by relevance (Ochoa & Duval, Jan. – Mar. 2008).

SCORM standards have been built upon now, with newer standards known as the Tin Can API (or the Experience API or xAPI). This sharing of learning objects, whether for free or for a fee, would promote efficiencies, so teams with similar interests would not reinvent similar learning objects. In this LO economy, the best-made learning objects would be adopted, and lesser ones would be ignored; in the long term, those who could create evocative learning contents would dominate, and those who could not would have their niche markets or would ultimately find other more rewarding work doing something else.

Learning objects are shared via repositories, referatories, digital libraries, learning management systems (LMSes), social media (like image- and video-sharing sites), and immersive virtual worlds. In many senses, digital collections are conceptualized as not "merely IT deployments but as social systems with contributors, owners, evaluators and users forming patterns of interactions on top of portals or through search systems embedded in other learning technology components" (Sicilia, Ochoa, Stoitsis, & Klerkx, 2013, p. 285). In this conceptualization, the authors cite "curated digital collections" which include referatories, "aggregated collections," "concrete initiatives," repositories, and "meta-aggregators" (Sicilia, Ochoa, Stoitsis, & Klerkx, 2013, p. 285). Broadly speaking, there are a number of types of learning objects in the sense that anything on the Web and Internet can have learning value.

While the concept of a learning object originated with object oriented programming, some suggests that there is a benefit to delinking learning objects from object oriented theory and defining learning objects on their own terms (Sosteric & Hesemeier, 2002, n.p.). Having a broader definition enables those who create and use LOs not to have to fit their visions in lockstep to others and may further enable innovations. There are multiple ways to build any sort of digital learning object (Churchill & Hedberg, 2006, p. 881).

At the simplest level, reusable learning objects consist of component parts within which may be disaggregated and remixed and reused for other learning uses. Some refer to the smallest learning objects as "atomistic" or "atomic" as in the sizes of atoms and the smallest indivisible units. Others refer to these smallest elements as "prims" (or "primitives") (Chikh, 2014, p. 34). "Prims" is a term from 3D virtual worlds in which the smallest building elements are polygon primitives.

The LOs themselves may be considered components of a larger learning sequence. LOs may be nested within other LOs. Each of these elements may be placed in different learning contexts and introduced in different ways. As of yet, there is no accepted defined sizes for learning objects. In the past, people have defined LO elements based on the relationships of the elements to other elements. A prim is necessarily subbed to learning objects, and learning objects belong in course sequences or courses. The challenge with defining unit sizes in other ways is that there is no standard accepted measure. There is an idea of "units of learning" (UoLs) (Chikh, 2014, p. 37) but the definition is elusive. There is no standard accepted definition of a "credit" or an "hour of study" in LOs. There is nothing standardly accepted except a general idea that an LO should have a defined learning objective, and every element of the LO should serve that learning objective, and the LO must be able to "deliver" that objective "independent of the reuse context" (Allen & Mugisa, 2010, p. 61). Of course, some LOs contain multiple learning objectives. Another type of delimiter may be the topic or learning outcome (Weller, Pegler, & Mason, 2003, as cited in Christiansen & Anderson, March 2004, p. 18). Learning objects have to be discrete, with clear limits.

While reusability is technologically feasible, reusability in educational practice may prove challenging in other ways (Vinha, 2005, p. 413). After all, instructors have a lot of requirements for teaching and learning, and their needs are not simple. A study of selected learning object repositories found that approximately 20% of reusable learning objects had been re-used (Ochoa & Duval, 2008). A fifth of LOs enjoy the so-called "Matthew effect," in the sense that those with many adopters tend to accumulate more adopters while those passed by by instructors continue to be ignored. (In the parable of the sower, Matthew 13:12 reads: "Whoever has will be given more, and they will have an abundance. Whoever does not have, even what they have will be taken from them," in the New International Version of the Bible. Robert K. Merton coined the "Matthew effect" in 1968 to capture the idea of "accumulated advantage" or "cumulative advantage" or "success breeds success".)

Further, the researchers found a "long-tail" phenomenon of learning object reuse, with a few objects used frequently and the majority used occasionally or not-at all based on niche adoption.

The main implication of the finding of a Log-normal distribution is that the "Long Tail" effect applies to reuse. Few objects are reused heavily while most of the reused objects are reused just once. However, the volume of reuse in the tail is at least relatively as important as the volume of reuse in the head. According to this result, federating repositories in order to provide a wider selection of objects is a good strategy to foster reuse. Objects present in small repositories have a high probability of being reuse at least once if they are exposed to a wider universe of users. (Ochoa, 2011, p. 5)

Since early 2000, there have been efforts to link and federate learning object repositories. One project used the IMS Digital Repository Interoperability (DRI) specification. This team worked to ameliorate the differences between the respective repositories. They write:

*In a perfect world there would be only one metadata protocol and we would
need only one repository and one search mechanism. However, this would
be a rather bland world. The reality of elearning is a hodge-podge of legacy
repositories, protocols, special interest groups and self-serving communities.
(Hatala, Richards, Eap, & Willms, 2004, p. 26)*

As an instructional designer for over a dozen years and a college- and
university-level instructor for even longer (during which various courses and
learning sequences were designed, developed, and deployed), this author
decided to combine her professional experiences in an autoethnography, in
order to study the state of digital learning objects.

In this chapter, two hypothesis are explored:

Hypothesis 1: In the current learning object economy, there is a discrepancy
between desired features by DLO adopters and DLO creators.
Hypothesis 2: There are practical strategies and tactics to narrow some of the
gaps between the desired features of DLO adopters and DLO creators.

To actualize the research, there are three stages to this work:

The first stage explores what factors inform the adoption of digital learning
objects for face-to-face, blended, and fully online learning contexts. This
stage includes an autoethnographic research piece involving the author's
instructional design work with instructors and her development work on
various types of digital learning objects and then a full literature review to
catch up on the topic. From this, an instrument is created that highlights the
ten top-level desirable features with the related sub-features (Table 1: Ten
Features of Digital Learning Objects that May Affect Adoption and Usage).
A related tool is also created help in the vetting of possible digital learning
objects (Appendix B: Assessment Questions to Evaluate a DLO or a DLO
Sequence (from "Ten Features of Digital Learning Objects that May Affect
Adoption and Usage").

The second stage involves analyzing how digital learning objects are
built for local contexts (in a university) to meet the local aims, based on the
ten desirable features of DLOs. In other words, do instructional designers
and design teams built to the issues that are of concern to those who might
inherit digital learning objects? In this stage, too, a convenience sampling of
LOs is analyzed to see how they fit within the ten desirable features of LOs.

The third stage is a gaps analysis that looks at what features of LOs
are desired by potential DLO adopters in the field...as contrasted to what

instructional designers and developer teams build to locally. While many learning objects created at a university are used in a closed way (without open sharing), there are some incentives to share more---partially to benefit the broader publics, partially to fulfill grant requirements for public sharing and publishing, and partially to burnish instructor and university reputations. This third step identifies gaps between what is being focused on as a DLO value and what potential inheritors of DLOs desire. Some ideas are shared to incentivize closing this gap, both improved reusability of digital learning objects. In this stage, a survey instrument that may be used to understand the uses of DLOs is created (Appendix C: "Adoption of DLOs": A Derived Survey Instrument for Assessing Potential DLO Adopter's Needs").

Based on the model created in the first stage, in the Appendices, there is a question list that may be used to systematically assess a DLO for possible use. There is also a survey instrument that may be used to explore this phenomenon of DLO inheritance further, to crowd-source insights of DLO adoption.

REVIEW OF THE LITERATURE

While digital learning objects clearly have promise, in the years since this concept has emerged, there is as-yet no consensus about what DLOs are and whether they are even beneficial or harmful to learning. It is helpful to use a life cycle view of learning objects. A learning object is conceptualized as going through various stages: obtaining, labeling, offering, selecting, using, and retaining (Strijker, 2003, as cited in Collins & Strijker, 2004, p. 9). At each of the steps are human concerns ("Why?" and "Who?") as well as technological ones ("How?" "What?" "Where?") (Collins & Strijker, 2004, p. 10).

Management of Learning Object Repositories

Digital collections of learning objects are collected in different ways. Some, such as those hosted by universities, are often curated or refereed and must meet certain guidelines before LOs may be shared there. Sometimes institutional peer review is applied to try to maintain the quality of digital learning objects (Nash, 2005, p. 220). There are pressures to populate learning object repositories while maintaining learning value. Some platforms are open to submittals but these may be rejected later if they do not meet the requirements for the system.

One research group examined major learning object repositories (LORs) and found that basic desirable functions were still elusive. They list six desirable features:

1. Knowing where to find the materials;
2. Finding the license/copyright position clearly stated (and preferably a recognized open use policy);
3. Finding at least some basic educational metadata;
4. LORs enforcing basic filters before RLOs are accepted (e.g., ensuring that there is some content, ensuring that copyright is stated, etc.);
5. LORs providing mechanisms for users to report broken links and support rating/feedback;
6. LORs providing a good search mechanism.

Obvious as these points may seem, they are not currently as widespread as would be hoped.

While the infrastructure is undoubtedly vital for the effective use of RLOs, in practice, the benefits of RLOs are also limited by what is available for the subject of interest. (Sinclair, Joy, Yau, & Hagan, 2013, p. 190)

There are middleware tools to help teachers find LO content (Yen, Shih, Chao, & Jin, 2010), evaluate that content, and organize the contents in a usable way. There is active work in designing effective recommendation tools in learning object repositories (Zapata, Menéndez, Prieto, & Romero, 2013). Another contemporary approach to identifying high quality and appropriate learning object for a particular context is to tap the wisdom of the crowd—by harnessing collaborative filtering and online word-of-mouth (Recker, Walker, & Wiley, June 2000). Crowd wisdoms are sometimes built into automated recommender systems, which suggest LOs to learning object repository (LOR) users (Zapata, Menéndez, Prieto, & Romero, 2015, p. 24). One benefit of harnessing fellow instructor experiences is that they can evaluate how an LO works in live contexts instead of just as an observed still-object. They can bring to bear learner feedback from the uses of LOs. There is also work toward developing LO recommender systems for groups of instructors collaborating around the building a course; one feature of such a system is to integrate "voting aggregation strategies and meta-learning techniques... to automatically obtain the final ratings without having to reach a consensus between all the instructors" (Zapata, Menéndez, Prieto, & Romero, 2015, p. 24).

For all the hopefulness of the efficiencies of LOs, some researchers have expressed skepticism about inroads based on "human" and "educational" reasons. They observe some natural constraints:

The reusability of an electronic learning resource depends on its fit with the language, culture, curriculum, computer-use practices, and pedagogical approaches of the potential learners and their instructors. Making this fit has proven to be very difficult. The major reasons for this difficulty relate to the way that electronic learning objects are used in practice, which in turn are directly related to the organizational settings of those who create, label, and offer learning objects on one hand, and of those who select and use them on the other. (Collins & Strijker, 2004, p. 1)

These researchers highlight the differences between university, corporate, and military educational and training contexts. Learning objects also show a "dominant adopted philosophy of learning" in learning objects (Collins & Strijker, 2004, p. 2), and various contexts have different learning philosophies.

Learner Acceptance of DLOs

In one study, researchers applied the technology acceptance model (TAM) to learner acceptance of digital learning objects. They studied both the LO characteristics and learner differences to see what effect these may have on learner acceptance of LOs:

The findings show that both perceived usefulness and perceived ease of use are determinants of behavioural intention to use learning objects. Learning object characteristics influence both perceived usefulness and perceived ease of use of learning objects; individual differences appear to have no influence upon intention to use learning objects. (Lau & Woods, 2009, p. 1059)

The particular features of LOs that were conducive to learner enthusiasms? "Learners who perceived that the learning objects had better turnaround time, were flexible, and provide a feeling of control over course content would indicate that the learning objects were easier to use. Moreover, learners who indicated that the learning objects fitted in with their learning contexts with comprehensive, up-to-date, easy to comprehend contents together with appropriate pedagogy features to support their learning goals helped them to become committed towards the learning" (Lau & Woods, 2009, pp. 1071 -

1072). An earlier work by this research team found a connection between user beliefs and attitudes towards LOs as having "significant positive relationships with behavioural intention and that behavioural intention accurately predicted the actual use of learning objects" (Lau & Woods, 2008, p. 685). Here, behavioral intention is a measure of "a person's attitude towards using the system and its perceived usefulness" (Lau & Woods, 2008, p. 687).

The idea of "learning objects" was popularized in 2000 (Sinclair, Joy, Yau, & Hagan, 2013, p. 178), and in the intervening years, there have been more objects made and distributed through various online venues.

Teacher Preferences for the Identification and Usage of Digital Learning Objects

For instructors who want to pursue the uses of learning objects, there is a cost in time and effort to seek out contents. Adopting learning contents may mean displacing prior contents, and there is a cost to working the various changes. There are varying levels of learning object availability depending on the topic (Christiansen & Anderson, March 2004, p. 1), with some LOs scant or non-existent. At the K-12, post-secondary, and tertiary levels of education, learning objects are used to varying effects. The instructors at these various levels may have differing levels of preparations to find and integrate digital learning objects into their teaching and learning. Updating and maintaining LOs over time will require even higher skills. Teachers must be prepared to accept digital learning objects (Bratina, Hayes, & Blumsack, Nov. – Dec. 2002). Even though instructors, particularly in K-12 levels, may be years away from direct professional expertise in certain subject areas, they will still be required to assess others' expertise and the work of subject matter experts (SMEs) and content experts. This is not to say that teachers do not bring their own expertise to the challenge; as others have noted, vast background knowledge is required to teach effectively with inherited digital learning contents (Sosteric & Hesemeier, 2002, n.p.). There is often no official preparation for how teachers and instructors find, vet, and integrate learning objects; it is considered generally part of the teaching work to find and harness learning resources.

A learning object approach offers teachers tradeoffs: "The learning object approach diminished instructor control, but improved graphics content, interactive capabilities and the opportunity to institute online student assessment with automated quizzes" (Christiansen & Anderson, March 2004,

p. 12). Not only do teachers give up some control, LOs may be adopted at a cost to the professional and personal ego.

Instructors and instructional designers are not egoless in the teaching process, nor do students want them to be. Formal learning can be seen as an interpersonal enterprise, a conversation between someone knowledgeable and someone seeking knowledge. ...Meaningful teaching may occur only when instructors have opportunities to express their personal knowledge. (Parrish, 2004, p. 55)

A research team conducted a study on teachers who searched for digital learning resources on Internet-based repositories, and they found that teachers used "a broad range of search strategies in order to find resources that they deemed were age-appropriate, current, and accurate" and generally planned to use such resources "with little modifications into planned instructional activities" (Recker, Dorward, & Nelson, 2004, p. 93). While this study focused on teacher needs in order to suggest improved functionalities in educational repositories, there were user insights. The teachers sought a range of materials, described as "background information, contact information, graphics, data sets, maps, worksheets, assessments, tools, interactive applications, real-world examples, and links to other sites (Recker, Dorward, & Nelson, 2004, pp. 98 – 99). Further, they preferred the atomistic level of information, for easier integration with the learning. Barriers to the use of inherited digital learning objects "primarily related to the quality of the resources, and the abilities of teachers and students to access and use them," specifically:

Digital resources that were out-of-date, slow, unavailable, charged a fee, or contained information that was too "simple" or too "advanced" discouraged study participants: "it can be very time consuming finding relevant, timely, and grade-appropriate material – it requires a lot of 'sifting' through search engine hits as well as the sites and resources they offer." One teacher noted frustration at "spending time on fruitless searches, which resulted in either lots of irrelevant resources or resources of less quality than that found in books." (Recker, Dorward, & Nelson, 2004, p. 98)

Interestingly, professionally edited contents in books were identified as the standard against which the instructors based their assessments of LOs. Also, the effort for the search was a major point of consideration. One study also found a preference for contents created by fellow teachers, aligned with state-set core standards (K-12), and with consideration for teacher needs (Recker, Dorward, & Nelson, 2004, p. 98), and they wanted full functionality with little or no modification required (p. 99). For some teachers, they want the ability to verify learner accesses to particular digital learning contents (Recker, Dorward, & Nelson, 2004, p. 100) and to see how learners performed when user-specific assessments are available. Technology adoption is not a final and absolute decision. The adoption may be a continuing one or not because teachers may always choose to discontinue usage of a technology at some point; further, initial or continuing rejection of a technology may change into later adoption (Gaffney, 2010, p. 5).

Learning Object Metadata Standards

Learning object metadata schemas seem to come from government funding (Heery, Johnson, Beckett, & Rogers, 2005), non-profits, and academia.

The Dublin Core Schema offers terms to describe web and physical resources. IMS Global has a Learning Object Discovery & Exchange (LODE) specification. The Learning Resource Metadata Initiative has a specification that describes various properties of educational resources. ISO/IEC has a standard for "information technology- learning, education and training-metadata for learning resources" as a multi-part standard. The Open Archives Initiative Protocol of Metadata Harvesting (OAI-PMH) is a protocol for harvesting metadata from a number of archives to enable federated services across platforms. Advanced Distributed Learning has offered sharable content object reference model (SCORM). Others, such as Learning Object Metadata (by IEEE), are built for specific use with XML (Learning object metadata, Aug. 16, 2016). There are metadata standards for mobile learning objects. While there has been some discussion in the research literature of potential LO metadata convergence, that has not yet happened, and there are likely reasons why a single convergence will not likely occur (differing interests, differing adoptions of LO metadata models in different technology systems, and others). Whatever the metadata schema used for indexing learning objects, the applied metadata should be as accurate as possible, so that the LOs may be accurately labeled and the desired learning objects may be found. In some cases, LO metadata may be enriched with overlays of other information to ensure that they have the semantic interoperability necessary to function within federated systems (Stefaner, Vecchia, Condotta, Wolpers, Specht, Apelt, & Duval, 2007, p. 327).

To improve the quality of metadata of learning objects, some researchers suggest that there should be collaborations between the resource authors and metadata specialists (Currier, Barton, O'Beirne, & Ryan, March, 2004).

Evaluating the Quality of Learning Objects: Manually and Computationally

An offhand approach to evaluating learning object quality would be characterized by the idea of "I know it when I see it." Some LO quality features described evoke common-sense concerns, including "clearness, ease of use and adequacy of the educational content" as important quality features of educational resources (Karolčik, Čipková, Veselskỳ, Hrubišková, & Matulčiková, 2015, p. 1).

Governments have an interest in standardization for quality measures of digital educational materials from government (Fernández-Pampillón, 2013). Some vehicles for LO quality standardization include instruments and models. One summary of the Learning Object Review Instrument LORI 1.5 identifies the following dimensions of learning object quality: content quality, learning goal alignment, feedback and adaptation, motivation, presentation design, interaction usability, accessibility, reusability, and standards of compliance. To be more specific, elaboratory information is included as follows:

- **Content Quality**: Veracity, accuracy, balanced presentation of ideas, & appropriate level of detail
- **Learning Goal Alignment:** Alignment among learning goals, activities, assessments, & learner characteristics
- **Feedback and Adaptation:** Adaptive content or feedback driven by differential learner input/modeling
- **Motivation:** Ability to motivate and interest an identified population of learners
- **Presentation Design:** Design of visual and auditory information for enhanced learning and efficient mental processing
- **Interaction Usability:** Ease of navigation, predictability of the user interface, & quality of interface help features
- **Accessibility:** Design of controls and presentation formats to accommodate disabled and mobile learners

- **Reusability:** Ability to use in varying learning contexts and with learners from differing backgrounds
- **Standards Compliance:** Adherence to international standards and specifications (Leacock, Richards, & Nesbit, 2004, p. 334)

Researchers have advanced schemas for assessing learning object quality. One example is the Learning Quality Metadata schema, which is "an extension of the IEEE LOM standard". This schema is applied in an automated way to estimate "the quality of digital educational resources" (Pons, Hilera, Fernández, & Pagés, 2016, p. 45).

Formally, there has already been some work done in this area of DLO quality analysis. Early work has focused on particular aspects of DLOs, which are important to get right for quality to be achieved.

...in the context of digital libraries, Custard and Sumner (2005) claim that concerns about quality are mainly related to issues of: 1) accuracy of content, 2) appropriateness to intended audience, 3) effective design, and 4) completeness of metadata documentation. In the specific field of learning multimedia resources, the so far most recognized instrument for quantitatively measuring quality, the Learning Object Review Instrument (LORI) (Nesbit et al., 2003), approaches quality from nine different dimensions: 1) content quality; 2) learning goal alignment; 3) feedback and adaptation; 4) motivation; 5) presentation design; 6) interaction usability; 7) accessibility; 8) reusability; and 9) standards compliance. (Cechinel, Sánchez-Alonso, & García-Barriocanal, 2011, p. 1256)

Another instrument is the Learning Object Attribute Metric tool, which considers three main categories: (1) environment (media type), (2) learner role, and (3) activity—along with related pedagogic attributes of all three (Sinclair, Joy, Yau, & Hagan, 2013, p. 186). This model includes five criteria: interactivity ("constructive activity, control, level of interactivity"), design ("layout, personalization, quality of graphics, emphasis of key concepts"), engagement ("difficulty level, theme, aesthetics, feedback, multimedia), usability ("overall ease of use, clear instructions, navigation"), and content ("accuracy, quality"), with the subcategories in parentheses directly following the category (Sinclair, Joy, Yau, & Hagan, 2013, p. 186).

In the study of intrinsic (and latent) measures of learning objects rated as high (by human raters) vs. low, the number of images in an LO was found to be a potentially important feature indicating quality (Garcia-Barriocanal &

Sicilia, 2009, as cited in Cechinel, Sánchez-Alonso, & García-Barriocanal, 2011, p. 1256). Follow-on research tried to identify "intrinsic metrics" that tended to appear in learning objects assessed (by human raters) as good vs. those assessed as poor in order to identify indicators LO quality; the authors used linear discriminant analysis to study the strength of various metrics when classifying LOs into quality categories. One insight was that differences in what was seen as "good" vs. "poor" differed based on the category of discipline (Cechinel, Sánchez-Alonso, & García-Barriocanal, 2011, p. 1255); they explain, "The good and not-good groups were considered to have different profiles regarding a specific metric when both the distributions and medians presented significant difference at 90% confidence level for the thresholds evaluated. When such a situation is observed it means that the evaluated metric is associated (or correlated) to learning object quality" (Cechinel, Sánchez-Alonso, & García-Barriocanal, 2011, p. 1260). Quality measures of learning objects may be automated and included as part of LO rankings inside a repository. One approach melds Duval's "Quality in Context" and Borlund's "Relevance Dimensions" (Ochoa & Duval, Jan. – Mar. 2008, Relevance…, p. 37) to try to bring together searcher's queries with the most fitting learning object matches on several dimensions, including topical relevance, pertinence, and "situational relevance" (Ochoa & Duval, Jan. – Mar. 2008, Relevance…, p. 37). Or such information may be a factor in which LOs are returned from a search query. A parallel idea involves using informational metrics to evaluate learning object quality in an automated way, in the same way that various fields apply bibliometrics, scientometrics, and webometrics to understand impact (Ochoa, 2011, p. 1), with the idea that quality attracts users. LO usage statistics may encapsulate DLO adopters' hard work in vetting LOs and then adopting them, and in that sense, these statistics show a costly signal based on the "wisdom of crowds." One researcher argues about how useful LO use data may be:

The captured opinions and descriptions of how learning objects are used could become more valuable to other users than the standard metadata, which may be too general to be of help. Nonauthoritative metadata, or "annotation metadata," could work much the same way that Amazon.com book reviews do, that is, helping buyers of books get more information and more varied opinions than those typically found on jacket covers or in published book reviews (Recker & Wiley, 2000). It can also create a history of use and users, which could stimulate learning object developers to create more useful objects. (Parrish, 2004, p. 64)

Infometrics involve not a single summary value but a mix of values: "Informetrics is focused on measuring and understanding processes that create, publish, consume or adapt information. Moreover, it is common that after the process has been analyzed, useful metrics are developed to summarize characteristics of the process and then used to create tools that can have a practical application to improve the studied or a related process" (Ochoa, 2011, p. 1). A research team combined both top-down formal expert evaluations of learning object quality and bottom-up learner-based measures of LO quality (Kurilovas, Serikoviene, & Vuorikari, 2014, p. 526). The authors write:

The research results show that the complex application of different methods, such as the principles of the multiple criteria decision analysis for identification of quality criteria, technological quality criteria division principle, the fuzzy group decision making theory to obtain final evaluation measures, normalisation requirement for the weights of quality criteria, and scalarization method are (1) applicable in the real life situations when the educational institutions have to decide on purchase of LOs for their education needs, and (2) could significantly improve the quality of the expert evaluation of LOs by noticeably reducing the expert evaluation subjectivity level.

On the other hand, bottom-up approach to LOs "travel well" quality evaluation focused on the user-driven approach through social tagging and parameters of interaction for measuring context as star ratings is applicable to harness and operationalise the acquired contextualised information to help the reuse across linguistic and national context. Bottom-up approach outlines the central role of learners' individual and social behaviour while working with LOs in the repositories. (Kurilovas, Serikoviene, & Vuorikari, 2014, p. 533)

Suffice it to say that there are a variety of theories and models and practices, which inform learning object metadata.

ADOPTION OF SHARED DIGITAL LEARNING OBJECTS FOR ONLINE LEARNING

To move the research forward, this work involves three steps. The first defines the required and desirable features of digital learning objects. The second section defines what instructional designers and development teams build to in DLOs. The third analyzes the gaps between what DLO adopters want and what DLO creators create and suggests some ways to possibly narrow the gap.

Part 1: Required and Desirable Features From Digital Learning Objects

The first step of this research involved defining main features of DLOs that are important for DLO adopters in online teaching and learning. Ten high-level features were arrived at, with a number of sub-features under each. The ten top-level features include: (1) pedagogical value, (2) learning engagement, (3) presentational (and interactional) features, (4) legal adherence, (5) technological features, (6) instructor (adopter) control, (7) applicability to the respective learning contexts (local conditions), (8) local costs to deploy, (9) labeling and documentation; contributor and informational source crediting, and (10) global transferability and adoptability. The ten features enables some level of parsimony to this approach although the sub-features add a lot of complexity.

The initial draft of Table 1 was done before the literature review and before other work on this project—in order to capture the author's main experiences with what faculty look for to enhance their online courses. This table is conceptualized as a rubric or checklist, although it may be transformed into either, but it is conceptualized as a data object to help those who work with DLOs—as adopters as well as creators. This can be a conversation starter about what features are desirable in a DLO or DLO sequence. While the table's main features are in order of general priorities for those inheriting DLOs, the ordering can clearly be changed. Also, this is conceptualized as a modularized instrument, from which segments may be subtracted and to which segments may be added. There are various other ways to use this, such as by defining what features are "required" vs. which ones are only "desired," the differences between "must have" and "would like." It is in the revision of this instrument for local purposes that its full strengths may be identified and expressed.

Table 1 has to be fairly general because there are too many specifics with particular learning domains and topics and related technologies. The table itself is complex and may be better unpacked with some elaborating text. The table has ten main high-level features. These include: (1) pedagogical value, (2) learner engagement, (3) presentational (and interactional) features, (4) legal adherence, (5) technological features, (6) instructor (adopter) control, (7)

Table 1. Ten features of digital learning objects that may affect adoption and usage

Ten Main Features of Digital Learning Objects (DLOs) and Related Sub-Feature	Specific Details	
1. Pedagogical Value		
Main Stakeholders (in descending order): Instructors, Learners, Institutions of Higher Education, LO Repositories		
1a Informational Accuracy	Accurate Information	Inaccurate Information
	• Clear presentation • Informational sufficiency • Various forms: textual, visual, auditory, video, and multimedia • Control for negative learning	• Unclear presentation • Lack of informational sufficiency • Various forms: textual, visual, auditory, video, and multimedia • Poor or no controls for negative learning
	Credible Sourcing / Clear Provenance	Non-credible Sourcing / Unclear Provenance
	• Clear source citations • Verifiable information sources • Reputable information sources	• Unclear or missing source citations • Non-verifiable information sources • Disreputable information sources
	Trustworthy Subject Matter Experts (SMEs)	Untrustworthy Subject Matter Experts (SMEs)
	• Identified SMEs • Respectable standing in the field • Trusted reputations • Trusted work methods (by professional peers) • Clear data framing	• Unidentified SMEs • Poor standing in the field • Untrustworthy reputations • Untrusted work methods (by professional peers) • Unclear data framin
1b Informational Value	Original Information	Derivative Information
	• Rare information or data access • Important tactical (method) information • Rare SME expertise	• Common information or data access • Unimportant tactical (method) information • Common SME expertise
1c Curricular Relevance	Relevant to the Learning Sequence	Irrelevant to the Learning Sequence
	• Important learning objectives	• Unimportant learning objectives
1d Contemporaneous and Up-to-Date Contents	Contemporaneous and Up-to-Date Contents	Non-Contemporaneous and Not Up-to-Date Contents
	• Inclusive of up-to-date learning in the field • Relatively "future-proofed" in terms of both information and time-based indicators	• Non-inclusive of up-to-date learning in the field (uses old paradigms, uses old technologies, uses debunked methods) • Is not "future-proofed" in terms of information and time-based indicators (is a clear time when the digital learning object will be erroneous, will appear dated, and will be irrelevant) ... but may be useful as a historical artifact
1e Unit Size	"Right"-Sized	"Wrong"-Sized
	• Logical unit size (to enable interchangeability across fields) • Proper length of the lesson • Ability to be integrated into a learning sequence with other DLOs for learning (without excessive gaps or excessive overlaps) • Editable if not properly sized	• Improper unit size • Improper length of the lesson • Inability to be integrated in a learning sequence • Not editable for proper sizing

continued on following page

Table 1. Continued

1f Learning Assessment	Valid Learning Assessment	Invalid Learning Assessment, Lack of Learning Assessment
	• Aligned with learning objectives • Aligned with learning contents • Ease of integration with the online learning environment • Clear grade reportage • Ability to change point values • Editable • Removable • Sufficiently easy to build an assessment if an assessment is not included or if the one included but is not appropriate? (Or, the DLO and DLO sequence(s) are so well designed that assessments are easy for the instructor or instructional designer to create.)	• Unaligned with declared learning objectives (if available) • Non-aligned with learning contents • Absent altogether • Poor integration with the online learning environment • No grade reportage; inaccurate grade reportage • Inability to change point values • Uneditable • Not removable • Difficult to build an assessment if one is not included or if the one included is not appropriate?
2. Learner Engagement		
Main Stakeholders: Instructors, Learners, Institutions of Higher Education, LO Repositories		
2a Learning Design	Effective Learning Design	Ineffective Learning Design
	• Informed by appropriate learning theory • Includes basic elements of an effective learning design: measurable learning objectives, proper and accurate contents, effective feedback, and assessment • Is sufficiently comprehensive in coverage • Includes proper learner supports • Includes clear learning sequence(s)	• Not informed by appropriate learning theory • Fails to include basic elements of effective learning design • Is not sufficiently comprehensive in coverage • Does not include proper learner supports • Does not include clear learning sequence(s)
2b Learning Value (to Learners)	Learner Aligned	Learner Non-Aligned
	• Alignment with learner level of knowledge and skill • High learner comfort level with the DLO(s) • Respect for learner time (no time-wasting redundancies which are without learning value)	• Non-alignment with learner level of knowledge and skill • Poor learner comfort level with the DLO(s) • Lack of respect for learner time (time-wasting redundancies, without learning value)
	Learning Enablements	Learning Constraints
	• Contains relevant lessons to the learner (such as target knowledge and / or skills) • Relates to learner needs	• Does not contain relevant lessons to the learner (such as target knowledge and / or skills) • Does not relate to learner needs
2c Supports for Learners	Learner Supports	Absence of Learner Supports or Poor Learner Supports
	• Cognitive scaffolding for those with weaker skills • Cognitive scaffolding for those with stronger skills • Access to context-sensitive learner supports (word definitions, navigation annotations, and other features) • Lead-up and lead-away resources to the DLO	• No support for those with weaker skills • No support for those with stronger skills • No access to context-sensitive learner supports (word definitions, navigation annotations, and other features) • Absence of lead-up and lead-away resources to the DL
2d Alignment to Learner Readiness	Aligned to Learner Readiness	Misaligned to Learner Readiness
	• Little to no need for additional preparation for learners to use the digital learning object(s) effectively	• High need for additional preparation for learners to use the digital learning object(s) • Poor overall fit for learners to use the digital learning objects

continued on following page

Table 1. Continued

2e Learner Immersion	Learner Immersion	Learner Non-Immersion
	• Virtual • 3D • Simulation • Roleplay • Games • Case studies • Project-based learning • High engagement • Longer time investment • Social and / or cohort learning	• Light or non-immersive learning
2f Succinctness	Succinct Learning Object	Non-Succinct Learning Object
	• Strategic repetition or absence of repetition • Respectful of learner time	• Unnecessary repetition • Lack of respect for learner time
3. Presentational (and Interactional) Features		
Main Stakeholders: Learners, Instructors, Institutions of Higher Education, LO Repositories		
3a Production Quality	High Production Quality	Low Production Quality
	• High level of human talent and professionalism • Clear audio, imagery, and video • Legible text • Clear writing • Authentic informational contents • Apparent high costs and investments to create • High-level revision and editing; level of care (little to no level of errors) (variable depending on forms and conventions)	• Low level of human talent and professionalism • Unclear audio, imagery, and video • Illegible text • Unclear writing • Inauthentic informational contents • Apparent low costs and investments to create • Low-level of revision and editing; low level of care (error-prone) (variable depending on forms and conventions)
3b Presentation Novelty	Unique or Memorable Presentation	Non-Unique / Non-Memorable Presentation
	• Innovative • Memorable	• Derivative, unoriginal • Non-memorable
3c Sequencing	Sequential	Non-Sequential
	• Article or Paper • Slideshow (classic) • Video	• Branching slideshow • Branching video (or video with outlinks)
3d Learner Interactivity	Interactive	Non-Interactive
	• Models • Simulations • Games • Branching websites • Branching slideshows • Branching videos	• Static models • Static imagery • Static articles and papers • Static slideshows
4. Legal Adherence		
Main Stakeholders: Institutions of Higher Education, Instructors, LO Repositories		
4a Intellectual Property Adherence	Respectful of IP	Not Respectful of IP
	• Intellectual property (copyright, trademark, patent, export restrictions, etc.) protections • Proper documentation	• Improper intellectual property • Improper documentation
4b Privacy Protections	Respectful of Privacy Protections	Not Respectful of Privacy Protections
	• Privacy protections (for media captures)	• Improper privacy protections processes and / or documentatio

continued on following page

Table 1. Continued

4c Accessibility Accommodations	Proper Accessibility Accommodations	Improper Accessibility Accommodations
	• Closed captioning or timed text and / or transcripting for audio and video • Alt texting for imagery • Accessible uses of color • Machine readable data tables • User controls for all "players" (games, simulations, audio, video, and so on) • Plain language (or even complexity but with eloquence and clarity) • Hierarchical text	• Missing accessibility features • Poor quality of accessibility features • Ornate or difficult-to-understand language, improper use of terminology • Non-hierarchical, non-tagged text
5. Technological Features		
Main Stakeholders: Instructors, Learners, Institutions of Higher Education, LO Repositories		
5a Technology Integration with Learning Environments	Technically Integrate-able	Technically Non-integrate-able
	• Easy integration with the technology environment(s) and devices • Easy integration with the F2F (face-to-face) environment(s) • Easy integration with the blended (online and F2F) environment(s)	• Difficult (or impossible) integration with the technology environment(s) and devices • Difficult (or impossible) integration with the F2F environment(s) • Difficult (or impossible) integration with the blended (online and F2F) environment(s)
5b Playability / Functionality	Playable and Functional	Non-Playable and Non-Functional
	• Intuitive user interface o Input devices o Touchscreen • Works as advertised	• Difficult user interface • Fails to work as advertised
5c Portability	Portable	Not Portable
	• Offline version • Mobile version	• No offline version • Poor offline version • No mobile version • Poor mobile version
6. Instructor (Adopter) Control		
Main Stakeholders: Instructors		
6a Ability to Edit and Update	Ability to Update	Inability to Update
	• Feedback channel to DLO creators • Direct technological access to the underlying source code (or the DLO in an editable format)	• No (or poor) feedback channel to DLO creators • No direct technological access to the underlying source code (or the DLO in a non-editable format)
6b Ease of Opt-out (Delinkage / Removal)	High Ease of Delinkage and Removal / Ease of Decoupling	Difficulty of Delinkage and Removal / Difficulty of Decoupling
	• Low cost of removal of the Digital Learning Object • No residual impacts of the former DLO or DLO sequence	• High cost of removal of the DLO • Residual impacts of the former DLO or DLO sequence
7. Applicability to the Respective Learning Contexts (Local Conditions)		
Main Stakeholders: Instructors, Learners, Institutions of Higher Education, LO Repositories		
7a Political Acceptability	Political Acceptance	Political Non-Acceptance
	• Messaging • Costs • Reputation	• Messaging • Costs • Reputation

continued on following page

Table 1. Continued

7b Alignment with Instructor Teaching Approach	Instructor Teaching Approach Alignment	Instructor Teaching Approach Non-Alignment
	• Consistent with the instructor's professional knowledge • Consistent with the instructor's pedagogical approaches	• Inconsistent with the instructor's professional knowledge • Inconsistent with the instructor's pedagogical approaches
7c Reputation of the DLO Maker(s)	Solid Reputation	Questionable Reputation
	• Quality reputation • High-trust • High transparency • Stability • Security	• Lack of a quality reputation • Low-trust • Low transparency, or lack of transparency • Instability, "fly-by-night" quality • Insecure DLO, known security problems (such as malware riding with the DLO or the hosted website)
7d Institutional Costs	High Institutional Costs	Low Institutional Costs
	• High institutional costs to deploy	• Low or negligible institutional costs to deploy
8. Local Costs to Deploy		
Main Stakeholders: Institutions of Higher Education, Instructors, Learners, LO Repositories		
8a Technological Requirements	Technological Expense	Low or No Technological Expense
	• Technological systems • Software • Expertise • Hosting costs	• No extra identifiable costs
8b Direct Costs and Indirect Costs	Direct and Indirect Cost(s)	Absence of Direct and Indirect Costs / Free
	• Outright purchase or subscription payments to a vendor (or other model of payment) • Additional cost-incurring dependencies required to deploy the DLOs effectively	• Open-source • Open-access • No additional costs
8c Costs over Time (Lifetime Costs)	Lifetime Cost(s)	No Anticipated Lifetime Costs
	• Updates • Other anticipated costs in the future	• Provided updates
8d Unwanted Advertising and Branding	Unwanted Branding	No Unwanted Branding, Neutral Design
	• Presence of advertising logos and watermarks (intrusive and non-intrusive) • Highly branded look-and-feel • Marked writing style • Marked visual style	• No advertising or branding • A more neutral look-and-feel • Neutral and objective writing style • Neutral visual style
8e Unwanted Dependencies: Proprietary Technologies, Remote Hosting	Proprietary Technologies, Remote Object Hosting	No Proprietary Technologies, Local Hosting
	• Requirement to use proprietary and closed-source technologies • Requirement to access DLOs through a remote hosted site (without the ability to download and locally host)	• No use of proprietary and closed-source technologies • No requirement to access DLOs through a remote hosted site (ability to use the DLO through local hosting)
8f Risks to Reputation	Potential Reputational Damage	Potential Reputational Enhancement or No Effect
	• Risks of reputational harm from poor DLO quality	• Potential for reputational enhancement from high DLO quality • No effect

continued on following page

Table 1. Continued

9. Labeling and Documentation; Contributor and Informational Source Crediting		
Main Stakeholders: Institutions of Higher Education, Instructors, Learners, LO Repositories		
9a Pedagogical Metadata	Metadata-ed for Pedagogical Applications	Non-Metadataed for Pedagogical Applications
	• Name of the DLO • Subject area • Resource type • Target learners • Level of learning • Main language(s) • Learning objectives • Main learning contents • Pedagogical approach(es) • Rights management data • Date of creation • Author information • DLO citation methods, • And others • Uses a defined structured metadata schema or system	• Any missing documentation (silence)
9b Contributor and Informational Source Crediting	Crediting	Non-crediting
	• All authors and contributors cited (by role) • All informational sources are credited	• No authors and contributors cited • No informational sources are credited
10. Global Transferability and Adoptability		
Main Stakeholders: Learners, Instructors, Institutions of Higher Education, LO Repositories		
10a Culturally Aligned (or Culturally Neutral)	Culturally Aligned or Culturally Neutral	Culturally Non-Aligned or Culturally Non-Neutral
	• Messaging (textual, visual, and others) • Representation of people • Respectful tone • Others	• Messaging (textual, visual, and others) • Representation of people • Disrespectful tone • Others
10b Multilingual Versioning Availability	Multilingual Versioning Available	Monolingual Versioning Available
	• Built-in language options • Available with third-party multi-language tools	• Multilingual language options not built in • Translations unavailable with third-party multi-language tools

applicability to the respective learning contexts (local conditions), (8) local costs to deploy, (9) labeling and documentation; contributor and informational source crediting, and (10) global transferability and adoptability.

Below each shaded label is a listing of the "main stakeholders" for the particular DLO feature. The stakeholders include four main groups: instructors, learners, institutions of higher education, and LO repositories. These are conceptualized as broad groups, with instructors including DLO adopters, learners of all stripes, institutions of higher education including administrators, and LO repositories including referatories, digital libraries, content management systems, learning management systems, and so on. Each of the respective 10 features have natural stakeholder groups who are invested in that feature. For example, "1. Pedagogical Value" is generally of primary importance to instructors first, whose roles require them to identify methods and materials that have teaching and learning value for their students. Next are the learners, who have a primary interest in learning. Then, institutions of higher education have an interest because of their primary interest in learner success and achievement. Finally repositories that host DLOs also have an interest because their reputations depend on the quality of the LOs they host and the numbers of views and downloads. "6. Instructor (Adopter) Control" is mostly an area of interest for Instructors. (Earlier, adopter control maybe referred more to the ability to chunk parts of a learning object for usage; in the present day, with so much sophistication in coding, and the importance of open-source, many inheritors of DLOs want access to the code, which gives them full control over the object's behaviors.)

It would help to break down each of the ten main feature areas and supporting sub-areas in Table 1.

Pedagogical Value

"Pedagogical Value" is a broad feature that includes, in descending order, informational accuracy, informational value, curricular relevance, updatedness, unit size, and assessment. The idea of pedagogical value is that a learning object has fundamental requirements in order to be valuable to learners. One of the largest "tells" of an amateur is the sharing of inaccurate information. Said another way, a self-respecting professional has to get the information right in the digital learning object. The information not only has to be correct but also relevant and non-trivial. In a learning sequence, the information has to have value. The information should reflect the latest research in the field, in part because new data are seen to challenge older data. If the learning object is not updated, it is easier to sometimes just start over (Parrish, 2004). For the sake of accuracy, whenever a learning object is updated, the correlating metadata should also be updated (Ochoa & Duval, 2009, p. 70). The size of the LO should be appropriate to the learning context or editable up or down to fit the length-of-learning needs. A key definition of an LO is that it "allows flexibility, independence and reuse of content in order to deliver a high degree of control to instructors and students" (Wiley, 2002, as cited in Zapata, Menéndez, Prieto, & Romero, 2013, p. 1). [Wiley (2000a) suggested that there is an "inverse relationship between the size of a learning object and its re-usability" (as cited in Christiansen & Anderson, March 2004, p.

3). In other words, the smaller a DLO, the more usable it may be in a variety of contexts. Since the initial theorizing, there have been studies that have supported this concept and others that have contradicted this assertion about DLO size and reusability. Ochoa (2001) found a mixed pattern of learning object re-use with the larger granularity ones re-used more (26.05%) than the medium (21.5%) and small granularity ones (18.05%) (p. 5). In this work, small granularity objects included components in slides and images; medium granularity ones included modules in courses and software in libraries; and large granularity ones included courses in curricula and Web APIs. There were some limits here in terms of the selection of repositories to use and the definitions of granularity; also the respective object counts varied greatly (with over a million small granularity objects and only a little over a thousand large granularity objects).

It may be argued that a small unit size of an object—such as a photo—may be too unprocessed and raw (not built out for learning) for learning value. Some teachers who were tasked as part of a research study to explore online learning objects found a "patchwork result" based on the granularity of learning objects (Christiansen & Anderson, March 2004, p. 17). If learning objects seem disjointed, more cognitive load may be required to process the information and learning. The authors elaborate:

Course developers must balance the value of a variety of learning resources, with different approaches to a subject and viewpoint being offered for consideration, against the need to provide coherence in the course materials. Variety may be beneficial to the learning process, but it does require students to alter their learning process as they approach the various materials. Weller, Pegler & Mason (Ibid.) state "a course that continually seems to shift dramatically in pedagogy, level or style would carry an overhead for students as they make the cognitive shift between objects and styles." (Christiansen & Anderson, 2004, p. 18)

A more practical way of conceptualizing granularity and adoptability may be as follows: "Objects that have a granularity immediately lower than the object being built are easier to reuse than objects with a much lower or higher granularity" (Ochoa & Duval, 2008, Measuring…, p. 3).

Also, for learning objects that are highly granular and atomistic / atomic, there may be a lot of competition in terms of other available contents—so such objects do not stand out if they are generic. If the images are unique—such as those of outer space by the National Aeronautics and space Administration

(NASA) or of emerging pathogens by the Centers for Disease Control and Prevention (CDC)—then they have inherent value.]

In the absence of fundamental features, the LO cannot be said to have pedagogical value. For example, if the information is inaccurate or misleading, an LO cannot be used (except as a negative example). If the information in an LO is commonplace, and there are a number of sources for the same data, the LO becomes less valuable. If the LO is not contemporaneously relevant and *au courant,* it will likely date out soon into irrelevance, it may not be worth the cost of integration in a learning context; to this end, LOs have to be future-proofed against irrelevancy. If the learning objectives are non-relevant in a learning sequence, that may also sideline an LO. While these sub-feature elements are important, it is helpful to note that even something as "small" as a typo may be enough to render a LO unusable.

Of the listed sub-features, only the absence of a pre-built LO assessment is not *de rigueur.* After all, anyone who inherits an LO can write his / her own assessment if the object is sufficiently well built.

Learner Engagement

In this context, learners are non-specialist users of digital learning objects. The second feature, "Learner Engagement," is comprised of the following sub-features: learning design, learning value (to learners), supports for learners, alignment to learner readiness, learner immersion, and succinctness. The learning design refers to how the DLO is structured and also to what learning theories may underlie the design. The learning value points to the potential benefits that learners may achieve with the use of the LO. Supports for learners are various types of help (both context-sensitive and those not) that learners may access during the use of the learning object. The "alignment to learner readiness" points to the fit between the object and the target learners—in terms of what the learners are assumed to know and what they are capable of learning (whether the LO is fitted to the particular Zone of Proximal Development, in Vygotsky's conceptualization). Another sub-feature is learner immersion, which is about the proper level of learner engagement with the topic. (A fact-based slideshow might be conceptualized as less immersive for learners than a case study or a simulation or a 3d virtual immersive environment for learning. The tools for building learning objects have gone well beyond authoring tools to create stand-alone learning objects. There are online systems that enable building born-digital contents for Web delivery. There are generators that enable auto-creation of learning objects. Virtual immersive worlds enable the creation of dynamic scenarios with interactive artificial intelligence agents.)

Finally, succinctness refers to the idea that an LO should be respectful of learner time, without excessive or unnecessary repetition of learning sequences and contents. At heart, this feature "Learner Engagement" involves how receptive learners are to engaging with the learning object as well as designed features that support the learners' use of the LO. LOs need to be attention-getting, memorable, clear, and well fitted to learner needs.

Presentational (and Interactional) Features

"Presentational (and Interactional) Features" (3) refers to the DLO's production quality, its novelty or originality, its sequencing features, and the design of learner interactivity. This feature would apply across platforms, operating systems, devices, small screens and larger screens, and various input devices (and modes of input and output).

Legal Adherence

"Legal Adherence" (4) addresses to the adherence to intellectual property, the privacy protections for the people represented in the DLO, and accessibility accommodations (closed captioning, alt-texting for imagery, readable data tables, and so on). Legal adherence is important because if these are not properly addressed, they create liabilities for all involved. This is especially so for a global environment where there are differences in intellectual property, privacy, accessibility, and other laws. Others have noted the importance of having accessible learning objects (de Macedo & Ulbricht, 2012) for the broadest ranges of possible users.

Technological Features

Fifth are "Technological Features." These include aspects of technology integration with learning environments (whether F2F, blended, or online; whether on mobile or other computational devices, and so on). The playability / functionality of the DLO is important, particularly with how it may be interacted with through various input devices (particularly those with small screens) and through touch-screen interfaces. The DLO also needs to be portable across ecosystems are also technological features of concern. Technology systems are in constant dynamic churn, and being more specific here would not be particularly helpful. The goal is to aim for ubiquity, so that an object plays on everything with ease.

Instructor (Adopter) Control

"Instructor (Adopter) Control" (6) is an extension of design and technology. This addresses how easy it is for inheritors of the DLO to edit and update the contents and capabilities. (Under Creative Commons licensure, whether or not users of others contents may create derivative works is a major factor in LO adopter control.) For many creators of contents, there is a sense of risk in allowing others to edit and update the original contents, particularly if that original creator's name and reputation are linked to the object. There is no guarantee that others will understand the original intensions or standards. Those who create learning objects may only want trusted others to edit and revise—if even them. A revision may create legal liabilities, which may somehow entangle the original creator (with the scattershot and broadly inclusive nature of many lawsuits).

Yet, if a person chooses to maintain control over whatever he or she has created, there is also an implied obligation to update the LO as more information becomes available. If not, that DLO will age out gracelessly or merely be a representation of that information during a particular slice-in-time. Users then bear the costs of swapping out that inherited learning object. In one framework, learning objects should be updated whenever there are changes in four areas: legal guidelines and relevant policies; the domain field; course curricular strategies / teaching and learning methodologies; and relevant technologies (Hai-Jew, Dec. 15, 2010).

This also includes the ease of opt-out, so if an adopter decides to switch out from using a DLO, how easy is it to de-couple from that object? Further, are there difficulties in disconnecting from tightly-coupled digital contents? Or even worse, are there potential harms in the decoupling? The concept is that commitment to a DLO is fragile and even at best is temporary and temporal. A decision for use may be made in a few seconds of consideration, but that may switch again with frustration or some light offense (like a misspelling or poor turn-of-phrase or poorly selected image or inconsistent font sizes).

Applicability to the Respective Learning Contexts (Local Conditions)

The next feature of DLOs is "Applicability to the Respective Learning Contexts (Local Conditions)" (7) This feature includes the following: political acceptability, alignment with instructor teaching approach, reputation of the DLO maker(s), and institutional costs. Each of these sub-features affects the political viability of accepting the target DLO(s) for the particular institutional context.

Local Costs to Deploy

"Local Costs to Deploy" (8) focuses on a variety of related costs (and risks) linked to the usage of inherited learning objects. This section involves the following elements: technological requirements, direct costs and indirect costs, and costs over time (lifetime costs). First, there are traditional concepts of costs. "Free" can be quite illusory. For example, there are "opportunity costs" in using others' learning objects because the objects will not be built locally, and the faculty and staff will not acquire the knowledge and skills from that work. While they are not going to incur the costs of time, content development, LO development, LO testing and revision, and other work, they lose opportunities for professional development and professional reputation building. The respective institutions of higher education fail to gain in-house capabilities of building DLOs.

There are also costs to using digital learning objects that have unwanted advertising and branding information. There are no-strings preferences when accepting learning objects; in the same way, users do not want to have to provide local information about the usage of the LO, and there is no desire to have to sign in to download an LO, and there is no acceptance of unwanted email reminders. Designers of learning object to share would benefit from keeping each as unmarked and unbranded as possible. Also, in terms of "Unwanted Dependencies: Proprietary Technologies, Remote Hosting," if there are potential access challenges, such as based on proprietary technologies used and the risks of having remote hosted digital learning objects (because such hosting can end at any time), those can be considered costs as well. Finally, another potential cost may be a risk to reputation if the DLO maker does not have a reputation of quality and integrity. To understand the sense of "costs" in this paragraph, it helps to understand the challenges with constraints.

Labeling and Documentation: Contributor and Informational Source Crediting

The ninth feature, "Labeling and Documentation; Contributor and Informational Source Crediting" relates to the availability of pedagogical metadata, and named contributors and sources. The contributor information is important since authorship may represent branding and related quality. As part of the online culture, many contributors to learning object repositories and social media platforms use handles, not real names. In some cases, it is possible to track a handle back to a real-world individual, an actual name, and a verified email, but not always. If an author cannot actually be identified, then the work is essentially an anonymized one and potentially risky—if the work is not backstopped by a legally liable identifiable person. Tracking authors adds more complexity and effort to the work of finding and vetting suitable digital learning objects. These data may help potential DLO adopters understand what the LOs are and how the informational contents of the DLO were sourced.

Global Transferability and Adoptability

Finally, "Global Transferability and Adoptability" (10) refers to how culturally aligned (or culturally neutral) a DLO is and also whether there is an ability to translate the contents into a different language. In other words, this is conceptualized as a geographical/cultural and a linguistic issue. To be successful, DLOs need to either be globally palatable because (1) the pedagogical approach and designs are culturally neutral or because (2) the geographically-specific cultural approach is understood and acceptable. One source of examples of such LOs may be globally-popular massive open online courses (MOOCs) because the learning contents are accepted and non-offensive to the learners from regions of the world.

At first look, it may seem that the ten features are a hodge-podge. These are the most essential requirements for learning object adoption—in the author's conceptualization. For example, a pedagogical approach is not generally mixed with content, but for this author, pedagogical value cannot be separated from the DLO content and information. Also, the features have some overlap between them. For example, the LO adopter's level of control over the contents are based in part on the technological features (Features 5 and 6 overlap to a degree). Depending on the decision-maker(s), there may be varying degrees of subjectivity in the evaluation of each of these ten features and the supporting sub-features. Depending on the role (instructor, learner, institutional administration, and LO repository owners) of the decision-maker, the individuals and groups will value particular features more than others. In many cases, there may be thresholds of sufficiency that will ultimately decide whether a DLO is acceptable or not for a defined learning context. (A systematic human-driven process may be automated someday.)

Of course, there is always room for subjective human decision-making based on something ineffable—such as an appreciation for some aspect of the LO that captures the imagination, such as an attractive design, a high number of mentions on social media, or an innovative design. There may be a preference for learning objects that conform to expectations and certain conventions of LO form; of course, the sense of an expectation is formed from prior experiences, which will vary. Serendipity and time-based factors may play a role as well. There may be professional considerations such as who made the DLO and resulting political implications in selecting that. Instructors may be seeking particular LO types—such as those that may be used in small groups, or those that are built in particular theories (such as competency-based learning), or those which use particular technologies. Adopted LOs need to interact well with a potential new LO and to cohere well. After all, there are numerous different types of learning contexts and innumerable learning contexts.

There are any number of factors beyond DLO quality that may inform the decision. When prospecting for DLOs, some may be looking for how an LO fits with the existing course-of-study. In one study, teachers were looking for learning objects that were sufficiently coherent to be packaged together (Christiansen & Anderson, March 2004, p. 14). There may be DLO adopter "pet peeves," which are automatic deal breakers even for LOs that are high-quality otherwise. In situations where there are systematic approaches by individuals and groups, though, this approach may have some value.

Other Options to DLO Adoption / Inheritance

If an inherited DLO is rejected, there are other options.

One involves developing an LO locally. The cost of developing LOs locally is non-minimal. Acquiring relevant information entails a high cost. There's research in subscription databases for the latest peer-reviewed published research by professionals whose hours are not inexpensive. Developing digital contents is expensive, too, with high-end equipment and skills required.

Software programs—for editing and authoring—can easily top in the thousands of dollars. If guest speakers are brought on to co-create learning object contents, there may be costs for that talent as well. The building of DLOs also involves data storage into the future because raw videos, raw audio, and other files, tend to be least "lossy" in their raw forms. By the time a digital file is revised and edited and compressed, there is often data loss. To enable future revisions of learning objects, the original raw files are usually kept as a matter-of-course, along with the legal sign-offs, official records, and other development-based contents. LOs have to be created under an umbrella of legal regulations; if not, they may become a legal liability to its creators and maybe even to its users. LOs themselves are generally only used for teaching and learning, and depending on the numbers of students taking the course, it may take many years to recoup the cost of investment, if recouping is even possible. LOs are creative contents, and as such, they are an extension of the various contributors' professional selves.

Another option to not using others' DLOs or creating one's own is to do without any altogether. In this latter case, instructors would go with a textbook or some other resource to address a learning objective. In higher education, there is much more of a tendency to go with third-party commercial publisher-created contents because publishing companies have professional editors to vet contents, and they bear the legal liabilities for the contents, and the instructors do not. For many digital learning contents created under the auspices of publishing, the bylines are either by the authors of the related academic textbooks or are written without bylines (by ghostwriters). Such contents are often branded with a corporate logo and the related reputation.

Finally, it may help to have a high-level outline overview of Table 1. The features are listed in descending order of importance in terms of consideration for usage. A failure to meet the thresholds for acceptance of any of the prior features may mean that the decision goes to no (conceptualized as a binary yes / no). One way to think about this sequence is as follows. Does this learning object have pedagogical value for my particular teaching and learning need? If so, is it sufficiently engaging for learners? Are the presentational and interactional features sufficiently attention-getting and engaging over time? Is the DLO street legal? Technologically, does the DLO work within the technological systems? If necessary, does the instructor have the capability to revise the DLO? Does the DLO fit with the local learning contexts? Are the anticipated costs manageable in the near-term, mid-term, and the future? Are the metadata for the DLO sufficiently informative? Finally, are there features that enable easy transferability and adoptability of the DLO in a global and multilingual context (for a variety of learners)? An outline of the top-level features of Table 1 and the sub-features may be viewed in Appendix A. These features are practical ones but of varying value depending on the potential DLO adopter. Also, there may be other features not identified in Table 1 that may change up considerations.

Part 2: What Instructional Designers Focus on in Designing and Developing LOs

In the prior section, ten features were defined for what instructors usually require when they adopt digital learning objects. In terms of these ten features, what do the technical designers of LOs actually focus on? Is there a gap? Figure 1, "Ten Features of Digital Learning Objects that May Affect Adoption and Usage," is a spider chart that shows the author's estimates of the weighted areas of focus for instructional designers in the design and development of DLOs in a university environment. The local conditions at various instructional design shops may be somewhat off of what is going on in other locations and in a global context. Different local designs will have strengths and weaknesses.

Figure 1. An instructional designer's focus in the design and development of digital learning objects

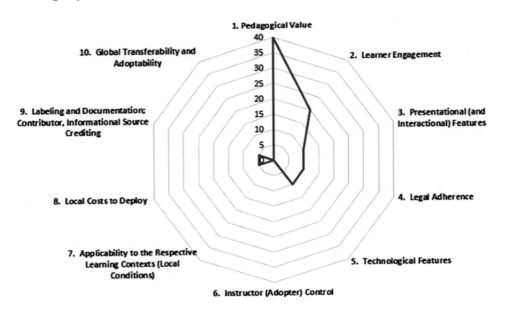

This information comes from decades of work in higher education in over a half-dozen institutions of higher education, both in the U.S. and abroad.

This shows that some of the 10 factors are given a large amount of attention and several are not given any. The three features that rank 0 are: instructor (adopter) control, applicability to the respective learning contexts (local conditions), and global transferability and adoptability. In an academic environment, instructors generally do not code or author digital contents, so while raw files are passed to clients, most are not re-edited by the instructors. Also, the applicability to others' local conditions are not of interest to the instructional designer because in this case, the ID is building to a particular context. Third, the global transferability and adoptability is generally not the issue, first, because of a cultural egocentrism (some would say "cultural arrogance") based on people's context-of-origin. Also, the multilingual aspect of global transferability and adoptability is not an area of focus because most higher education is conducted in English. While digital learning objects may— as a byproduct—by translated in other languages through Google Translate, there is not often direct design to multiple-language use. One insight here is that digital learning objects are often designed for particular local or targeted "use cases" and not considered for general public release.

The current "state of the art" in the field is somewhat elusive. While there are still high ambitions for the potential of digital learning objects and a culture in which open-source and open-access both have traction, there are financial pressures on institutions of higher education and other organizations that might support the building of open digital learning objects. In workplace contexts, digital learning objects are created as part of people's mainline work, but it is difficult to find endeavors for creating DLOs without funding. When university faculty have any spare time, attention often seems to go towards research and publishing before digital learning object creation because tenure and professional rewards go to peer-reviewed publication (to fulfill the knowledge production role of university faculty) well before any recognition for LOs. Being able to broadcast a byline is generally not monetizable and does not include a lot of reward.

A light "environmental scan" of the LO environment was taken as part of this research work. In this perusal, there were high-quality and trusted sites as well. They include government sites: data.gov, National Aeronautics and Space Administration [NASA TV, NASA for Students, and NASA for Educators)], United States Geological Survey (USGS), Centers for Disease

Control and Prevention (CDC), United States Department of Agriculture (USDA), and others. SlideShare, recently acquired by Microsoft along with LinkedIn, works as a strong escrow site for quality digital learning objects. There are educational channels on social media platforms that offer learning value: Google's YouTube, TED Talks, Vimeo, BigThink, and others. Some educational non-profits also offer high value learning objects and learning experiences: Khan Academy, the National Science Digital Library (ISKME), Code.org, W3C, and others. On the virtual immersive world, Second Life, there are some designed spaces with learning value. Also, Wolfram Mathematica offers some strong Wolfram Demonstrations Projects. NetLogo offers a creative library of agent-based modeling learning objects. Mainline massive open online courses (MOOCs)-providers offer strong learning objects and experiences. These include Coursera, edX, Udacity, and others. The Massachusetts Institute of Technology has the MIT Open Courseware site that enables access to quality learning materials as well. This is not a comprehensive list. The learning objects included everything from single photos to full virtual immersive simulations and experiences.

If there is a pattern here, about quality, it is that the organization has to have clear quality standards and then has to back up those standards by enforcing quality. In this environment scan, there were many lesser learning objects— either hosted on individual sites. While there are more contents available then when this author conducted earlier environmental scans (for various instructional design projects), the quality varied, and some of the contents were quite dated. Some LO referatories pointed to objects that pointed to web pages with "404/Page Not Found" messaging. This may suggest also that local developers of learning objects would benefit by working in a more competitive and global environment, so that they are challenged to create more competitive contents. Also, there is a correlation between reputable organizations, professionals, and funding, to enable the creation of effective digital learning objects. If the "power law" and "long tail" holds in terms of learning object usage, it is because DLO users flock to quality, and objects with lesser quality will simply exist for niche uses, if any.

Another insight from this review is that many of these "learning objects" are not particularly metadata-ed in any of the extant LO metadata models. The various technological systems used to deliver these LOs have varying levels of accommodation for metadata. This is not to say that LO metadata systems are not relevant in the current available LOs but only that development has proceeded without metadata labeling in some cases.

Part 3: Building DLOs for Sharing (A Gaps Analysis)

Instructors may adopt learning objects for any number of purposes. They may select a video to showcase insights by a professional speaker. They may select several short interactive simulations to highlight different aspects of physical in-world phenomena or other systems behaviors. They may identify a particular topic that is elusive to learners and bolster their learning by providing multiple examples.

It would seem reasonable that there would be some gaps between receivers and producers of digital learning objects. Receivers may want particular features in the DLOs that they seek, but have to settle for less. In an analogical way, developers of learning objects may aim towards delivering particular features but have to settle for less. In both contexts, there will be naturally occurring gaps. However, having some objectives and standards is a net positive and may result in more optimal decision-making on the adoption of digital learning objects and more optimal building of DLOs.

In Table 2, there are some disparities identified, with the largest ones in pedagogical value (a high focus for developers but maybe less so for DLO

Table 2. Gaps analysis between DLO adopter criteria and ID design and development focuses

	DLO Adopter Criteria	Instructional Designer Design and Development Focuses	Disparity between the DLO Adopter vs. the Creator in Terms of Focus
1 Pedagogical Value	20	40	-20
2 Learner Engagement	30	20	+10
3 Presentational (and Interactional) Features	15	10	+5
4 Legal Adherence	5	10	-5
5 Technological Features	10	10	0
6 Instructor (Adopter) Control	5	0	+5
7 Applicability to the Respective Learning Contexts (Local Conditions)	5	0	+5
8 Local Costs to Deploy	10	5	+5
9 Labeling and Documentation; Contributor, Informational Source Crediting	0	5	-5
10 Global Transferability and Adoptability	0	0	0
Total	100%	100%	--

adopters), learner engagement (more important for adopters than creators), presentational features (more important for adopters than creators), and so on.

A visualization of the gaps between DLO adopter criteria and ID design and development focuses follows in Figure 2.

So what does this discrepancy mean for those who would build digital learning objects for sharing? What are some practical ways to close the gap? To summarize, instructional designers need to focus more on learner engagement, presentational (and interactional) features, instructor (adopter) control, and local costs to adopt the DLO. How these accommodations look will differ depending on the respective contexts and DLOs. Does this mean that they should focus less on features that adopters of DLOs ranked as less important? Not quite. This is not to say that designers and developers should focus less on pedagogical value or legal adherence or "labeling and documentation; contributor, informational source crediting," because those are all important features both professionally and legally.

DISCUSSION

So what was learned in this work? Both Hypotheses 1 and 2 were generally validated. Hypothesis 1 reads "In the current learning object economy, there is a discrepancy between desired features by DLO adopters and DLO creators." Hypothesis 2 reads, "There are practical strategies and tactics to narrow some of the gaps between the desired features of DLO adopters and DLO creators." The first hypothesis was borne out with the identification of some gaps between what DLO adopters want and what DLO creators create. For the second hypothesis, there are some practical strategies and tactics to narrow the gap, so ideally, a larger percentage of extant learning objects may be adopted. It is still to be seen what DLO designers and developers will create and what changes may occur from this work. Also, there is interest in whether the "Ten Features of Digital Learning Objects that May Affect Adoption and Usage," "Assessment Questions to Evaluate a DLO or a DLO Sequence (from "Ten Features of Digital Learning Objects that May Affect Adoption and Usage")," and "Adoption of DLOs" Survey Instrument have value beyond this particular work.

The research work, as noted, is based on a review of the literature, autoethnographic research (based on decades of online teaching and learning, and instructional design work), analyses of available learning objects from

Figure 2. Gaps analysis between DLO adopter criteria and instructional designer design and development focuses

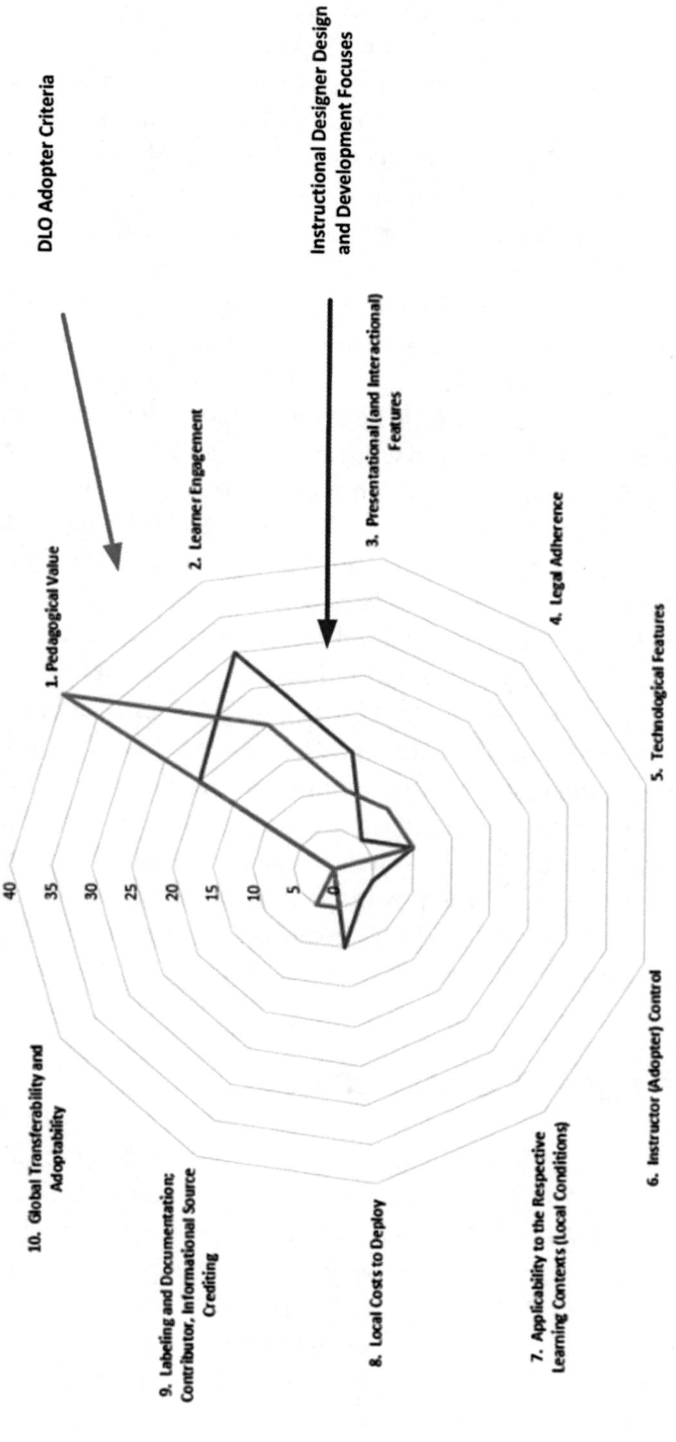

some mainline repositories and other spaces, and analytical work. The focus here has been on pragmatic and applied ideas.

What has not been discussed yet is a challenge in the learning object economy. For a designer and developer of LOs, the value proposition generally goes like this: Would you build a digital learning object from scratch to full legal and professional specifications, taking on responsibility for all costs and taking on potential liabilities, for your local use and then share the learning object broadly with the world for free? Further, would you continually update and revise this LO to ensure its accuracy and appeal to learners? The proposal is already a tough one, and it is hard to see designers and developers wanting to accept even more rigorous standards for learning object quality for secondary and tertiary users. This ask would be even tougher if one were to ask developers and designers to accept the hard work and costs and risks of designing learning objects only for public usage (without local benefits). In the same way that a lot of images and videos are uploaded and then "orphaned," this is a factor with learning objects, which are often dated. At core, learning objects are not cost-free. They require high levels of skill to create. The incentives to share broadly are low, particularly when there are many in the larger environment who are willing to reputationally- and commercially- benefit off the work of others. Practically speaking, identifying gaps between user interests and those of developers may not make much difference because the initial underlying incentives and interests have not changed. The imbalance in incentives in the LO economy means that such exchanges may not be sustainable over time. (As a side note, not all content experts have the skills to create digital learning objects. Even if there is interest in the LO creation endeavor, many do not have the knowledge, skills, resources, information, or other required resources to make this happen.)

FUTURE RESEARCH DIRECTIONS

Three "instruments" were created as a part of this work—the "Ten Features of Digital Learning Objects that May Affect Adoption and Usage," "Assessment Questions to Evaluate a DLO or a DLO Sequence (from "Ten Features of Digital Learning Objects that May Affect Adoption and Usage")," and "Adoption of DLOs" Survey Instrument—and it may be helpful to pilot test these in different contexts and to see what revisions and adjustments may be done to enhance these. The survey, in particular, has not been pilot-tested, and that may be a logical next step.

A more formal analysis of extant DLOs may be done to see if those align more with what DLO adopters apparently want vs. what designers and developers build. There are about three dozen repository and referatory sources of DLOs in the research literature that may be explored. On the Internet and Web, there are a large number of hosted digital learning objects.

Another approach may involve the design of models that may enhance how instructional designers build learning objects to share. Ozdilek and Robeck (2009) showed that the ADDIE Model may be used as a standard against which instructional designers describe their work in order to identify areas in which such instructional designers fall short. In their work, the researchers found that instructional designers may better focus on why learners' needs to engage with particular learning ["why the learner needs to learn the material—what might (be) called relevance"], and the context in which the learning content will be applied (Ozdilek & Robeck, 2009, p. 2049). This work here provides a checklist for considerations but nothing as developed as a model.

CONCLUSION

To conclude, this chapter involved an update to digital learning object research, foremost to better understand what features adopters of DLOs are interested in, what designers and developers of DLOs focus on, and what gaps may exist. May the LO economy thrive!

ACKNOWLEDGMENT

Thanks to Colleague 2 Colleague for accepting a presentation based on this topic for the 2017 Summer Institute on Distance Learning and Instructional Technology (SIDLIT, pronounced "sidelight"), at Johnson County Community College, from Aug. 3 – 4, 2017. The presentation is "Adoption of Digital Learning Objects (and What it Means for DLO Designers and Developers Who Share)." The related slideshow is available on SlideShare at https://www.slideshare.net/ShalinHaiJew/adoptionof-digitallearningobjects.

REFERENCES

Allen, C. A., & Mugisa, E. K. (2010). Improving learning object reuse through OOD: A theory of learning objects. *Journal of Object Technology*, *9*(6), 51–75. doi:10.5381/jot.2010.9.6.a3

Benkler, Y. (2006). *The Wealth of Networks: How Social production Transforms Markets and Freedom*. Yale University Press. Retrieved Jan. 3, 2017, from http://www.benkler.org/benkler_wealth_of_networks.pdf

Berners-Lee, T., Hendler, J., & Lassila, O. (2001, May 17). The Semantic Web. *Scientific American*. Retrieved Jan. 23, 2017, from https://pdfs.semanticscholar.org/566c/1c6bd366b4c9e07fc37eb372771690d5ba31.pdf

Bratina, T. A., Hayes, D., & Blumsack, S. L. (2002, Nov. – Dec.) *Preparing teachers to use learning objects*. The Technology Source Archives at the U. of N. Carolina. Retrieved Jan. 4, 2017, from http://technologysource.org/article/preparing_teachers_to_use_learning_objects/

Cechinel, C., Sánchez-Alonso, S., & García-Barriocanal, E. (2011). Statistical profiles of highly-rated learning objects. *Computers & Education*, *57*(1), 1255–1269. doi:10.1016/j.compedu.2011.01.012

Cechinel, C., Sánchez-Alonso, S., & Sicilia, M. A. (2009). Empirical analysis of errors on human-generated learning objects metadata. In F. Sartori, M. A. Sicilia, & N. Manouselis (Eds.), *MTSR 2009, CCIS 46. Springer-Verlag*. doi:10.1007/978-3-642-04590-5_6

Chikh, A. (2014). A general model of learning design objects. *Journal of King Saud University—Computer and Information Sciences, 26*, 29 – 40.

Christiansen, J.-A., & Anderson, T. (2004, March). Feasibility of course development based on learning objects: Research analysis of three case studies. *International Journal of Instructional Technology and Distance Learning*. Retrieved Jan. 3, 2017, from http://www.itdl.org/journal/mar_04/article02.htm

Churchill, D., & Hedberg, J. (2008). Learning object design considerations for small-screen handheld devices. *Computers & Education*, *50*(3), 881–893. doi:10.1016/j.compedu.2006.09.004

Collis, B., & Strijker, A. (2004). Technology and human issues in re u s i n g learning objects. *Journal of Interactive Media in Education*, (4), 1 - 32. Retrieved Jan. 4, 2017, from http://www-jime.open.ac.uk/2004/4

Currier, S., Barton, J., OBeirne, R., & Ryan, B. (2004, March). Quality assurance for digital learning object repositories: Issues for the metadata creation process. *ALT-J Research in Learning Technology*, *12*(1), 5–20. doi:10.3402/rlt.v12i1.11223

De Macedo, C. M. S., & Ulbricht, V. R. (2012). Accessibility guidelines for the development of learning objects. *Procedia Computer Science*, *14*, 155 – 162. doi:10.1016/j.procs.2012.10.018

Fernández-Pampillón, A. M. (2013). A new AENOR project for measuring the quality of digital educational materials. *TEEM '13*, 133 – 139. doi:10.1145/2536536.2536557

Gaffney, M. (2010). *Enhancing teachers' take-up of digital content: Factors and design principles in technology adoption*. National Digital Learning Resources Network. Retrieved Jan. 7, 2017, from http://www.ndlrn.edu.au/verve/_resources/enhancing_teacher_takeup_of_digital_content_report.pdf

Hai-Jew, S. (2010, Dec. 15). An instructional design approach to updating an online course curriculum. *Educause Review*. Retrieved Jan. 16, 2017, from http://er.educause.edu/articles/2010/12/an-instructional-design-approach-to-updating-an-online-course-curriculum

Hatala, M., Richards, G., Eap, T., & Willms, J. (2004). The interoperability of learning object repositories and services: Standards, implementations and lessons learned. *WWW 2004*, 19 – 27.

Heery, R., Johnston, P., Beckett, D., & Rogers, N. (2005). JISC metadata schema registry. *JCDL '05*, 381. doi:10.1145/1065385.1065484

Hill, J. R., & Hannafin, M. J. (2001). Teaching and learning in digital environments: The resurgence of resource-based learning. *Educational Technology Research and Development*, *49*(3), 37–52. doi:10.1007/BF02504914

Karolčik, S., & Čipková, E. (2015). Veselský, M., Hrubišková, H., & Matulčiková, M. (2015) Quality parameterization of educational resources from the perspective of a teacher. *British Journal of Educational Technology*, 1–19.

Kiu, C.-C., & Lee, C.-S. (2006). Ontology Mapping and Merging through OntoDNA for Learning Object Reusability. *Journal of Educational Technology & Society*, *9*(3), 27–42.

Kizilec, R. F., Pérez-Sanagustín, M., & Maldonado, J. J. (2017). Self-regulated learning strategies predict learner behavior and goal attainment in Massive Open Online Courses. *Computers & Education, 104*, 18–33. doi:10.1016/j. compedu.2016.10.001

Kurilovas, E., Serikoviene, S., & Vuorikari, R. (2014). Expert centred vs learning centred approach for evaluating quality and reusability of learning objects. *Computers in Human Behavior, 30*, 526–534. doi:10.1016/j. chb.2013.06.047

Lau, S.-H., & Woods, P. C. (2008). An investigation of user perceptions and attitudes towards learning objectives. *British Journal of Educational Technology, 39*(4), 685–699. doi:10.1111/j.1467-8535.2007.00770.x

Lau, S.-H., & Woods, P. C. (2009). Understanding learner acceptance of learning objects: The roles of learning object characteristics and individual differences. *British Journal of Educational Technology, 40*(6), 1059–1075. doi:10.1111/j.1467-8535.2008.00893.x

Leacock, T. L., Richards, G., & Nesbit, J. C. (2004). Teachers need simple, effective tools to evaluate learning objects: Enter Elera.net. *Proceedings of the IASTED International Conference "Computers and Advanced Technology in Education*, 333 – 338.

Learning object metadata. (2016, Aug. 16). In *Wikipedia*. Retrieved Jan. 21, 2017, from https://en.wikipedia.org/wiki/Learning_object_metadata

Margaryan, A., & Littlejohn, A. (2008). Repositories and communities at cross-purposes: Issues in sharing and reuse of digital learning resources. *Journal of Computer Assisted Learning, 24*(4), 333–347. doi:10.1111/j.1365-2729.2007.00267.x

McCormick, R., Scrimshaw, P., Li, N., & Clifford, C. (2004). *CELEBRATE Evaluation report*. Retrieved Jan. 13, 2017, from http://celebrate.eun.org/ eun.org2/eun/Include_to_content/celebrate/ file/Deliverable7_2Evaluation Report02Dec04.pdf

McGreal, R. (2004). *Online Education Using Learning Objects*. London: RoutledgeFalmer.

Minguillón, J., Rodríguez, M. E., & Conesa, J. (2010). Extending learning objects by means of social networking. *LNCS, 6483, 220 – 229*. doi:10.1007/978-3-642-17407-0_23

Nash, S. S. (2005). Learning objects, learning object repositories, and learning theory: Preliminary best practices for online courses. *Interdisciplinary Journal of Knowledge and Learning Objects, 1,* 217–228.

Ochoa, X. (2011). Learnometrics: Metrics for learning objects. *LAK '11,* 1 – 8.

Ochoa, X., & Duval, E. (2008). Measuring learning object reuse. *Proceedings of the Third European Conference on Technology Enhanced Learning (EC-TEL '08), 322 – 325.* doi:10.1007/978-3-540-87605-2_36

Ochoa, X., & Duval, E. (2008, January – March). Relevance ranking metrics for learning objects. *IEEE Transactions on Learning Technologies, 1*(1), 34–48. doi:10.1109/TLT.2008.1

Ochoa, X., & Duval, E. (2009). Automatic evaluation of metadata quality in digital repositories. *International Journal on Digital Libraries, 10*(2-3), 67–91. doi:10.1007/s00799-009-0054-4

Ozdilek, Z., & Robeck, E. (2009). Operational priorities of instructional designers analyzed within the steps of the Addie instructional design model. World Conference on Educational Sciences. *Procedia: Social and Behavioral Sciences, 1*(1), 2046–2050. doi:10.1016/j.sbspro.2009.01.359

Parrish, P. E. (2004). The trouble with learning objects. *Educational Technology Research and Development, 52*(1), 49–67. doi:10.1007/BF02504772

Pons, D., Hilera, J. R., Fernández, L., & Pagés, C. (2016). A learning quality metadata approach: Automatic quality assessment of virtual training from metadata. *Computer Standards & Interfaces, 45,* 45–61. doi:10.1016/j.csi.2015.12.001

Recker, M., Dorward, J., Dawson, D., Mao, X., Liu, Y., Palmer, B., & Park, J. et al. (2005). Teaching, designing, and sharing: A context for learning objects. *Interdisciplinary Journal of Knowledge and Learning Objects, 1,* 197–216.

Recker, M. M., Dorward, J., & Nelson, L. M. (2004). Discovery and use of online learning resources: Case study findings. *Journal of Educational Technology & Society, 7*(2), 93–104.

Recker, M.M., Walker, A., & Wiley, D.A. (2000). Collaboratively filtering learning objects. In D.A. Wiley (Ed.), *Designing Instructional with Learning Objects.* Academic Press.

Rustici, M. (2009, Jan. 6). *Benefits of SCORM. Rustici Software*. Retrieved Jan. 17, 2017, from http://scorm.com/scorm-explained/business-of-scorm/benefits-of-scorm/

SCORM. 2004 4th Edition: SCORM Users Guide for Instructional Designers. Version 8. (2011, Sept. 15). Advanced Distributed Learning. Retrieved Jan. 18, 2017, from https://adlnet.gov/wp-content/uploads/2011/12/SCORM_Users_Guide_for_ISDs.pdf

SCORM Overview. (2015). Advanced Distributed Learning. Retrieved Jan. 17, 2017, from https://www.adlnet.gov/adl-research/scorm/

Sicilia, M.-A., Ochoa, X., Stoitsis, G., & Klerkx, J. (2013). Learning object analytics for collections, repositories & federations. *LAK '13*, 285 – 286. doi:10.1145/2460296.2460359

Sinclair, J., Joy, M., Yau, J. Y.-K., & Hagan, S. (2013, April – June). A practice-oriented review of learning objects. *IEEE Transactions on Learning Technologies*, 6(2), 177–192. doi:10.1109/TLT.2013.6

Sosteric, M., & Hesemeier, S. (2002, October). When is a learning object not an object: A first step towards a theory of learning objects. *The International Review of Research in Open and Distributed Learning*, 3(2). doi:10.19173/irrodl.v3i2.106

Stefaner, M., Vecchia, E. D., Condotta, M., Wolpers, M., Specht, M., Apelt, S., & Duval, E. (2007) MACE—enriching architectural learning objects for experience multiplication. Creating New Learning Experiences on a Global Scale. *European Conference on Technology Enhanced Learning*, 322 – 336. Retrieved Jan. 7, 2017, from http://link.springer.com/chapter/10.1007%2f978-3-540-75195-3_23

Vinha, A. (2005). Reusable learning objects: Theory to practice. *ITiCSE '05*. Retrieved Jan. 23, 2017, from https://www.w3.org/2001/sw/

Wiley, D. A. (2000, June). *Learning object design and sequencing theory* (Dissertation). Brigham Young University. Retrieved Dec. 31, 2016, from http://opencontent.org/docs/dissertation.pdf

Wiley, D. A. (2002). Connecting learning objects to instructional design theory: a definition, a metaphor, and a taxonomy. In D.A. Wiley (Ed.), The Instructional Use of Learning Objects. Agency for Instructional Technology.

Yalcinalp, S., & Emiroglu, B. (2012). Through efficient use of LORs: Prospective teachers views on operational aspects of learning object repositories. *British Journal of Educational Technology*, *43*(3), 474–488. doi:10.1111/j.1467-8535.2011.01212.x

Yen, N. Y., Shih, T. K., Chao, L. R., & Jin, Q. (2010, July – September). Ranking metrics and search guidance for learning object repository. *IEEE Transactions on Learning Technologies*, *3*(3), 250–264. doi:10.1109/TLT.2010.15

Zapata, A., Menéndez, V. H., Prieto, M. E., & Romero, C. (2013). A framework for recommendation in learning object repositories: An example of application in civil engineering. *Advances in Engineering Software*, *56*, 1–14. doi:10.1016/j.advengsoft.2012.10.005

Zapata, A., Menéndez, V. H., Prieto, M. E., & Romero, C. (2015). Evaluation and selection of group recommendation strategies for collaborative searching of learning objects. *International Journal of Human-Computer Studies*, *76*, 22–39. doi:10.1016/j.ijhcs.2014.12.002

KEY TERMS AND DEFINITIONS

Accessibility: Ensuring multimodal ways of perceiving informational contents (through visual, auditory, tactual, and other streams).

Adoption: Acceptance, integration, and usage (of a learning object).

Application Programming Interface (API): Tools that enable computers to intercommunicate and share data (as well as other defined functions).

Atomistic (or Atomic): At the smallest essential unit level.

Autoethnography: Qualitative research in which selected parts of the author's life experiences are explored for broader insights.

Blended Learning: The combination of F2F and online learning in a "blend."

Courseware: Learning materials instantiated in software or code; a portmanteau term consisting of "course + software."

Curriculum: The subject matter in a course of study.

Digital Learning Object (DLO): A discrete unit of learning in digital format.

Digital Library: An online space in which informational contents are made available on loan.

F2F (Face-to-Face) Learning: In real-space learning.

Federation: Combining learning object repositories (LORs) to enable LO searches, queries, and other functions across a number of LORs simultaneously.

"Ilities": A list of features ending with "ility" in the name (originally coined by Advanced Distributed Learning in the rollout of SCORM).

Learning Management System (LMS): A computer system that enables various functionalities related to formal learning: enrollment, study, intercommunications, digital file sharing, live- and recorded- presentations, and others.

Metadata: Data about data.

Pedagogy: A method of teaching.

Portability: Able to be transferred with relative ease.

Resource-Based Learning Environment (RBLE): A learning site built around the access to learning resources albeit with supporting tools for self-directed learners.

Referatory: A website that contains metadata about digital learning objects by which points to the hosted contents but does not directly host digital learning objects (these may also offer a range of services, such as tools for virtual community building, collaborative DLO co-design and development, crowd-source review of DLOs, and others).

Repository: An online storage site for digital learning objects.

SCORM (Sharable Content Object Reference Model): A set of standards and specifications to enable the reusability of digital learning objects.

Self-Regulated Learning (SRL): Learner-driven and directed learning, requiring learner self-discipline.

Tin Can API (Experience API, xAPI): A set of successor standards and specifications to SCORM which enable the capture of deeper information from digital learning objects.

APPENDIX A

1. Pedagogical Value
   1a Informational Accuracy
   1b Informational Value
   1c Curricular Relevance
   1d Contemporaneous and Up-to-Date Contents
   1e Unit Size
   1f Learning Assessment
2. Learner Engagement
   2a Learning Design
   2b Learning Value (to Learners)
   2c Supports for Learners
   2d Alignment to Learner Readiness
   2e Learner Immersion
   2f Succinctness
3. Presentational (and Interactional) Features
   3a Production Quality
   3b Presentation Novelty
   3c Sequencing
   3d Learner Interactivity
4. Legal Adherence
   4a Intellectual Property Adherence
   4b Privacy Protections
   4c Accessibility Accommodations
5. Technological Features
   5a Technology Integration with Learning Environments
   5b Playability / Functionality
   5c Portability
6. Instructor (Adopter) Control
   6a Ability to Edit and Update
   6b Ease of Opt-out (Delinkage / Removal)
7. Applicability to the Respective Learning Contexts (Local Conditions)
   7a Political Acceptability
   7b Alignment with Instructor Teaching Approach
   7c Reputation of the DLO Maker(s)
   7d Institutional Costs

8. Local Costs to Deploy
   8a Technological Requirements
   8b Direct Costs
   8c Costs over Time (Lifetime Costs)
   8d Unwanted Advertising and Branding
   8e Unwanted Dependencies: Proprietary Technologies, Remote Hosting
   8f Risks to Reputation
9. Labeling and Documentation; Contributor and Informational Source Crediting
   9a Pedagogical Metadata
   9b Contributor and Informational Source Crediting
10. Global Transferability and Adoptability
    10a Culturally Aligned (or Culturally Neutral)
    10b Multilingual Versioning Availability

Appendix A: Outline of Elements in "Ten Features of Digital Learning Objects that May Affect Adoption and Usage"

APPENDIX B

1. Pedagogical Value

1a. Informational Accuracy:
  - How accurate is the information in this digital learning object?
  - Is there clear provenance of the information?
  - Are the information sources credible or not? Are there clear source citations? Are the informational sources verifiable? Are the information sources reputable?
  - Are there objective ways to validate or invalidate the digital learning object?
  - Who is/are the subject matter experts (SMEs)? Do they have standing in the field? Are they trustworthy as professionals? Are their work methods well respected? Do they frame a domain topic with appropriateness and clarity (within the field)?
1b. Informational Value
  - What is the informational value of the contents of the digital learning object? Why?

- ○ Is this information rare or common? Is this information broadly accessible by the public through other sources or not?

1c. Curricular Relevance
- ○ Does the digital learning object contribute to the learning sequence?

1d. Contemporaneous and Up-to-Date Contents
- ○ Are the domain contents of the digital learning object contemporaneous and up-to-date?
- ○ Or if the DLO is dated, does it have historical value?
- ○ Is the DLO relatively "future-proofed" in terms of both information and time-based indicators?

1e. Unit Size
- ○ Is the unit size of the learning object conducive for usage in the online learning context?
- ○ If it is too large, is it possible to break apart the LO into smaller pieces for appropriate learning?
- ○ If the DLO is too small, is it possible to add lead-up materials and lead-away materials to complement the contents? (re-contextualization of the DLO)
- ○ If the DLO is too large, is it possible to edit it to the proper size (or only use part of it)?

1f. Learning Assessment
- ○ Does the digital learning object (DLO) have any built-in learning assessment?
- ○ If so, does this assessment link well to the online learning environment? (Does it report directly to the gradebook? Are the point values editable?)
  - If so, is this built-in assessment aligned with the digital learning object?
- ○ Does the assessment highlight information that is relevant to the learning domain?
- ○ If the learning assessment is not desirable, is it easy to de-couple it from the digital learning object? Or is it easy to edit and modify?
- ○ If there is no related learning assessment, is it relatively easy to create a learning assessment linked to the digital learning object?

2. Learner Engagement

2a. Learning Design
  ◦ Is the DLO informed by appropriate learning theory?
  ◦ Does the DLO include basic elements of an effective learning design: measurable learning objectives, proper and accurate contents, effective feedback, and assessment?
  ◦ Is the DLO sufficiently comprehensive in terms of coverage?
  ◦ Does the DLO include proper learner supports?
  ◦ Does the DLO define clear learning sequence(s)?

2b. Learning Value (to Learners)
  ◦ Is the digital learning object aligned with the learning needs of the target learner audience? How so? How not?
  ◦ If the DLO is not sufficiently aligned, is it sufficiently editable in order to make it more appropriate for the target learner group(s)?
  ◦ Is the DLO designed to respect learner time?
  ◦ Does the DLO contain relevant lessons to the learner, such as target knowledge and / or skills?
  ◦ Does the DLO relate to learner needs?

2c. Supports for Learners
  ◦ Is there "cognitive scaffolding" to support learners who are not sufficiently prepared to engage the topic? Is there "cognitive scaffolding" to support learners who already have some exposure or learning in the target lesson topic?
  ◦ Are there designed context-sensitive learner supports (such as word definitions, navigation annotations, and other features)?
  ◦ Are there lead-up and lead-away resources to the DLO?

2d. Alignment to Learner Readiness
  ◦ Is there little to no need for additional learner preparation to use the DLO effectively?

2e. Learner Immersion
  ◦ Is the DLO classically immersive (virtual, 3D, simulated, role-play-based, gaming-based, case study-based, or project-based)?
  ◦ Is the DLO designed to be high-engagement, with longer learner time investment?
  ◦ Is the DLO designed to be social and cohort-based?

2f.   Succinctness
   ◦   Is the DLO sufficiently succinct and without unnecessary repetition?
   ◦   Is the learner's time respected?
      ▪   If ancillary materials are included, are they relevant?

3. Presentational (and Interactional) Features

3a.   Production Quality
   ◦   Does the DLO or DLO sequence show a high level of human talent and professionalism?
   ◦   Are the audio, imagery, and video clear and coherent?
   ◦   Is the text legible?
   ◦   Is the writing clear?
   ◦   Are the informational contents authentic?
   ◦   Are there apparent high costs and investments to create the digital learning objects?
   ◦   Is there a high level of revision and editing quality and a high level of care (with no or few errors)?
3b.   Presentation Novelty
   ◦   Is the presentation of the DLO innovative?
   ◦   Is the presentation of the DLO memorable?
3c.   Sequencing
   ◦   Is the DLO sequenced (article or paper, slideshow, or video) or non-sequenced (branching slideshow, branching video with outlinks, and others)?
3d.   Learner Interactivity
   ◦   Is the DLO designed to be highly interactive (models, simulations, games, branching websites, branching slideshows, branching videos, e-books, and others)?
   ◦   Or is the DLO more non-interactive (static models, static imagery, static articles and papers, static slideshows, static e-books, and others)?

4. Legal Adherence

4a.   Intellectual Property Adherence
- Have the rules for intellectual property (copyright, trademark, patent, export restrictions, and others, etc.) been assiduously followed?
- Have the IP releases been properly documented?

4b.   Privacy Protections
- Have the privacy protections of those who have participated in the video captures, audio captures, and other work been respected?
- Have these privacy protection measures been documented (e.g. have the signed media releases been recorded and saved appropriately?)?

4c.   Accessibility Accommodations
- Have all audio and video been closed captioned (timed text) accurately? Or if closed captioning is not available, is there transcripting or stand-in text (like a machine-readable slideshow) for the audio / video contents?
- Is there accurate information-equivalent alt-texting for imagery?
- If color is used, is it used in a high-contrast and accessible way? Are there multiple channels for the conveying of data beyond color?
- If data tables are used, are these machine-readable in a coherent way? (Is it clear what data is in each cell and what the proper measures are?)
- Does the learner have control over all "players" (games, simulations, audio, video, and so on)?

5. Technological Features

5a.   Technology Integration with Learning Environments
- Is the DLO or DLO sequence easy to integrate in the respective technology environments and devices?
- Is the DLO easy to integrate in the face-to-face (F2F) environments?
- Is the DLO easy to integrate with the blended (online and F2F) environments?

5b.   Playability / Functionality
- Is there an intuitive user interface or not?

- ▪ Are there accommodations for input devices?
- ▪ Are there touchscreen functionalities?
  - ◦ Does the DLO work as advertised?
5c. Portability
  - ◦ Does the DLO work offline?
  - ◦ Does the DLO work via mobile devices?

6. Instructor (Adopter) Control

6a. Ability to Edit and Update
  - ◦ Is the DLO editable and updatable in terms of having a feedback channel to the DLO creators?
  - ◦ Is the DLO editable and updatable due to direct technological access to underlying source code?
6b. Ease of Opt-out (Delinkage / Removal)
  - ◦ Is there a low cost of removal of the DLO?
  - ◦ Is the DLO removable without residual impacts?

7. Applicability to the Respective Learning Contexts (Local Conditions)

7a. Political Acceptability
  - ◦ Is the messaging in the DLO politically acceptable in the local context?
  - ◦ Are the costs of the DLO politically acceptable in the local context?
  - ◦ Is the reputation of the DLO and the DLO maker acceptable in the local context?
  - ◦ Or if not, are the political concerns and issues mitigatable?
7b. Alignment with Instructor Teaching Approach
  - ◦ Is the DLO consistent with the instructor's professional knowledge?
  - ◦ Is the DLO consistent with the instructor's pedagogical approaches?
7c. Reputation of the DLO Maker(s)
  - ◦ Does the DLO maker have a quality reputation?
  - ◦ Is there a high level of trust between the DLO maker and various users of the DLO?
  - ◦ Is there high transparency in the work of the DLO maker?

  ○ Is there high stability in terms of the DLO maker's history and quality?
  ○ Is there a sense of security in working with the DLO maker?

7d. Institutional Costs
  ○ Are there "high" institutional costs to deploy the DLO?

8. Local Costs to Deploy

8a. Technological Requirements
  ○ What technological systems are required to deploy the DLO(s)? How much support is required to enable the technological tools?
  ○ What software is required? (These may include authoring tools and other creation and editing tools.)
  ○ What expertise is required?
  ○ What hosting costs are required?

8b. Direct Costs and Indirect Costs
  ○ What are the outright purchase costs or subscription payments to a vendor for the DLO(s)?
  ○ What are indirect costs such as additional requirements to deploy the DLO(s)?

8c. Costs over Time (Lifetime Costs)
  ○ What are the lifetime costs to "ownership" of the DLO? Costs for updates? Unanticipated costs in the future?

8d. Unwanted Advertising and Branding
  ○ Is there presence of advertising logos and watermarks that are intrusive? Non-intrusive?
  ○ Is there a highly branded look-and-feel to the DLO(s)?
  ○ Is the writing style neutral (objective) and as "unmarked" as possible?
  ○ Is the visual design style neutral and as "unmarked" as possible?

8e. Unwanted Dependencies: Proprietary Technologies, Remote Hosting
  ○ Are proprietary and closed-source technologies required to the use the DLOs?
  ○ Are the DLOs hosted (and controlled) by their being hosted remotely (and unusable in a locally downloaded way)?

8f. Risks to Reputation
  ○ Are there risks to reputation in the usage of the DLO(s)?

9. Labeling and Documentation; Contributor and Informational Source Crediting

9a. Pedagogical Metadata
- Are the main pedagogical metadata included, such as the following: name of the DLO, subject area, resource type, target learners, level of learning, main language(s), learning objectives, main learning contents, pedagogical approach(es), rights management data, date of creation, author information, DLO citation methods, and others?
- Does the digital learning object use a defined structured metadata system?

9b. Contributor and Informational Source Crediting
- Are all authors and contributors cited (by role)?
- Are all informational sources credited?

10. Global Transferability and Adoptability

10a. Culturally Aligned (or Culturally Neutral)
- Is the messaging in the DLO culturally aligned (or culturally neutral)?
- Is the representation of people in the DLO culturally aligned (or culturally neutral)?
- Does the DLO have a respectful tone (as perceived by its users)?
- Is the DLO culturally aligned in other ways?

10b. Multilingual Versioning Availability
- Are there built-in language options in the DLO (or DLO sequence)?
- Are there available accesses to third-party multi-language tools?

Appendix B: Assessment Questions to Evaluate a DLO or a DLO Sequence (from "Ten Features of Digital Learning Objects that May Affect Adoption and Usage")

APPENDIX C

Survey Instrument: Adoption of DLOs

Part 1: Survey Respondent Information

What subject area(s) do you teach?

What level(s) do you teach at?

How long have you been teaching at the university level?

How familiar are you with the concept of a "digital learning object" (DLO)? [For our purposes here, DLOs are any digital contents—created for any purpose—that may be used to support learning.]

Have you ever created a digital learning object?

If so, what was the topic / were the topics?

What costs are there for creating a digital learning object? (Please consider staff hours, technologies, content acquisition, and so on.)

What are the main challenges in the creation of digital learning objects?

Does your workplace ever outsource the development of digital learning objects for online learning?

Is there a way to understand how frequently your workplace outsources the development of digital learning objects for online learning?

Do you teach F2F?

In your F2F teaching, do you use others' digital learning objects?

Do you teach in a blended modality?

In your blended teaching, do you use others' digital learning objects?

Do you teach via online?

In your online teaching, do you use others' digital learning objects?

What are your standards for selecting DLOs? (open-ended question, with a text response option)

What are grounds for accepting or rejecting a particular found DLO? (open-ended question, with a text response option)

Part 2: Desired Learning Object Features in the Adoption of LOs (DLOFALOs)

In terms of selecting digital learning objects created by others, what do you look for? (open-ended response)

When you search for DLOs for your teaching, what is the typical likelihood that you'll find some resources that you can use?

Where do you usually go to look for DLOs?

When you fail to find DLOs, what are the main reasons for the failure? (open-ended response)

Does your institution of higher education have a shared repository or digital library space for DLOs?

Do you tend to find what you need from the institution space?

In terms of selecting digital learning objects created by others, how important are the following factors? (sum to 100%, ability to set any to 0)

1. **Pedagogical Value**: The digital learning object's informational accuracy, informational value, curricular relevance, up-to-datedness of contents (and future proofing), and unit size (including a possible learning assessment)

2. **Learning Engagement**: The learning design, learning value, supports for learners, alignment to learner readiness, learner immersion, and DLO succinctness

3. **Presentational (and Interactional) Features**: Production quality, presentation novelty, sequencing, and learner interactivity

4. **Legal Adherence**: Intellectual property adherence, privacy protections, and accessibility accommodations

5. **Technological Features**: Technology integration with learning environments, playability / functionality (various input devices, touch interactivity), and portability (such as capability for offline use, mobile device playability)

6. **Instructor (Adopter) Control**: Ability to edit and update, ease of opt-out (de-linkage / removal)\

7. **Applicability to the Respective Learning Contexts (Local Conditions)**: Political acceptability, alignment with instructor teaching approach, reputation of the DLO maker(s), and institutional costs

8. **Local Costs to Deploy**: Technological requirements, direct costs and indirect costs, costs over time (lifetime costs), unwanted advertising and branding, unwanted dependencies like proprietary technologies and remote hosting, and risks to reputation

9. **Labeling and Documentation; Contributor and Informational Source Crediting**: Pedagogical metadata, contributor and informational source crediting

10. **Global Transferability and Adoptability**: Culturally aligned (or culturally neutral), multilingual versioning availability

Part 3: Local Creation of DLOs

Do you create digital learning objects (offer a broad definition) as part of your work?

If so, what are some names of DLOs that you have created?

Byline for the sharing of LOs

How much time does an average LO take to create and finalize?

If you were to add up all the costs for creating a DLO, what would the average cost be (in today's dollars)? (Consider the hours of all the contributors to the DLO, the costs for contents, the costs for technologies, and so on.)

Do you share your DLOs publicly through referatories or repositories or digital libraries?

Why or why not?

If you share, what sort of copyright do you apply to your DLOs? (full copyright protections, Creative Commons licensure, release to the public domain, etc.) (show on a continuum)

Are there incentives that would change your mind about sharing DLOs?

If you were to share your DLOs publicly, who do you see as the main users? Why?

In a global context, your digital learning objects would be competing with those that others have created. What would be the competitive advantage of the DLOs you create vs. those created by others?

Does your workplace leadership support the public sharing of DLOs?

What sort of workplace funding is provided for the building of DLOs?

Is it important that your DLOs are available in a sequence or not?

Appendix C: "Adoption of DLOs": A Derived Survey Instrument for Assessing Potential DLO Adopter's Needs

Conclusion

A year and a half is a long time to spend on evolving a text. As noted earlier, one begins with a set of hopes and ambitions and objectives, but the world and circumstances will have an effect on human will and the limits of human talent and capabilities. At the beginning of this project was just the observation that digital and analog data—as imagery, as multimedia—are everywhere and plentiful. As extracted from social media platforms, such data is broad-reaching and big. There are any number of ways to collect, code, and analyze such data, but foremost, an analyst has to start from areas of expertise and familiarity but to branch from there.

In looking at how this book has evolved, I notice that the issues explored through data are somewhat academic in some cases (technology manifestos, renunciation of U.S. citizenship, assignment assessment), but mostly very human (selfie humor, mass surveillance, and snacking). In the same way, this book is both for academics and for citizen data analysts. After all, everyone living today is living in an age of massive information flows, and adapting to this is part of human survival and human thriving. We have to engage the world in a more selectively datafied way if we are to get to our subjective "ground truths." How we code what is around us says something about the world and something about the coder. Any way we can improve this work of engaging data, and the world through data, we are the better for it.

So what was learned in the research and writing of "Techniques for Coding Imagery and Multimedia: Emerging Research and Opportunities"?

1. *Starting with the familiar.* When working on a "new(ish) problem," it helps to begin with something that is somewhat familiar. There is a benefit to knowing the territory to some degree, so there is a basis against which to understand "ground truth" and to compare data exploration results. Oftentimes, researchers know a lot more inherently than they are aware

of, and often, the work is to surface these subliminal and otherwise-hidden insights, so they may be useful for learning and analysis.

2. *The role of the imagination.* Imagination has a critical role in coding imagery and multimedia because it is important to conceptualize what one thinks is important before even the first digital object is observed in order to maximize what is learnable from multimedial datasets and collections. This work is by people and for people, ultimately to provide constructive insights and to improve the human condition.

   The imagination has to inform pre-analysis hypothesizing for the proposal of testable posits. The imagination has to provide research questions of interest and peculiarity. In other words, the imagination lays the groundwork. Certainly, there is direct discovery from multimedia data, which requires analysts to recognize what is relevant (the whispers of inferences, the shimmers of maybe-patterns), but it is important to note that such insights are post hoc and likely quite constrained by the dataset(s). A broad imagination-informed approach begins before the data is even available. It enables conceptualizing expectations and then observing what is *not* found.

3. *The importance of documenting research methods and techniques.* While there are numerous ways to approach the analysis of imagery and multimedia—and to code what is relevant—it is important to record and report on the methods and techniques. This is not to try to set standards for analysis but to document for researcher self-awareness and critique, for posterity, and for some transferability to other researchers who may benefit (and who may further refine others' methods). Knowing what is valuable and why from data may also inform how to create programs and to automate such methods with computer code.

4. *Multidimensional data is eminently interpretable.* If one were to look at one image alone or one multimedia object alone, one analyst can convincingly interpret the object in a number of ways from various perspectives. This is much more so when numerous individuals with numerous disciplinary backgrounds and varying skills apply their attention to the respective works. The point of analysis is to surface understandings not lock down one viewpoint at the exclusion of all others. This is not about any "curse of dimensionality" but more about the "gift of dimensionality." Very human methods of engaging complex unstructured or semi-structured data involve evolving a plan and iterating over the image and multimedia sets in depth.

5.   *Computational analytics plays a complementary role to human analysis.*
Data may be created for particular designed purposes, but they always
may be analyzed in other ways to create value and understanding. A
person's "coding fist" is unique to the individual and his/her background
and interests and training, but that approach may also be captured and
remembered technologically and applied by others who are "read into"
the approach. Manual methods do not have to remain such, and the
converse is also true, that computational coding methods do not have
to remain such. Manual and computational methods of coding may
complement each other.

6.   This text is an early and rough work on how to manually and pseudo-
manually (with some computational assists) code imagery and
multimedia. Certainly, computer scientists have been working on thorny
issues of object recognition in computer vision research through machine
learning…and have applied various aspects of artificial intelligence
(AI) to the analysis and sorting of digital imagery and videos and other
multimedia objects. What is less explored is human analysis and coding
of imagery and multimedia. Researchers should not cede the space to
computers and their pattern seeking alone. After all, computer algorithms
and their design benefit from human insights and intuitions. There is
information in unstructured data that is not seeable by computers alone.
Human interpretation in their diverse subjectivities is valuable and
irreproducible between people without inordinate amounts of training
and documentation (and even then is limited, given the breadth of
human thinking, experience, imagination, and background). Also, why
would people give up the pleasure of the analysis of unstructured data?
My sense is that such work, even if it is naïve and early and rough-cut,
would benefit other researchers and programmers. My further sense is
that such coding will be informed by both the human touch and by the
machine touch, in a strategic tradeoff of complementary and competing
strengths.

About the Author

Shalin Hai-Jew works as an instructional designer at Kansas State University (K-State). She has taught at the university and college levels for many years (including four years in the People's Republic of China) and was tenured at Shoreline Community College but left tenure to pursue instructional design work. She has Bachelor's degrees in English and psychology, a Master's degree in Creative Writing from the University of Washington (where she was a Hugh Paradise Scholar), and an Ed.D in Educational Leadership with a focus on public administration from Seattle University (where she was a Morford Scholar). She reviews for several publishers. She has authored and edited a number of books. She presents at a number of professional conferences annually. Dr. Hai-Jew was born in Huntsville, Alabama, in the U.S.

Index

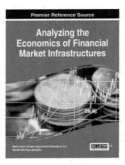

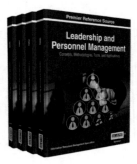
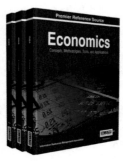
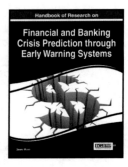

Stay Current on the Latest Emerging Research Developments

Become an IGI Global Reviewer for Authored Book Projects

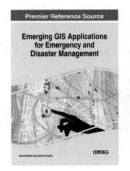

Premier Reference Source

Emerging GIS Applications for Emergency and Disaster Management

Premier Reference Source

Managerial Strategies and Green Solutions for Project Sustainability

Premier Reference Source

Comparative Approaches to Using R and Python for Statistical Data Analysis

Premier Reference Source

Solutions for High-Touch Communications in a High-Tech World

The overall success of an authored book project is dependent on quality and timely reviews.

In this competitive age of scholarly publishing, constructive and timely feedback significantly decreases the turnaround time of manuscripts from submission to acceptance, allowing the publication and discovery of progressive research at a much more expeditious rate. Several IGI Global authored book projects are currently seeking highly qualified experts in the field to fill vacancies on their respective editorial review boards:

Applications may be sent to:
development@igi-global.com

Applicants must have a doctorate (or an equivalent degree) as well as publishing and reviewing experience. Reviewers are asked to write reviews in a timely, collegial, and constructive manner. All reviewers will begin their role on an ad-hoc basis for a period of one year, and upon successful completion of this term can be considered for full editorial review board status, with the potential for a subsequent promotion to Associate Editor.

If you have a colleague that may be interested in this opportunity, we encourage you to share this information with them.

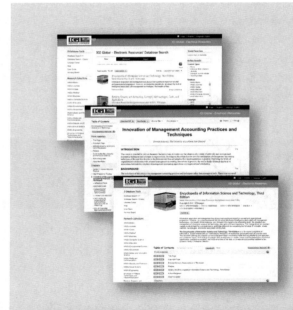

Printed in the United States
By Bookmasters